A Decade of Radio Advertising

HERMAN S. HETTINGER

ARNO PRESS and THE NEW YORK TIMES

New York • 1971

Reprint Edition 1971 by Arno Press Inc.

Reprinted from a copy in The Newark Public Library

LC# 70-161150
ISBN 0-405-03569-1

HISTORY OF BROADCASTING: RADIO TO TELEVISION
ISBN for complete set: 0-405-03555-1
See last pages of this volume for titles.

Manufactured in the United States of America

A DECADE OF RADIO ADVERTISING

THE UNIVERSITY OF CHICAGO PRESS
CHICAGO, ILLINOIS

THE BAKER & TAYLOR COMPANY
NEW YORK

THE CAMBRIDGE UNIVERSITY PRESS
LONDON

THE MARUZEN-KABUSHIKI-KAISHA
TOKYO, OSAKA, KYOTO, FUKUOKA, SENDAI

THE COMMERCIAL PRESS, LIMITED
SHANGHAI

A DECADE OF
RADIO ADVERTISING

By

HERMAN S. HETTINGER, PH.D.

Merchandising Department, Wharton School of Finance and Commerce
University of Pennsylvania

THE UNIVERSITY OF CHICAGO PRESS
CHICAGO · ILLINOIS

INTRODUCTION

Broadcast advertising is still a very new business. The regular broadcasting of programs is in itself little more than twelve years old, while the use of broadcasting as an advertising medium has just reached the decade mark.

In the spring of 1920, the late H. P. Davis, vice-president of the Westinghouse Electric and Manufacturing Company,[1] was attracted by an advertisement of a Pittsburgh department store calling attention to a sale of equipment which could be used in listening to the company's experimental station 8-XK, located in the home of Dr. Frank Conrad, one of the Westinghouse research experts. At this time Mr. Davis was trying hard to find some means of realizing upon the huge war-time investment of the Westinghouse Company in facilities for manufacturing radio equipment, and the advertisement suggested to him that, instead of developing radio principally along the lines of point-to-point communication, receiving sets could be sold to listeners desirous of hearing programs broadcast from various stations, still to be established. Out of this idea a new medium of mass communication was born, and on November 2, 1920, Station KDKA, Pittsburgh, initiated the first regular program service by broadcasting the Harding election returns. Two years later the American Telephone and Telegraph Company, then owners of Station WEAF, in turn wondered how this new, expensive broadcasting equipment could be made to pay for itself.[2] Early in 1923 it attempted to solve the problem of revenue by issuing a circular to advertisers which stated that sales messages would be broadcast at the nominal charge of $100 for a ten-minute talk, during which time it was estimated that approximately 750 words could be delivered. Thus broadcast advertising modestly came into being.

Though the development of broadcasting as an agency of mass communication was so swift and revolutionary as to arouse

[1] From pamphlet A-04914, issued by the Westinghouse Electric and Manufacturing Company.

[2] *Radio in Advertising*, O. G. Dunlap (Harper & Bros.), pp. 21–22.

universal public interest and to challenge the attention of Congress and the courts, the rise of broadcast advertising was slow and uncertain until the formation of the first of the great national networks late in 1926 transformed radio into a medium of national proportions. From then on the use of radio broadcasting for advertising purposes grew with amazing rapidity. Annual advertising expenditures increased from a scant four or five million dollars to approximately eighty million dollars.[3] A structure for broadcast advertising—including agencies, stations, networks and subgroups, regional networks, and the various middlemen functioning between the individual station and the agency or program sponsor—grew up within a few short years, while broadcasters and advertisers together developed the technique for a new medium with little or nothing to guide them. All this occurred with a rapidity which gave no opportunity for looking backward over the ground traversed, or for generalizing as to the principles which might guide the future development of the industry.

Today there are signs that the industry is beginning to develop form, substance, and guiding principle. A fairly efficient structure is emerging from the chaos which ruled the years of 1929–30, when so-called spot broadcasting first competed with national networks. The groundwork of scientific advertising technique is being laid in the work of agencies, networks, and individual stations, and in the infrequent research by universities and similar organizations. The early indiscriminate rush of sponsors to the new medium is subsiding in favor of a steady growth in use by companies and industries to whose needs broadcast advertising is adapted.

The newness of the industry affords at once a splendid opportunity and a serious problem to the student of broadcast advertising desiring to make a contribution to the knowledge of the field. Thus far, investigation regarding broadcast advertising has been limited to a few scattered and tentative studies. Work in this field, therefore, is, to a large degree, purely a pioneering undertaking. This is true with respect to both its extensive and intensive aspects. As regards the former, no comprehensive study of broadcast advertising has ever been made, so that even

[3] See chap. vi for details as to expenditures.

the groundwork for an appreciation of the field as a whole does not exist in organized form today.

With respect to the intensive aspects of possible investigation, similar difficulties present themselves. Station records are so incomplete, the data collectable from different sources so uneven as to extent and period of years covered, that there arises a serious question as to the depth to which the intensive study of one particular phase of broadcast advertising can be carried.[4] It is quite true that interesting and valuable case studies could be carried on with the co-operation of advertising agencies and program sponsors primarily, and, to a lesser extent, of stations and networks. However, unless the investigator be engaged daily in the industry, these at present are extremely difficult. Studies in psychology, dealing with attention, imagery, memory, and similar factors as applied to broadcast advertising, provide an important field of investigation for the psychologist, but not the economist. Consequently, much of the research done in this field must remain, for the time being at least, of an extremely tentative and experimental nature.

In view of the extreme scarcity of information regarding the field as a whole, it seems that the outstanding need of the industry is for a broad, general survey of broadcast advertising in an attempt to describe, define, and evaluate the basic elements of its structure, the underlying principles of its technique, and the economic and social rôle which it plays in the modern business community.

A study of this nature is important for several reasons. In the first place, a general knowledge of the functioning of the broadcast advertising structure as a whole and its evaluation in terms of fundamental principles are necessary to the broadcaster, advertising agency, and program sponsor alike, if each of the three parties to broadcast advertising is to function intelligently with regard to each other and to broadcast advertising as a whole.

---

[4] It is rare indeed to find a station whose records exist in satisfactory form even as far back as 1929, while even considerable network data prior to that date become fairly tentative in nature. Other than Denney's *National Advertising Records*, giving advertising expenditures for time over networks, the report on Commercial Radio Advertising prepared by the Federal Radio Commission for the U.S. Senate in 1931 under the Couzens-Dill Resolution and a few scattered studies by other agencies (often of doubtful methodology), there are no summarized data available. The incomplete station records —existing in the rawest conceivable state—therefore become the chief source of information, making satisfactory intensive study difficult and often impossible.

Moreover, broadcast advertising is the keystone of the so-called "American System" of broadcasting, which in turn implies a broadcasting structure privately owned and competitively operated, and deriving its revenue from the sale of "time" to advertisers. Since broadcasting itself is more than a mere advertising medium, being also a potent agency of mass communication—just as the public press is a vitally important agency for the dissemination of information and free speech as well as probably the most important advertising medium of all—it is impossible to evaluate the degree to which broadcasting in the United States fulfils the "public interest, convenience and necessity" as prescribed in the Radio Act of 1927 without carefully studying its workings from all angles.

It is for these reasons, therefore, that a broad comprehensive study of the use of radio broadcasting as an advertising medium in the United States has been essayed. Following intensive research in the field of listener habits and reactions with regard to broadcasting, the direction of broadcasting programs for several years, and consultation with network and station executives, advertising agencies, and government officials regarding the most fruitful fields of radio research, it has been this problem which always has loomed uppermost. Finally, this study was undertaken at the suggestion of Philip G. Loucks, managing director of the National Association of Broadcasters, and with the encouragement and assistance of the Hon. Harold A. LaFount, acting chairman of the Federal Radio Commission, James W. Baldwin, former secretary of the Commission, and Dr. Herbert W. Hess, chairman of the Merchandising Department of the Wharton School of Finance and Commerce of the University of Pennsylvania.

Specifically the objectives of the present investigation are as follows: (1) to determine the extent and manner of the use of radio broadcasting as an advertising medium in this country; (2) to evaluate the trends in broadcast advertising structure and procedure in terms of such fundamental principles as thus far may be discernible; and (3) to analyze and evaluate the American system of broadcasting in the light of the degree to which it fulfils the "public interest, convenience and necessity."

Material to be studied in the course of pursuing these three objectives will include (1) a general analysis of the psychological aspects underlying the popularity of radio broadcasting with the listening public; (2) a similar investigation of the psychological aspects of its adaptability to convey effectively the advertising message; (3) a study of the extent and nature of the listening audience to which the advertiser may address his program and message; (4) a description and analysis of the broadcasting structure existing to reach the potential audience, together with the various middlemen who function between the agency or advertiser and the individual station; (5) an investigation of the extent to which broadcasting is used for advertising purpose and by whom it is employed; (6) a study of the entire question of the manner in which radio broadcasting is utilized in advertising, involving such matters as program construction, the choice of the time of day and season at which to broadcast, commercial announcement technique, the use of special offers, contests and similar items; and finally a comparison of the service rendered the listener by the American broadcasters and advertisers as compared with that of principal foreign broadcasting countries, notably England and Germany, whose broadcasting problems are most closely akin to our own, and whose facilities are the best developed among the countries so situated.

Data for the investigation have been collected from practically every available source of information, including two years of experience as director of the broadcasting efforts of the University of Pennsylvania and by research experience in the general field of broadcast advertising.

A great deal of the fundamental, factual, and statistical information has been collected directly from the records of the two great national network companies, the Columbia Broadcasting System, Inc., and the National Broadcasting Company, both of which have been more than generous in their co-operation. Most of the data procured from these sources have been completely "raw" in nature so that first tabulations and summarizations have had to be made from it.[5] Where this has been necessary, classification and summarization have been undertaken only

[5] The rawness of the data can be judged by the fact that all program information had to be tabulated from the network program sheets themselves, no summaries existing except in remote instances and for limited periods. The length of commercial announcements—except in the case of 1931, where information was requested by the Federal Radio Commission—could only be determined by actually counting the words in a representative sample of announcements.

after consultation with the proper network authorities and experts, this procedure likewise having been followed with regard to all other data employed in the investigation. In addition to the factual material gleaned from network records, various executives have been interviewed regarding specific phases of the study. Indeed, wherever possible, material and conclusions have been checked with experts in the field, to insure accuracy of statement and soundness of interpretation.

Information regarding the money expenditures for network broadcasting time has been secured from *National Advertising Records* through the courtesy of its publishers, the Advertising Records Company, formerly known as the Denney Publishing Company. These records constitute the sole source of information regarding money expenditures for broadcast advertising available at the present time, and as such are invaluable to the student of the industry.

Information regarding individual station experience was gathered in a variety of ways. At the outset an attempt was made to secure a sample of 35 representative stations from which data could be secured, comparable in completeness to those furnished by the networks. A base year of 1929 was taken, however, since the writer was counseled that it would be impossible to procure information for an earlier date. Even this attempt was only partially successful. Detailed data finally were procured from 10 stations, whose generosity and interest are deeply appreciated. The remaining stations failed not because of interest or willingness but because the necessary records were not available in practical form. The detailed information supplied by the 10 stations in turn has varied greatly so that no combined tabulations have been possible, the data being used rather in the form of individual examples rather than in summary form.

This initial attempt at securing individual station information was supplemented by a questionnaire sent to the managers of 165 stations (other than the original 10 furnishing data), asking for their experience and opinion upon certain questions pertinent to the investigation. Replies were received from 52 stations of varying size and scattered throughout the entire country, thus constituting in themselves a representative cross section of the broadcasting industry.[6] This information in turn was supplemented by visits to 14 stations situated in New England, the Middle Atlantic states, Middle West, and Maryland. In this manner a total of 76 stations were reached by one or another of the methods outlined above.

The advertising agency viewpoint in turn was secured through interviews with radio executives in leading advertising agencies,[7] while time-brokers, special station representatives, electrical transcription companies, and other factors in the broadcast advertising structure were covered in a similar manner.

All classifications and tabulations in the study (e.g. program classification), have been made after careful consultation with qualified authorities in the field, both as to the propriety of the classifications and the actual practice of placing certain items under specific classifications when tabulation was begun. Tabulation of musical programs was done either by Irene Hewes or Sarah S. Hettinger of the library of the Curtis Institute of Music, Philadelphia, or by members of the network staff, the details of classification having been worked out in advance with network officials and also approved by Morrison S. Boyd, of the music faculty of the University of Pennsylvania, who also was consulted regarding the other musical phases of the study.

Partly because of their present dominance of broadcast advertising, and because of the greater availability of their records, the national networks have been used as the starting point of this discussion in this study, analysis then proceeding to the questions of national and local advertising over individual stations. Likewise, because of the inadequacies of data prior to that date, 1927 has been used as the initial year, though, wherever possible, a background has been given for developments prior to that period. Most data end June, 1932, since the me-

---

[6] A list of the stations answering the questionnaire, as well as those co-operating either through supplying detailed records or providing information when the writer visited them, is found in Appendix A. The questionnaire itself appears in Appendix B. Questions submitted to networks and the 35 stations are not listed since they are requests for specific records and as such are covered by a presentation of the records themselves. These will appear as the study is developed.

[7] Eleven of the most important agencies, as far as broadcast advertising is concerned, were interviewed. These were selected after consultation with competent authorities in the field.

chanics of collection and tabulation have precluded extending the study to any later date.

In addition to the acknowledgments already made in the course of this Introduction, the writer wishes to voice his deep appreciation to the invaluable advice and assistance afforded by Paul W. Kesten, director of sales promotion, and John Karol, director of market research of the Columbia Broadcasting System, E. P. H. James, sales promotion manager and Paul F. Peter, chief statistician of the National Broadcasting Company, both in collecting the necessary data and in the planning and development of the study. To Dr. Leon Levy, president of the WCAU Broadcasting Company, goes the writer's gratitude for having first interested him in the field of broadcast advertising. Likewise, he extends his thanks and appreciation to Dr. J. Russell Doubman, associate professor of merchandising in the Wharton School, for his valuable assistance at all stages of the study, to Dr. J. Parker Bursk, assistant professor of statistics, for his advice in the matter of statistical presentation, and to Dr. Sherman S. Oberly, assistant professor of psychology at the University, for his counsel regarding the psychological aspects of the analysis. Finally, a special word of appreciation is due to Philip G. Loucks, managing director of the National Association of Broadcasters, at whose suggestion this study first took form and without whose kind assistance much of the information hardly could have been collected; and to Sarah S. Hettinger, whose continued help and encouragement smoothed many a rough place in an arduous but highly interesting road.

LOGAN HALL
UNIVERSITY OF PENNSYLVANIA
MARCH 31, 1933

TABLE OF CONTENTS

xiv TABLE OF CONTENTS

LIST OF TABLES

LIST OF TABLES

LIST OF CHARTS

PART I. THE PSYCHOLOGICAL AND ECONOMIC BASES OF BROADCAST ADVERTISING

CHAPTER I

THE PSYCHOLOGICAL BASIS OF BROAD-CASTING: SATISFACTION AFFORDED TO THE LISTENER

In considering radio broadcasting, there is a great temptation to take it too much for granted. Though a few years ago it was the latest wonder of the age, broadcasting by now has become a fairly commonplace matter. A program from Europe or distant Asia is received with little more interest or enthusiasm than was evinced a decade ago by the lucky Philadelphian who had tuned in on Chicago. Radio is no longer a miracle; and, in consequence, the fundamental utility of radio broadcasting too often is overlooked by the various parties concerned with it.

Nevertheless, this fundamental utility of radio broadcasting to the listener must constitute the starting-point of any analysis of broadcasting or broadcast advertising. What is the potential satisfaction which can be derived by the listener from the use of his receiving set? Until this question is answered it is impossible either to criticize broadcasting for what it has failed to give the listener of his due or to praise it for the bounties which it has provided. Nor is it possible to evaluate the hold which it has upon the listener, and which in turn lies at the heart of its value as an advertising medium. It is, therefore, with such an analysis that our investigation begins.

Mechanically, broadcasting is the transformation of sound impulses into electrical energy and its radiation far and wide through the ether. This energy is sent in all directions as light rays from an electric-light bulb, and, indeed, there seems to be a fundamental relationship between the two. The electrical energy, in turn, is picked up by the listener's receiving set and re-transformed into sound, with the resulting program. Thus far, broadcasting has been limited to the transmission of sound, though the advent of television in more than experimental form undoubtedly will extend its range of activity into the realm of

3

sight as well, with ensuing radical modifications of broadcasting structure and procedure.

Two basic results of the fundamental characteristics of broadcasting should be borne in mind from the outset. The first of these is that, because of the radiation of the broadcast electrical energy over wide areas, the radio station becomes one of the most potent agencies of mass communication to have been developed since the printing press. A second result is that, limited as it is at present to the transmission of sound, radio broadcasting depends primarily upon two agencies of expression—(1) the spoken word and (2) musical expression, both vocal and instrumental. To this should be added a supplementary medium of auditory expression which has arisen out of radio broadcasting itself, namely, sound effects; whereby the imagery of the individual is reinforced by the appropriate sounds which suggest to him the presence of objects (the whir of an airplane), forces (wind or rain), or activities on the part of actors (pouring water, footsteps).

The first of these two results achieves importance only when the structure of broadcasting in relation to the listening audience served is taken into consideration. The second, however, is of immediate concern. Because of it, radio broadcast programs are restricted to various forms of musical presentation, ranging from symphonic orchestras to pianos and accordions, and from Stravinsky to Tin Pan Alley; and to vocal presentations including informal talks on interesting subjects, formal lectures and debates, accounts of news events, broadcasts of public occasions, dramatic programs from Shakespeare to the drolleries of Ed Wynn, and various other features.

Functionally, this vast body of program material may be divided into two principal categories, by no means mutually exclusive: (1) entertainment and (2) useful information. This classification possesses validity primarily with respect to the listener's attitude toward the program, rather than with regard to programs themselves, where one program may have an utterly different significance to two different groups. Thus a symphonic broadcast may have a definite utilitarian value to a student of music over and above the aesthetic enjoyment which it affords. It is also well to keep in mind the fact that there are varying degrees of useful information. The daily crop, market, and weather reports are of decided practical value to the farmers to whom they are broadcast throughout the country. Recipes for housewives likewise are of value, though not as intensely or materially so as the agricultural broadcasts. Finally, news reports, such as those of Lowell Thomas and political analyses exemplified by the work of Frederick William Wile, most decidedly are useful information even though they have little so-called practical value.

To the program sponsor the above classification has a decided significance. Entertainment and information are the two great reasons for listening to the radio. Unless the information possesses great basic utility indeed, as in the case of crop and market reports, there will be little interest in the program unless it is presented with especial attractiveness. Other than those objects of universal interest, namely, time, news, and weather reports, the broadcaster of useful information is faced with a restricted audience composed of the special-interest group or groups to which his subject appeals the most strongly. True, this circle may be enlarged by good showmanship, but there still are limits which cannot be transcended. Moreover, since man would rather be entertained than edified, the principal interest in broadcasting, at least under any democratized system, will be in entertainment.

Of the program types sketched briefly in the preceding paragraphs, music thus far has loomed most important, as it probably will continue to do as long as broadcasting is confined to the realm of sound. Therefore, in order to appreciate fully the satisfaction which the use of a radio receiving set affords the listener, and which constitutes the service rendered by broadcasting to the public, it becomes necessary to understand the fundamental aspects of the pleasure derived by the listener from hearing music. This, in turn, involves a brief excursion into the psychology of music, which, though it may seem abstract at the outset, is of great practical importance to all parties concerned with broadcasting (as will be seen later in the chapter).

It is not without reason that listener surveys indicate 60 per cent of the people of a community such as Buffalo, New York,[1] prefer musical programs to all others, and that in Philadelphia

[1] *The Buffalo Radio Audience*, compiled for Station WBEN, Buffalo, New York, by Dr. Robert Riegel, of the University of Buffalo (1932).

99.8 per cent of listeners should find musical programs accept-able.[2] As a form of expression music is one of the oldest and most universal known to man. From earliest days certain of its tones have been associated with feelings of pleasantness and others with feelings of unpleasantness. Its rhythm has assisted in in-ducing motor activity in man, and often has been used by him in organizing his muscular activity either individually or in groups. Finally, its melodic and harmonic structure has been shaped into one of the most sublime agencies for the expression of human emotion. A more detailed analysis of the psychology of music will indicate what pleasure and satisfaction the listener derives from its various aspects.

The basic elements of music are sound, rhythm, and form. Sound in turn subdivides itself into pitch, volume or intensity, and timbre or quality. Rhythm, in turn, may be defined as a "periodicity of sound and some organizing principle which we call stress,"[3] which stress, in turn, is secured either by a change in the intensity, duration, or pitch of the dominant note; and which has the effect of grouping single notes into units with the accenting of one or more of the individual notes. The units into which the notes are grouped are known as the measure and the musical phrase. Finally, form implies melodic line, harmony, counterpoint, and the rearing of the entire complicated struc-ture which finds its culmination in the symphony.

True, the listener may not recognize these elements in their technical habiliments, but he will note them just the same. "I don't like sopranos," he may comment, for the high notes grate upon his ears. He is commenting upon sound. "That march has a nice swing. It makes me want to tap my foot," says the listen-er as the rhythm catches hold of him. "It's a beautiful tune," continues the listener, "and I especially like the end where, in the closing chord, the cornet sings high above the whole band."

[2] *An Analysis of the Summer Radio Audience in the Philadelphia Buying Area,* by Herman S. Hettinger and Richard R. Mead, University of Pennsylvania, compiled for Station WCAU, Philadelphia. The same preference was indicated in a similar study conducted in the early part of 1930—*A Study of Habits and Preferences of Radio Listen-ers in Philadelphia,* Herman S. Hettinger—thus seeming to point to the conclusion that listener habits in this respect are generally stable.

[3] *The Borderland of Music and Psychology,* by Frank Howes, M.A. (Oxon.) (Kegan Paul), p. 94. The reader is recommended to both Mr. Howes's chapter on "Rhythm" and the one on "Emotion in Music" as especially illuminating discussions of these two ques-tions.

He is commenting upon melody, harmony, and orchestration. Musically unsophisticated as he may be, if his musical experience has reached even the most elementary stages, and granting a normal "ear" for music, these elements will have meaning to him.

This meaning will vary with the listener's auditory imagery and the degree of his musical education, formal or informal, and it therefore may be well to examine this question briefly. The simplest form of musical experience is the appreciation of sound by itself, devoid of rhythm or form. In the field of sight it is analogous to experiencing unrelated colors one at a time. In sound it relates to the pleasantness or unpleasantness of the pitch, intensity, or timbre of individual sounds. The listener's appreciation is purely sensory. It is limited to a feeling of restfulness upon hearing soft music, or to the stimulation afforded by a crash of sound; to delight in the full rich notes of the 'cello as against the thinner tones of the violin, or a preference for the middle pitch as against either extreme. Though all musical appreciation rests upon the sensory as its basis, it is only in the most unmusical that it fails to rise above these heights.[4, 5]

Thus, little musical experience remains at this level. Organization is the basic law of mental activity, and sound becomes organized in consciousness even as individual color sensations are blended into a picture. The non-voluntary attention of the sensorial experience soon becomes the more or less voluntary attention of following melody and form; while even earlier the sensory experience of pleasure or displeasure at hearing different tones transfers itself to chords, where thirds and sixths—abounding in such numbers as "Holy Night," Beethoven's "Minuet in G," barber-shop harmony, and popular music[6]—are found to be the most acceptable. Here the borderline between the purely

[4] An excellent discussion of the levels of musical experience will be found in the essay on "Types of Listeners," by Otto Ortmann, appearing in *Types of Music*, edited by Max Schoen (Kegan Paul). The writer has borrowed from Mr. Ortmann's classification though reducing it to more elementary form, and enlarging upon certain aspects considerably from other sources.

[5] Anent the sensory type Mr. Ortmann finds a marked preference among young children for sounds of middle pitch, duration, and intensity as compared with the extremes (*ibid.*, pp. 43–44). Dr. Charles S. Myers also describes the sensory impressions of the most unmusical vividly in his essay, "Individual Differences in Listening to Music," *ibid.*, pp. 20–22.

[6] Ortmann, *ibid.*, p. 50.

sensory and higher forms of musical experience becomes extremely vague. Now rhythm asserts itself in consciousness. The listener, mostly through chance experience, has come to recognize certain phrases and progressions, so that melodic structure begins to have meaning for him. The perceptual and imaginal levels of musical experience now have been attained.

Simplest and most elemental of these forces is rhythm, next indeed to sound itself as a fundamental force in music. A tentative definition already has been given of rhythm,[7] and it is a sufficiently well-known phenomenon to require no additional description. Its probable origin and its effect upon the listener, however, are of considerable interest because of the light that they shed upon the satisfaction which the listener derives from pronouncedly rhythmic music, of which our modern dance tunes are such an important example.

Several theories have been advanced in explanation of rhythm. One of these is that rhythmic movements are inseparable from bodily activity,[8] and that all physical activity tends to take on a rhythmic form if repeated. From these rhythmic activities, in turn, came the dance, and with the dance was associated music. Closely allied to this is the theory that rhythm, especially as found in music, arose out of a need for some organizing principle in effecting concerted group action.[9] Still another approach is offered by the theory based on the observation that most of the factors which induce accentuation also give rise to attention,[10] and that therefore rhythm aids in keeping up the level of attention. All of these theories possess merit and probably constitute partial explanations of rhythms, each finding confirmation in certain phases of experience. The rhythmic aspects of bodily movement are matters of commonplace knowledge to anyone who has indulged in athletics, while the work songs of primitive tribes confirm the relation of rhythmic music to concerted group action. The last-mentioned theory is more difficult to illustrate in terms of simple daily experience, and therefore will be dismissed without further comment.

More important than the origins of rhythm are the effects

[7] See p. 6.

[8] *The Fundamentals of Psychology*, by W. B. Pillsbury (Macmillan), p. 349.

[9] *The Rhythmic Conception of Music*, by Margaret Glyn.

[10] Pillsbury, *op. cit.*, p. 350.

which different rhythms exert upon the listener. These are of marked nature and can be measured specifically. The motor stimulus of a stirring rhythm, a matter of common experience, has been found definitely to heighten the systolic and pulse pressures and increase the velocity of the blood flow.[11] This type of music therefore is valuable in counteracting depressed reactions, in removing fatigue and arousing muscular activity. Likewise, a lullaby played on a violin was found to have a sedative and regularizing effect upon the body processes. The restful effect of certain definite rhythms also is well illustrated by an anecdote of Howes,[12] regarding a friend to whom the music of Bach, with its clear-cut mathematical tempo, was physically refreshing. Similarly, certain musicians have noted a desire, when fatigued, to play music of a regular rhythmic pattern, such as Bach, Haydn, or the early Beethoven sonatas. A seeming increase was noted in the tempo and accuracy of work on the part of student tabulators when popular dance music was being played in the tabulating room.

From rhythm, musical experience progresses to melody and the simple perception of tonal progression. Melody is closely related to rhythm, and it will be found that most folk tunes combine simple melodic line with clearly pronounced rhythm. In this connection it is interesting to note the evolution which is taking place in modern dance music where the melodic and even the harmonic is taking a much more important place as against the purely rhythmic aspects than was the case a decade ago.

Finally, from the appreciation of melody it is a comparatively short psychological step to an understanding of the higher forms of composition, a knowledge of which is predicated more upon habituation than talent. Now the perceptual and imaginal levels of musical experience have been reached, and, with the latter of these, music becomes the potent medium for the expression of feelings and emotions which it is. It is with a brief discussion of this aspect that we conclude our analysis of the psychology of music as it relates to the listener.

[11] "The Effects of Music upon Electro-Cardiograms and Blood Pressure," by Ida H. Hyde, in *The Effects of Music*, edited by Max Schoen (Kegan Paul), pp. 184–97. The essay deals with the effect of other aspects of music than merely rhythm and it should be noted that major and minor chords, for instance, also exert an influence on the body processes, the former stimulating, the latter depressing.

[12] Frank Howes, M.A. (Oxon.) *op. cit.* (Kegan Paul), p. 137.

Psychologically, the question of emotion is a thorny one, related as it is to affection and feeling on the one hand, and to instinct on the other.[13] Important in the present instance, however, is the fact that, on the one hand, emotion possesses a close relation to feelings of pleasantness and unpleasantness,[14] and, on the other hand, with bodily changes by which nature has contrived to prepare the individual for strenuous effort in overcoming danger or difficulty.[15] These latter, in turn, are called into action, not only by the presence of acute physical danger, but from a thwarting of purposes, or the mere need for motor activity without the presence of a corresponding channel of expression. As an example of the latter, we can take the theoretical case of watching a romantic motion picture. The drama is drawing to a close; the obstacles have been overcome, virtue is about to receive its due, and the course of love soon again will run smoothly. Throughout the course of events we have been living the drama vicariously. We have strained in an attempt to overcome the seemingly insuperable odds, and, now that success is at hand, a warm glow of satisfaction suffuses us. In the drama we have recognized situations which demanded action, and instinctively we have tried to act regarding them; but the outlet being missing, the only result which we attained was one of emotional disturbance, pleasant or unpleasant, depending upon the situation and our relation to it. Thus does drama stir our emotions; with the additional feature that if any of the experience portrayed is analogous to some which we have faced, the emotional appeal of the unfolding story will be heightened by the memory of the analogous emotion which we in turn felt at some past time. Out of these relatively simple elements, then, the whole complex structure of human emotion is constructed.

The close relation of music to emotion is a matter of common experience. However, the exact relationship is more difficult to determine. Music probably is related, directly or indirectly, to both of the fundamental aspects of emotion previously de-

[13] Pillsbury, *op. cit.*, p. 480, defines emotions as either a complicated feeling or the subjective side of an instinct. For present purposes this will do as well as any other definition.

[14] *Ibid.*, p. 480.

[15] *Ibid.*, pp. 487–90; also *Bodily Changes in Pain, Hunger, Fear and Rage*, by Walter B. Cannon, M.D. (Appleton).

scribed. The pleasantness or unpleasantness of certain tones or tonal combinations already has been noted, as has been the relation to motor activity and bodily changes of the rhythmic aspects of music. Similar changes, it should be noted, are induced by music in major and minor keys, the latter generally depressing and the former exerting a constructive effect;[16] the exact effect probably being determined by the combination of tonality and rhythmic pattern. Because of these relations, music possesses the ability to induce feelings and emotional states.

This, however, is but the groundwork. As has been pointed out previously, the individual recollects[17] or recognizes how he or she felt in a given situation at some past time. Because of its ability to induce feelings, music produces an emotional reaction which the listener, referring to past experience in an endeavor to classify the impression which the music makes upon him, terms as "sad," "happy," "fierce," or "restful,"as the case may be.

Now to this is added all of the associations which a given "gay" or "sad" composition may have for him, all coloring and reinforcing the original mood created by the music. A certain composition may thus remind the listener of a past experience, or it may revive an image which has become associated with the number in question. Finally, if the listener is conversant with the literature of music or possesses especially strong musical imagery, he may find in the composition a projection of the personality and strivings of the composer; and, if these be analogous to his own, past or present, a picture of his own life, painted in tonal colors and shades. It is then that the highest level of imaginal musical experience is reached; and it can be said of all music as Storm has written of folk music: "Our own doings and sufferings are in these songs; it is as if we all had helped with their making."[18] In conclusion, it should be noted, first, that an individual tends to listen to different types of music at different levels, popular dance music seldom if ever rising above the perceptual level; and, second, that the richer content of

[16] Ida H. Hyde, op. cit., pp. 184–97.

[17] Pillsbury, op. cit., pp. 499–500; Howes, op. cit., has an especially fine analysis of the relation of emotion and music, based largely upon this concept, and borrowing largely from Ribot and MacDougall.

[18] Immensee, by Theodore Storm, p. 36.

imaginal listening causes the music inducing it to wear much better than that appealing to the lower levels of experience.[19]

The preceding discussion of the psychology of music, abstract as it may seem, has a concrete bearing upon the question of the satisfaction which the listener derives from the use of his radio; for it helps to explain the types of music which he likes, and what he gets out of them. It is not without sound psychological foundation that popular music should indeed be "popular." Most listening to music is probably at the perceptual level, where mere enjoyment of the sound patterns without broader associations is the chief characteristic, or at best of a rather elementary imaginal type where the associations raised by the music are of a simple and homely nature. Consequently, if the broadcaster is to give the great body of the public the music it desires, he must provide music at a level which the listener is capable of appreciating. This means, therefore, that dance music, folk music, the more simple classical numbers, and the more elementary program music (music which tells a story) will be the types most appreciated by listeners as a whole. This is fairly well substantiated, at least for metropolitan centers, by Table I, showing the proportion of listeners in Philadelphia and Buffalo liking various types of music.[20] Thus, assuming that the radio broadcasting system should be operated for the great mass of the public, it is evident that the lighter types of music must continue to predominate.

Lest this be interpreted as meaning that we should condone the exclusive broadcasting of the cheap and meretricious, several additional aspects should be noted. In the first place, there is a variety of quality among popular, light classical, and the simpler classical compositions. The work of Grofe and Gershwin and the arrangements used by Paul Whiteman are a far throw from the monotonous rendition of the average dance band, while the

[19] "The Immediate and Long-Time Effects of Classical and Popular Phonograph Selections," by A. R. Gilliland and H. T. Moore in *Effects of Music* (ed. Max Schoen), pp. 211–22.

[20] Based upon studies made by the writer in Philadelphia in 1932 for WCAU, and by Dr. Robert Riegel, University of Buffalo, for WBEN of that city in 1932, and reproduced from "Metropolitan Radio Audiences" by the writer in *Broadcast Advertising*, December, 1932. The inclusion of Polish music in the Buffalo table is because of the large Polish population in that city. Likewise, the high percentage of people liking old-fashioned music is explained mainly on the basis of the large German population together with the Polish group already noted.

old folk songs, Haydn, and the more readily understandable of the works of composers such as Beethoven and Tschaikowsky possess unquestionable merit, even if they do not contain the complexity of Strauss' "Zarathustra" or Stravinsky's "Oedipus Rex." Moreover, it already has been remarked that it is the music appealing to the imaginal level of listening which wears best. If this is true, is there not a possibility that the radio listener's taste, familiarized with all forms of music, should not turn more toward the higher types? This is the opinion of some of the most expert broadcasters. Finally, the opinion is ven-

TABLE I

TYPES OF MUSIC LIKED BY PHILADELPHIA AND
BUFFALO RADIO AUDIENCES

TYPE OF MUSIC	PERCENTAGE OF LISTENERS LIKING TYPE	
	Philadelphia	Buffalo
Classical...................	31.4	36.1
Semi-classical..............	39.9	39.0
Dance.....................	73.4	69.0
Sacred.....................	27.7	15.7
Old-fashioned..............	27.7	42.7
Polish.....................	....	8.3

tured that it would be interesting to know exactly what has been the effect on public taste of the broadcasts of such organizations and periods as the New York Philharmonic and Philadelphia Orchestras, the Damrosch Musical Appreciation Hour, and the Metropolitan Opera, wherein, devoid of the awesome qualities of the concert hall, and in the intimacy of one's own home, one can hear the world's great music as one pleases. Though popular music will always predominate in public demand, the trend of popularity over the next decade, as far as proportion of various types of music is concerned, will be extremely interesting to observe.

The question of the levels of listening, however, is but one of the aspects of musical psychology of interest to the broadcaster. The value of dance music, for instance, lies not only in the ease with which its melodic line and structure is perceived but in the physical and psychological effects which its pronounced rhythm engenders. It stimulates and is pleasant and helpful to work to, even though one barely is aware of its existence; whereas music of a higher type tends to require more concentrated listening and consequently distracts from the task at hand. It aids in motor activity and arouses a desire for such activity. This may be the reason why, in their surveys, investigators have found a relatively large proportion of housewives who have voiced a preference for more dance music broadcast during the morning and afternoon hours.[21]

This leads to a still broader question. Perhaps stimulating music broadcast in the morning possesses a constructive value to the listener. Likewise, restful music at the end of the day, or at the evening dinner hour (now abdicated to the children), may render valuable service to many listeners. This may be the psychological reason underlying the popularity of the Slumber Hour in its heyday. Finally, if music can stir emotions it may be of interest to the advertiser to study his musical program carefully to determine whether the correct emotional state has been built up before his sales message is delivered, or whether the type of music and performing group chosen is in keeping with the emotional background or feeling-tone which he wishes his product to possess. This indeed may be a fruitful field for additional investigation.

The discussion of the listener's satisfaction derived from musical programs having been completed, it now remains to see with what, other than song, the human voice can provide the owner of a radio receiving set. This, in turn, requires an analysis of the types of programs which can be translated into speech. Since the adaptability of broadcasting to the advertising message is primarily a matter of comparing the spoken and the printed word as means of influencing people to purchase goods, any discussion of the psychology of language necessary to this study will be postponed until this matter is considered. However, several general features should be mentioned tentatively.

[21] Though the writer has never made a tabulation of this situation, it always has been of great interest to note the large proportion of the women voicing any desire for a change in program set-up (and they are relatively few out of the total listening audience) who demanded more dance music in the morning or afternoon. On the other hand, the requests for more classical music have been negligible at any period. Other investigators have noted the same trend.

The programs, which are conveyed to the listener through speech, represent events and objects through the medium of sound alone, the speech in turn reinforced either by sound effects or the actual noises of the occasion. There are no pictures or direct visual impressions to assist the spoken word, though visual imagery may be stimulated by the words utilized in the description. A second factor of importance is the ability of the voice to portray, at least partially, the personality of the speaker. Thus a gruff, friendly, masculine voice engenders confidence, while the unctuous tone, which women find so hard to overcome when speaking on the radio, makes the listener feel unconsciously that he is being patronized, and, as such, probably has a great deal to do with the marked unpopularity of women lecturers or announcers.[22]

Finally, individuals tend to associate certain types of voices with specific types of people, so that voice stereotypes are created. It is this stereotype of voice pattern which makes possible radio drama, where voice is the sole means of identifying the actors other than the descriptive lines worked into the script.

All of this in turn can be utilized through the age-old process of story-telling, practiced long before the first pictures were produced. In it, the imagination of the listener is free to create ideal characters out of the figment of his mind, unhampered by literal images, a sobering thought for those who some day may be obliged to create programs for television.[23]

With these preliminary remarks regarding non-musical programs to the rear, it may be well to analyze somewhat more

[22] This does not mean that women cannot be successful as speakers over the radio. Some of them have been decidedly so. It merely signifies that the number of women capable of making a favorable impression over the radio is definitely and seriously limited by their voice personalities, irrespective of how charming they might be if one were to meet them face to face.

[23] In this respect, Mrs. Loring Dam, of the University of Pennsylvania Museum, makes an interesting observation regarding the "Magic Carpet," a children's story hour which she conducts on Saturday mornings during the winter. It has been her observation that stories recounted without the aid of pictures, and preferably with the children taking part, have always been the most successful, while motion pictures presenting similar stories in detail have been decidedly less popular. Quite probably this is not entirely confined to children, and some of the untrammeled imagination of youth may withstand the onslaught of the years. In radio the writer has observed the same reaction in his personal experience with the program "Chandu, the Magician," which delighted him over the air and bored him completely in motion-picture form where it seemed utterly improbable and ridiculous.

thoroughly than thus far has been done what programs of this sort are available to the listener. At the outset these may be divided into two principal groups: (1) talks of different kinds, and (2) dramatic presentations. Under the first heading come programs such as news, market, and weather reports; editorial comments on aspects of the news such as those made by William Hard; educational talks, debates, and symposiums; eye-witness accounts of athletic and public events, where the talking is given added dramatic value by the crowd sounds; direct broadcasts of public events, such as national conventions and speeches by the President; miscellaneous talks on interesting subjects including religion, food, household hints, sports, and a variety of topics; and, finally, poetic readings. With regard to these, radio broadcasting becomes at once a magazine, class periodical, newspaper —in highly attenuated and hardly competing form to be sure —and economic bulletin.

In the field of drama, the material offered is of an equally wide variety. In presentations such as those of the Radio Guild, broadcasting reproduces the best traditions of the legitimate stage, though, of course, skilful adaptation is necessary to compensate for the lack of visual presentation, and not all stage works are capable of being successfully presented over the air. Dramatized stories in turn make broadcasting its own fiction magazine, various stories appealing to various classes. In this field the "Adventures of Mary and Bob" (the *True Story* program of several years ago), "Real Folks," "Red Adams," and the "Country Doctor" and "Seth Parker" are notable examples. If programs of this sort have any particular leaning, it is toward folk drama of the "Real Folks" and "Country Doctor" type. The comic strip, initiated by "Amos 'n' Andy," is another type of drama which has gained wide popularity, while the mystery story and melodrama—ideally suited for broadcasting in the play it gives the imagination and the wild results which can be achieved through sound effects—also are coming into their own. Finally, there are children's dramatic programs, mostly melodrama to be sure, but one program, "The Adventures of Helen and Mary," contains some delightful dramatizations of well-known fairy tales.

The relation of sound effects to successful dramatic broadcasting already has been mentioned several times. However, a complete appreciation of its importance in creating vivid impressions for the listener requires a somewhat more detailed description of procedure in this field. Probably the most simple approach is to describe the sound effects in a specific program, as noted and recorded by the writer. The program in question was a dramatization of the life of Alexander the Great, broadcast by the Columbia School of the Air.[24] As the scene opens, Alexander and his generals are banqueting following one of their victories. Music and the noise of the banquet hall are used to create the original atmosphere. The music is soft in the background, while the shouting of the men grows louder until individual voices are heard. It is as if one is moving nearer to the scene of festivities. Then, with the mental picture created, the sound effects fade before the voices of the principal actors, and finally pass away completely. The illusion is so complete, however, that it requires definite concentration to notice that the sound effects are no longer in use. Later, messengers approach, and one hears the sound of horses coming nearer; then the approaching and, later, the retreating footsteps of the messenger himself. In another episode of the sketch, Alexander burns his wagon train before marching into India. The wagon train is some distance away from the main camp and the semi-mutinous Macedonians. Here the illusion of distance is beautifully created by two trumpet calls, the second echoing far away, as well as by the usual device of approaching and retreating couriers on horseback, the hoof-beats thundering on the hard earth. Still later, Alexander reviews the Persian troops which he has ordered trained in the Macedonian manner of fighting, and the sound of marching suggests thousands of men passing in review. Here again the spatial aspect is exceptionally well handled. In addition to these principal devices, numerous small sound effects, such as the scraping of a sword when it is drawn from its sheath, also are employed with great effectiveness. As one program manager once remarked, sound effects such as these are the lifeblood of the dramatic presentation over the radio.

By now we should have received a fairly clear appreciation of the potential satisfaction derived by the listener from the use of his receiving set. There is, however, one additional satisfaction which he secures, though its present importance is difficult to

24 *Broadcast*, November 21, 1932.

estimate; namely, the thrill of conquering time and space. This thrill is decidedly less than it was in the early days of broadcasting when it probably constituted the principal reason for listening. Nevertheless, there is incipient and often realized drama in being present, at least in hearing, at the performances of the Metropolitan Opera, when a new President of the United States is being inaugurated in Washington, or in Geneva on an occasion such as the one when the representatives of China and Japan pleaded their respective causes before the world, following the hostilities in Shanghai. It is a thrill which, to some extent at least, will remain with radio as long as radio exists.

And so, in summary, radio broadcasting renders a wide variety of services to the listener. It is the symphony hall and opera house; salon and music hall; vaudeville stage and the realm of the legitimate drama; the fiction magazine and the more serious periodical; the newspaper (abbreviated, to be sure), farm journal, and woman's magazine; and, at times, even functions as a supplement to the formal school system, though its service in the field of adult education is vastly more important. Every station of any size or pretension fulfils the majority of these rôles for its listeners at least once during each week, and often daily. It is this service, and its utility to the listener, that constitutes the cornerstone of successful radio broadcasting.

CHAPTER II

THE PSYCHOLOGICAL BASIS OF BROADCAST ADVERTISING: ADAPTABILITY OF BROADCASTING TO THE ADVERTISING MESSAGE

The various factors which underlie the satisfaction derived by the listener from radio broadcasting, and which constitute the basis for its widespread popularity, were discussed in the preceding chapter. These are of fundamental importance to the radio broadcast advertiser, since they constitute the foundation of any sound program policy, a matter which he, as well as the station and network executive, must consider at all times. It is the purpose at this time to carry the analysis of the use of radio broadcasting as an advertising medium one step farther, and to inquire into the extent and nature of its ability to present effectively the advertising message to the listener. In the early days of broadcast advertising, when good will was the sole objective of program sponsors and the active selling message was seldom employed, this matter received little if any attention. Today, when the advertiser seeks to accomplish practically the same purposes through his radio campaign as by the use of any other medium, the adaptability of broadcasting to a definite selling message has become a question of no small concern. In considering its various aspects, the psychological approach again constitutes the soundest method of getting to the core of the problem, and has therefore been employed.

The specific uses of advertising are many,[1] but throughout all of them runs one fundamental purpose: To induce the sale of a given commodity, service, or proposition by successfully appealing to the consumer to purchase it. The appeal is a general one, designed for many readers or listeners; not as in the case of salesmanship, being created by a given seller to meet a

[1] Kleppner lists some sixteen in all (*Advertising Procedure*, by Otto Kleppner [Prentice Hall], chap. ii), including linking a family of products together, dispelling malimpressions regarding the product, securing the support of the trade, to be recognized as a leader in the field, and numerous others. Other writers approach the problem differently but with equal variety.

specific contingency in which he is trying to influence an individual buyer to purchase the article in question.[2]

Fostering the sale of the commodity involves, in turn, the overcoming of the resistance of the potential buyer by showing, through the means open to the advertiser, the desirability and even necessity of possessing the product, and by doing this so vividly that action will be stimulated and the purchase made. Moreover, since purchase may not be effected until some time after the potential customer has seen the advertisement, or since the advertiser may wish to have the purchaser continue to buy his brand when once the original stock has been exhausted, he must be certain that his message is remembered, which he accomplishes both through the vividness of his presentation and the number of times it is repeated.

From the viewpoint of the ideal, however, each individual advertisement should be strong enough to impel immediate purchase—obviously a very distant goal indeed. It is from this viewpoint, though, that an analysis of the psychology of advertising best can be undertaken. Continuing, therefore, with the question of making the advertisement sufficiently dynamic to cause the reader or listener to buy the thing advertised, the commonly accepted manner of describing the steps involved in this process is to say that the advertisement must attract attention, arouse interest, stimulate desire, and impel action. Walter Dill Scott visualizes this task[3] by describing three circles which the advertising message must penetrate before the individual can be made to buy. First, his attention must be attracted by the advertisement. Second, the message must be such that he can comprehend it. Finally, his inner springs of action must be touched, so that he will want the article enough to buy it. Psychologically, attracting the attention involves following the laws relating to the focus, margin, duration, and range of attention. Making one's message understood revolves

---

[2] This generalization is by no means water-tight. Strong arguments can be advanced for calling direct-mail advertising selling in spite of the fact that the same letter is sent to large numbers of people, no matter how artfully this is camouflaged. Likewise, it is argued by a few that broadcasting is selling because an individual announcer speaks, theoretically, to an individual listener, even though his message is keyed to the psychology of a group of listeners. The line between selling and advertising is not and never will be clear-cut, and the above distinction becomes one of degree.

[3] *The Psychology of Advertising*, by Walter Dill Scott (rev. ed.), chap. i.

about the related problems of perception, imagery and association, and comprehension. Securing action requires the creation of a motive to purchase through an appeal to the instinctive tendencies of the individual, together with his feelings and complexes; and, in addition, investing the product with the correct feeling-tone to give it the maximum compatibility with the motive which has been aroused.

Thus far in advertising, this process has been carried out almost exclusively in relation to the sense of sight.[4] Therefore, the laws of attention, imagery, perception, and the other related phases of psychology have been applied exhaustively to visual advertising. However, to date, practically nothing has been done with regard to the interpretation of these laws in terms of an approach to the listener through the sense of audition. Experimental work carried out in this field with special regard to broadcasting and broadcast advertising is so rare and so tentative as to be negligible.[5] The approach to the subject in this instance, therefore, must be in the nature of a reinterpretation of existing data in terms of radio broadcasting experience.

Since individuals are accustomed to think of advertising largely in terms of magazines and newspapers, and since the psychological principles relating to advertising have been worked out primarily with regard to these two media, the present discussion will consist mainly of a comparison of them with broadcast advertising, from the psychological point of view. One decided word of caution should be added at this point; namely, that in this comparison no attempt will be made to show the psychological superiority of one medium over the other, but it will aim merely at pointing out the similarities and dissimilarities, so that a clear understanding may be had of the strength and limitations of broadcast advertising as far as its

[4] The writer, however, knows of one instance where a chain of bakeshops created a synthetic smell of cooking which was wafted in front of the individual store, though the baking was done far away. Sales in the stores where the experiment was tried actually increased.

[5] A number of educational institutions, notably Ohio State University and the Teachers College, Columbia University, have been carrying on experiments in radio education which ultimately will be of value to all broadcasters from the psychological point of view. As yet though, they seem too tentative. The only volume of value in this field is *Voice and Personality as Applied to Radio Broadcasting*, by T. H. Pear, professor of psychology in the University of Manchester, England.

fundamental psychology is concerned. Careful study of psychology as it relates to this problem, combined with broadcasting experience, has convinced the writer that a comparison of sight and sound advertising with a view of determining the general superiority of one or the other is a complete impossibility. The choice of any medium depends upon the specific task to be accomplished and the market to be reached—a principle which applies to the relative use of broadcast advertising as against other media as much as anywhere else.

At the outset it may be well to discuss briefly the component parts of the typical magazine or newspaper advertisement and radio broadcast advertising program, in order that a clear understanding may be had of what is being compared. In visual advertising the principal component parts are the illustration, copy, mechanical aids such as color, borders, type face, kind of paper used, and similar features. In broadcast advertising the chief elements are the program itself, the commercial announcement, and the dramatization or sound effects used in combination with the commercial announcement to make it more vivid and attractive.[6]

A comparison between these elements reveals a rough similarity between the commercial announcement and the printed copy; between the type of voice, pronunciation, and delivery of the announcer and the type face; and between the dramatization or sound effects used in connection with the commercial announcement and the illustration of the printed advertisement. Though these points of correspondence are extremely tentative and by no means exact, they are of considerable value in attaining a clear appreciation of the elements of the broadcast advertising program.

This leaves the program proper to be accounted for, and to be placed in its proper category. Some broadcasters and advertisers have claimed that the program of the radio advertisement and the illustration of the printed advertisement are analogous. This seems to be an erroneous view. The real analogy is between editorial material of the periodical and the program of the

---

[6] What is meant in the last instance is in the nature of the sound of someone pouring himself a drink of ginger ale in the midst of a ginger ale announcement, or where the announcement is introduced in a conversation between two characters rather than directly. These factors, it will be seen, possess a separate and distinct relation to broadcast advertising as against similar effects used in the program proper.

broadcast. This confusion of reasoning at times has had unfortunate effects in that it has induced certain advertisers to value direct product tie-up in a program too highly, and occasionally to sacrifice the entertainment value of the program to that end.

The matter of comparing the program to editorial material, however, is not as simple as it appears at first glance. In constructing the program, it often is possible to shape the entertainment into what is functionally a very close replica of the illustration of a printed advertisement. Thus, in a series of broadcasts by Thomas Cook and Sons, the program consisted of a travelogue describing one of the many places which the company was attempting to persuade the listener to visit, and was practically in the nature of an illustration of the commercial announcements which preceded and followed it. Such a complete tie-up between product and program seldom is possible, nor is it even politic for all companies in a given field to attempt it. Thus another travel company may present a program of South American dance music in an attempt to direct the listener's interest to that part of the world. Here the relation between the entertainment and the commercial announcement is not as direct, though an aspect of the illustration still remains in the program. Finally, a third travel company may sponsor a famous opera singer with no thought other than that of attracting the attention of the economic and cultural class comprising its principal clientèle. Here the illustration aspect of the entertainment has passed away completely, and only the editorial phase remains.

In the foregoing analysis, no attempt is made to argue the relative merits and disadvantages of a close and direct program-product tie-up, but merely to clarify thinking as to the fundamental significance of the various parts of the broadcast advertising program. Product-program compatibility is vitally necessary to successful broadcast advertising in many instances but it can be achieved indirectly, through the creation of the appropriate feeling-tone, just as effectively as by a direct dramatization of the product itself during the course of the entertainment. The principal relationship between the program proper and the advertising message always must be basically one of editorial material to advertisement; and such illustrative aspects as are possible must remain decidedly secondary.

This situation, where the advertiser furnishes the editorial material appearing immediately opposite his sales message, constitutes an important advantage of broadcast advertising. In the first place, it enables the advertiser to select the type of entertainment most certain to appeal to that part of the listening public which he is most interested in reaching, and to place it next to his own advertising message. Moreover, if he possesses the requisite enterprise and showmanship, it is possible for him to construct the best feature of its type to be broadcast, and thus to be doubly sure to hold his audience in competition with the programs of other advertisers. Potentially, then, the broadcast advertiser always has the possibility of placing his sales message immediately opposite the outstanding feature article or story in the issue (here, in the day's broadcast). This characteristic of broadcast advertising makes it an especially effective medium for the daring and enterprising advertiser, who, because of it, can win huge audiences for his message. Moreover, the advertiser and not the medium gets the credit for the presentation.

It must be remembered, however, that the broadcast advertiser does not furnish all of the editorial material in which the listener is interested, much of which indirectly affects the reaction to his own program. He has little or no control, except as to his choice of the hour of broadcasting, over the programs which immediately precede and follow his own, and with regard to which too great similarity or contrast may adversely affect his own work. Moreover, it is the sum total of the editorial material— in other words all of the programs broadcast over a station—which constitutes the station's appeal to the public, and which therefore is an important factor in determining the proportion of listeners habitually tuning in on the station. Consequently, an outstanding program broadcast over an outstanding station will secure, on the whole, a much wider reception by listeners than the same program broadcast over a mediocre station of the same power and coverage.

It is the foregoing elements of visual and auditory advertising, therefore, which must be compared if a clearer understanding of the psychological aspects of the use of radio broadcasting as an advertising medium is to be achieved. As the basis for this comparison, Scott's three circles of attention, comprehension, and motivation[7] will be employed.

A comparative analysis of the attributes of visual and auditory attention yields little of practical value. One learns, for instance, that the eye takes in from four to five objects at a time, while the ear apprehends as high as eight ticks without rhythm and forty ticks if grouped.[8] One also notes that the auditory perception of space, both with regards to distance and direction, is inferior to visual,[9] which leads to the speculation as to whether there may not be less auditory distraction since the ear does not seem to be able to move over the periphery of sound as fast as can the eye over that of sight. It also is possible to speculate to the end that there are fewer auditory stimuli of like intensity present in the environment of an individual at a given moment than visual stimuli, again tending to lessen the potential distraction in the case of the former. However, this is largely conjecture. Indeed, sight and sound are so unlike that a discussion of this sort eventually ends nowhere.

There are a number of specific broadcasting considerations which may yield a more satisfactory approach to the attention phase of broadcast advertising, especially as far as the aspect of relative distraction is concerned. As to the number of items which can be attended by the average listener during the course of a broadcasting day, assuming normal listening habits, there is a definite limit. Surveys indicate that the typical set owner uses his radio from three to six hours a day, and likewise that he usually confines his listening to three or four stations to which he habitually resorts.[10] Since most programs are either fifteen or thirty minutes in length, with the former predominating, this means that, on the average, a listener will hear from nine to eighteen programs daily; probably nearer the former than the latter. These, in turn, are selected out of the thirty-six to

[7] See p. 20.

[8] *The Fundamentals of Psychology,* by W. B. Pillsbury, p. 273.

[9] *Ibid.,* p. 325.

[10] Listener studies such as the 'Elder studies" of the Columbia Broadcasting System, the Starch researches for the National Broadcasting Company, the writer's own researches in Philadelphia, and similar studies confirm these generalizations, all of which are generally accepted by the industry.

seventy-two programs broadcast during the period of listening by the stations usually employed. In so far as more of this listening will be done in the evening than in the daytime, it is safe to assume that approximately 50–60 per cent[11] of the programs heard will be commercially sponsored. This means that the average listener will hear from four or six to ten or eleven commercial programs and their accompanying advertising messages daily. Thus there seems to be a greater potential isolation existing on the part of the average radio broadcast advertisement than with respect to an advertisement appearing in a publication, where a great many appear in one issue and more than one publication (magazine and newspaper) may be read daily. This is offset in part by the fact that the periodical (especially a magazine) is inspected a number of times with a resulting increase in the probability of a given advertisement being noticed by the reader.

This rather restricted competition between advertisements in the radio broadcasting field is of considerable importance to the broadcast advertiser, especially when combined with the fact that the listener tends to make a habit of turning to a program which has pleased him once, without any preliminary sampling of the other programs being offered at the hour in question. Thus the advertiser builds up a loyal listening group who immediately turn to his program, and who are lost to any other commercial sponsor competing for the same audience at the same hour. Thus the advertiser secures almost perfect isolation for his message as far as his habitual audience is concerned, the aspect of previous interest at once directing their attention toward his program. Moreover, the advertising effort as a whole, though not the commercial announcement in particular, is actually sought after by the listener.[12] This is a tremendous advantage to the enterprising advertiser with courage and showmanship, though it imposes a penalty upon the mediocre broad-

[11] See chap. vi for estimates as to the proportion of commercial to total programs broadcast. It should be remembered that listening is concentrated between the hours of seven and ten at night, as are commercial advertising programs.

[12] It might be argued here that the listener tends to tune in on the program and out on the commercial announcement. Without doubt this sometimes happens. This, however, does not invalidate the foregoing psychology, but is merely a challenge to the creation of sufficiently interesting commercial announcements to hold the listener interest. As an example, Ed Wynn's buffoonery during the Texaco announcement is as funny to the writer as any part of the program, if not more so.

caster whose efforts cannot secure an audience from among the listeners already pre-empted by the outstanding programs, a penalty which is probably greater in broadcasting than in the case of other media.

Another aspect of the question of the relative distraction existing with respect to a broadcast advertising program is found in the fact that, in point of time, the advertisement proper does not compete with the editorial material. They are not on the same or opposite pages, but follow each other, each presented by itself. This indeed may give rise to unfavorable reactions in case of a poorly done announcement interrupting the tenor of the entertainment; but again this becomes a question of skilful announcing and not of the fundamental psychology involved. One aspect of printed advertising, however, should not be overlooked; namely, that in the case of certain periodicals people actually buy them as much to inspect the advertisements as for the articles contained.

Thus, because of the relatively few competing advertisements during the course of the broadcasting day as far as the listener is concerned, the item of previous interest, and the relatively slight competition between the sales message and editorial material (the program), the radio broadcasting advertisement seems to possess a relatively low amount of distraction when once the listener has decided to use his radio at all.[13]

This question, however, cannot be answered with any finality without additional experimentation. With regard to visual advertising, factors such as habit regarding the inspection of the advertisements (e.g. thumbing over the periodical), counter-attraction between advertisements and between the editorial matter and the advertisement, and the mental level (concentration or reverie) of the reader at the time of perusal must be kept in mind. In the field of broadcast advertising, room noises and receiving set heterodyne, the possibility of engaging in other activities such as reading or work while listening to the radio, and competing visual impressions are among the factors which must be considered.

[13] It is interesting to note that all of the foregoing factors have been mentioned by advertising executives in leading agencies. For the most part these men have not been concerned exclusively with the medium of radio broadcasting, so that their opinions possess cbjective value.

The ability to attend radio broadcasting, and therefore the broadcast advertising programs, while engaged in other activities, is a matter of considerable interest. Regarding it Paul W. Keston, director of sales promotion of the Columbia Broadcasting System, has raised an interesting psychological question in his conversations with the writer. With regard to most broadcasts of popular music, the listener does not give the program his undivided attention, but makes it the background for other activities. His general mental level therefore is one of diffused attention. Thus, when the commercial announcement is delivered, it constitutes a sufficiently pronounced stimulus to focus the listener's attention involuntarily upon the announcement. The resulting effectiveness possibly may be greater than in the case of a program—such as a dramatic broadcast—wherein the listener has been concentrating upon the entertainment, and where the announcement at times may constitute a distraction from the main purpose of listening. It is practically impossible to state this observation in the form of a conclusion, but rather, as a question illustrating the type of problem to be solved in broadcast advertising psychology. Its importance probably lies primarily in the realm of commercial announcement technique, where it may reveal guiding principles as to the construction of announcements for various types of programs, rather than with regard to programs proper.

Another observation illustrating existing problems in attention as related to broadcast advertising, which may bear mention at this time, is that of M. A. Howlett, president of Station WHK, Cleveland, Ohio. Mr. Howlett's view is that, since the majority of listening occurs at the end of the day's work, when the individual desires to relax and avoid difficult mental effort, his mental level is one primarily of diffused attention, ready to be focused by some stimulus. Because of the ease involved in attending the broadcasting program (all one does is to sit and listen), it furnishes an ideal subject to attend. However, since the listener is aware, at least dimly, that what he is hearing will not be repeated, once having decided to give the program his attention, he concentrates to catch it all the more. It can readily be seen that such a psychology will relate primarily to programs other than dance music, where active listening is a prerequisite to enjoyment, and to commercial announcements. It is an interesting observation, and, if nothing else, again aptly illustrates some of the questions regarding the attention given to broadcasting programs, which can only be answered by further research.

Analysis of the second aspect of advertising psychology, namely, the problem of securing comprehension of the sales message on the part of the reader or listener, involves a comparison of the visual and auditory means of communication represented in written and spoken language. The illustration, extremely important to printed advertising in the securing of comprehension, will be reserved for later mention.

At the outset, it is necessary to comment briefly upon the nature of language itself. Language may be described as a means of communicating thought, including ideas and emotions.[14] There are two principal forms of language: ear and eye. Of eye language the written word is the most important, though facial expression and gesture as forms of language may not be overlooked completely. Spoken language developed first, probably arising out of instinctive expressive movements which affected the placing of the speech organs and consequently the sounds that emanated from them. These sounds later came to be repeated to describe similar situations and to be formed into the foundations of language. Written language came later, appearing first in the form of picture writing, and later developing through successive steps into a more or less faithful representation of the spoken language underlying it. Thus spoken language is the living, changing language, of which the written word is merely representative.

Since the communication of thought is the chief purpose of language, its relation to thought in the mental process requires consideration. Here three alternative possibilities exist: (1) thought may precede language in definite and detailed imagery; (2) it may consist merely of language, and (3) it may be a mixture of the two. The intermediate condition is probably the most frequent and may consist of an alternation between thought in language and in images, or there may be a generalized

[14] *The Psychology of Language*, by Pillsbury and Meader (Appleton), p. 4. The author is indebted to this volume for the fundamental material presented here regarding language especially to chap. v, "Mental Processes in Speech," and chap. viii, "Language Receptors: Reading and Listening."

idea of what is being considered existing in the vaguest terms, which in turn may be developed directly into words.[15] With regard to the manner in which the words themselves are thought or imaged in the mind, auditory-kinaesthetic imagery (the sound of the word combined with the muscular feeling resulting from its enunciation) seems somewhat to predominate, though both this form and visual imagery are possessed in varying degrees by different individuals.[16] Finally, it must be remembered that the language of an individual is largely conditioned by his general imagery. Words are but symbols, even though at times they are used interchangeably with the objects and ideas which they represent in the general thought-process. Behind every word stands an idea or concrete object, pictured in the mind of the individual for the most part in terms of his predominant imagery, or in a combination of several imaginal types. For these images language is but a symbol, though sometimes it serves as a short-circuit substitute for them.

This relationship between language and the objects or ideas which it represents becomes clearer, especially as it relates to the perception and understanding of the broadcast advertising message, when the respective psychological aspects of reading and listening are analyzed. Of these two, reading will be considered first.[17]

Two types of reading require discussion; reading for words and reading for sense. In reading for words it is the word itself, as it has been seen on the printed page, supplemented frequently by the sounds of the words had they been pronounced, which constitutes the basis of the reading process.[18] This type of reading finds its most typical expression in proofreading. At the other extreme, is reading for sense, wherein the principal object is to grasp the thought of the author. Pillsbury says:

In this case the supplementing may not be words at all, but ideas of a non-verbal character. One may become so lost in a description that the words are practically not noticed. Pictures or other content are suggested by the word and come to consciousness instead of the words—again an illustration of the

---

[15] *Ibid.*, p. 99.   [16] *Ibid.*, pp. 101–2.

[17] The source of data for this discussion, other than the interpretation of its advertising significance is chap. viii, "Language Receptors: Reading and Listening," from Pillsbury and Meader. The chapter in question is the work of Professor Pillsbury.

[18] *Ibid.*, p. 138.

law of perception that one may appreciate meanings which depend upon very definite sensory impressions without being aware of the impressions themselves.[19]

The pictures referred to in the above passage are in terms of the individual's specific imagery as described earlier in the discussion.

It is interesting to note the relationship existing between reading for words and reading for sense as it is found in the process of learning to read. This is described by Pillsbury as follows:[20]

In learning to read, the printed symbol becomes associated with the spoken word in the same sort of repetition.[21] At first the sight recalls the sound and the sound the object or the idea, but with growing familiarity, the process becomes short-circuited as all mental processes tend to do, and the object may come at once on seeing the word. This mechanical association is fundamental for sense reading of all other types.

Thus it becomes evident that the progression is from reading by words to reading by sense, with many intermediate stages existing. The actual stage in a given situation depends upon a variety of factors such as the reading ability of the individual (many people seem never to have learned to read with facility); the imagery of the reader in relation to the subject matter at hand; the mental level at which reading takes place (e.g., forcing one's self to read when sleepy and when the mental level is one of diffused attention), the relative concreteness or abstraction of the subject matter; the reader's familiarity with the subject and vocabulary of the author, and similar considerations. According to Pillsbury,[22] probably the most prevalent intermediate stage is the one in which "one reads words and seems with the consciousness of the words to have the meaning in pictures or other mental content added to them." In his opinion most reading is probably of this type.

The foregoing analysis, therefore, seems to point to the fact that most reading involves both the auditory-kinaesthetic or visual imagery of the word itself and the image of the object or idea which it represents, so that two steps are involved in per-

---

[19] *Ibid.*, p. 139.   [20] *Ibid.*, p. 140.

[21] Pillsbury refers here to the manner in which a child learns to associate a word with the object it designates by hearing it repeatedly when he sees the object.

[22] Pillsbury, *op. cit.*, p. 142.

ception through reading, varying in degree with the individual and the situation in question.

Listening follows a closely parallel course to reading so far as its psychology is concerned except that here, in the opinion of Professor Pillsbury,[23] the tendency, at least in the case of the mother-tongue, is to have the sentences supplemented directly by whatever imagery is natural to the individual. Visual imagery of printed words comes only when there is some question of spelling or other difficulty.

If the writer interprets the situation correctly, the foregoing data indicate that, for a large number of people, the effort involved in the perception of the spoken message must to some measure be less than in the case of the printed message, necessitating as it does, in many instances, one less mental step. It is probable, however, that no final conclusion can be reached on this matter without additional experimental evidence; though, if this observation is correct, it constitutes an important advantage for broadcast advertising.

Several additional features regarding the perception and comprehension of the broadcast advertising message should be mentioned at this point. The first of these is the part played by the inflection of the human voice in aiding in the understanding of the spoken message, in turn assisted materially by the facial expression and gestures where the speaker is visible to the listener. Another feature to be noted is the fact that effective printed and spoken vocabularies differ greatly. Many words which look well and are readily understandable when presented in print (polysyllables for instance) militate seriously against comprehension when employed in speech, largely because of their cumbersomeness. It also should be noted that it is not possible with the spoken word to retrace one's steps over a perplexing passage, nor is it possible, in point of time, to cover the same amount of material by listening as can be achieved in the case of printed language. Nor does the spoken word offer the facilities for detailed and intricate description, necessary in the discussion of mechanical appliances and similar goods, that are open through the use of the printed word. This is probably of considerable importance in industrial advertising, but, in gen-

[23] *Ibid.*, p. 146.

eral consumer advertising, where sufficient clarity so that "he who runs may read" is necessary, it is of doubtful significance.

In conclusion, one phase of the printed advertisement remains to be discussed, namely, the illustration. There is no means by which perception and understanding is achieved more readily than through the use of pictures—concrete presentations of the product or the situation with regard to which the advertiser wishes to impress the prospective customer. Indeed, this is the most potent form of visualization open to the advertiser and constitutes an advantage of visual advertising which cannot be duplicated in any other manner. In certain cases it is almost indispensable. It is about the only way to present a clear picture of a complex product. At times it is vitally necessary in showing vividly certain characteristics of a product; as, for example, in pointing out the beauty of design of a certain brand of oil burner, where it would have been utterly impossible to have conveyed the same idea by purely verbal means. It is especially valuable in the dramatization of situations revolving about the use of the product, as is well testified by the number of advertisements in our leading magazines wherein the illustration, perhaps aided by the headline, tells the whole story, and there the copy performs few if any functions other than assisting in the construction of a balanced layout. In this regard it is especially valuable as an opening wedge for the securing of reader interest, and as a means of appealing to the instinctive tendencies upon which the creation of the motive for purchase depends. Broadcast advertising has no illustration except to the extent that the program can be used in this fashion, or to the limited degree, thus far at least, that dramatization of the commercial announcement itself has been effected.

Thus far the questions of attention and comprehension have been discussed from the viewpoint of the psychological aspects of broadcast and printed advertising. The problem of the appeal to the instinctive tendencies, whereby a motive to purchase the article is created in the mind of the prospective customer, requires little comment. It is chiefly a problem of using the tools at one's disposal for securing a complete appreciation of the advertising message on the part of the reader or hearer, a matter which already has been discussed in considerable detail. The final question, therefore, is the problem of investing the advertisement with the requisite emotional appeal to produce action on the part of the potential buyer.

In this respect the copy approach itself, that is, the content and development of the message, is of fundamental importance. Herein there is no difference between visual and auditory advertising except with regard to the limitations of visualization imposed by the characteristics of one as against the other; and it is this matter which therefore must be discussed. In the case of the development of the copy, there is little difference between the printed advertisement and broadcast advertising. True, the vocabulary of the latter must be more simple and theoretically shorter. On the other hand, renditions of narrative copy have been heard over the air within recent months which were beautifully done from the viewpoint of listener interest and which were every bit as long as could have been employed in a printed advertisement. It is believed that this difference has been over-emphasized in the past, and that its true significance lies in the fact that the listener will object vociferously to lengthy broadcast advertising copy, while merely quietly refusing to read lengthy printed copy.

In the matter of presentation and visualization, a more pronounced difference exists between the two forms of advertising. The printed advertisement possesses the advantage of the illustration, which, for the purpose of dramatizing the message, is probably unequaled. Likewise, the type of illustration—pen and ink, wash drawing, or photograph, etc.—can be of material assistance in the creation of the appropriate feeling-tone—one of substantiality and dependability, of quality and workmanship, or whatever the case may be—for the advertisement as a whole. The type face, borders, layout, use or non-use of color and the paper, where this is controlled, can be employed to a similar end.

In the case of the broadcast advertisement, though the illustration aspect is definitely limited, other compensating factors are available for use. True, the work of the illustration can be accomplished in part through the dramatization of the product or situations revolving about the use of or need for the product, as has been mentioned previously, but these opportunities are limited. More important is the possibility of achieving the same effect indirectly by constructing the program so that its personality will suggest emotionally to the listener the qualities which it is desired that he should impute to the product advertised. Thus the famous Atwater Kent program dramatized, better than any illustration could have done, the feeling of high quality and pre-eminence imputed to the radio receiving sets of that name. Finally, a limited, but probably increasing, degree of the illustrative aspect can be achieved through the dramatization of the announcement. This can be done either through the use of sound effects, as was done by Canada Dry Ginger Ale, by humorous interludes, as in the case of Ed Wynn and Graham MacNamee on the Texaco program, or finally by leading into the commercial copy through anecdote or similar means, as is splendidly carried out by Heywood Broun on the General Electric program. Since the scientific construction of commercial announcements is just beginning to be achieved, this form of visualization is probably endowed with considerable future potentialities. All of these means therefore can be utilized effectively for building up the correct emotional appeal on the part of the broadcast advertising program.

One final attribute of the broadcast advertising program remains to be discussed: the human voice. From earliest days language, and especially spoken language, has been employed as a means of conveying emotions as well as ideas. Genetically, it probably was emotion, which was the first to be transmitted through articulate sound. Thus, today, the human voice still remains the most potent instrument of emotional expression, and one which, like the illustration in printed advertising, cannot be duplicated in any other manner. This seems to be one of the greatest advantages open to broadcast advertising, and one which thus far, largely from lack of adequate study, has been developed to a very slight degree.

The problem of vocal expression in relation to the broadcast advertising message is twofold. It involves, first, the creation of the correct emotional attitude on the part of the listener to ensure a proper reception of the message itself. Just prior to the recent Christmas holidays, David Wark Griffith, the motion picture director, broadcast an appeal over the Dromedary Date program. The appeal, incidentally, required the purchase of the dates in question, and promised that for every Dromedary Date box top mailed to the listener's station one box of dates would be provided the local Salvation Army free for distribution among the poor. The appeal was one to charity as well as utility, and for that purpose Mr. Griffith's delivery was almost perfect. Low, well-modulated tones, with decided emotional intonation to the delivery, synchronized perfectly with the purpose at hand. Again, in the case of the Texaco program, the enthusiasm of Graham MacNamee is the delivery best adapted to create a feeling of prestige for the product and of confidence in its ability to produce the satisfaction which has been promised the listener. The matter of appropriate delivery of a message, varying with the product and copy approach, and with a persuasive or imperative ending, is of tremendous importance in broadcast advertising, and when done correctly possesses marked value to the advertiser.

The second aspect of vocal expression, as it pertains to the broadcast advertising message, is with relation to the creation of an appropriate voice personality on the part of the announcer —one which will establish confidence and authority for what he says. Here, if anywhere, broadcast advertising most closely approximates personal salesmanship; for the delivery must be such that the listener receives the impression of one very specific individual, with a definite and marked personality, talking to him as man to man. Preachment goes even less in radio than on the printed page, and the personal relationship must be established without fail. This is, indeed, the secret of the success in the field of radio announcing, one announcer having created so popular a radio personality for himself that recently when he appeared at the studio rather late and out of breath, with a resulting impediment to the usual quality of his delivery, he received several thousand letters inquiring as to his health and prescribing a wide variety of remedies for colds and sore throats. It should be noted that the question of voice personality on the part of the announcer is a matter over and above the delivery of a given announcement in keeping with the emotional content of its message and of the program.

Because of the importance of the question of voice personality to broadcast advertising, it may be well to devote some time to discussing it. At the outset it is well to remember the potentialities of the voice as a form of gesture. "It is clear," writes

Professor Pear,[24] "that sometimes the characteristics of the voice are used consciously—more often unconsciously—as a form of gesture. If someone refuses or delays to perform a duty, he may be ordered to do so in a tone which is as effective as a whip. The conscious use of blandishment needs no more than mention." This aspect of voice seems to be more closely related to the delivery of a given announcement than to the matter of voice personality itself.

The problem of voice personality revolves about two principal aspects. The first of these is that, language being a social phenomenon, there is an element of social pattern in all use of the voice. This pattern in turn gives rise to the formation of voice stereotypes, or so-called "typical" voices representing to the average listener general types of individuals such as lawyers, teachers, ministers, laborers, and the like. The second aspect of voice personality is that of the individual variation from the social pattern, which constitutes the true expression of the personality of the speaker.[25]

Both of these aspects of voice personality operate in the field of the following voice dynamics: intonation, of which there are three levels—individual, racial and class; rhythm, pronunciation, vocabulary, and style. In addition to these qualities, voices are judged by listeners to have other individual qualities such as color and brightness, shape in the sense of well-rounded tones and texture—rough, smooth, and coarse. This synaesthesia, or predisposition to describe auditory stimuli in terms of other imagery, was reported by Professor Pear to have occurred in 24 per cent of 76 students employed in one experiment, and in 23 per cent of a group of 112 students in another instance.[26]

As far as voice stereotypes are concerned, they are probably developed by listeners on the basis of racial, class, and cultural standards, operating with regard to the various voice dynamics listed in the preceding paragraph. It is necessary, therefore, for the announcer to possess the correct voice pattern appealing to a

[24] *The Voice and Personality as Applied to Radio Broadcasting,* by T. H. Pear, professor of psychology, University of Manchester, England (Wiley), p. 9. This volume is used as the basis for the ensuing discussion of voice personality.

[25] In the present discussion personality is interpreted as meaning "the effect upon others of a living being's appearance, behavior, etc., so far as they are interpreted as distinctive signs of that being" (*ibid.,* p. 37).

[26] *Ibid.,* p. 112.

definite class audience. The reader need merely compare the announcer on the National Farm and Home Hour to the Broadway sophistication of Ben Bernie, or listen to the programs of Dr. Brinkley, goat-gland expert and almost-governor of Kansas, over his Mexican station, XER, to grasp the significance of this phase of announcing. For this reason, certain voices, like that of Milton Cross and Ted Husing, are best suited to specific types of programs. The question of voice stereotype becomes even more important where a fictitious character, such as the Old Counsellor on the Halsey Stuart program of some time ago, is introduced to present the commercial copy. Here the voice must be indisputably in character, for the slightest slip is enough to destroy the impression. This pertains equally to the field of the radio drama. A final aspect of voice stereotypes, bordering closely on individual characteristics, is the question of commonly accepted voice patterns believed to be indicative of certain types of personality. Thus a gruff, masculine voice is supposed to typify honesty, probity, and ability, with the result that the speaker is believed merely because of this one characteristic. All of the foregoing aspects are of prime importance in the art of radio announcing, and in the psychological adaptability of broadcasting to the advertising message.

If voice stereotypes are constructed on the basis of the racial and class standards of the listener, then the individual voice personality is the result of its variations from a given accepted standard. Where not too pronounced and sensorially pleasing, as for instance a slight southern drawl in a northern community, the effect is probably to increase the vividness of the impression made upon the listener. On the other hand, a too great variation from the accepted pattern militates against the speaker. These then are some of the considerations which must be kept in mind when adapting the voice to the presentation of the advertising message over the radio.

Before summarizing the preceding discussion of the psychological phases of broadcast advertising, brief mention should be made of the memory aspect of radio, especially as it relates to repetition. Because of the nature of broadcasting, programs are without exception broadcast at time-intervals no greater than one week, while many of them are presented several times during the week or even every day. This insures a continuity of effort and resulting deep impression of the program upon the listener, which in the estimation of several advertising research experts is one of the important factors in such success as radio broadcast advertising thus far has achieved.[27]

The question may properly be asked as to what this psychological analysis of radio broadcast advertising has revealed. The following conclusions summarize the situation as it appears in the light of present knowledge:

1. With regard to the component parts available for use in the presentation of the advertising message, visual advertising possesses the advantage of the illustration, which can only be approximated in part by broadcast advertising, either through direct or indirect product dramatization, or the dramatization of the commercial announcement. From the psychological point of view the indirect dramatization of the product and that of the commercial announcement seem to possess the greatest potentialities.

2. On the other hand, broadcast advertising possesses the appeal of the human voice, which, if used correctly in terms of correlation with the emotional appeal contained in a specific announcement, and also in terms of existing voice stereotypes and the principles governing the development of individual voice personality, constitutes one of the most potent selling forces at the disposal of radio, one which can only partially be approximated by visual advertising through vividness of the written copy.

3. Because of the nature of broadcasting, requiring programs repeated at regular intervals, there seems to be a greater impetus toward regularity of advertising effort, usually at weekly and often more closely recurring intervals, thus tending to give broadcast advertising a relatively greater effectiveness as regards the remembering of its sales effort.

4. Because of the item of previous interest, aroused by listener interest in the program proper, as well as because of a number of less conclusive factors, broadcast advertising seems to have a slightly less distraction than may be the case with regard to visual advertising. Additional experimental data are necessary before any certain conclusions can be drawn in this field. In the

[27] This will be discussed more thoroughly in the chapters dealing with current broadcasting practice.

matter of perception existing material offers still less conclusive results.

5. Because of the presentation of both the sales message and editorial material (entertainment part of the program) by the advertiser, broadcast advertising seems to offer especially great potential rewards to the enterprising and able advertiser, and to impose a similar penalty upon the mediocre sponsor. This also cannot be stated with complete conclusiveness until detailed case studies are available upon which a final judgment can be based.

6. As far as is revealed by an examination of the psychological aspects of the situation, and taking into consideration the present state of knowledge in the field, no comparison can be made regarding the relative general supremacy of visual as against broadcast advertising or vice versa. It probably will never be primarily a question of comparison on this basis, but rather of specific abilities to meet individual contingencies, decision being based upon a knowledge of the similarities and dissimilarities of the two types of media.

CHAPTER III

ECONOMIC BASES: EXTENT AND NATURE
OF THE LISTENING AUDIENCE

Thus far a discussion has been presented, first, of the basic satisfaction derived from radio broadcasting, and which in turn constitutes the reason for its widespread public appeal; and, second, of the psychological factors underlying the ability of broadcasting effectively to present the sales message to the listener. However, the successful functioning of radio broadcasting as an advertising medium depends upon more considerations than merely a basic popularity and a psychological adaptability to carrying the advertising message. Advertising involves mass appeal, and before it can be said with certainty that broadcasting constitutes a satisfactory medium, it must be determined, first, that the fundamental appeal of radio has created a sufficiently large potential listening audience economically to justify its use for advertising purposes, and, second, that an adequate broadcasting structure exists whereby this audience may be reached by the advertiser. An answer to the first of these questions constitutes the subject matter of this chapter, while the second problem will be discussed in those which immediately follow.

The rise in the radio listening audience in the United States during the past decade is presented in Table II.

In so far as it is estimated that there are between 35,000,000 and 37,000,000 receiving sets in the world,[1] this means that approximately 45 per cent of all sets in operation are located in the United States. Because of the very tentative nature of the annual estimates, it is difficult to make any generalization regarding the annual rate of growth other than to point out that it has been comparatively steady. From April, 1930, when the radio census was taken, to April, 1932, there was a gain of 38.4 per cent in the number of sets in operation in this country. A general conception of the increase in the diffusion of radio receiving

[1] *Radio Markets of the World, 1932,* U.S. Department of Commerce, p. 27.

41

set ownership among the population can be secured from the fact that in 1932 in the neighborhood of 55.7 per cent of the families in the United States possessed radio sets, as compared with 40.3 per cent in 1930.

Total figures, in themselves, are of little use to the broadcast advertiser. Vastly more important are factors such as the relative distribution of radio set ownership between different sec-

TABLE II
ESTIMATED NUMBER OF RECEIVING SETS IN USE IN THE UNITED STATES, 1922–32*

Year	Number of Sets in Use
1922	60,000
1923	1,500,000
1924	3,000,000
1925	4,000,000
1926	5,000,000
1927	6,500,000
1928	7,700,000
1929	9,000,000
1930	12,048,762
1931	15,000,000
1932	16,679,253

* Source of data for 1922–29, inclusive, and for 1931 is *Radio Retailing*, published by the McGraw-Hill Company. The 1930 figure is taken from the United States Census, and the 1932 figure from *Radio Markets of the World, 1932*, published by the Department of Commerce. In each case the source selected has constituted the most accurate available. The general comparability of sources is indicated by the fact that in the instance where comparable data are available, 1932, the McGraw-Hill estimate for March 1 is 16,545,245 sets, while the Department of Commerce estimate for April 1 is 16,679,253. A discrepancy of dates should be noted: 1922–29 and 1931 being as of January 1 and 1930 and 1932 as of April 1. Since all the figures are estimates and contain a good deal of error at best, this is unimportant statistically.

tions of the country, as regards urban and rural areas, communities of different size, as well as by economic, racial, national, and similar groups. A factor of equal interest is the extent to which the advertiser may expect to make his potential audience into an actual one, a matter which depends primarily upon listener habits with respect to the use of the radio, and other like features.

Data seem to indicate that, with respect to receiving set ownership, the United States divides itself into three relatively distinct and internally homogeneous areas.[2] The first and most

[2] All data presented regarding geographical distribution of set ownership are taken from the Census of 1930, and therefore are as of that year. These are the most recent data available on the subject.

important of these may be called the Northern Area and comprises the great district lying north of the Mason and Dixon line and extending westward to Kansas, Nebraska, and the Dakotas, which are included within its boundaries. Thus this area embraces all of New England, the Middle Atlantic states, and the North Central district of the country. In 1930 there were located in it 76.4 per cent of the receiving sets in the United States. The second radio listening area might be termed the Southern Area, and includes the territory lying south of the Mason and Dixon line and having as its western extremities the states of Texas and Oklahoma. According to 1930 Census figures, 11.9 per cent of the total radio-owning families in the country reside in this region. The third and final area, the Far Western Area, includes the Mountain and Pacific states, and contains 11.7 per cent of the radio families in the United States. The proportion of radio-owning to total families within each of these major areas was as follows in 1930: in the Northern Area 51.1 per cent of all families owned radios; in the Southern Area 16.2 per cent, while in the Far Western Area, 43.9 per cent possessed receiving sets. These percentages are comparable to the national average of 40.3 per cent for the same year.

Thus the Northern Area is seen to be the most important radio listening district in the country both with regard to total number of listeners and the proportion of total families which can be reached by means of radio broadcasting. While the Southern Area ranks second in the matter of number of listeners, it is a very poor third as far as the percentage of families owning radios is concerned. Though the limited population of the Far Western Area makes it relatively unimportant from the viewpoint of total listeners, the diffusion of radio receiving set ownership is above the national average in this region.

The comparative homogeneity of set ownership, within each of the three areas defined above, is indicated in Table III, which shows the percentage of families owning receiving sets for the areas in question as well as for the Census districts and states contained within them.

It will be noted from Table III that, in the case of both the Northern and Southern areas, there is little variation between the percentage of receiving set ownership for the area as a whole and of the individual census districts comprising it. This is not the case in the Far Western Area, where a greater lack of uniformity is evidenced. This apparent lack of homogeneity is

TABLE III

RELATIVE PROPORTION OF FAMILIES HAVING RADIO SETS
IN VARIOUS STATES AND AREAS*

Division and State	Percentage of Families With Radios	Division and State	Percentage of Families With Radios
United States........	40.3	South Atlantic—	
NORTHERN AREA....	51.1	Continued	
New England.......	53.8	Virginia.........	18.2
Maine...........	39.2	West Virginia....	23.3
New Hampshire..	44.4	North Carolina...	11.2
Vermont.........	44.6	South Carolina...	7.6
Massachusetts....	57.6	Georgia.........	9.9
Rhode Island....	57.1	Florida..........	15.4
Connecticut......	54.7		
		East South Central..	12.3
Middle Atlantic.....	55.3	Kentucky........	18.3
New York........	57.9	Tennessee.......	14.3
New Jersey......	63.4	Alabama........	9.5
Pennsylvania.....	48.1	Mississippi.....	5.4
East North Central..	50.2	West South Central..	16.5
Ohio...........	47.7	Arkansas........	9.1
Indiana.........	41.6	Louisiana.......	11.2
Illinois..........	55.6	Oklahoma.......	21.6
Michigan........	50.6	Texas..........	18.6
Wisconsin.......	51.0		
		WESTERN AREA......	43.9
West North Central..	43.1	Mountain..........	30.9
Minnesota.......	47.3	Montana........	31.9
Iowa...........	48.5	Idaho..........	30.3
Missouri........	37.4	Wyoming........	34.1
North Dakota....	40.9	Colorado........	37.8
South Dakota....	44.2	New Mexico.....	11.5
Nebraska........	47.9	Arizona.........	18.1
Kansas.........	38.9	Utah...........	41.1
		Nevada.........	30.6
SOUTHERN AREA....	16.2		
South Atlantic......	19.0	Pacific...........	49.1
Delaware........	45.9	Washington......	42.3
Maryland........	42.9	Oregon.........	43.5
District of Colum-		California........	52.0
bia...........	53.9		

* Data here given are taken from the U.S. Census (1930). The percentage of families owning radios in various areas, such as the Northern Area, or districts such as New England, represents the proportion of all radio-owning to total families within the area or district.

explained by the fact that the Pacific states, which enjoy the greater diffusion of radio ownership, embrace approximately 70 per cent of the total families in the area and 80 per cent of the radio families. The lack of homogeneity between states, however, is more pronounced, though not sufficient to nullify the validity of the basic areas. The variations in set ownership percentage in this case are explained primarily by the relative urbanization of the various states, and on racial and economic considerations.

TABLE IV

COMPARISON OF THE PROPORTION OF TOTAL FAMILIES, RADIO FAMILIES, NET RETAIL SALES, RETAIL OUTLETS, INCOME TAX RETURNS, AND TOTAL RADIO FACILITIES IN EACH OF THREE MAJOR RADIO LISTENER AREAS

Radio Listener Area	Percentage of Total Families*	Percentage of Radio Families*	Percentage of Net Retail Sales†	Percentage of Retail Outlets†	Percentage of Income Tax Returns‡	Percentage of Total Radio Facilities§
Northern................	60.0	76.4	67.5	72.5	63.7	52.2
Southern...............	28.9	11.9	20.5	15.1	25.5	29.3
Far western.............	11.1	11.7	12.0	12.4	10.8	18.5
Total...............	100.0	100.0	100.0	100.0	100.0	100.0

* Census of Population, Radio Division, mimeographed reports.
† Census of Distribution, *Preliminary Reports*, p. 9.
‡ *Sales Opportunities 1931* (Curtis Publishing Co.).
§ *Fifth Annual Report of the Federal Radio Commission* (1931). Based on Table II, pp. 42–43. Under the allocation plan now in force, stations of varying power and hours of operation are assigned different units of value (based thus on service rendered), and each of the five administrative zones are theoretically allotted an equal number of units of such facilities. The radio facilities referred to in the table are in terms of these units.

As has been noted previously, no accurate data on receiving set ownership by different geographical units exist as of a date later than 1930, so that it is impossible to state what changes have taken place in this respect since the time of the radio census. In the case of all ensuing information, the national increase has been prorated among the various states according to their previous set ownership, and not on the basis of actual sales within their respective boundaries.

A comparison of the relative economic importance of the three major listener areas is found in Table IV, and presents an even clearer picture than thus far has been indicated of their comparative significance to the advertiser and distributor of goods.

From Table IV it becomes evident that, at least as far as the

potential audience is concerned, radio broadcasting is capable of
reaching a larger proportion of families in the economically most
important Northern Area than in any other district. This area,
accounting for more than two-thirds of the annual net sales, almost
three-fourths of the retail outlets, and 60.0 per cent of the total
population, in turn embraces more than three-quarters of the
radio families in the country. It is only in the Southern Area
that the potential audience is relatively weak. The significance
of this fact will become more evident when rural-urban and racial variations in set ownership are analyzed.

Before entering upon a discussion of these factors, however,
one additional table will be presented which should be of especial interest to broadcasters and advertisers accustomed to
thinking of radio in terms of the five administrative zones established under the Radio Act of 1927, and which will indicate the
relative importance of each of them from the distributive viewpoint. These zones, it should be noted, were created originally
merely as administrative subdivisions, but took on added significance under the Davis Amendment[3] which required that
broadcasting facilities be distributed equally among them. They
are based upon a division of the total population of the country
into five almost equal parts; however, taking no account of the
fact that radio receiving set ownership is unevenly distributed
among the total population.

The First Zone comprises all of New England, New York,
New Jersey, Delaware, Maryland and the District of Columbia.[4]
Pennsylvania, Virginia, West Virginia, Kentucky, Ohio, and
Michigan constitute the Second Zone. All of the South Atlantic
and South Central states, with the exception of the two located
in the First Zone and three in the Second Zone, are allocated to
the Third Zone. The entire North Central district of the country, other than Ohio and Michigan, lies in the Fourth Zone,
while the Fifth Zone embraces the Mountain and Pacific states

[3] 45 Stat. L. 373. Passed March 28, 1928. The degree to which its provisions have
been followed, and the economic and social significance of both its underlying theory
and actual results, will be discussed later in the study.

[4] Territorial units such as the Virgin Islands and Porto Rico, Hawaii, and Alaska are
included in the First and Fifth zones, respectively, but their facilities are too meager to
be of any significance. An amendment is now before Congress to exclude them from the
zone structure.

and is analogous to the Far Western Area in the economic divisions.

The relative proportion of radio families, net sales and similar factors located within each of them in 1930, will be found in Table V.

Since the First, Second, and Fourth Zones lie mostly in the Northern listening area, and the Third Zone comprises the major portion of the Southern Area, the same conclusions regarding the location of the potential listening audience is to be drawn from this table as from the preceding one.

TABLE V

COMPARISON OF THE PROPORTION OF TOTAL FAMILIES, RADIO FAMILIES, NET RE-
TAIL SALES, RETAIL OUTLETS, AND TOTAL RADIO FACILITIES IN EACH OF THE
FIVE ADMINISTRATIVE ZONES OF THE FEDERAL RADIO COMMISSION*

Radio Zone	Percentage of Total Families	Percentage of Radio Families	Percentage of Net Retail Sales	Percentage of Retail Outlets	Percentage of Total Radio Facilities
I.	23.0	31.3	27.8	25.1	17.3
II.	22.0	23.0	21.9	22.4	16.9
III.	23.0	7.2	14.9	19.1	21.3
IV.	22.0	26.7	23.2	22.7	23.2
V.	10.0	11.8	12.2	10.7	21.3
Total.	100.0	100.0	100.0	100.0	100.0

* Sources of data for this table are the same as for the preceding one.

A comparison of radio receiving set ownership in urban and rural districts, as well as with respect to communities of different size, also is of interest. Thus it was revealed in the 1930 Census that 50.0 per cent of the urban families of the country possessed receiving sets, 20.8 per cent of the rural farm families, 33.7 per cent of rural non-farm families (including many suburban residents not included in the urban areas as understood by the Census), and that 21.0 per cent of all farm families owned radios.

From this it might be assumed that radio broadcasting constitutes a rather poor medium wherewith to reach the farm market of the country. This, however, is only a half-truth since geographical variations in farm receiving set ownership seriously modify this conclusion. Thus, in 1930, the average ownership of radio sets among farm families in the Southern Area constituted but 5.0 per cent of all farm families in the region. These in turn, numbered 3,390,798 and comprised 50.8 per cent of the entire farm population of the United States—to be sure, the poorer half of our farm population. In the case of the other half of the country's farm population, located primarily in the Middle Atlantic and North Central states, the percentage of set ownership was 45.2 per cent as compared with 40.3 per cent for the country as a whole. Similar marked differences exist with respect to the urban set ownership in the Southern Area, which was revealed as being 28.6 per cent of total families, as against 54.7 per cent in other parts of the country.

Differences in the diffusion of set ownership in communities of different size also exist. In New York City the percentage of set ownership in 1930 was 59.1 per cent; in Philadelphia 56.3 per cent; and in Chicago 63.2 per cent. In a sample chosen at random from among the ninety cities of more than 100,000 in population, exclusive of the three mentioned above, the average percentage of set ownership[5] was 50.3 per cent, while the proportion of radio to total families in fifty towns of from 10,000 to 25,000 in size, scattered throughout the country, was 47.1 per cent.

An analysis of the relative proportion of radio to total families among the foreign and native white families, and among negroes, affords a partial indication of the reason for the relatively low degree of set ownership in the Southern Area. This is presented in Table VI.

From the table one notices a number of interesting tendencies. From the viewpoint of potential circulation, radio is a poor medium to reach the negro population, the low proportion of set ownership of which also goes a long way to explaining the situation in the Southern Area. This is clarified to an even greater degree when one compares the national average degree of receiving set ownership among native white farm population, 24.2 per cent in all, with the 45.2 per cent ownership of farmers in the Northern and Far Western areas. Since in this case the comparison is between native white farmers for the most part—the total number of foreign-born farm families in this country being relatively unimportant—the almost inevitable conclusion is

[5] The average referred to here is a weighted one, each city entering into the computation to the extent of the number of its families, radio and non-radio.

that the southern farmer is on the average less liable to own a radio than is a farmer in some other section of the country.

Finally, the question arises as to the diffusion of receiving set ownership among various economic classes. Data regarding this point are difficult to secure, while those which do exist are so slight as to be relatively inconclusive. From it, though, it may be possible to gain at least some inkling of what may be the trend in this field.

In the study of 18,024 families conducted by Dr. Daniel Starch for the National Broadcasting Company, and published by them in 1929 and in revised form in 1930, it was indicated

TABLE VI*

COLOR AND NATIVITY OF FAMILIES HAVING RADIOS

TYPE OF FAMILY	PERCENTAGE OF TOTAL FAMILIES IN GROUP HAVING RADIOS		
	Urban	Farm	Total
Native white............	56.3	24.2	44.4
Foreign-born white.........	46.2	32.2	43.6
Negroes.................	14.4	.3	7.5
Entire country.........	50.0	21.0	40.3

* *Radio Census*, Census of Population, 1930.

that the monthly rental of homes of radio-owning families was 41.0 per cent higher than in the case of non-radio families.[6] From this fact it seems that there is a tendency for receiving set ownership to be concentrated in the upper or at least higher than average income levels. Since the data on which the study was based were collected primarily in the spring of 1928,[7] this conclusion may have been quite correct for that period, even though the smallness of the sample deprives it of a certain amount of finality.

However, there is considerable doubt as to whether the figure

[6] *Revised Study of Radio Broadcasting*, by Daniel Starch, Ph.D. (National Broadcasting Co., 1930), pp. 18–20A.

[7] Of the total interviews 17,099 were made between March 15 and April 15, 1928, while the remaining 925 were secured between November 15, 1929, and January 1, 1930. The latter were confined to the Pacific and Mountain states which had not been covered in the previous survey.

of relative rental value of the home, as found in the Starch report, accurately describes the situation of receiving set ownership today, as it applies to various economic groups. Ownership of automobiles and use of telephones are commonly accepted as indicating a more than average, but by no means excessively high, standard of living. For this reason, a comparison of the relative degree of receiving set ownership to that of the foregoing articles is of interest. The comparison is confined to the primary listening areas of Yankee Network stations in a number of New England cities, these areas including in each case the city

TABLE VII

COMPARATIVE RADIO RECEIVING SET, AUTOMOBILE OWNERSHIP AND RESIDENCE TELEPHONES IN USE IN REPRESENTATIVE NEW ENGLAND TOWNS AND THEIR IMMEDIATE LISTENING AREAS*

City	Number of Radio Sets	Number of Telephones	Number of Automobiles
Boston, Mass.............	631,738	458,376	532,340
Providence, R.I..........	130,540	81,448	109,091
Worcester, Mass.........	87,849	61,718	76,997
Hartford, Conn..........	89,598	66,995	91,485
Springfield, Mass........	63,171	46,294	58,605
New Bedford, Mass......	55,694	39,202	50,544
Manchester, N.H........	29,827	26,606	33,224
Bangor, Me.............	26,971	24,982	36,159

* *The Yankee Network of New England* (Shepard Broadcasting Service, Inc., 1932), pp. 45–47.

in which the station was located and the several adjoining counties wherein it was listened to regularly by a moderately large proportion of the listening public. As such, they embrace primarily an urban and suburban population, with a small number of rural families added to them. The number of receiving sets, residence telephones, and automobiles in the listening area centering around each of the towns is shown in Table VII. From the table it is evident that, at least as far as New England is concerned, radio receiving set ownership is more widely scattered throughout the community than either that of telephones or automobiles. This, in turn, seems to point to a rather wide distribution of radio ownership among all segments of the community. This conclusion finds additional support in a comparison of receiving set ownership and the number of residence telephones in use in Pennsylvania, the other area for which information has been available. Data regarding a number of representative Pennsylvania communities are found in Table VIII.

Though receiving set ownership does not exceed the number of residence telephones in use in all cases, the two parallel each

TABLE VIII

COMPARISON OF RADIO SET OWNERSHIP AND ESTIMATED NUMBER
OF RESIDENCE TELEPHONES IN USE IN REPRESENTATIVE
PENNSYLVANIA COMMUNITIES AS OF JULY, 1930*

Town	Number of Receiving Sets	Estimated Number of Residence Telephones
Philadelphia........................	258,640	198,551†
Pittsburgh.........................	81,279	90,030
Scranton...........................	12,902	15,490
Reading............................	15,553	14,477
Allentown..........................	14,293	10,649
Harrisburg.........................	12,053	12,458
Altoona............................	8,913	11,532
Wilkes-Barre.......................	8,024	7,518
Lancaster..........................	7,572	8,507
Bethlehem..........................	7,443	5,684
New Castle.........................	5,047	7,637
Pottstown..........................	3,108	2,117
Washington.........................	2,957	4,205
Sunbury............................	2,253	2,133†
Carbondale.........................	1,933	2,170
Monessen...........................	1,591	1,217
Jeanette...........................	1,505	1,449
Clairton...........................	1,273	975†
Mt. Carmel.........................	1,263	740†

* The number of residence telephones has been furnished by the Bell Telephone Company. Since these are given as of the base rate area which often includes more than the city proper, it has been necessary to estimate the number of residence telephones in the city as against the base rate area. Since the total population was known in each instance for both the city proper and the base rate area, it has been possible to compute the number of city telephones by a simple proportion, assuming a similar degree of use of telephones in the city and its immediate environs. Since these environs are chiefly suburbs and above the average income level, this assumption seems a sound one, erring if at all on the side of conservatism. Set figures are from the U.S. Census.

† Actual count. Base rate area coincides with town.

other very closely with few exceptions. It also is interesting to note that in the majority of instances wherein receiving set ownership lags behind the number of residence telephones in use (Altoona, New Castle, Washington, Carbondale and Lancaster), the towns in question are situated in the mountainous parts of Pennsylvania, where reception is notoriously poor. Thus in the case of Altoona, it is almost impossible to secure satisfactory reception of any except a very few outside stations during the daytime, and only these when conditions are especially favorable.[8] Since Lancaster does not lie in such territory, the explanation of its low set ownership may be found in the large number of Amish or so-called "plain people" who live there, and to whom the radio is quite probably unacceptable on religious grounds.

From the two instances just cited, it seems that the Starch survey no longer describes the situation with respect to radio receiving set ownership among various economic groups within the community as it is today. This is all the more probable when one considers the introduction of the midget set and the radical downward revision of all receiving set prices that was experienced by the industry shortly after the Starch survey was completed. Radio broadcasting can therefore be said to reach all economic classes within the community that are of any interest to the advertiser.

It is now possible to summarize the situation with respect to the potential listening audience for radio broadcasting programs. It has been seen that the radio audience of the country totals approximately seventeen million people and that more than one out of every two families owns receiving sets, thus virtually affording half of the American public as a potential group to be reached and affected by broadcast advertising. Since geographical variations are of more interest than is the mere number of total listeners, the relative distribution of radio set ownership throughout the country is of especial significance. Here it was shown that three major listener areas existed: the Northern Area containing 76.4 per cent of all radio sets and accounting for 67.5 per cent of the country's retail trade; the Southern Area with 11.9 per cent of the sets and doing 20.5 per cent of the nation's retail business; and the Far Western Area, wherein are found 11.7 per cent of the radio sets, and where 12.0 per cent of the retail trade of the country is transacted. Because of its relatively low degree of urbanization, its unfavorable economic situation, and its large negro population—only 14.4 per cent of the urban and 0.3 per cent of the farm negroes own receiving sets—the South can be least effectively reached by means of broadcast advertising. In addition to variations with respect to the radio audience in different parts of the country, it was re-

[8] Roy F. Thompson, manager of Station WFBG, Altoona, in interview.

vealed that there was a slight tendency toward a larger proportion of radio to total families in the larger cities than in the
smaller towns, and for the average set ownership in urban areas
to be slightly greater than in farming districts. In the case of
the more important half of the country's farm population situated primarily in the Middle Atlantic states and North Central
region, radio broadcasting constituted a satisfactory medium of
approach, 45.2 per cent of farm families owning radios. In the
Southern Area this was not the case, only 5.0 per cent of all farm
families owning radios, and with sound reasons existing for believing that the percentage of set ownership among the native
white farmers in this area was materially lower than in other parts
of the country. Finally, evidence was produced pointing to the
probability of a widespread ownership of radio receiving sets on
the part of all income classes in the community.

The potential radio audience, however, is but the groundwork of the effective circulation provided the user of broadcast
advertising. The actual circulation for a given program depends
upon a variety of factors, the most important of which include
the following: (1) the general listening habits of the population;
(2) the average circulation of the individual station or stations
over which the program is broadcast; (3) the inherent appeal of
the sponsor's own program both as to the adaptability of its
basic type to the psychology of the audience and as to the showmanship employed in its presentation; and (4) competition from
other programs broadcast in the same territory at the same
hour. All of these factors operate both nationally and with regard to specific variations in different parts of the country.
Only the first of them, however, constitutes appropriate subject
matter for our present discussion.

Habits regarding the use of the radio vary considerably,
depending upon a number of circumstances. They differ with
respect to hours of the day at which the radio is used,
and show some slight variation on the basis of days of the
week and seasons of the year. Likewise, different basic program types, such as comedy, sports broadcasts, and the like,
tend to meet with varying acceptance on the part of the
radio public, and, especially, particular segments of it. Differences in behavior with regard to these matters in themselves
will vary as between urban and rural areas, towns of dif-

ferent size, different sections of the country, sex, age, racial, cultural, and other special interest groups within the community. Finally, minor variations exist for specific localities depending upon local customs, such as the night usually reserved for church socials and similar matters.

At the present time there is a great need for fundamental data in this field which are of sufficient comprehensiveness and detail to make possible the presentation of definite conclusions regarding listener behavior. The field of research itself is so new,[9] the diversity of methods employed so great, and the angle of approach to the problem in itself so diversified as to make the comparison of existing data a most difficult task, while there is no single study which combines comprehensiveness of data and soundness of method to warrant its use as a basis for generalization in this field.[10] This does not mean, however, that no research of fundamental value has been done in the field of broadcast advertising. Many of the pioneer efforts in the field are of extreme interest, and, lacking any better information, of considerable value.[11] Moreover, all of the work done has contributed materially to the growing knowledge of the problem of research technique in the broadcast advertising field, a result of no small importance to the industry. However, the fact remains that lis-

[9] The newness of the field may be judged from the fact that the Starch study referred to previously was the first to be made, while one conducted by the writer in December, 1928, probably was the second.

[10] Methods of listener study vary greatly. Some investigators analyze fan mail, some use mail questionnaires, others telephone calls, and still others house-to-house surveys. The basic approach varies even more greatly. Some measure habits, asking listeners what they habitually do; others measure behavior at a series of specific moments with habits deduced therefrom. Similar disparity exists in the choice of sample, and indeed at almost any stage of the work.

[11] In this category should be placed the "Listening Area" and "Price Waterhouse" studies of the Columbia Broadcasting System, and the very excellent studies on "Does Radio Sell Goods" made for them by Professor Robert E. Elder, of the Massachusetts Institute of Technology. The "Price Waterhouse studies" are of relative network popularity and are probably as sound as can be accomplished in this field within the limits of practical expenditure of money. The "Listening Area studies" define qualitative areas of regular listening to Columbia stations, and are not quite as acceptable from the viewpoint of pure research. Other studies of interest include the Crossley surveys made for the Association of National Advertisers, the method of which is open to some question as to its adaptability to the scope of the study; work such as that of Dr. Robert Riegel, of the University of Buffalo, and, on the engineering side, though closely related to listener studies, the very important and provocative work on station coverage done by Dr. C. M. Jansky of Washington, D.C.

tener data are lamentably weak, and that, as a result, little conclusive evidence can be presented in this field.[12] In view of this, one of the most valuable things which could occur in the industry would be the scientific analysis of existing methods of research with a view of determining both their basic value and their specific fitness for securing information regarding given subjects of investigation, together with the general application of these methods to an extent which would make possible the comparison of results. Not only would such a step be of marked value within the industry itself, but much money would be saved which is now wasted in useless research. Significant results of practical value would also be secured and in addition it would aid materially in fostering a clearer appreciation of the potentialities of broadcast advertising on the part of the general public and advertiser alike.

In so far as a comprehensive survey of listener behavior would entail a most expensive and detailed research of its own, the discussion will here be limited to a presentation of the items regarding which there seems to be more or less common agreement, and to studies conducted in Buffalo and Philadelphia, by methods which insure a comparability of results.[13] Thus the groundwork will be afforded for an appreciation of the forces which shape the actual listener audience from the entire potential group of receiving set owners.

The variation in number of listeners at different hours of the day is probably the most important single item of listener data.

[12] The chief difficulties with present research in this field are: (1) a tendency to deduce results for the attainment of which the methods employed are psychologically and statistically unsuited; (2) inadequate samples, especially in national studies and where behavior is measured at given moments; (3) a desire to cover too wide areas rather than study a localized district thoroughly, and (4) too great concentration on competitive aspects such as station popularity rather than upon the fundamentals which will sell radio as a whole. The lack of comparable localized studies already has been mentioned.

[13] *A Merchandising Interpretation of Listener Reaction and Habits with Respect to Radio Broadcasting*, by Herman S. Hettinger (manuscript, 1929); *A Study of the Habits and Preferences of Radio Listeners in the Philadelphia Buying Area*, compiled for and published by the WCAU Broadcasting Company, 1930; *Analysis of the Summer Radio Audience in the Philadelphia Buying Area*, also for WCAU, by Herman S. Hettinger in collaboration with Richard R. Mead (1931). An almost identical method was applied by Dr. Robert Riegel, of the University of Buffalo, in the *Buffalo Radio Audience*, compiled for Station WBEN, 1932. The high degree of correlation existing between different years and with respect to the two towns indicates the general satisfactoriness of the method.

With regard to it, there are at least several features in which all of the researches that have been done seem at least basically to be in agreement. The first of these is the fact that the evening audience is on the average two to three times as great as the daytime audience when measured on an hourly basis. The second point of agreement is that in most cases the number of listeners tuned in during the morning and afternoon hours are almost the same, with somewhat greater variations existing as between towns and methods of research in this instance than in the former.[14] The general aspect of the listening-audience curve during the average weekday is indicated in Chart I.[15] The chart indicates the average proportion of total listeners tuned in at various hours of the day on any day from Monday to Friday, inclusive.[16]

From the chart it will be noted that with the exception of the noon and evening meal periods, together with a slight lag in the evening audience in Buffalo, the two curves are practically identical. Since the Philadelphia curve is for the summer and the Buffalo curve for winter, it is difficult to tell how much of the variation is on a seasonal basis. The 1930 Philadelphia curve fits the Buffalo one even more closely, but, since it represents the entire week rather than merely Monday to Friday, it would be less sound to compare it than to use the 1931 Philadelphia curve.

Several other thoughts are suggested at least tentatively by a comparison of the Philadelphia and Buffalo studies. The first of these is that Saturday listening varies very slightly from that of

[14] In this case the researches of Herman S. Hettinger and Richard R. Mead in Philadelphia, the Buffalo study of Dr. Riegel, the work of Mr. Benjamin Soby for the Westinghouse stations in Pittsburgh and Springfield, Massachusetts, and the Crossley survey are all in extremely close agreement as to the contours of the listening curve if not with regard to actual percentages. As will be noted in the chart, Philadelphia and Buffalo are practically identical. There is less agreement on the morning-afternoon variation. Philadelphia and Buffalo show greater afternoon audiences. Some of the other studies show the opposite.

[15] "Metropolitan Radio Audiences," by Herman S. Hettinger; *Broadcast Advertising*, December, 1932.

[16] In *A Merchandising Analysis of Housewife Radio Listening Habits*, made under the writer's direction by Halsey D. Kellogg and Abner G. Walters, the variation at specific hours on various days mentioned are shown to be seldom more than 2 to 3 per cent. Other studies confirm this. See *Broadcasting*, April 15, 1932, for summary of the study.

CHART I

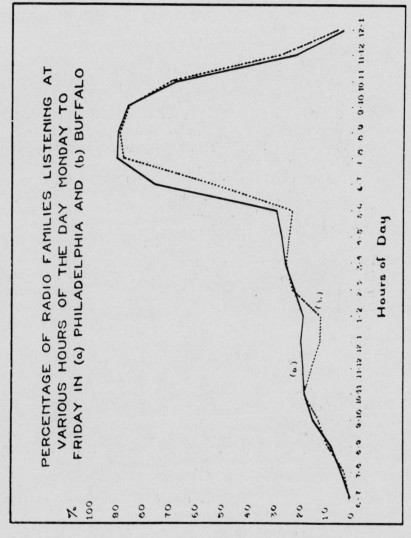

PERCENTAGE OF RADIO FAMILIES LISTENING AT
VARIOUS HOURS OF THE DAY MONDAY TO
FRIDAY IN (a) PHILADELPHIA AND (b) BUFFALO

other week days as far as the hourly listener load is concerned, the only difference of note being a slight tendency toward a smaller evening audience. It is the writer's own belief, though he has no means of substantiating it, that this is probably more true of metropolitan centers than of smaller towns.

Another conclusion drawn from the studies is the relatively greater discrepancy between different communities as to the matter of Sunday listening. Here the Buffalo study showed a very different tendency, the number of listeners being much lower than Philadelphia in the morning and much higher in the afternoon. Again, how much of this is seasonal and how much of year-round duration is impossible to say at the moment. However, it is worth noting as a matter deserving careful consideration. The same tendency, however, is noted in Chart II, which indicates the difference of listening in Philadelphia proper, its immediate suburbs, and small outlying towns such as West Chester, Norristown, and similar communities in Pennsylvania and New Jersey. This tendency toward towns of different size to have rather marked variations in the hours of habitual listening is to be noted for weekdays as well as on Sunday, and is found in Chart III.[17] It is quite reasonable to assume that the Sunday variation would be greater than the weekday one, since, in the case of the former, life is less circumscribed by the necessities of daily living. Differences likewise are to be noted in both studies on the part of men and women, with women constituting the great daytime audience, as well as on the basis of income classes, though the latter are of relatively lesser significance. The writer has noted some slight tendency toward variations in age groups, but, except with regard to the younger children, these are of little importance. Thus, probably, differences in listening at various hours of the day arise mainly with regard to communities of different size, men and women, and with regard to Sunday. Differences on various days of the week are of no importance with the exception of Sunday, which is important both as regards to general trend and special seasonal differences. The average number of hours the radio is used by listeners is between four and six, with the former figure favored.[18]

[17] "Metropolitan Radio Audiences."

[18] *An Analysis of the Summer Radio Audience in Philadelphia Buying Area*, by Herman S. Hettinger and Richard R. Mead, p. 15.

CHART II

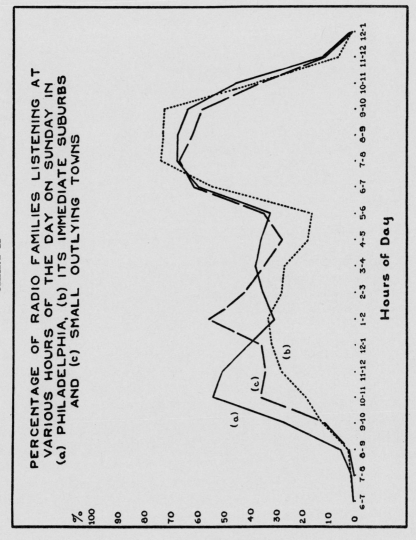

PERCENTAGE OF RADIO FAMILIES LISTENING AT
VARIOUS HOURS OF THE DAY ON SUNDAY IN
(a) PHILADELPHIA, (b) ITS IMMEDIATE SUBURBS
AND (c) SMALL OUTLYING TOWNS

CHART III

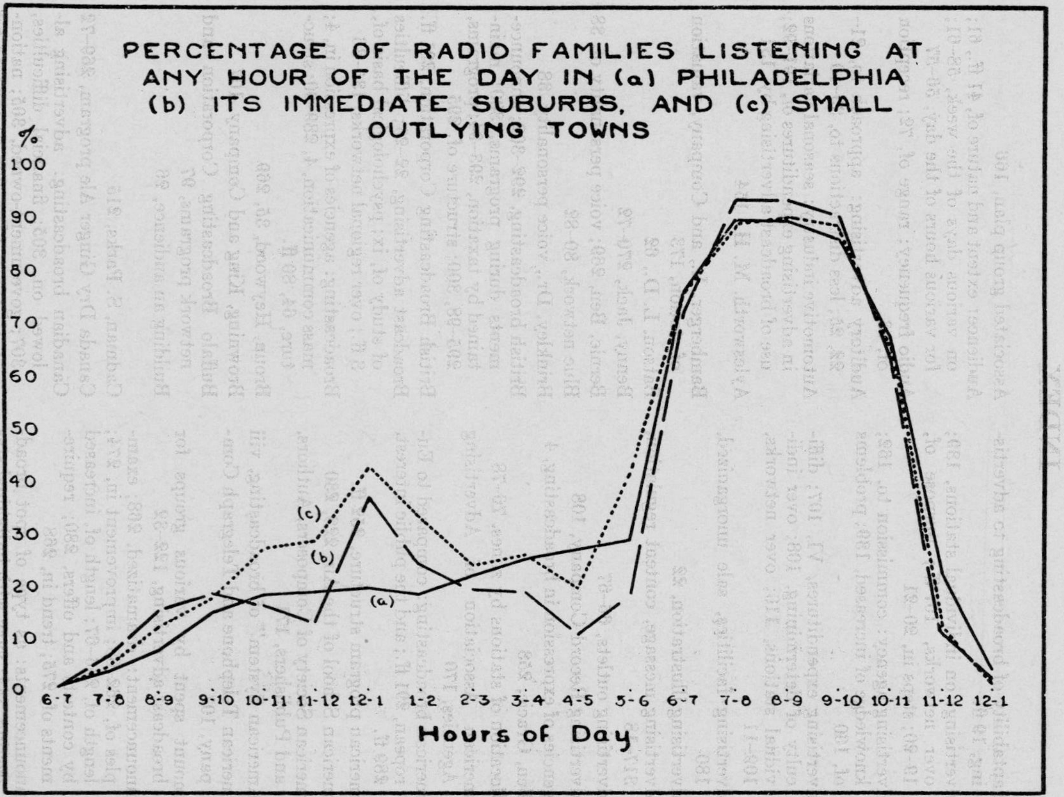

PERCENTAGE OF RADIO FAMILIES LISTENING AT
ANY HOUR OF THE DAY IN (a) PHILADELPHIA
(b) ITS IMMEDIATE SUBURBS, AND (c) SMALL
OUTLYING TOWNS

%

100

90

80

70

60

50

40

30

20

10

0

6-7 7-8 8-9 9-10 10-11 11-12 12-1 1-2 2-3 3-4 4-5 5-6 6-7 7-8 8-9 9-10 10-11 11-12 12-1

Hours of Day

(a)

(b)

(c)

With respect to the proportion of people listening on various days of the week, most studies are of general agreement that there is little difference on this subject. Most estimates vary from 60 per cent to 80 per cent as to the number of listeners prone to use their radio some time during every day of the week. The chief variation of importance seems to be in the case of week ends during the summer, where the Sunday audience is approximately 90 per cent that of the Monday to Friday average in Philadelphia.[19] This is a factor which probably will vary greatly between towns, especially in the summer, depending upon existing recreational facilities and similar features.

Seasonal variation in the size of the listening audience has been a moot question with broadcasters since the beginning of the industry. Though the evidence available is rather slight, there seems to be sound reason to believe that the dropping off in size during the summer months has been exaggerated. The tendency seems too much to have been one of executives visualizing the summer in terms of their own vacation and forgetting the great number of jobs where the vacation period was either nonexistent or limited to a few days. In this case estimates and researches available seem to indicate a decline in audience of little more than 10 per cent on the average weekday and reaching the lowest figure of approximately 80.0 per cent normal on the last Sunday in July and first Sunday of August when vacationing is at its peak.[20] In this case there are decided differences with regard to income groups with approximately two-thirds of the $5,000 and above class going away on vacations and only 21.1 per cent of the low income group, under $2,000, going away for any period of time at all. This factor probably is conditioned to a high degree by the nearness of resorts, so that in communities such as Boston the decline in the summer audience probably will be greater than in a city such as Philadelphia. The foregoing information, thus, is extremely tentative and no final and widely applicable conclusions can be drawn from it other than the barest general trend.

In addition to differences in listening on the basis of varying

[19] The Philadelphia surveys of Herman S. Hettinger and Richard R. Mead, the Buffalo survey of Professor Riegel, and the Elder surveys of the Columbia Broadcasting System—all are in general agreement on this matter.

[20] Crossley (1930) and the Philadelphia researches previously mentioned.

hours of the day, days of the week, and seasons of the year, each in turn interpreted in the light of varying communities, towns of different size, sex, age, and income groups, the determination of the actual audience for a given program is further conditioned by listener habit with regard to the choice of stations. Research authorities are in general agreement on the fact that the average listener tends to use three to four stations regularly, turning to the others, if at all, only when these have failed to give enjoy-

TABLE IX

PROPORTION OF PHILADELPHIA AND BUFFALO LISTENERS LIKING
VARIOUS TYPES OF PROGRAMS

TYPE OF PROGRAM	PERCENTAGE OF LISTENERS LIKING PROGRAM	
	Philadelphia (Per Cent)	Buffalo (Per Cent)
Music..............................	99.8	*
Comedy............................	74.6	76.6
Drama.............................	66.1	83.5†
News..............................	54.7	53.1
Sports............................	62.4	63.4
Religious..........................	39.9	46.9
Educational.......................	19.3	43.7
Special features...................	27.6	43.1
Women's programs.................	15.0	21.2
Children's programs...............	47.6	51.7

* Not mentioned except in first choices due to wording of question.
† Approximation combining several Buffalo classifications.

ment. This is well summarized in a statement by L. D. Batson, of the Electrical Equipment Division of the Department of Commerce:[21] "Ultimately the owner tends to reach a stage where the one or two stations most easily tuned will be sampled, and if one has a satisfactory feature the dial is set for it and left until something discordant with the listener's mood develops, when the set will be shut off or another station tried." This means, therefore, that if the broadcaster is not on one of the regularly used stations in the area he will fail to reach a large portion of the people. Likewise it signifies that if he is on any of the two or three most popular stations, provided no too great

[21] *Radio Markets of the World 1932*, p. 25.

discrepancy exists between them, he is using a potentially satisfactory medium, and upon his program in competition with
others broadcast rests the burden of winning the audience.

This leads to a brief discussion of the final limiting factor with
respect to the actual audience, namely, the program likes and
dislikes of the audience. At the outset it is well established that
listeners seldom indeed prefer one type of program to the exclusion of all others. Therefore, their relative liking of certain types
of programs will determine the basic number of listeners a given

TABLE X

MUSICAL PREFERENCES OF PHILADELPHIA AND
BUFFALO RADIO AUDIENCES

Type of Music	Percentage of Listeners Liking Type of Music	
	Philadelphia (Per Cent)	Buffalo (Per Cent)
Classical............................	31.4	36.1
Semi-classical......................	39.9	39.0
Dance..............................	73.4	69.0
Sacred.............................	27.7	15.7
Old-fashioned......................	27.7	42.7
Polish.............................		8.3

program can hope to reach at all. Those not interested in sports
broadcasts are never part of the circulation, actual or potential,
of a sports program. Variations in this field are so great and
data so extremely tentative that no generalization is possible except with regard to decidedly local areas. A comparison of
two of these, Buffalo and Philadelphia, is found in Tables IX
and X.[22]

These tables at least are illustrative of the type of data revealed in this field. As in the case of all other listener information, a great deal more fundamental material is required before
listener behavior can be measured with any degree of conclusiveness.

[22] Buffalo and Philadelphia studies previously referred to.

CHAPTER IV

ECONOMIC BASES: THE AVAILABLE BROAD-
CASTING STRUCTURE—INDIVIDUAL
STATIONS

There are two principal elements in the broadcasting structure of the United States, by means of which programs are carried to the approximately seventeen million listeners who comprise the potential audience for the medium, and out of whose
number the advertiser carves his own particular circulation.
The first of these is the individual broadcasting station. The
second factor, until recently completely overshadowing the first,
is the grouping and operation of a number of individual stations
into networks, either national or regional in scope, and making
possible the simultaneous presentation of a program over a wide
territory. Regarding the middlemen such as time-brokers, station representatives, transcription companies, and similar organizations who function between the station and the advertising agency or program sponsor, no mention will be made. Discussion of them will be reserved until analysis is made of the
actual use of the radio broadcasting structure as an advertising
medium. The immediate analysis will be devoted, therefore, to
the broadcasting structure existing for the purpose of transmitting programs to the listener, and of the significant factors of
this structure as they involve broadcast advertising.

A knowledge of the structure available for reaching the potential circulation of the medium is of more than usual importance
in the case of radio broadcasting. In the first place, radio broadcasting structure is of such recent development that even today
it is in a comparative state of flux. Moreover, because of its
newness, the full significance of the existing broadcasting structure is neither completely understood nor appreciated by the
advertiser or the public at large. In addition, radio broadcasting technique itself is in a state of relative infancy so that the
possibility of sweeping inventions or new applications of existing knowledge is by no means remote. Finally, since the radio

broadcasting structure is definitely limited by the number of available wave-lengths, and not merely by the demand for facilities as in the case of magazines or newspapers, and, since the apportionment of these wave-lengths is a matter of governmental regulation and international treaty, it becomes a very much more complex question than does the structure of other media.[1] For these reasons a brief elementary discussion of the nature and trends in broadcasting structure must be considered, the individual stations being treated first and the question of network broadcasting being considered afterward.

At the present time there are approximately 600 broadcasting stations in the United States serving the American listening public.[2] Of these stations all but 40 are privately owned and operated. The exceptions to private ownership are stations owned either directly or indirectly by states and municipalities, including in this number the various state universities and similar institutions, but not privately owned schools and colleges.[3]

These stations operate on a total of ninety channels or wave-length assignments, lying within the 550–1,550 kilocycle band reserved exclusively for broadcasting by international convention. With regard to the power of stations and the proportion of wave-lengths assigned to each type of station, the following is the situation at the present time: (1) There are 237 so-called local stations, having a maximum power of 250 watts in daytime and 100 watts at night, and occupying six of the total ninety frequencies available to American broadcasters. These stations are designed primarily to give localized service within the immediate environs of the communities in which they are located. (2) Low-power regional stations, possessing a maximum night power of 1,000 watts and day power of 2,500 watts, com-

---

[1] If the rumored North American Conference occurs, and a widening of the wave band ensues, a major reallocation of stations in this country is certain to occur, with resulting fundamental modifications of structure of importance to all parties concerned in broadcasting.

[2] *The Sixth Annual Report of the Federal Radio Commission*, p. 25, lists 604 stations under its jurisdiction as of June 30, 1932, of which 5 are outside the immediate boundaries of the country, 1 in Porto Rico and 2 each in Hawaii and Alaska. Also *Radio Broadcast Stations of U.S.*, January 1, 1932.

[3] *Commercial Radio Advertising*, Federal Radio Commission (December, 1931), p. 13. With regard to most of the features herein reported the situation has not changed materially since that date.

prise a total of 272 stations and occupy forty wave-lengths. A small number of these stations are reduced to lower operating power at certain intervals of the day to make way for Canadian stations on the same wave-length. Most of the stations of this class are either 500 or 1,000 watts in power and are designed for immediate local use over a slightly wider territory than those of the first class, in this case reaching at least some short distance into the rural areas. (3) High-power regional stations, of which there are 8, possessing power up to 5 kilowatts, and occupying four wave-lengths. Finally 90 clear channel stations ranging in power from 5 to 50 kilowatts and occupying forty wavelengths, being designed to serve wide urban and rural areas, complete the structure.[4] There are 90 stations on these clear channels, approximately half of which were in simultaneous operation at night in 1931. Part-time stations include transmitters operated only during daylight at the location of the dominant station, and at night when the dominant station is silent, in which cases the power of the stations range from 50 watts to 20,000 watts. Of these stations, because of the allocation activities of the Federal Radio Commission to be discussed later in the chapter, no more than 397 are in simultaneous nighttime operation.[5] These stations insure satisfactory daytime reception to approximately 94.0 per cent of the population of the United States and nighttime reception to about 89.6 per cent of the country.[6] They represent an investment of over $49,000,000.[7]

Of these stations more than 90 per cent are available to use by the broadcast advertiser on the days and at the hours during which they are in operation.[8] This includes substantially all of the important stations in the country. All of the high-powered stations, those above 5,000 watts, are available for advertising purposes; while 88.8 per cent of the stations of over 1,000 watts and under 5,000 watts in power, 85.0 per cent of stations over 100 and under 1,000 watts, 95.0 per cent of the local 100-watt stations, and 79.0 per cent of those under 100 watts in power

[4] *Commercial Radio Advertising*, Federal Radio Commission, p. 13.

[5] *Sixth Annual Report of the Federal Radio Commission*, p. 25.

[6] *Commercial Radio Advertising*, Federal Radio Commission, p. 12.

[7] *Ibid.*, p. 43.   [8] *Ibid.*, p. 22.

similarly accept broadcast advertising.[9] In addition to the strictly commercial stations, operated exclusively for private profit, 7
of the 12 state or municipally owned stations, 5 of the 28 religious stations, and 12 of the 44 educational stations accepted
commercial advertising programs in December, 1931.[10] Due to
the decline of state aid and other revenue experienced by many
educational institutions, the number of educational stations accepting commercial programs has definitely increased, though
the exact extent of this tendency is not known.[11]

In order to achieve a clearer picture of the development of the
radio broadcasting structure in the United States, it will be
profitable to review, first, the trend in the number of stations
during the past decade; second, the rise in station power and the
other improvements of a technical nature which have resulted
in increased range and quality of station service; and, finally, to
discuss briefly the work of allocation of broadcasting facilities
which has been carried on by the Federal Radio Commission
and upon which the complexion of the present radio broadcasting structure of the country largely depends.

The trend in the number of broadcasting stations in operation
in the United States is indicated in Table XI.

From the table it will be noted that there was a marked decline in stations during the period 1927–29, and that, since that
date, there has been a tendency for the number of stations to
remain comparatively static. The greatest number of stations
existing in the country probably was higher than any figure appearing in the chart, since the most pronounced rise in station
ownership was between the period June 30, 1926, and June 30,
1927, reaching an estimated peak of 732 stations during the
early months of the latter year.[12]

---

[9] *Ibid.*, p. 23.

[10] *Commercial Radio Advertising*, Federal Radio Commission, p. 22.

[11] Philip G. Loucks, managing director of the National Association of Broadcasters,
to the writer.

[12] This rise was brought about by the breakdown of government radio regulations in
April, 1926, when the United States Court for the Northern District of Illinois decided
(*U.S.* v. *Zenith Radio Corporation*) that the Department of Commerce had no express
power to establish broadcast regulations, the general tenor of which decision was further
affirmed by an opinion of the attorney general. There followed a wild scramble for
broadcasting stations (*The Federal Radio Commission*, by L. F. Schmeckebier [Brook-
ings Institute], pp. 12–13, 23).

The decline in stations has been due to a number of reasons. Probably the principal one of these has been the matter of increasing costs of operation as radio has become stabilized and has taken on a definitely commercial aspect. Increased station power, together with other rising costs of operation including talent, program service, management and similar items, improved equipment required by the Commission, increased copy-

TABLE XI

NUMBER OF BROADCASTING STATIONS IN THE UNITED
STATES, JUNE 30, 1922—JUNE 30,1932*

Year	Number of Stations
1922	382
1923	573
1924	535
1925	571
1926	528
1927	681
1928	677
1929	606
1930	618
1931	612
1932	604

* Figures for the years 1922–26. inclusive, are from the annual reports of *Commercial and Government Radio Stations of the United States,* published by the Radio Division of the Department of Commerce. Data for the following years are from Table I of the Report of the Chief Engineer, *Sixth Annual Report of the Federal Radio Commission,* 1932, p. 25. Station totals in all cases include a few broadcasters in the territorial possessions ranging annually from about five to seven stations. Since it has been almost impossible to separate these for the earlier years in a satisfactory manner, they have been left in for all years. It should be noted that estimates of stations do not always agree, those of the Department of Commerce varying from those of the Commission in certain instances. In these cases the latter have been taken as authoritative. Data for early years probably are very tentative.

right fees, and similar factors, combined with the absence of the necessary revenue on the part of the poorly managed and often uneconomically located marginal stations, constituted one blade of the shears which cut many of them out of the broadcasting structure. The other blade was the direct work of the Commission, both in its early allocation work and in the continual weeding out of stations whose operation was not, in the "public interest, convenience and necessity," a matter which needs further detailed discussion. A conception of the financial requirements of broadcasting can be secured from the fact that it is estimated that the average capital required for a 1-kilowatt station is $44,900, with an annual maintenance expense of $64,400 exclusive of programs. The capital cost of a 5-kilowatt station is in the neighborhood of $127,000, and the annual maintenance charge, exclusive of talent, is $159,000; while for a 50-kilowatt station the capital charge is no less than $338,000, and the basic maintenance expense $296,150.[13]

More important than the trend in the number of stations has been the great increase in power on the part of broadcasting stations as a whole, as well as the marked rise in the number of stations of higher power. Thus, while the total stations in the country increased approximately 60.0 per cent since 1922 and 5.4 per cent since 1923, the total watt power at nighttime has increased fourteen and one-half times since 1923, or almost three hundred times faster than the number of stations. The general situation in this respect is indicated in Table XII which shows the relative proportion of stations of different power in the United States, annually since 1923, when power data first were available.

Several things should be noted concerning this table. The first of these is the very decided decline in the number of stations of less than 50 watts in power within recent years. A second feature of interest is the fact that it nevertheless is in the lower-powered stations, 100 and 500 watts primarily, where the greatest increase has taken place. Another factor of special note is that though the high-power stations comprise a very small proportion of the broadcasting stations of the country, they are of basic importance when it comes to serving large rural areas, or to covering complete metropolitan trading districts as in the case of the larger cities. The favorable attitude of the Federal Radio Commission toward high power and the consequent granting of 25- and 50-kilowatt status to 6 and 9 additional stations respectively on October 1, 1931,[14] will greatly increase the service rendered by this type of station when the various power increases finally go into operation early in 1933, and should be

---

[13] *Present and Impending Applications to Education of Radio and Allied Arts* (National Advisory Council on Radio in Education, 1932), pp. 80–90. The estimates in question are by a committee composed of the leading radio engineers in this country. The reader is cautioned as to their tentativeness, however, since items such as real estate and wages will vary so greatly between towns as to be extremely difficult to typify in a common figure. The above estimates are undoubtedly extremely low if one were to apply them to New York stations.

[14] *Broadcasting Magazine*, October 15, 1931, p. 8.

of considerable assistance to the listeners in the areas affected. Finally, it should be noted that the decreased proportion of 1-kilowatt stations in 1932 does not represent a falling away of stations of this class, but rather indicates the consolidation of part-time stations.[15]

The increase in station power described above should be interpreted with care, since it merely constitutes a rough general

TABLE XII

RELATIVE PROPORTION OF STATIONS OF DIFFERENT
POWER, JUNE 30, 1923—JUNE 30, 1932*

YEAR	PERCENTAGE OF STATIONS OF DIFFERENT POWER IN WATTS†							
	Under 100	100–400	500–900	1,000–4,000	5,000–10,000	11,000–25,000	30,000–50,000	Total
1923	48.9	33.8	16.7	0.6				100
1924	47.6	30.9	19.5	2.0				100
1925	38.3	30.9	24.9	4.8	1.1			100
1926	29.3	27.4	27.8	11.7	3.8			100
1927	27.9	32.8	26.0	9.2	4.1			100
1928	23.5	34.3	24.7	11.0	5.6	0.3	0.6	100
1929	13.1	36.4	22.5	16.7	9.0	1.4	0.9	100
1930	9.5	40.4	23.1	15.2	9.1	1.5	1.2	100
1931	6.5	41.9	19.6	21.3	7.7	0.9	2.1	100
1932	5.2	45.2	21.5	17.7	7.3	1.0	2.1	100

* The percentages in question are based upon counts made of stations of different nighttime power as found in *Commercial and Government Radio Stations of the United States*, 1923–31, and *Radio Broadcast Stations in the United States*, 1932, which continues the Department of Commerce work under the auspices of the Federal Radio Commission.

† Headings for station power are misleading, since power tends to group itself very decidedly at certain points: 100, 250, 500, 1,000, 2,500, 5,000, 10,000, 25,000, and 50,000 watts, with a few stations having intermediate power.

measure of improved station facilities, though it probably is the best common denominator available. Station power is but one of a number of factors upon which station service, in turn, is conditioned; others of importance including the location of the transmitter, the type and efficiency of antenna employed, topographical and similar conditions with regard to the location of the station, freedom from interference from disturbances created by other stations and non-radio electrical disturbances, the fundamental carrying characteristic of the wave-length used, and the hours of station operation. Since many of these con-

[15] Mr. Loucks to the writer.

siderations revolve around the matter of technical improvements in broadcasting within the past several years, it is this question which next will be discussed briefly.

These technical improvements have been of equal if not greater importance than the general increase in power, and have affected favorably both the clarity, quality, and range of station reception. One of the most interesting improvements in broadcast transmission has been that of the general increase in efficiency of modulation. In order to understand the effect of this factor upon station reception it is necessary to remember that a radio broadcast wave really possesses two aspects: the carrier wave, which is merely the basic emanation of electrical energy at the assigned frequency or wave-length, and the modulation, which constitutes the impression of the sound impulses, translated into electrical energy, thereby changing the characteristics of the carrier wave itself. It is the modulation which constitutes the usable signal and which the receiving set translates into the program heard by the listener.[16] Moreover, it is the modulated portion of the carrier wave which is responsible for most station interference. By a high degree of modulation it is possible to extend the service area of the station wherein its programs can be heard into territory wherein it previously merely constituted a nuisance to other stations. Thus, it is estimated that an increase from 40 per cent to 80 per cent modulation gives the same result in increase of signal delivered, as if the power were increased four times. The effect of the added modulation upon a 500-watt station is the same as if the power of the station had been increased to 2,000 watts; with the important difference that, in the instance of the greater modulation, the nuisance area of the station has not been increased as would have been the case had the carrier output been quadrupled.[17] It should be noted that, since the issuance of General Order 111 by the Federal Radio Commission on April 30, 1931, broadcasting stations have been required to maintain a modulation of over 75 per cent.[18]

[16] Dr. C. B. Joliffe, chief engineer of the Federal Radio Commission, at the Eighth Annual Convention of the National Association of Broadcasters, Cleveland, 1930 (*Proceedings*, p. 35).

[17] *Fifth Annual Report of the Federal Radio Commission*, Report of the Chief Engineer, p. 23.

[18] *Ibid.*, p. 97.

Improved frequency monitoring is another technical improvement which has been of great service in reducing interference between stations. In General Orders 116 and 117 issued by the Commission in June, 1931,[19] it was required of stations to remain within ±50 cycles per second of their assigned wavelength and to instal monitoring equipment capable of producing that result. This was enforced on June 22, 1932, and by December of that year was practically in complete operation, with noticeable beneficial results. The increased service range possible to broadcasting stations, with all broadcasters maintaining a frequency deviation tolerance of no more than ±50 cycles, is illustrated by the fact that it is estimated that the ensuing freedom from interference by other stations will increase, on the average, the effective service range of a 1-kilowatt station approximately 4.6 times.[20]

Not only have marked improvements been made in the quality of station output which in turn have resulted in decided increases in the average station service range,[21] but improvements also have been effected in the audio frequency range, with respect to both broadcasting transmitters and telephone lines used in connecting network stations. The result has been that a much more faithful representation of tone has been made possible, with a consequent greater naturalness in the reproduction of the program. The trend in this field is evidenced by the fact that today the most up-to-date transmitter can successfully broadcast tones ranging from 30 to 10,000 cycles, while the average modern station can reproduce from 30 to 7,500 cycles. When compared to the tonal range of a piano, which is from 16 to 4,608 cycles, the station of today is seen to be capable of reproducing a tonal range considerably exceeding that instrument and indeed including almost all of the tones of the symphony orchestra. In addition, modern telephone lines, which are being installed widely at the present time, are capable of carrying

[19] *Ibid.*, p. 104.

[20] *Fifth Annual Report of the Federal Radio Commission* (1931), p. 24. The effect has been extremely satisfactory according to a statement by the Commission printed in the *National Association of Broadcasters News Bulletin* on November 26, 1932.

[21] Daytime service range for a 100-watt station in a city residential section is estimated at 10 miles, and rural at 30 miles; for a 1,000-watt station 26 and 63 miles, respectively; a 5,000-watt station 44 and 93 miles; and a 50,000-watt station 78 and 160 miles (*ibid.*, pp. 30–31).

from 50 to 8,000 cycles as compared to the standard line used in transmitting broadcasting programs, which possesses a range of from 50 to 5,000 cycles. This potentiality of sound transmission is compared to an average audio frequency reception of from 50 to 5,500 cycles for a good modern receiving set with a dynamic speaker, and to a frequency range of from 256 to 2,200 cycles on the part of a pre-screen grid receiver.[22]

Marked improvements likewise have occurred in the matter of microphones, upon whose pick-up sensitivity depends the amount of the program conveyed to the station to be broadcast. Following the introduction of the carbon microphone in 1927 the next important improvement was the development of the condenser microphone in 1930, while in 1931 the dynamic or moving-coil microphone was first employed, the occasion being a broadcast of the Philadelphia Orchestra in the fall of that year. The advantages of the dynamic microphone lie in the fact that it possesses a tonal range of from 20 to 10,000 cycles, is not affected by humidity, temperature, or barometric pressure as have been some of its predecessors, and that it is small and sturdy as compared with the bulky and extremely delicate condenser microphone.[23] During 1932 the parabolic microphone, used for large gatherings, and the ribbon microphone have been developed. Both of these microphones are too new and their use still too limited to enable conclusive evaluation of their respective merits. Among the points of superiority claimed for the ribbon microphone are that it is directional and therefore has a greater freedom from interfering noise or reverberation, that it possesses a bilateral pick-up which adds to its versatility, and finally its extreme sensitiveness.[24]

Other technical improvements which should be noted are: (1) the development of half-wave, or single mast, antennae which serve to reduce the sky wave, resulting in less interference and consequent improve service range;[25] (2) the development of directional antennae making possible the reduction of interference

[22] *Radio Retailing*, August, 1931, p. 13.

[23] *Broadcasting*, October 15, 1931, p. 16.

[24] "The Ribbon Microphone—Its Application," by J. Weinberger, *Electronics*, November, 1932, p. 337.

[25] Installed by WABC, New York, WNAC, Boston, and WCAU, Philadelphia. Also see *Fifth Annual Report of the Federal Radio Commission*, p. 26.

in specific areas;[26] (3) improved knowledge of transmitter location[27] in relation to the service area desired, which is one of the most important developments of all; (4) improved studio design, especially with regard to acoustic properties; and, finally, the development and marked improvement in the quality of rebroadcasts from European and other foreign countries to a point where regular intercontinental service of this type has become commonplace.[28] The net result of these technical improvements has been a vastly superior broadcasting service on the part of the stations of the country, as compared with several years ago, and a consequent widening of the circle of listeners who can be reached effectively by individual stations or groups of stations. The principal difficulty today lies not in broadcasting apparatus but in the receiving sets, which have tended to lag materially behind the sending apparatus especially as regards the quality of reproduction. The shift to the small midget set in 1931 with the ensuing price war reduced the average price of receiving sets from $133 in 1929 to $62 in 1931.[29] This in turn has brought with it an overemphasis of price and a consequent reluctance to experiment with or introduce superior models which could be produced profitably only at prices above the current market level.[30]

The final question involved in a consideration of the individual station structure of the country is the part which has been played by the Federal Radio Commission in the development of broadcasting structure of the United States. The Radio Commission was established under the Radio Act of 1927,[31] and its five commissioners were empowerd to regulate broadcasting in the "public convenience, interest and necessity"[32] which, under the law, included the following specific duties: (1) to classify stations; (2) prescribe the nature of the service for each class of station and for any individual station; (3) assign wave-lengths; (4) determine location of stations; (5) regulate kind of apparatus

[26] *Sixth Annual Report of the Federal Radio Commission*, p. 29.

[27] *Ibid.*, pp. 30–31.

[28] *Ibid.*, p. 29.   [29] *Electronics*, March, 1932, p. 101.

[30] See the issues of *Radio Retailing* for 1931 and 1932, especially, for data on this matter.

[31] 44 Stat. L. 1162.

[32] Section 4 of Act, opening paragraph. Duties comprise body thereof.

used; (6) regulate the elimination of interference; (7) establish areas of service for individual stations; (8) make special regulations applicable to stations in network broadcasting; and (9) issue regulations regarding station records.

In actual practice the regulatory efforts of the Commission have tended to fall into several categories: (1) improvements in the standards of transmission, already covered to a considerable degree in the discussion of the technical improvements which have taken place in broadcasting; (2) general regulatory activities with regard to the quality of station service under the "public convenience, interest and necessity"; and (3) allocation of station facilities under the Davis Amendment referred to previously.

With regard to the first type of activity, the Commission not only has rendered an important service through the issuance of general orders, such as those mentioned under technical improvements, but also has tended to accomplish the same purpose through the supervisory influence it exerts over equipment by means of the specifications of engineering requirements as regards the issuance of construction permits, and through the general research carried on by its technical staff.

The Commission's part in maintaining generally high standards of service for the "public convenience, interest and necessity" is well illustrated by a summarization of its own statement, issued August 23, 1928, of what it considered to lie in that province.[33] Among the items included were: (1) that stations should be equipped and financed so as to give as high an order of service over as large a territory as possible; (2) that where a number of stations render the same type of service in a given area, consideration should be given the station whose service does not constitute a duplication; (3) freedom from heterodyning should be effected to the maximum degree; (4) advertising should be secondary to the entertainment service of programs; (5) transmitter location should be regulated so that blanketing will be reduced to a minimum; (6) the financial responsibility of station owners should be complete and specific; (7) private controversy is forbidden on the air; (8) stations must operate on a regular schedule so announced; (9) adequate frequency control

---

[33] *First Annual Report of the Federal Radio Commission*, pp. 167–70. This still seems to be the attitude of the Commission.

must be maintained; and (10) the right to continue to operate a broadcasting station is conditioned upon the service rendered.

It will be noted that the majority of the Commission's items deal with engineering, and evidence points to the fact that this field has been the most important phase of regulation. However, when necessary, the Commission also has regulated with respect to other matters. Though by no means infallible, it has steered a fairly steady course through the troublesome formative years of broadcasting.

The most important work of the Commission has been the allocation of facilities to various parts of the country, under the Davis Amendment.[34] The groundwork for this allocation was laid in General Order No. 40 assigning the various stations to the different wave-lengths reserved for specific types of service. As was noted at that point a total of ninety channels were provided for: six channels being reserved for local broadcasting, forty for low-powered regional stations, four for high-powered regional stations, and forty for cleared channel stations.[35] The effectiveness of this order was further reinforced by General Orders 41 and 48 dividing stations on the basis of day- and nighttime operation, resulting ultimately in a reduction of the number of nighttime stations from 82.9 per cent of the total in 1927 to 65.7 per cent or 397 stations in 1932.[36] This was of great assistance in improving station service. Conditions, however, are still far from ideal, as is shown by the fact that the nighttime range of the average station is less than its day range because of interference from other stations in the overcrowded ether, whereas the physical conditions with respect to broadcasting reception are much better at night.

The Federal Radio Commission has been severely criticized numerous times with regard to its allocation of station facilities. What has actually taken place in this field since the formation of the Commission is indicated in Table XIII which reveals the relative percentage of broadcasting facilities, calculated on the Commission's unit basis, existing in each zone as compared to

[34] See chap. iii, p. 41.

[35] *First Annual Report of the Federal Radio Commission*, pp. 49–50. The plan was put into operation November 11, 1928.

[36] *Ibid.*, pp. 50–54. For statistics see *Sixth Annual Report of the Federal Radio Commission*, p. 25.

the total population and the percentage of radio-owning population.

From the table it becomes evident that the Commission has followed the Davis Amendment, and that, if criticism there be, it should be leveled primarily at the amendment itself. Analysis reveals that there is little indeed which can be said for the amendment, and it is not without reason that the Standing Committee on Communications of the American Bar Associa-

TABLE XIII

COMPARISON OF THE PERCENTAGE OF RADIO FACILITIES ALLOCATED TO
VARIOUS ZONES AS COMPARED TO THOSE EXISTING THEREIN PRIOR
TO REALLOCATION UNDER THE DAVIS AMENDMENT*

| ZONE | PERCENTAGE OF TOTAL FACILITIES AS OF JUNE 30 | | | | |
	1927	1931	1932	Percentage of Total Radio Families	Percentage of Total Families
I	20.2	17.5	17.2	31.4	23.0
II	15.5	16.7	16.9	23.0	22.0
III	14.0	21.3	21.3	7.2	23.0
IV	32.7	23.0	23.1	26.7	22.0
V	17.6	21.5	21.2	11.7	10.0

* The 1927 figures were calculated on the basis of the list of stations appearing in *Commercial and Government Radio Stations of the United States* for that year. The 1931 and 1932 percentages were based on tables regarding quota units appearing in the *Annual Reports of the Commission* for those years.

tion recently issued a statement recommending the repeal of the amendment and declaring that it had "proved impossible of enforcement."[37] One is almost tempted to state that the 1927 situation regarding facilities was a more logical one than that existing at the present time under the Davis Amendment, as far as the major distribution of facilities is concerned. It is quite true that both the area to be served and the population residing within it must be considered in any scheme of allocation, so that the Mountain District in particular requires more than its proportionate share of facilities if distributed on the basis of radio families. However, it is difficult if not impossible to justify the high proportion of total facilities existing in the Third Zone on

[37] *Broadcasting*, November 15, 1932, p. 13.

any basis, or indeed the decided underquota condition of the Second Zone.

The inadequacies of the Davis Amendment become even more apparent when one examines state quotas, which, according to its provisions, should be kept fairly even. Here we find certain states decidedly over quota, such as Illinois by 53 per cent, Iowa 57 per cent, Nebraska 80 per cent, Texas 40 per cent, Florida 107 per cent, and Tennessee 76 per cent; while other states are equally under quota, as in the case of Pennsylvania by 27 per cent, Michigan 22 per cent, Indiana 22 per cent, Connecticut 21 per cent, and Massachusetts 12 per cent, to cite a few examples. Likewise it is found that, even on the basis of the Davis Amendment itself, the First Zone is 6 per cent under quota and the Second Zone 9 per cent, while the Third Zone is over quota by 11 per cent, the Fourth 26 per cent, and the Fifth 18 per cent.[38] From these figures, it is almost necessary to conclude that as far as state allocations are concerned the Davis Amendment has failed completely, and that it has achieved only a slightly greater degree of success in the various zones. This conclusion is further reinforced by the observation that many of the principal cities, wherein are located the most powerful stations, are located on state boundaries, thus further disrupting both the zone and state allocations. It seems therefore that the Davis Amendment constitutes a definite attempt to legislate in the face of economic law, which dictates that supply can only exist profitably where demand is found in sufficient quantity and intensity. Moreover, it is based on the false premise that receiving set ownership tends to follow total population. In so far as the whole question of a reallocation of facilities may be raised in the near future by the rumored North American conference, it seems desirable that thought be given to the construction of some possible method of station allocation which will be more in keeping with the actual needs of the listening public of the country.

A final matter which requires mention regarding the individual station structure, which is at the service of the broadcast advertiser, is the tendency toward a specialization of stations as to types of service. This tendency to specialize upon either a spe-

[38] From official tabulations of the Federal Radio Commission published in *Broadcasting*, December 1, 1932, p. 26.

cific type of clientèle or business is distinctly noticeable to anyone conversant with the broadcasting industry. The specialization of stations as to the extent of area covered is an inherent
feature of the very allocation of American broadcasting facilities themselves. This specialization is observed in actual practice where stations such as WLW, Cincinnati, and WOR, Newark, tend to assume regional scope, similar to the large newspapers in the publication field. Likewise, class and racial stations
are springing up throughout the country, of which Henry
Field's well-known farmer station KFNF, Shenandoah, Iowa,
and WLS, the Prairie Farmer station of Chicago, are class examples, while WRAX, Philadelphia, constitutes an excellent
and interesting example of a station appealing to various foreign groups within the community. There is a similar tendency
on the part of small local stations in large cities to specialize
with regard to certain economic and cultural levels in the community where competition is less keen. There is no clear line of
demarcation regarding this specialization of stations, but it is a
tendency which seems to be definitely on the increase, and
which should eventually give broadcasting structure greater
flexibility and versatility as to reaching special interest groups,
over and above the general circulation which it affords.

CHAPTER V

ECONOMIC BASES: BROADCASTING STRUCTURE —NATIONAL AND REGIONAL NETWORKS

The rise of the national network was an economic necessity to the development of the broadcasting industry in the United States. This was so primarily for two reasons: first, that only national advertisers possessed the funds necessary to finance broadcast advertising, and without broadcast advertising, in turn, the American system could not have developed; and second, the fact that only through a network program service could entertainment of a suitable standard be furnished by the individual station in the earlier years, and even to a surprisingly marked degree today. The rise of national networks not only provided program service to the struggling individual stations, but, in addition, gave them a source of ready revenue. It was a small revenue to be sure but nevertheless it was at least something, at a time when it was most sorely needed—a situation which still exists in many cases.

Broadcasting networks, consisting of a group of stations connected by telephone circuits and broadcasting the same program simultaneously from a central key station, arose in 1924 when stations WJAR, Providence, and WEAF, New York, were first linked together; station WSAI, Cincinnati, being joined to the other two at a slightly later date. Experimentation along these lines had been going on since early in 1923 but it was not until the following year that these efforts took permanent form.

By June 30, 1925, the original network had grown to 12 stations, located in New York, Hartford, Providence, Worcester, Philadelphia, Pittsburgh, Cleveland, Detroit, Cincinnati, Buffalo, Boston, and Davenport, Iowa. On November 1, 1926, the National Broadcasting Company was formed and there were added to the original WEAF Network, as it was called, 5 more stations, located in Portland, Maine, Chicago, St. Louis, Kansas City, Missouri, and Minneapolis. The so-called Red and Blue networks of the National Broadcasting Company were formed late in 1926 as were a number of the subsidiary groups covering the more remote parts of the country. In November, 1928, the Columbia Broadcasting System came into existence with 17 stations, and the foundation for the present national network structure was completed. By June 30, 1932, a total of 171 stations were associated with national networks, while at least another 16 were connected with permanent regional networks,[1] to say nothing of the probably larger number of stations functioning together as regional networks on a temporary basis and only when the occasion of a commercial program demanded. Thus, of the total number of stations in the country, 28.5 per cent are connected with national and regional networks.

At the present time there are two great network companies in the field—the National Broadcasting Company and the Columbia Broadcasting System, Inc. The National Broadcasting Company includes two basic networks, the Red and the Blue, rendering duplicate service to New England, the Middle Atlantic states, and the North Central district, exclusive of Wisconsin, Minnesota, and the Dakotas which constitute a group of four stations comprising one of the regional sub-networks of the system. The Red Network, of which WEAF is the key station, includes 26 stations, of which 4 Chicago stations serve alternately on both basic networks. The Blue Network, with WJZ, New York, as key station, serves the same area, and, including the 4 stations in Chicago, possesses 17 outlets in all. These are, on the average, of somewhat higher power than the Red Network stations though the latter has a numerical superiority. In addition to the two basic networks, which cover the major portion of the Northern Area, there are eight sub-networks, which can be bought in conjunction with either basic network: (1) the Northwestern group, mentioned previously; (2) the South Central group, embracing 6 stations in the East South Central states; (3) the Southwestern group, including 7 stations in the West South Central states; (4) the Southeastern group, containing 7 stations along the South Atlantic seaboard; (5) the Mountain group, comprising 4 stations in that area; (6) and (7)

---

[1] National networks figures are from fundamental data supplied the writer by the network companies themselves. The total number of network stations is from *Commercial Radio Advertising*, Federal Radio Commission, p. 14, and is as of December, 1931, though equally applicable to the later date.

two Pacific Coast networks of 5 stations each, known as the Orange and the Gold networks, respectively; and (8) two Canadian subsidiaries, 1 in Toronto and 1 in Montreal. On June 30, 1932, this structure comprised 84 stations in all.

The Columbia Broadcasting System structure is somewhat less complex than that of its competitor. The fundamental unit is a basic network of 26 stations covering the same area as that reached by the two National Broadcasting chains. The second unit of importance is a group of 48 supplementary stations scattered throughout the entire country—in addition to being fairly strong in the basic network area—which can be bought in any combination along with the basic network. Of the entire number, 13 stations are located in basic network territory. The only areas not covered by the supplementary stations are the Pacific Coast and the extreme Southeastern region, in both of which cases a separate sub-network exists to serve the territory in question. In the case of the Pacific Coast, the Don Lee Network, a semi-independent regional network comprising 7 stations, constitutes the Columbia System outlet. The extreme Southeastern territory is covered by another separate group comprising 3 Florida stations and 1 in Savannah, Georgia. Finally, 2 Canadian stations, 1 in Montreal and 1 in Toronto, complete the structure. Since June 30, 1932, a third Canadian station CKOK, Windsor, Canada, directly opposite Detroit, has supplanted the local Columbia outlet in that city. On June 30, 1932, the Columbia Broadcasting System included 87 stations other than its short-wave units. It should also be noted with respect to this network that the Yankee Network stations of New England are connected with it, and comprise its outlet in that territory. There also are a number of stations connected with the Columbia System on a temporary basis, bringing the total potential number of stations to 95 in all. Earlier in its history the Columbia System possessed an organization of regional sub-networks similar to that of the National Broadcasting Company, but abandoned these several years ago.

The development of the network structures of both companies is found in Table XIV.

A somewhat better appreciation of the relative growth of national networks and of their relation to the total number of stations in the country is found in Table XV.

TABLE XIV

STRUCTURE OF THE TWO NATIONAL NETWORK COMPANIES SINCE THEIR FORMATION*

Columbia Broadcasting System, Stations and Power of Various Basic and Subsidiary Networks, 1928-32

YEAR	BASIC NETWORK		SUPPLEMENTARY STATIONS		SOUTH ATLANTIC GROUP		DON LEE PACIFIC COAST UNIT		CANADIAN SUPPLEMENTARIES		TOTAL STATIONS	TOTAL POWER
	Total Stations	Total Power	Total Stations	Total Power	Total Stations	Total Power	Total Stations	Total Power	Total Stations	Total Power		
1928	17	24,400	....	....	....	....	....	....	....	....	17	24,400
1929	24	66,500	22	49,750	3	1,750	....	....	....	....	49	118,000
1930	24	97,500	25	42,500	3	1,750	5	5,000	2	9,000	59	155,750
1931	24	142,250	41	61,850	4	3,000	6	6,000	2	9,000	77	223,100
1932	26	202,750	48	71,850	4	2,750	7	6,500	2	9,000	87	292,850

* Taken from original network records, as of June 30th, annually.

TABLE XIV—*Continued*

National Broadcasting Company, Stations and Power of Various Basic and Subsidiary Networks, 1926-32

Year	Red Network		Blue Network		Southeastern Group		South Central Group		Southwestern Group		Northwestern Group	
	Total Stations	Total Power	Total Stations	Total Power	Total Stations	Total Power	Total Stations	Total Power	Total Stations	Total Power	Total Stations	Total Power
1926	18	29,250	....	....	....	....	....	....	....	....	....	....
1927	21	125,250	7	90,500	1	1,000	4	3,000	1	1,000	....	....
1928	23	160,000	10	117,500	2	6,000	4	7,000	4	12,000	2	2,000
1929	25	164,250	10	117,500	5	9,000	6	17,000	6	32,000	3	12,000
1930	26	267,000	12	177,500	6	14,000	7	27,000	6	32,000	3	12,000
1931	26	312,500	13	178,500	5	9,000	7	27,000	6	77,000	5	14,000
1932	26	292,000	13	174,500	7	10,500	6	17,000	7	78,000	6	14,500

TABLE XIV—*Continued*

YEAR	MOUNTAIN GROUP		CANADIAN SUBSIDIARIES		PACIFIC ORANGE NETWORK		PACIFIC GOLD NETWORK		PACIFIC SUPPLEMENTARY NETWORK		HAWAIIAN SUBSIDIARY		TOTAL STATIONS	TOTAL POWER
	Total Stations	Total Power	Total Stations	Total Power	Total Stations	Total Power	Total Stations	Total Power	Total Stations	Total Power	Total Stations	Total Power		
1926	....	....	....	....					....	....	....	....	18	29,250
1927	....	....	....	....	6	16,500	1	1,000	....	....	....	....	41	238,250
1928	1	5,000	....	....	5	15,500	1	1,000	....	....	....	....	52	326,000
1929	2	17,500	1	5,000	5	15,500	1	5,000	....	....	....	....	63	389,750
1930	2	17,500	2	6,650	5	15,500	2	6,000	2	1,000	....	....	72	574,500
1931	2	17,500	2	6,650	5	15,500	2	6,000	2	1,000	....	....	75	664,650
1932	4	19,000	2	6,650	5	60,500	5	21,000	2	1,000	1	1,000	84	695,650

From this table it is evident that the growth of network affiliation on the part of stations has been a comparatively steady one, with the Columbia System growing more rapidly in order to make up for the start possessed by the National Broadcasting Company and its predecessors. A rather more than ordinary increase in network affiliation is shown in 1932, probably due to the battle for outlets which was waged between the two networks that year and which resulted, among other things, in the

TABLE XV

RELATIVE PROPORTION OF NATIONAL NETWORK TO TOTAL STATIONS IN THE UNITED STATES, JUNE 30, 1924—JUNE 30, 1932*

Year	Total Stations in U.S.	Total Network Stations	Percentage of Network to Total Stations	Total N.B.C. Stations	Percentage of N.B.C. to Total Stations	Total C.B.S. Stations	Percentage of C.B.S. to Total Stations
1924	535	3	0.6	3	0.6		
1925	571	12	2.1	12	2.1		
1926	528	18	3.4	18	3.4		
1927	681	41	8.0	41	8.0		
1928	677	69	10.2	52	7.7	17	2.5
1929	606	112	18.4	63	10.4	49	8.0
1930	618	128	20.7	71	11.4	57	9.3
1931	612	148	24.2	73	12.0	75	12.2
1932	604	167	27.8	82	13.8	85	14.0

* *Commercial and Government Radio Stations of the U.S.* (1922–26) and *Sixth Annual Report of the Federal Radio Commission* (1927–32) for individual station figures; network data from basic network records. Canadian stations are not included.

switch of WGN and WMAQ, Chicago, from the National Broadcasting Company to the Columbia System, and vice versa; and of a similar situation with respect to stations KSL and KDYL, Salt Lake City, the former shifting to Columbia and the latter swinging the other direction.

The proportion of total facilities available for broadcasting which are possessed by network stations is of considerably greater importance than is the question of the mere number of stations affiliated with the two great national companies. The relative proportion of network to total broadcasting facilities in each of the five zones is found in Table XVI. Though the data given here are for November, 1931, it should be noted that no fundamental changes occurred in this respect until after June

30, 1932, so that the figures given here are comparable with those presented in other charts in the chapter.

From the table it becomes evident that though the networks contain but a small proportion of the total stations, they control, or at least have affiliated with them, the cream of the nation's broadcasting facilities. As will be seen later, any control

TABLE XVI

PROPORTION OF TOTAL FACILITIES AFFILIATED WITH NETWORKS
AS OF NOVEMBER, 1931*

ZONE	NON-NETWORK STATIONS		ALL NETWORK STATIONS							
	Total Non-network Facilities in Units	Percentage of Total Facilities	Total Network Facilities in Units	Percentage of Total Facilities	Total Station Facilities	Percentage	Total N.B.C. Facilities in Units	Percentage of Total Facilities	Total C.B.S. Facilities in Units	Percentage of Total Facilities
I.........	22.76	30.1	53.00	69.9	76.76	100.0	34.10	45.0	18.90	24.9
II........	15.50	22.3	56.18	77.7	72.31	100.0	35.32	48.8	20.86	28.9
III.......	27.90	30.1	64.64	69.9	92.54	100.0	40.32	43.5	24.32	26.4
IV.......	30.23	30.3	69.49	69.7	99.72	100.0	32.14	32.2	37.35	37.5
V........	38.39	41.3	54.64	58.7	93.03	100.0	43.02	46.2	11.62	12.5
Entire country.	135.41	31.3	297.95	68.7	433.36	100.0	184.90	42.6	113.05	26.1

* Based on *Commercial Radio Advertising*, pp. 66–69. The units in the table are based upon assigned values given to stations of varying power and hours of operation by the Federal Radio Commission as found in Rule 109 of its Rules and Regulations.

which exists is very tenuous indeed. The tendency to have affiliated with them the most powerful stations of the nation will be even more pronounced when the high-power assignments of October, 1931, finally are all put into effect. When this is completed 30 of the 32 stations of 25,000 or more watts in power in the country will be affiliated with the two national network companies. The 2 independent stations will be WOR, Newark, and KNX, Hollywood. Of the total high-powered stations, the National Broadcasting Company will have affiliated with it a total of 21 stations, and the Columbia Broadcasting System 9 stations. The National Broadcasting Company will gain a total of 277,500 watts in the power increases, while the Columbia System will gain 214,000 watts.[2]

Not only is Table XVI interesting as an indication of the fact that the national networks have affiliated between them practically all of the important stations of the country, but a comparison of the relative proportion of the facilities controlled by either network in the various zones will enable the formation of conclusions regarding the relative strength of the two companies in different parts of the country. At the outset it must be remembered, however, that the National Broadcasting Company possesses two basic networks in the Northern Area, which in turn embraces practically all of the First, Second, and Fourth zones, while the Columbia System has only one basic network. When a comparison is made of the First and Second zones, especially, it is only sound procedure to take this fact into consideration. Doing so, indicates that in these areas there is a slight predominance of facilities in favor of the National Broadcasting Company networks. In the Fourth Zone where the National Broadcasting Company Chicago stations, comprising a large portion of their total facilities in that zone, are interchangeable between the two basic networks, the dual coverage requires less consideration. In this instance, however, the Columbia System shows a rather marked superiority, while, in the Third Zone, the National Broadcasting Company possesses the greater facilities. In the Fifth Zone the possession of two networks on the part of the National Broadcasting Company makes comparison difficult, but a superiority in facilities is again indicated in its direction.

Though there seems to be some quantitative superiority in the matter of facilities on the part of the National Broadcasting Company, it must be remembered that this is but a very rough measure of the relative effectiveness of the two networks to serve the national advertiser. All of the numerous factors regarding station circulation hold for networks as well, and because of this no conclusive answer is possible regarding the relative effectiveness of the various national networks. In all probability there is but the slightest shade of difference between the

[2] Based on *Broadcasting*, October 15, 1931, p. 8, and December 1, 1932, p. 12.

three basic networks[3] and all of them are about equally effective from the viewpoint of the audience served. Some conception of the thoroughness with which the national networks probably cover the country may be gained from the estimates of the Columbia System as of January 1, 1932, to the extent that 82.4 per cent of the listeners tended to employ Columbia stations with at least a fair degree of regularity.[4] This situation is fairly typical with regard to other national networks.

The relations between the central network organizations and their affiliated stations are of considerable interest to the advertiser, and basically affect the efficient functioning of the network structures. In the case of the Columbia Broadcasting System, the following description indicates the salient points regarding the station-network relations of this organization.

Stations affiliated with the Columbia Network receive one of two classes of service, "permanent" or "temporary." Virtually all of the stations fall in the first class, which means that program service is available from the opening of the network each day until sign-off in the late evening, except commercial programs not requiring a particular station's facilities. Stations in the temporary class are those without regular affiliation tied in at the specific order of an advertiser desiring their coverage. These stations receive only one hour's service on any night they are used for a commercial program and are entitled to any sustaining service falling within that hour.

All permanent stations are on a contract basis, in which they are required to pay a predetermined monthly charge for wire facilities entitling them to all sustaining service which might be available to them. Such charges vary in accordance with the expense to the System for leased wire rental. If a station denotes inability to meet the terms of the System during negotiations, a more reasonable charge may be arranged, in exchange for which the station agrees to accept a stipulated number of commercial program hours per week without charge to the System.

Practically all sustaining programs (i.e. programs whose cost is met by the Network and not by a commercial sponsor) sent to

[3] An opinion formed by one of the experts originally consulted regarding the Price, Waterhouse surveys of the Columbia System.

[4] *Radio Listening Areas*, by Columbia Broadcasting System.

affiliated stations may be sold by the individual managements for sponsorship by local advertisers. The Columbia System makes no additional charge to the station for such use of sustaining features. However, there is a hazard to the station in this, for there is no obligation to the System to preserve a set time for sustaining programs; so the practice of local sponsorship has not become widespread except on certain programs which have been broadcast regularly at a specified time for a long period. A number of features, such as the New York Philharmonic Symphony concerts, World Series baseball games, and intercollegiate sporting contests, are restricted and may not be sponsored under any conditions.

Contracts with associated stations vary in individual cases as regards payment for the acceptance and transmission of sponsored programs. In exchange for a special reduction in charge for facilities, as explained previously, certain stations broadcast commercial programs without charge for a specified number of hours per week, and, on all subsequent commercial programs accepted by them, are paid a contract rate per hour. This rate is not uniform with all stations but varies with factors such as the size and importance of the market served and the demand for coverage of that market by national sponsors of programs. There is, therefore, a wide spread in rates paid affiliated stations for the same time, the difference being accounted for primarily by the circulation or potential audience. The minimum rate of payment to affiliated stations for acceptance of a commercial broadcast is $50 per evening hour and $25 per daytime hour, with shorter periods commanding proportionate sums.

Contracts with stations on the Columbia Basic Network provide for the delivery of all time between eight and eleven at night, current New York time, to the Columbia System upon two weeks' notice. In some instances, all time is under option, while, in others, specified hours other than the period generally arranged for are included in the time commanded by the network. The majority of contracts with supplementary stations provide for option on virtually every hour.

The National Broadcasting Company's relations with its affiliated stations are somewhat more simple than those of the Columbia System. At present, two types of arrangements exist. The older and probably more prevalent of the two is one wherein the station is paid $50 for every hour of commercial broadcasting done between six and twelve o'clock at night, while the station in turn pays the National Broadcasting Company $25 for every hour of sustaining programs accepted from it. The daytime rates for the same periods are $30 and $15, respectively.[5] Recently a new arrangement with affiliated stations has been announced whereby the affiliated station has the option either of purchasing its sustaining programs under the system previously outlined or of paying the flat sum of $1,500 per month, or $18,000 a year, for sustaining programs, thereby receiving the right to broadcast as many of these as it desires.[6] It was stated at the time the announcement was made that the new arrangement would constitute a considerable saving for a number of affiliated stations. It also should be noted that, while the Columbia affiliated stations contribute to the payment of the line charges, this cost is met directly by the National Broadcasting Company. Finally, certain programs, such as addresses by the President of the United States, broadcasts of the Metropolitan Opera Company, and the Damrosch Hour, are furnished stations free of charge, the National Broadcasting Company assuming all expenses.

Any discussion of station-network relations, however, would be incomplete without mention of some of the more important problems which exist in this field today, and which promise to affect seriously future network structure and practice. Practically all of these problems revolve about the thorny question of the payment received by the individual station from the network for broadcasting a commercially sponsored program. The criticism of the present systems in vogue is especially strong on the part of the managers of the more powerful stations, with high operating costs and overhead. A number of such managers have stated that it is impossible to make money on network commercial programs at the standard rate of payment. Two large stations were estimated to lose approximately $150 on each hour of network commercial programs broadcast. This situation is further aggravated by the fact that even where a fairly profitable business is built up on network commercial programs, the cost of sustaining service eats up much of the revenue. Thus one

[5] *Commercial Radio Advertising*, Federal Radio Commission, p. 30.

[6] *Broadcasting*, July 15, 1932, p. 15.

large station reports that out of $50,000 received for broadcasting network programs, 60 per cent was paid back to the network in the form of sustaining program fees.

This situation is more serious with respect to the National Broadcasting Company, because of its relatively inelastic system of payment, than in the case of the Columbia Broadcasting System, where greater leeway is possible. The result is that there are a number of important National Broadcasting network stations which constitute chronic sources of dissatisfaction. It should be remarked, in fairness to all parties concerned, that this dissatisfaction is strictly limited to economic matters, and that in other spheres of activity the most cordial co-operation and spirit of friendliness maintains.

Though the Columbia Broadcasting System is faced with somewhat less difficulty in this field because of the greater elasticity of its system of station payment, it must not be assumed that its method constitutes the ultimate solution to the problem. There are instances where the network command of evening broadcasting hours acts as a curtailing factor with regard to station revenue, making impossible the acceptance of local business at the higher evening rate and forcing the acceptance of network business. Thus in the case of one station, which may be cited as an example of the potentialities of this form of arrangement, but four out of twenty-eight of the choice evening hours were available monthly for local sponsorship. The solution of the problem, indeed, demands a more far-reaching modification of network structure and practice than that thus far effected by either network, and concerning which, at present, only the barest ventures of opinion are possible.

The practical results of this problem, however, are of more immediate interest. One of the most important of these is the question of station delivery. Because it is the large stations, covering wide areas and usually located in important buying centers, which constitute the chief source of dissatisfaction, the situation arises, more frequently than desirable for the network, where a leading station may refuse to accept a sponsored program which conflicts with a local and more profitable broadcast. Since the market covered by this station may be of especial importance to the broadcast advertiser, the entire undertaking may be abandoned or shifted to a competing network, as has been the case in at least several instances. When a number of stations on one basic network refuse to clear time for a program, the situation becomes virtually impossible. This is exemplified by the experience of one space buyer, who attempted to secure a group of 18 stations of which only 8 could be cleared at the hour and on the night desired. Obviously, such a situation seriously impairs the efficiency of the network, unless steps, such as having two outlets in the town in question, are taken to counteract it.

A second problem which has been greatly accentuated by the station payment problem has been that of the shifting of stations from one network to the other. The real root of this problem lay in the jockeying of the two great network companies for competitive position in the more important territories. However, it became a relatively more simple matter to secure a competing station for one's own network, when that station was dissatisfied with the revenue it was receiving for network advertising programs from one's competitor. This, it is said by experts in the field, has been behind the majority of the 11 station shifts which have taken place between networks within recent years, beginning with the shift of WCCO, Minneapolis, to the Columbia Broadcasting System in 1929, and concluding, at least to date, with the exchange of network affiliations of stations KSL and KDYL, Salt Lake City, during the summer of 1932, whereby the Columbia System gained the former, a 50-kilowatt station, for the latter which is only 1 kilowatt in power. In this series of shifts the National Broadcasting Company gained stations WMAQ, Chicago, 5,000 watts; KOIL, Omaha, 1,000 watts; WWNC, Asheville, North Carolina, 1,000 watts; and KDYL, Salt Lake City, 1,000 watts; and lost WGR, Buffalo, 1,000 watts; WGN, Chicago, 25,000 watts; KFAB, Lincoln, Nebraska, 5,000 watts;[7] WBT, Charlotte, North Carolina, 25,000 watts; WHAS, Louisville, Kentucky, 25,000 watts; WCCO, Minneapolis, 50,000 watts; and KSL, Salt Lake City, 50,000 watts. With the exception of the Minneapolis and Charlotte shifts, all of the changes of network affiliation occurred either in 1931 or 1932. It should be noted that most of the stations involved are important regional outlets. In addition to the aforementioned stations, the National Broadcasting

[7] Station possesses a construction permit for 25,000 watts.

Company in 1932 secured stations KEX, Portland, Oregon; KJR, Seattle, Washington, and KGA, Spokane, Washington, as outlets for its newly formed Pacific Gold Network. These stations had been Columbia outlets prior to 1929 when that network made the Don Lee chain its far-western subsidiary. Other than the shifts in network affiliation mentioned above there have been no changes of importance in network structure since the formation of the Columbia System in 1928.

Thus far the network difficulties arising primarily out of the problem of station compensation have been discussed. Several additional comments, however, are necessary with regard to the station viewpoint in the matter. Much as the larger station may find the relatively low recompense secured for broadcasting national network programs a matter of difficulty, it also is faced with the fact that in most cases it cannot do without the network sustaining services. In few, if any, instances have stations been able to maintain their popularity with the listening audience after they have severed their network connections.[8] The cost of securing comparable talent, and in many cases the virtual impossibility of so doing, combined with the high overhead of program creation, have been more than the station could overcome successfully.

The question of network payment for commercial programs, and the allied problems of station delivery and the shifting of affiliation from one network to the other, is a matter of concern only to the larger broadcasting stations. For the most part the small network affiliate is quite content with his lot. The network constitutes a ready source of program material on which he may build his local popularity. In addition, the revenue secured from network commercial programs is especially acceptable, since it forms the foundation of his revenue in many instances, while, with his small expenses, it probably will be a source of considerable profit. On this basis, the smaller station then builds its local clientèle, who broadcast mostly in the daytime, and capitalize as much as possible upon the popularity which has been built up by the network programs.

It is impossible to say at the present moment what is the an-

---

[8] Though station popularity is a difficult matter to measure, it might be ventured that WOR, Newark, has enjoyed probably the greatest success as an independent station competing directly with network key stations for listeners.

swer to this perplexing question of station-network relations. The elements, however, are clear. If the network compensation is not better adjusted, increasing difficulty will be experienced with important outlets, and if this occurs, serious modifications of network structure may arise. With regard to the solution of this problem a number of trends are noticeable, which may shed some light on the probable future of network practice and structure in this regard; while the speculative opinion of experts in the field may also be ventured, not with the purpose of indicating a definite solution as much as of suggesting some of the potentialities contained within the present situation.

That the trend in the direction of a readjustment of network rates is indicated, is shown by the proposed solution of the WLW problem, which was almost accepted by the National Broadcasting Company.[9] Under this arrangement, the advertiser was to receive station WSAI, Cincinnati, Ohio, on the Red Network, and WCKY, Covington, Kentucky, on the Blue Network at the regular card rate; though it would be possible to substitute station WLW in either case by paying an additional sum so as to equal that station's own card rate. This arrangement was revoked at the final moment by the network. Had it been put into effect it would have constituted a significant recognition of the principle of payment of stations according to their economic importance. In addition, if any number of stations had been able to force similar concessions, it would have introduced an element of uncertainty into network costs which would have seriously impaired the selling of network time.

Such an arrangement therefore cannot be said potentially to constitute even a partial solution of the problem at hand. A much more fundamental readjustment of network rates is necessary. Indeed, it is probable that the entire theory of network rates may be open to question. For the most part, the national network is analogous to the national magazine. An advertiser does not buy one part of the circulation separately, but the entire circulation of the magazine. In some towns this circulation may be weak, and in others it may be especially strong. However, the principal interest of the advertiser is its general rather than specific coverage. If this is satisfactory he will buy space in the periodical in question. If not he will use another maga-

[9] *Variety*, January 1, 1933, p. 37.

zine. However, in the broadcast advertising field too much emphasis has been placed on the component parts of the national circulation, the individual station, and too little on the functioning of the network as a whole. Consequently the advertiser has come to look upon the network much more as an association of individual stations than as one national medium, simultaneously reaching millions of people. In building up this impression the networks have been partly to blame, since they have emphasized the competitive control of key outlets much more than they have the general aspects of their coverage. It would seem that the time has come to place the emphasis upon the latter aspect. Though a network is no stronger than its individual stations, it nevertheless is the complete network which is of primary importance to the advertiser, and in terms of which he logically should think.

Though the changing of the theory of network rates is largely a matter of sales presentation, unless one wishes to go as far as one executive and to charge for networks as a bloc rather than by individual station charges added together, there is one concrete step which can be taken that would relieve the situation to a marked degree. This step is the basic readjustment of network rates to the advertiser on the basis of the economic importance of the stations and the areas they covered, and an ensuing readjustment of network compensation to stations on the same basis. At the present time the advertiser is paying a ridiculously low sum for his key station and metropolitan coverage, and too much, at least correspondingly, for his outlying coverage. This is illustrated by Table XVII which presents a few rates for National Broadcasting and Columbia Network stations, together with the number of radio families within the city confines of the towns wherein each station is located, and the power of the station. The unscientific basis of present rates would be even more strikingly illustrated were it possible to present accurate coverage data for each station, and with respect to which the New York key stations would be shown to reach no less than 5,000,000 radio families in the retail trading area of that metropolis.

Table XVII raises the question of whether or not the advertiser is being charged too much for his outlying coverage and too little for his key station and metropolitan coverage. This seems to be the case. It therefore should be possible to revise the rates so that more equitable charges would be made for stations of varying importance. Were this done, it is the opinion of some experts that the cost of radio broadcasting actually would be lowered in many instances, at least to the buyer of a complete national network, since he would save more from reduced outlying station charges than he would be charged additional for

TABLE XVII

COMPARISON OF NETWORK CHARGES, POWER, AND NUMBER OF RADIO FAMILIES IN CITY WHEREIN STATION IS LOCATED FOR REPRESENTATIVE NETWORK STATIONS*

Station	City	Network	Power in Watts	Charge for One Hour Nighttime	Number of Radio Families in City
WEAF.......	New York, N.Y.	NBC	50,000	$900	1,021,651
WABC......	New York, N.Y.	CBS	50,000	800	1,021,651
KSD........	St. Louis, Mo.	NBC	500	210	108,267
WHO........	Des Moines, Iowa	NBC	5,000	190	19,621
WOW........	Omaha, Neb.	NBC	1,000	190	28,835
WDAY......	Fargo, N.D.	NBC	1,000	150	3,108
WKRC......	Cincinnati, Ohio	CBS	500	200	59,756
WFEA.......	Manchester, N.H.	CBS	500	125	7,562
WLAC......	Nashville, Tenn.	CBS	5,000	190	11,130
WHEC......	Rochester, N.Y.	CBS	500	170	45,814
KRLD or....	Dallas, Tex.	CBS	10,000	100	27,119
WRR.......	Dallas, Tex.	CBS	500	100	27,119

* The station data are from *Standard Rate and Data*, November, 1932, while the population data are from the *Census of 1930*. Station power has been secured from basic network records. The stations selected are representative of the situation as a whole, since rates do not fluctuate greatly between individual outlying stations.

the metropolitan facilities. Whether this would happen is difficult to say. At least a more scientific and, in the long run, more satisfactory rate structure would have been evolved. It is safe to venture the opinion that some readjustment of this sort will occur in network rates and station compensation.

Another attempted solution which has arisen out of the problem of station compensation and network time control has been the practice on the part of individual broadcasters to control two stations in a given town and to shunt the network programs between the two. This is exemplified by the Buffalo Broadcasting Corporation, owners of stations WGR and WKBW, Buffalo, New York. In this case, the two stations between them carry almost the entire Columbia Broadcasting System schedule, still allowing open time for local advertisers. Though this constitutes a most satisfactory solution to the problem of time control where it can be applied, the number of instances where it would be possible to secure control of two stations is so small as to make it of doubtful value except in a few scattered cases. However, it is relatively more possible in the larger communities, which are the real sore spots, though here its applicability is limited by the number of stations of sufficiently high power to be satisfactory as network outlets.

Still another trend, which is certain to be even more pronounced in the future than it has been in the past, is that toward network ownership and financial control of outlets in key cities. This has arisen for a number of reasons, the principal ones of which have been the problem of station delivery, and the battle to secure competitive advantages in the larger metropolitan markets on the part of the two networks. The number of stations either owned or controlled by the two network companies are found in Table XVIII.

In addition to the stations financially controlled by networks there are at least two stations wherein officials of the Columbia Network are listed as being holders of more than 10 per cent of the station's stock—WCAU, Philadelphia, 50,000 watts; and WDRC, Hartford, Connecticut, 500 watts.[10] How much this affects network control it is impossible to say. The National Broadcasting Company, on the other hand, operates the program service for the Westinghouse Electric and Manufacturing Company stations, WBX-WBZA, Boston-Springfield, 25,000 watts, and KDKA, Pittsburgh, 50,000 watts. It is stated that the network control is limited only to program service in the case of these stations. Finally, station WGY, Schenectady, is owned by the General Electric Company, which, though divesting itself of its Radio Corporation stock in accordance with the consent decree recently issued by the United States District Court, still owns a large block of the stock of the National Broadcasting Company's parent concern.

It will be noted in Table XVIII, that both of the great broadcasting companies possess a substantial financial interest in

[10] *Broadcast Reporter*, October 17 and 24, 1932.

high-powered stations located in the leading buying areas of the country, and that these stations, in turn, tend to constitute the nucleus of their basic networks to a rather large degree, though not completely so. If the pressure of competitive jockeying for position and the problem of station delivery continues, a further

TABLE XVIII

STATIONS OWNED OR FINANCIALLY CONTROLLED
BY NATIONAL NETWORKS*

Station	City	Power in Watts	Network by Which Controlled	Nature of Control
WEAF	New York, N.Y.	50,000	NBC	Owned
WJZ	New York, N.Y.	30,000	NBC	Owned
WENR	Chicago, Ill.	50,000	NBC	Owned
WTAM	Cleveland, Ohio	50,000	NBC	Owned
WRC	Washington, D.C.	500	NBC	Owned
WMAQ	Chicago, Ill.	5,000	NBC	Financial interest
KEX	Portland, Ore.	5,000	NBC	Financial interest
KYA	San Francisco, Calif.	1,000	NBC	Financial interest
KJR	Seattle, Wash.	5,000	NBC	Financial interest
KGA	Spokane, Wash.	5,000	NBC	Financial interest
KOA	Denver, Colo.	50,000	NBC	Leased
KGO	San Francisco, Calif.	7,500	NBC	Leased
KPO	San Francisco, Calif.	50,000	NBC	Leased
WABC	New York, N.Y.	50,000	CBS	Owned
WJSV	Alexandria, Va.†	10,000	CBS	Owned
WBBM	Chicago, Ill.	25,000	CBS	Owned
WCCO	Minneapolis, Minn.	50,000	CBS	Owned
WKRC	Cincinnati, Ohio	500	CBS	Owned
KMOX	St. Louis, Mo.	50,000	CBS	Financial interest
WPG	Atlantic City, N.J.	5,000	CBS	Leased

* This table is based on *Commercial Radio Advertising*, Federal Radio Commission, pp. 15, 19, and has been brought up to date from *Radio Broadcasting Stations in the United States 1932*. It is probably correct as of the spring of 1932.

† Adjacent to Washington, D. C.

increase in network ownership and control of stations may be expected. There is much to be said for such an arrangement. Logically the networks are the magazines of the air, and as such they require definite unitary aspect which will enable them to cover at least the major listening areas of the country at all times and on all occasions. It is even possible that such a structure would be more in keeping with the public interest, since it would insure the reception of both network sustaining and commercial programs over a wide area, and would do away with the possibility, and often actuality, of a local station refusing to take an important sustaining program because the hour in question had been sold to a local advertiser.

Whether this development will go so far as to create a situation wherein the networks will own all of their stations, at least on the basic chain, is hard to say. From the viewpoint of the sale of broadcast advertising facilities, the development of a distinct network personality with which to win the loyalty of the listening public, and the ability to distribute the cost of operation of individual stations over the network as a whole, such an arrangement is economically the most desirable. There are, indeed, a number of experts in the field who believe that the integrated network will constitute at least one of the elements in the broadcasting structure of the future. There is reason to doubt whether such a development will extend farther than the basic networks and coast subsidiaries, since the high upkeep of stations in areas where network facilities are in relatively less demand will tend unduly to raise the general network overhead. Coast subsidiaries probably would be retained as part of the integrated network since they could be used as regional chains when not broadcasting national programs. Likewise, it is probable that non-basic network areas could be covered through some form of affiliation with independent stations similar to that at present in force. However, this is purely a matter of speculation at the present time, the most important aspect of which is not so much the actual direction which future network development will take but rather the potentialities for structural change inherent in the situation.

Another interesting possible addition to the network structure of the country, which has been suggested to the writer in various forms by different broadcasters, is the formation of a co-operatively owned network by independent stations. This network would function in the program field similar to the Associated Press with regard to the newspapers of the country, in that it would provide station service in the broadcasting of public events, and quite probably to some extent would act as a clearing house for sustaining programs broadcast by individual station members within certain specified limits. This would coincide with the opinion of some individuals well versed in the field of broadcasting who believe that the network primarily should be a program service rather than a definite ruling entity. With regard to broadcast advertising, the co-operatively owned network would function in the double rôle of a national advertising medium and a clearing house of national and regional spot business.[11] Many practical problems would have to be solved,[12] if indeed they could be, before such a network could be brought into existence. It is interesting, however, to find even the suggestion being made in representative circles. However, in view of the great probability that the broadcasting band will be widened to at least 380 kilocycles during the next decade at the latest—thus making way for more stations—there undoubtedly would be room for both the integrated and the co-operative form of networks in the broadcast structure, each fulfilling a specific function and rendering a unique type of service to the public.

Thus the ultimate future of network structure is extremely uncertain. For the immediate future, however, one may safely predict: (1) readjustments in rate structure along more scientific lines, which should benefit station, network, and advertiser alike; and (2) a trend toward increased network ownership and financial control of stations, especially in the larger and strategically more important centers.

A final aspect of network development, which remains to be discussed before a complete appreciation is possible of the present and potential network structure available to the advertiser, is the regional network. There has been a marked rise within the past two years of formal and informal networks of this type, each designed to serve a particular segment of the country. It is estimated by one authority in the field[13] that there must be more than ten such networks in operation at the present time.

The Yankee Network, serving the New England territory,

[11] Chap. viii will discuss this aspect.

[12] Some of the difficulties visioned are: (1) the question of the extent of sustaining service rendered; (2) the rendering of sustaining service to competing stations, if any existed in the structure; (3) the rather high line charges which might ensue from a complicated sustaining program service; and (4) the problem of clearing time for national accounts if these were handled.

[13] Howard S. Meighan, Scott Howe Bowen, Inc. It is almost impossible to secure any accurate information on this point from any source, so that the best estimate is somewhat tentative. Because of his wide contact with the regional and spot broadcast advertising field, Mr. Meighan's estimate is probably the best available.

is one of the best examples of this form of network. It was organized in 1930 by the Shepard Broadcasting Service, owners of station WNAC, Boston, and several other adjacent outlets. By the close of the first year of its existence the network came to include 5 stations located in Boston, Providence, New Bedford, Worcester, and Bridgeport. Since that time Hartford, Manchester, New Hampshire, Springfield, Bangor, and a second station in Providence have been added to the Yankee Network.

The Yankee Network also is affiliated with the Columbia Broadcasting System, which enables it to furnish its member stations with both Yankee and Columbia sustaining program service. The Columbia System has the usual option on evening broadcasting hours, so that only about 15 per cent of the Yankee Network nighttime programs are their own commercial endeavors, these coming mostly after ten o'clock. However, at least 60 per cent to 70 per cent of the daytime broadcasts are Yankee Network programs. This arrangement has been described by officials of the network as being very satisfactory.

The Don Lee Network is somewhat similarly constructed and operates in the Pacific Coast area, primarily in California. It owns stations in San Francisco, Los Angeles, San Diego, and Santa Barbara, the first two stations acting as the key stations for the network. In addition, it possesses a franchise on the McClatchy stations in Bakersfield, Stockton, Fresno, and San Diego, and has a working arrangement with outlets in Portland, Seattle, Tacoma, and Spokane. Like the Yankee Network, it has enjoyed a high degree of success. A third network similar in many aspects to the two previously mentioned is the Southwest Broadcasting Company, operating stations in eight cities in Texas and Oklahoma. This network has experienced serious difficulties in the way of the high line charges required for linking together such widely separated stations as comprise its structure. A fourth regional network, the New England Network, comprising National Broadcasting Company affiliated stations, has been organized recently, largely under the sponsorship of station WTIC, Hartford, which acts as the key station for the group.

Several years ago a class network was attempted, however, with little success. The attempt in question was the Quality Group, originated by stations WOR, Newark, and WLW, Cincinnati, and including at different times various Chicago stations, WHAM, Rochester, WCAU, Philadelphia, and later WIP-WFAN, Philadelphia. The network was unsuccessful, not because the market for such service did not exist, but rather because the wire charges were too heavy in proportion to total cost of broadcasting, and payment for individual stations at the local card rate, which was the practice, brought the cost of the Quality Group too near that of broadcasting over the basic network of a national company.

A very recent development which promises to be even more pronounced in the future is the rise of the informal network, wherein several stations are associated merely for the duration of a given program. With agency knowledge of the individual station field increasing to a marked degree, more of this type of thing may be expected. Moreover, opportunities for regional functioning by this type of organization often present themselves. Thus WLW, Cincinnati, WCAE, Pittsburgh, WGAR, Cleveland, and WXYZ, Detroit, have been functioning periodically in this fashion for advertisers interested in the North Central district. At least one foreign-language program has been broadcast over an informal network of this type, Father Justin's Rosary having sponsored a program in Polish, over stations in Buffalo, Chicago, Cleveland, Detroit, Pittsburgh, Wilkes Barre, and Scranton.[14] According to agency executives a wide variety of these informal network arrangements exist in the broadcasting industry today.

[14] *Broadcasting*, March 15, 1932, p. 9.

PART II
THE USE OF BROADCASTING BY ADVERTISERS

CHAPTER VI

THE DEVELOPMENT AND PRESENT EXTENT OF ADVERTISING OVER NETWORKS

The first broadcast advertising effort was carried on over station WEAF, New York, early in 1923. At that time the American Telephone and Telegraph Company, owner of the station, announced that it would permit advertisers to broadcast messages at the nominal charge of $100 for ten minutes, during which time, it was estimated, approximately 750 words could be delivered.[1] As far as is known, the first commercial venture to be undertaken over station WEAF was a ten-minute talk under the auspices of the Queensborough Corporation, promoters of the Jackson Heights development in Long Island City. Among the first advertisers to combine the sponsorship of an entertainment program with a commercial announcement was the Browning, King and Company, well-known clothing establishment, which sponsored an hour of dance music. The first feature to be handled on anything approximating a national basis was the broadcast of the Victor Company on New Year's night, 1925, at which time a large number of stations were linked temporarily to the WEAF network to carry the program.[2] Out of these beginnings there grew, in the short space of nine years, the broadcast advertising of today.

In order to establish a perspective with which to approach subsequent detailed analyses of the development of advertising over various parts of the broadcasting structure, it may be well, first to examine briefly, the probable total expenditures for broadcast advertising in the United States. This is a difficult task. Regarding many of the items involved, little information exists in usable form. Even where data are available there is a great deal of duplication between items, so that only the most tentative estimate is possible.

In order to estimate the total expenditures in the broadcast

[1] *Radio in Advertising*, by Orrin G. Dunlap (Harper Bros.), p. 22.
[2] *This Thing Called Broadcasting*, by Goldsmith and Lescaboura (Holt), pp. 151–53.

advertising field, it is necessary to know the expenditures over national and regional networks, as well as individual stations. In addition to time expenditures, payments for talent likewise must be considered, since these loom much larger in proportion to the total broadcast advertising expense than does art work and mechanical reproduction in the periodical field. Finally, miscellaneous items, such as wire charges—where paid by the program sponsor—also enter into the total. These and similar considerations, however, are probably a negligible percentage of the grand total.

With respect to the available data in this field, the only summarized information existing over any period is with regard to annual expenditures for time over national networks, collected by the Advertising Record Company, formerly the Denney Publishing Company, and presented in its *National Advertising Records*. The only data existing for other than national networks are found in the Federal Radio Commission's survey of commercial radio advertising in 1931, made in response to the Couzens-Dill resolution. Because of this fact and of the impossibility of securing even so simple a figure as gross revenue from any representative number of stations,[3] it is possible only to present data regarding total expenditures for broadcast advertising as of 1931. Even in this case the result achieved is merely a very rough approximation. Notwithstanding its tentative nature, however, it may prove of marked assistance in achieving a general appreciation of the probable total extent of broadcast advertising, and of the relative importance of the expenditures over the various elements of the broadcasting structure.

Gross receipts of broadcasting stations and networks, derived principally from the sale of time to advertisers, were reported by the Federal Radio Commission to be as follows for the year of 1931:[4]

[3] An attempt to do this was abandoned, upon advice of experts, because of the chaotic state of many station books even in recent years, and because the turnover of station ownership further complicated the matter.

[4] *Commercial Radio Advertising*, Federal Radio Commission, pp. 43–44.

National networks

National Broadcasting Company	$25,895,959.34	
Columbia Broadcasting System	11,621,424.31	
Total expenditures over national networks		$37,517,384.65

Regional networks*

Don Lee Network	$ 999,832.79	
Yankee Network	779,529.94	
Total expenditures over regional networks		1,779,362.73
Expenditures over 525 individual stations†		38,461,302.41
Grand total		$77,758,048.79

* Other regional networks, formal and informal, are included in the individual station revenue, but constitute so small a sum as to be negligible, in all probability.

† This does not include all of the approximately 550 stations engaged in commercial broadcasting, about 90 per cent of the 604 stations carrying advertising programs. However, the missing ones are the very small ones, which constitute a negligible feature in broadcast advertising (*Commercial Radio Advertising*, p. 23)

This figure, however, is but an approximate approach to the actual total expenditures for broadcast advertising during the year of 1931. In the first place, there is a certain amount of talent expenditure, in addition to time expenditure, contained in both the network and individual station figures as given above. In the case of the networks, the total revenue as reported to the Commission was seen to be $37,517,384.65, as compared to the figure of $35,787,299.00 reported by *National Advertising Records*. Though it would be extremely unwise to assume the entire difference of $1,730,085.00 existing between the two figures to constitute an accurate measure of network receipts from the sale of talent,[5] it nevertheless is conservative procedure to accept the lower of the two totals and to attribute at least part of the discrepancy to the talent factor. In the case of the Yankee Network, no talent is included in the revenue, though it is impossible to tell what is the case with regard to the Don Lee Network. Likewise there is some talent payment found in the individual station total; but it probably is small, due to the fairly prevalent practice of stations in booking talent at cost and not including that charge as part of their general revenue. There is, however, no way in which to separate this talent figure from the total station revenue.

[5] Information as to actual revenue derived by networks from the sale of talent is not available.

A more important duplication is found in the question of network payments to individual stations for the broadcasting of network commercial programs, which appear as part of both the network and individual station revenue. It is possible to eliminate this duplication at least roughly, by subtracting an estimated total network payment to individual stations of $5,967,837.62 from their total revenue. This figure is secured by assuming that approximately one-third of the item of "Other Expenses"[6] on the national network expense sheets after programs, regular employees, equipment, replacement, line charges, international broadcasting, research, and development, totaling in all $17,903,512.85, have previously been accounted for. After making this deduction, a figure of $32,493,464.79 remains, and represents roughly the revenue derived from individual stations from other than network sources.

On the basis of these corrections, it becomes possible to restate, with slightly greater accuracy, the probable total amount spent by advertisers primarily for broadcasting time, though talent purchases from individual stations still are included in the station figure.

Expenditures over national networks, including payment to individual stations but excluding talent payment	$35,787,299.00
Expenditures over regional networks	1,779.,362.73
Expenditures over individual stations by national advertisers spotting programs, and by local advertisers	32,493,464.52
Total expenditures for broadcast advertising 1931, time primarily	$70,060,126.52

This figure is comparable to expenditures for space in other media, and, though it is only an approximation, it furnishes a better basis for comparison than does the *National Advertising Records'* network figure by itself. One other matter, the expenditure for talent, still remains to be considered. This is of much greater importance in achieving an appreciation of broadcast

[6] This figure is secured from a summary of expenses appearing on page 50 of *Commercial Radio Advertising*. It includes, in addition to payments to member stations, expenses such as agency commissions, cost of talent for outside sale, rent, and some overhead. It is the opinion of Paul F. Peter, chief statistician of the National Broadcasting Company, that about one-third of the total figure represents payments to stations.

advertising than in the analogous matter of art and production costs in the publication field, since, there, costs average 5 per cent to 10 per cent of space charges, while, in broadcasting, talent may cost from 25 per cent to 200 per cent as much as time. Though talent costs are almost impossible to estimate with any accuracy, experts seem to be in fair agreement that the average cost of talent on a broadcast advertising program is from one-quarter to one-third of time.[7] On this basis, talent expenditures of broadcast advertisers should range between $17,515,033.63 and $21,353,375.51, making a total broadcast advertising expenditure for 1931 of approximately from $87,575,158.15 to $91,413,502.00.[8]

Another interesting approach to the amount of broadcast advertising carried on in the United States in 1931 is found in the compilation of the Federal Radio Commission as to the total and commercially sponsored hours broadcast over 582 stations in the country during the second week of November of the year in question.[9] Of the 43,054 hours and 58 minutes of programs broadcast during the seven-day period under observation, 15,561 hours and 42 minutes, comprising 36.14 per cent of the hours broadcast, were devoted to commercial programs. Network commercially sponsored programs constituted 7.9 per cent of the total hours broadcast by the stations, while commercial programs originating in the individual stations and broadcast by them[10] amounted to 28.24 per cent of the total hours broadcast. Viewing the matter from another angle, the total commercial hours broadcast by a sample comprising 95.1 per cent of the stations of the country stated that 21.87 per cent were devoted to network programs and 78.13 per cent were utilized for the broadcasting of commercially sponsored programs originating in individual stations. The foregoing percentages are comparable to the relative proportion of total money expenditures devoted to network or individual station

[7] This is the consensus of opinion of fifteen station managers and several network officials.

[8] This is compared to the usual estimate of an approximate total expenditure of nearly two billion dollars for all advertising annually during the 1929–30 period.

[9] *Commercial Radio Advertising*, Federal Radio Commission, p. 31.

[10] Network programs include both national and the two regional networks reported. Individual station hours include all regional network hours other than those of the Yankee and Don Lee networks, probably a negligible amount.

broadcasting, which, for networks, amounts to 53.6 per cent of
the money spent for broadcast advertising—51.1 per cent over
national networks and 2.5 per cent over regional networks, and
46.4 per cent over individual stations. The discrepancy between
the proportion of commercial hours and the money expenditures over individual stations is explained by the extremely low
charges made by the smaller broadcasting stations for the use
of their facilities. Thus the average rate per quarter-hour nighttime throughout the country for a less than 100-watt station is
$15.32, for 100-watt stations $18.80, for 5,000-watt stations
$99.28, and for higher-powered stations $172.95.[11]

With this estimate of total broadcast advertising expenditures as a starting point, it now becomes possible to enter upon
a detailed analysis of the development of advertising over the
various parts of the broadcasting structure; and of these,
national network advertising will be the first to be considered.
A number of factors combined to make this form of broadcast
advertising the most important one. The national networks
were the first part of the broadcasting structure to make available organized facilities for broadcast advertising to the prospective program sponsor. They could do this because they were
best equipped both from the viewpoint of financial resources and
management to develop adequate program service and to contact the potential users of radio as an advertising medium.
Moreover, the networks early came to dominate the broadcasting structure of the country. This they did because the individual station sorely needed both the program service and such
business as the network office could throw its way. Neither
from the viewpoint of program development nor as regards
contacting the advertiser could the individual station make
much headway until increased advertising agency knowledge of
broadcasting, an improved middleman structure for contacting
the agency, and better program facilities arising out of more
scientific station technique and the rise of electrical transcriptions made possible the development of so-called spot broadcasting in 1929 and 1930. Finally, the development of national
broadcast advertising found an equally cogent reason for its
priority and dominance of the field in the fact that it was the
large national advertiser who could benefit most from this new

[11] *Commercial Radio Advertising*, Federal Radio Commission, pp. 24–25.

medium of mass communication—reaching millions of people
scattered far and wide throughout the country—and that, in
addition, it was he who financially was best equipped to make
the large expenditures required; for though radio may be a
cheap medium when cost is matched versus circulation, it does
require the outlay of large absolute sums when undertaken on
any extended scale or over a long period of time.

The growth of broadcast advertising over national networks
is indicated in Table XIX, which represents annual expenditures for time over the two national network companies.

TABLE XIX

TIME EXPENDITURES FOR BROADCAST ADVERTISING
OVER NATIONAL NETWORKS*

Year	Money Expended for Time	Percentage of Increase over Previous Year
1927	$ 3,832,150	....
1928	10,252,497	167.5
1929	19,729,571	80.6
1930	26,819,156	43.2
1931	35,787,299	33.5
1932	39,106,776	9.3

* *National Advertising Records.* The foregoing figures are at the contract rate
of one broadcast, discount for longer periods not having been subtracted. This
would average slightly over 5 per cent if computed. *National Advertising Records* is the source of practically all of the network figures in this chapter, though
some of the industrial summations have been taken from special presentations
made by the National Broadcasting Company.

The table is an interesting example of the rise of a new industry, wherein it must find its normal level in the competitive
structure before it becomes subject to all of the cross currents
prevalent in the field. In spite of the depression, radio broadcast advertising has forged steadily ahead until 1932 when the
first indications became evident that it was beginning to reach
the limit of its spectacular growth and to enter the second period
of its history, that of an established medium, capable of further
growth to be sure, but not at the same high rate which it previously had experienced. Even with respect to 1932, it is interesting to note that the first six months of the year were one of
the most successful periods in the history of network advertising.
Money expenditures over networks, at least, were approximate-

ly 50 per cent greater than during the same period of the preceding year during January and February, 1932, as also had been the case during the closing months of 1931. This rate of growth, however, declined as the summer approached, reaching a low ebb of 5.7 per cent in June. During the last six months of 1932 network broadcast advertising was about 10 per cent below the figure for the previous year, though still considerably above total expenditures for the same period in 1931.

A second comment is necessary regarding the interpretation of the foregoing table, which observation, in turn, possesses significance. It must be remembered at all times that radio broadcast advertising has experienced the major portion of its growth during one of the most severe depressions this country has faced. Had prosperity continued, or the business decline been less severe, both the rate at which broadcast advertising has grown and the variety of the industries which have employed it as a medium probably would have presented a very different picture from that of the present time. It is especially important that this fact be kept in mind when an attempt is being made to judge the efficacy of the medium from the present extent of its use, or to deduce who should employ it.

Another interesting approach to an analysis of the growth of advertising over national networks is found in a comparison of the number of hours of commercial programs broadcast by networks to the total hours broadcast. This is found in Table XX for the three key stations of the NBC Blue (WJZ), NBC Red (WEAF), and Columbia networks as of the second week in November, annually.

Other than the decline in commercial hours broadcast in November, 1932, mentioned previously, the most interesting feature of the table is the fact that the commercial hours broadcast over network key stations have tended to increase more slowly than the total money expenditures for broadcast advertising over networks. One of two factors may explain this tendency. Either network rates have increased sufficiently to cause the discrepancy or else advertisers are making wider use of network facilities, employing more stations. Examining the former, one finds that network charges for time have increased approximately 28.5 per cent since 1928,[12] and about 11.1 per cent since 1930. Thus increased national network charges explain but a small part of the more rapid growth of money expenditures over national networks than actual commercially sponsored hours broadcast. As a digression it is interesting to note that while basic network rates were increasing 28.5 per

TABLE XX

PROPORTION OF COMMERCIAL TO TOTAL HOURS BROADCAST OVER THE KEY STATIONS OF THE RED, BLUE, AND COLUMBIA BASIC NETWORKS, ANNUALLY, DURING THE SECOND WEEK OF NOVEMBER, 1927–32*

Year	Average Number of Commercial Hours Broadcast per Key Station	Percentage Increase or Decrease over Previous Year	Percentage of Commercial to Total Hours Broadcast
1927	14.65	. . . .	20.5
1928	19.84	+35.5	27.7
1929	29.46	+48.5	24.7
1930	35.24	+19.6	29.2
1931	42.22	+19.8	36.5
1932	31.50	−25.4	25.5

* The second week in November was selected because, in the opinion of the Federal Radio Commission, it constitutes a representative period in the broadcasting year. It was used as the base of the Commission's study of commercial radio advertising, and therefore possesses the advantage of comparability to that work. In other parts of this work similar tabulations have been employed for the second week of February, May, and August, respectively, but these are more significant with respect to seasonal trend than in indicating growth over a long period. The representativeness of November is further attested to by the fact that the percentages for this month are practically identical to those of the ensuing February, which lies within the same broadcasting period, most contracts beginning in October or November and continuing until April or May. It was impossible to tabulate data from more than four weeks of the year since the process involved an actual count of every hour from the original program sheets, a severe and costly task even for the period covered.

cent, the number of stations purchased on this basis had increased 14.0 per cent, and the total watt power represented by these stations had risen 88.6 per cent, while the number of receiving sets reached by the various basic networks had been augmented by no less than the national rate of growth or 38.4 per cent. Thus, on the basic networks, the advertiser of today receives more facilities and circulation per dollar expended than did the advertiser of five years ago.

[12] The foregoing rate estimate is based upon the charge of one-half hour evening time on the basic network, a unit which has probably been the most frequently purchased during the period under investigation. The rate is as of August, 1932.

However, with regard to the question at hand, the more rapid growth of total money expenditures for network advertis-

TABLE XXI

AVERAGE NUMBER OF STATIONS USED PER COMMERCIAL PROGRAM BROAD-
CAST AFTER SIX P.M. OVER THE RED, BLUE, AND COLUMBIA BASIC NET-
WORKS DURING THE SECOND WEEK OF NOVEMBER, 1927–32*

National Broadcasting Company

YEAR	RED BASIC NETWORK			BLUE BASIC NETWORK		
	Number of Stations on Network	Average Number Used per Program	Percentage More or Less than Basic Network	Number of Stations on Network	Average Number Used per Program	Percentage More or Less than Basic Network
1927........	21	14	−33.3	7	7	Equal
1928........	23	18	−21.7	10	10	Equal
1929........	25	25	Equal	10	13	+30.0
1930........	26	28	+ 7.7	12	13	+ 8.2
1931........	26	26	Equal	13	15	+15.4
1932†......	26	26	Equal	13	19	+46.1

Columbia Broadcasting System Basic Network

Year	Number of Stations on Network	Average Number Used per Program	Percentage More or Less than Basic Network
1927................	....	....	....
1928‡..............	17	....	....
1929..............	24	15	−37.6
1930..............	24	20	−16.7
1931..............	24	24	Equal
1932†..............	26	33	+26.9

* Source: Network program sheets. Basic networks have been used for comparison because they are the fundamental unit of purchase and as such constitute a
relatively steady base of comparison. Only programs after 6 P.M. have been considered since these constitute the great majority of broadcast advertising endeavor and are most typical of practice, looming much the largest in total expenditure.

† The second week in May, the latest data available for 1932.

‡ The Columbia Network was formed the latter part of this year, at which
time there was no division between basic and supplementary networks, nor are
data available as to the number of stations used.

ing than of commercial hours broadcast seems to find its chief
explanation in a wider use of the network facilities. This conclusion finds confirmation in Table XXI which indicates the

average number of stations used on commercially sponsored programs on the Red, Blue, and Columbia Basic networks, as compared with the total number of stations on each of these networks.

In spite of the fluctuations between networks and various years, a steady upward trend is noticeable in the data. The general effect of the increased use of the various station outlets for the average broadcast is illustrated in Table XXII, which shows the relative growth of the average commercially spon-

TABLE XXII

RELATIVE GROWTH OF COMMERCIALLY SPONSORED AS AGAINST TOTAL
STATION HOURS BROADCAST OVER NATIONAL NETWORKS
DURING THE SECOND WEEK OF NOVEMBER, 1927–32

Year	Average Station Hours of Commercial Programs	Percentage Increase or Decrease over Previous Year	Average Station Hours of All Programs	Percentage Increase or Decrease over Previous Year
1927..................	136.40	....	275.55	....
1928*.................	313.69	+130.0	708.63	+157.2
1929.................	655.03	+108.9	1540.41	+117.5
1930.................	772.19	+ 10.3	2285.70	+ 48.4
1931.................	1013.43	+ 40.3	2697.01	+ 13.6
1932†................	861.75	− 14.9	3251.69	+ 10.6

* The Columbia System first entered in this year, which accounts for the sudden rise in the following year, when it first operated over a wide area.

† May, 1932, the last data available. Part of this decrease is seasonal.

sored station hours as against the average of all station hours[13] broadcast over the three major networks—the two of the National Broadcasting Company and the one of the Columbia Broadcasting System—including supplementary units as well as basic networks.

In spite of the many contradictory forces at play, the general

[13] "Station hours" is a measure similar to ton miles and is derived by multiplying the length of a given program by the number of stations over which the program is broadcast. It is the ideal measure of network broadcast showing, as it does, the extent to which programs are broadcast over the whole network, and thus indicating complete network behavior. However, because of the extreme difficulty of calculation, it is impractical for wide application unless the resources of a large statistical department are at one's disposal. In the case of the total network station hours, *this is not the total hours broadcast by affiliated stations, but only of the hours originating on the network.* The former would make the perfect base for a measurement of the proportion of commercial to total hours broadcast, but unfortunately cannot be computed with any accuracy.

trend toward a swifter growth of commercial station hours than
of commercial hours broadcast by key stations stands forth
clearly, thus confirming the trend noted in Table XXI, dealing
with the average number of stations used per broadcast. The
importance of the network sustaining service to member stations is indicated by the fact that, with the exception of one
year, 1931, the total station hours increased more rapidly than
did the commercial station hours, indicating a continually wider
use of the network sustaining programs. The full significance
of this fact will be discussed in greater detail in the chapter dealing with program practice.[14]

TABLE XXIII

NUMBER OF COMPANIES BROADCASTING ANNUALLY OVER NATIONAL NETWORKS,
TOGETHER WITH AVERAGE EXPENDITURE PER COMPANY, 1927–32*

Year	Number of Companies	Percentage Increase or Decrease over Previous Year	Average Expenditure per Company	Percentage Increase over Previous Year
1927............	81	....	$ 48,298	....
1928............	160	+99.9	64,078	32.7
1929............	237	+48.1	79,028	23.3
1930............	297	+25.3	90,302	14.1
1931............	384	+29.3	93,208	3.2
1932............	303	−21.1	129,065	38.4

* Source: Tabulations of the National Broadcasting Company for both networks.

Of equal interest to the trend in total expenditures and general use of network as advertising media, is the question of the
number of companies broadcasting over networks, the length
of time these companies remain on the air, and the turnover
among them. The trend regarding the first-mentioned of these
features is found in Table XXIII.

It will be noted that the rate of increase in the number of
advertisers over national networks was proportionately less
each year until 1930, following which it remained comparatively
steady until 1932, when the first decline in program sponsors
was experienced in the history of network broadcast advertising. The slowing up of the rate of growth in number of advertisers in 1928 and 1929 was merely the usual corollary of the

[14] Chap. xi.

early years of an industry. Though the absolute growth continued to be great, it could hardly be expected to be proportionate in later years to what it had been at the outset.

The decline in the number of network advertisers is explainable only when the average expenditure per advertiser also is taken into consideration. With regard to this factor, the rate of increase lagged uniformly behind that of the number of clients, indicating that much of the growth in network broadcast advertising during the period of 1929-31 was due to the entrance into the field of a large number of smaller concerns with limited appropriations. However, in 1932, the situation reversed itself, and, though the number of advertisers declined by more than one-fifth, the average expenditure for network advertising rose by almost 40 per cent. Thus it becomes evident that the smaller program sponsor is tending to discontinue his broadcast advertising.

The trend in the length of time during which network broadcast advertisers remain on the air during a given season is indicated in Table XXIV.

The most interesting feature of this table is the fact that the number of accounts running nine months and over have been increasing more rapidly than other types of business. Thus today, one-fifth of the concerns, and undoubtedly much more of the money expenditures, remain on the air throughout the entire year. This not only indicates a probable smoothing of the seasonal curve for radio broadcast advertising, which will be discussed in a later chapter,[15] but also that broadcasting is attracting a more stable type of clientèle annually. The full significance of this, in turn, will become more evident when the type of industries engaging in broadcast advertising is discussed later in the chapter. Of equal interest to the decided growth in the number of long-term accounts has been the steady decrease in the number of concerns broadcasting for periods under three months in duration. This probably is the strongest indication of all that the experimental broadcast advertiser of the early days of radio is passing from the air.

The general conclusion that national network business is becoming more stable as to its base is further reinforced by an examination of the clients dropping broadcast advertising dur-

[15] See chap. x.

ing the season 1931–32. During the period ending June 30, 1932, a total of 134 concerns discontinued broadcast advertising, while 20 concerns entered the field, leaving a net loss of 114 companies. Much of this loss was seasonal in nature, the companies planning to resume in the autumn. Of the companies discontinuing broadcasting, 26 or 22.8 per cent had been on the air since 1929 or earlier, and were largely manufacturers of radios, typewriters, and other industries which have been es-

TABLE XXIV

NUMBER OF COMPANIES BROADCASTING OVER NATIONAL NETWORKS FOR PE-
RIODS OF DIFFERENT LENGTH, 1927–32 (JUNE 30–JUNE 30)*

DURATION OF BROAD-CASTING SERIES	1927–28		1928–29		1929–30		1930–31		1931–32	
	Number of Companies	Percentage of Total	Number of Companies	Percentage of Total	Number of Companies	Percentage of Total	Number of Companies	Percentage of Total	Number of Companies	Percentage of Total
Under 3 months......	37	33.6	43	23.1	51	18.6	64	18.9	61	17.9
3 months and under 6 months...........	29	26.3	62	33.3	88	32.2	94	27.9	104	29.9
6 months and under 9 months...........	20	18.1	28	15.1	47	17.2	71	21.0	62	17.4
9 months and under 12 months...........	11	10.0	20	10.7	37	13.6	38	11.2	48	13.8
12 months..........	13	12.0	33	17.8	50	18.4	71	21.0	73	21.0
Total..........	110	100.0	186	100.0	273	100.0	338	100.0	348	100.0

* The reader will notice that the present table is constructed on the basis of June 30–June 30 instead of the calendar year. This was done to avoid splitting up programs and showing series of shorter duration than actually existed, since the broadcasting season usually extends from October to April or May, with the midsummer months the low ebb. Other tables have not been presented on this basis because of two reasons: (1) The fact that data regarding other media are presented on a calendar basis, and using any other form would destroy the possibility of comparison, and (2) because important broadcasting data, such as those of the Federal Radio Commission study, cannot be reduced to the June 30 basis.

pecially hard hit by depression. Another 30 concerns, or 26.3 per cent, had been on the air less than three months, and constituted the "floating" portion of the broadcast advertising business. The remaining 50.9 per cent had been on the air, for the most part, either a year or less, and constituted to a large extent the seasonal decline in the industry. Thus the vast majority of the network drops are shown to be either seasonal in nature or, on the part of experimental advertisers, the older and more established users of broadcast advertising continuing today as in previous years.

Two additional features remain to be discussed regarding network advertising as a whole, before entering upon an analysis of the industries comprising this advertising. The first of these is the question of shifts of clients from one network to another, and the second, the trend regarding the same company sponsoring programs over both the National Broadcasting Company and Columbia Broadcasting facilities. With regard to the former, these have been surprisingly few, and such as there have been were rather evenly distributed between the two great network companies. In 1929 there were five shifts,[16] the National Broadcasting Company gaining two, and the Columbia Broadcasting System gaining three concerns from its competitor. In 1930, the eight shifts which occurred were evenly divided between the two networks, as was again the case with the six shifts which occurred in 1931. In 1932, up to June 30, the National Broadcasting Company had gained three clients from its competitor, and the Columbia Broadcasting System two concerns. In five years, there were a total of fifty concerns who discontinued broadcasting on one network, and at a later date resumed activities on the other. Of these companies, 50 per cent resumed broadcasting with no more than a summer season intervening;[17] another 26 per cent returned to network broadcasting during the following year; 20 per cent resumed their broadcast advertising efforts on a competing network after a two-year lapse, while the remaining 4 per cent did so after an interval of three years. There were relatively few companies who had broadcast on one network, and who returned to the same network after a longer interval than five months ensuing between broadcasts.

Though the number of companies sponsoring programs over both the National Broadcasting Company and Columbia Broadcasting System facilities still is small, there has been a marked trend in this direction within the past few years. The concerns broadcasting over both networks have been primarily either holding companies, advertising several products, or food, soap,

[16] A shift is here interpreted as a company which leaves one network and resumes broadcasting on a competing network during the same calendar year, with not more than a five-month interval, e.g., from the end of April to beginning of October (the long seasonal lay-off) between broadcasts.

[17] Twenty-four of these shifts were discussed at the outset of this part of the chapter. The twenty-fifth instance occurred in 1928 when the Columbia System was first established.

and toilet good companies seeking to reach the maximum audience. In 1928 two companies made this their practice; in 1929 six concerns; ten in 1930; twenty in 1931; and, during the first six months of 1932, seventeen concerns sponsored broadcasts over both networks.

Having discussed the general aspects of the use of national networks as advertising media, the next question which arises is as to what industries avail themselves of network facilities. Basic information with regard to the amounts spent by various industrial groups is found in Table XXV, while their relative rate of growth is depicted in Charts IV to VIII, inclusive.

A brief word of explanation regarding the various classifications of goods is in order. The classification itself is a standard one adopted by *National Advertising Records* for all media, including broadcasting. Since the original records were for the periodical field, some of the classifications pertain more definitely to magazines and newspapers than to broadcast advertising. The meaning of other groupings, however, is sufficiently clear to require no explanation. Among the less definite classifications are the following, whose significance in broadcast advertising is primarily of the nature herein indicated: (1) garden, which is largely confined to broadcasts such as the Davey Tree program; (2) machinery and mechanical supplies, devoted almost exclusively to electrical household equipment and contains no industrial goods; (3) hardware and paints, primarily the latter rather than the former; (4) shoes and leather goods, which in the case of broadcast advertising are almost exclusively shoes; (5) magazines, books, and stationery, wherein magazines predominate almost to the exclusion of the other two; (6) office equipment, consisting largely of typewriters and fountain pens; (7) travel and amusement, which is predominantly the motion-picture industry but at times has included to a much lesser degree concerns such as Thomas Cook and Sons; and (8) miscellaneous, wherein are grouped most of the experimenters and smaller advertisers who are scattered far and wide throughout industry and trade.

An examination of Table XXV, and of Charts IV-VIII, reveals that it is the food, drug, and toilet goods, and tobacco industries which constitute the backbone of American broadcast advertising, accounting for approximately two-thirds of the

TABLE XXV

BROADCAST ADVERTISING EXPENDITURES FOR TIME OVER NATIONAL NETWORKS*

	1927	1928	1929	1930	1931	1932
Foods and food beverages	$ 427,830	$ 733,476	$ 2,025,176	$ 5,264,116	$ 8,957,021	$11,297,227
Drugs and toilet goods	310,447	977,553	1,940,562	3,239,753	6,106,667	8,526,268
Cigars, cigarettes, and tobacco	37,000	385,030	1,348,502	2,076,114	5,371,117	6,245,223
Automobiles	433,063	1,249,000	1,702,803	1,355,414	1,313,923	1,939,094
Lubricants and petroleum products	21,940	311,279	961,439	1,495,338	1,183,346	2,303,331
Confectionery and soft drinks	260,402	701,164	563,984	839,070	1,359,919	1,635,096
Insurance and Financial	471,006	656,147	923,377	1,209,644	1,493,351	1,251,977
Soaps and housekeepers' supplies	90,759	182,146	238,372	532,998	1,419,883	1,119,592
Magazines, stationery, and books	171,187	602,478	886,044	1,421,922	1,359,001	750,296
Shoes, trunks, bags, etc.	45,150	190,135	367,293	834,392	1,261,430	396,151
Machinery and mechanical supplies	9,900	13,830	592,947	910,151	727,041	657,615
Paints and hardware	18,393	29,092	143,054	198,696	727,243	435,955
Furniture and furnishings	205,758	409,589	581,326	626,283	795,841	255,672
Clothing and dry goods	11,593	61,787	315,179	581,051	575,139	395,144
Radios, phonographs, and musical instruments	1,143,364	2,081,776	3,740,762	2,402,508	909,957	167,757
Sporting goods	18,180	44,500	75,593	167,228	269,003	97,678
Building materials	30,000	42,144	233,704	683,065	387,749	18,296
Jewelry and silverware	26,580	45,595	41,120	432,049	113,770	150,638
Garden		4,748	936	91,664	87,380	60,690
Travel and amusement	23,342	99,243	866,906	1,359,618	170,821	41,551
Office equipment	79,485	22,760	43,626	77,053	83,522	35,653
Schools, camps, and correspondence courses	6,258			20,379	17,237	
Miscellaneous	7,217	1,407,023	1,118,566	997,670	1,096,938	1,325,870
Total	$3,832,492	$10,251,495	$18,729,571	$26,816,156	$35,787,299	$39,106,776

* National Advertising Records (Denny Publishing Co.)

CHART IV

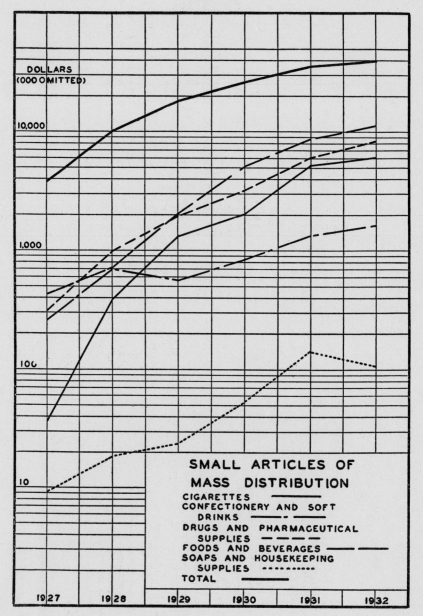

DOLLARS
(000 OMITTED)

10,000

1,000

100

10

SMALL ARTICLES OF
MASS DISTRIBUTION

CIGARETTES ————
CONFECTIONERY AND SOFT
    DRINKS ——— · ———
DRUGS AND PHARMACEUTICAL
    SUPPLIES ——— ———
FOODS AND BEVERAGES ——— ———
SOAPS AND HOUSEKEEPING
    SUPPLIES ············
TOTAL ————

1927   1928   1929   1930   1931   1932

CHART V

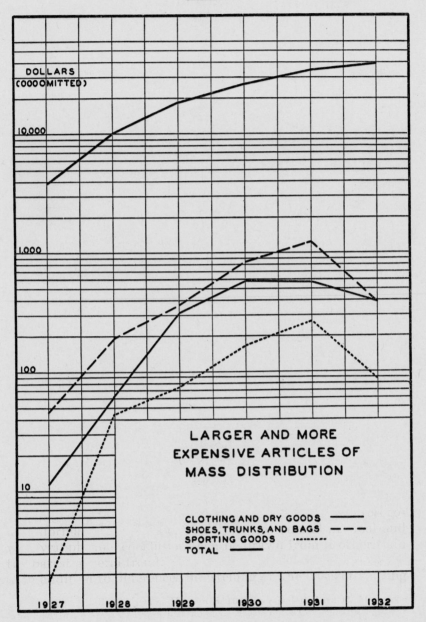

DOLLARS
(000 OMITTED)

10,000

1,000

100

10

LARGER AND MORE
EXPENSIVE ARTICLES OF
MASS DISTRIBUTION

CLOTHING AND DRY GOODS ————
SHOES, TRUNKS, AND BAGS — — —
SPORTING GOODS ·········
TOTAL ————

1927   1928   1929   1930   1931   1932

CHART VI

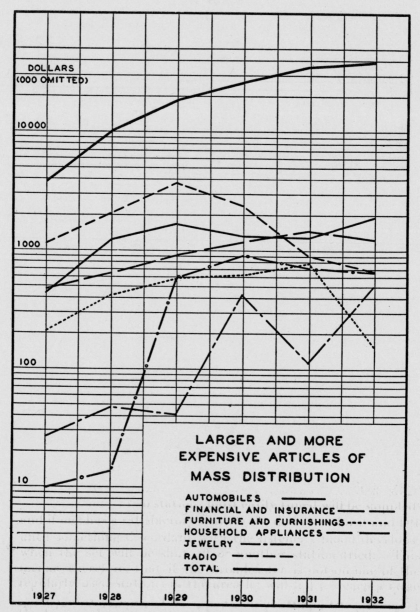

DOLLARS
(000 OMITTED)

10000

1000

100

10

LARGER AND MORE
EXPENSIVE ARTICLES OF
MASS DISTRIBUTION

AUTOMOBILES ————
FINANCIAL AND INSURANCE ——— ——
FURNITURE AND FURNISHINGS ·········
HOUSEHOLD APPLIANCES ——— ———
JEWELRY —·—·—·
RADIO ——— ———
TOTAL ————

1927   1928   1929   1930   1931   1932

CHART VII

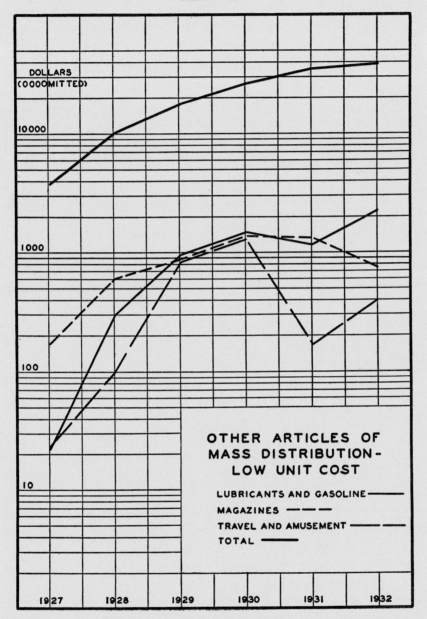

DOLLARS
(000OMITTED)

10000

1000

100

10

OTHER ARTICLES OF
MASS DISTRIBUTION-
LOW UNIT COST

LUBRICANTS AND GASOLINE————
MAGAZINES ———
TRAVEL AND AMUSEMENT ——— —
TOTAL ————

1927   1928   1929   1930   1931   1932

CHART VIII

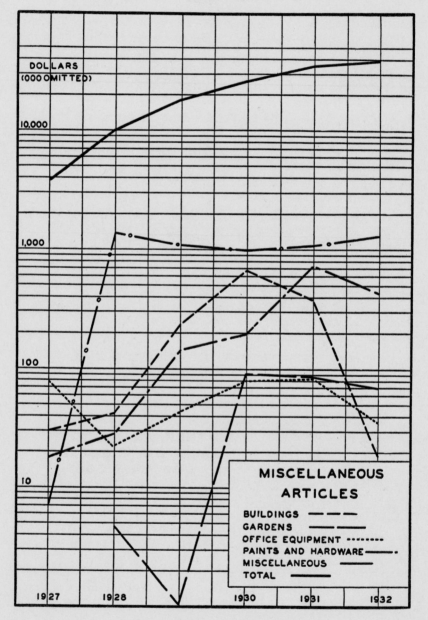

DOLLARS
(000 OMITTED)

10,000

1,000

100

10

MISCELLANEOUS
ARTICLES

BUILDINGS — — — —
GARDENS — · —
OFFICE EQUIPMENT ········
PAINTS AND HARDWARE —— · —
MISCELLANEOUS ————
TOTAL ————

1927   1928   1930   1931   1932

total expenditures for network time. This is even more vividly presented in Chart IX, which shows the relative proportion of total broadcast advertising expenditure for time over national networks represented annually by these industries.

Of these three leaders in network advertising, food looms the most important, and has enjoyed the steadiest growth. In 1927 expenditures by the food industry for broadcast advertising totaled $427,830, which placed it a close fourth to the automotive group. Since then the industry has increased steadily in importance as a broadcast advertiser, until in 1932 it topped the entire field with a total expenditure of $11,297,227. The number of food concerns on the air likewise have grown from 7 companies in 1927 to 76 in 1931. Of the total expenditures for broadcast advertising by the food industry in 1931, approximately 45 per cent was by the flour and cereal group; 22 per cent by beverages, such as coffee and tea, and dairy products; 14 per cent by the canned goods group; 11 per cent by chain stores, almost exclusively the Atlantic and Pacific Tea Company; and 8 per cent by condiments and relishes.[18]

The drug and toilet goods industry ranks second in 1932 with a total expenditure of $8,526,268. This group rose from fifth place as to network advertising expenditures in 1927 to its present high position, the number of advertising companies increasing from 11 to 52 in the year of 1931. Of the sponsor concerns, approximately 67 per cent were manufacturers of toilet articles, with dentifrices and mouth washes constituting almost half of the expenditures in this sub-group. Toilet soaps accounted for about 20 per cent of the network advertising expenditures by the group, while drugs and cosmetics completed the picture.

Cigarette and tobacco advertising over networks is highly concentrated, totaling but 12 sponsoring companies in 1931. This group as a whole started comparatively late in the field of broadcast advertising, but since 1928 has shown a greater growth in broadcast advertising expenditures than any other industry.

The insurance and financial group constituted one of the first

18 The sources of the data throughout this discussion of network advertising are *National Advertising Records* and the *Industrial Reports* prepared by the Statistical Department of the National Broadcasting Company. The number of concerns is given as of 1931 since these are the last compilations available at the present writing.

CHART IX

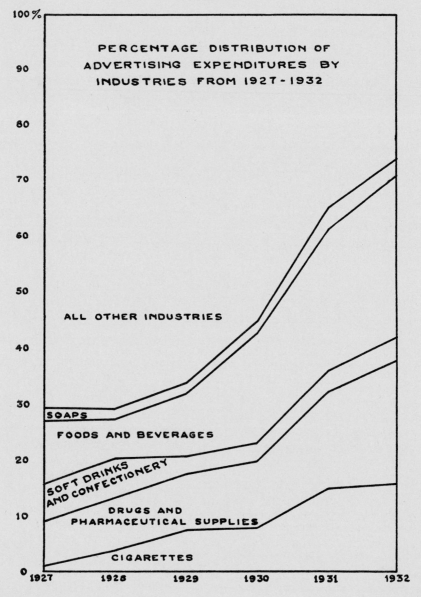

PERCENTAGE DISTRIBUTION OF
ADVERTISING EXPENDITURES BY
INDUSTRIES FROM 1927-1932

ALL OTHER INDUSTRIES

SOAPS

FOODS AND BEVERAGES

SOFT DRINKS
AND CONFECTIONERY

DRUGS AND
PHARMACEUTICAL SUPPLIES

CIGARETTES

users of broadcast advertising. Beginning with the Metropolitan Life Insurance Company in 1926, and the Cities Service Company in 1927, this group has shown a steady but not especially spectacular growth in broadcast advertising expenditures. The effort in this field is highly concentrated, being limited to 7 companies in 1931. Most of the advertising done by these concerns is institutional in nature and on an especially dignified plane.

Soaps again are confined to a few large companies, such as Lever Brothers and Procter and Gamble. From eighth place in 1927, the broadcast advertising expenditures of this group have risen steadily until soap manufacturers promise to become among the most important users of network facilities.

Confectionery and soft drinks, especially ginger ale, were one of the earliest users of broadcast advertising over networks. Their growth has been sporadic, and broadcasting by this group is at present confined to several ginger ale companies and Wrigley's Chewing Gum, with an occasional candy manufacturer.

The automotive industry is especially interesting, from the viewpoint of its broadcast advertising expenditures. Network advertising has always been highly concentrated in this field, with only 8 companies, in all, having participated since 1927, and with General Motors the only consistent user of radio. At no period have there been more than two or three automobile manufacturers broadcasting at the same time, so that figures for this group largely represent General Motors Corporation expenditures. In the magazine field, *Collier's*, *True Story*, and *Time* have been the outstanding examples, with the last-mentioned the only one remaining on the air today. Both *Collier's* and *True Story* experienced considerable success with their broadcast advertising effort, but declining advertising revenue in their own magazines forced curtailment of broadcasting in spite of increased circulation gained by means of the radio network.

The radio set manufacturing industry is probably the most interesting of all broadcast advertisers. Starting in first place in 1927 with an expenditure for the year of $1,143,364, it reached a peak of $3,740,762 in 1929 and since then has declined to almost insignificant proportions. Only one company remains on the air today, while the industry stands as an example of the evils of excessive expansion of productive capacity, overemphasis of price, unregulated competition, and a monopolistic system of license fees.

Having completed a general survey of the types of industries which have employed broadcast advertising over national networks in the past and who are doing so at present, it now becomes possible to summarize the trends with respect to the use of these networks as advertising media.

With regard to network advertising as a whole there seems reason to believe that it constituted approximately 54 per cent of the total broadcast advertising business of the country in 1931. What the proportion is today, it is impossible to tell, though there are reasons for believing that the individual station business has suffered from the depression more than have the networks.

There seems reason to believe that the future growth of network advertising will be at a considerably slower rate than in the past and that broadcast advertising has definitely emerged from the pioneer stage, as far as its acceptance is concerned, and is now facing the problem typical of an established medium in a period of declining advertising appropriations.

More important than the tendency toward an increased number of sponsors has been the greater use of existing network facilities by broadcasting companies, as reflected in the increased number of stations utilized per broadcast, and the more rapid rise in the number of commercial station hours, as against the number of commercial hours broadcast by the key stations of the various networks.

A marked tendency toward decreasing fluctuations in sponsorship is to be noted in the increasing proportion of companies remaining on the air throughout the entire year and the steadily declining proportion of companies broadcasting for periods of less than three months, as well as in the relatively low percentage of older broadcasters discontinuing their network effort.

Though still small numerically, there is a marked tendency for more advertisers to sponsor programs over the facilities of both great network companies. This trend is largely confined to holding companies distributing a variety of products, or to food, drug, and toilet good, and soap manufacturers, attempting to reach a maximum market.

As to the types of industries employing broadcast advertising over networks, the great majority of companies and products, as well as of total expenditures, were found to fall in the category of convenience goods: articles of small unit size, low price, high repeat sales, mass consumption, and which are distributed through a large number of outlets. These articles, such as canned foods, flour and cereals, dentifrices and mouth washes, cigarettes, soaps, ginger ale, and similar items, are goods which, though nationally advertised and branded, require constant sales effort to build up and hold any measure of consumer insistence, preference, or even acceptance. Likewise they are consumed throughout the year. Because of its widespread appeal and large circulation, its personal element, and potentialities for dramatization of the product and the brand name, radio broadcasting has constituted an effective advertising medium for industries of this type; and it probably is in this field where the greatest strength of broadcast advertising will always lie, though by no means exclusively so.

A second category of goods advertised extensively over the national networks at the present time are larger and higher-priced articles of mass consumption such as automobiles, electric refrigerators, and similar products. These again are sold to large segments of the public, and though the repeat sales are not as frequent in point of time as in the case of convenience goods, this fact is compensated for by a high degree of consumer loyalty to a given brand. Such goods are often termed specialty goods, largely because they tend to be distributed through specialized distributive agencies, and because of the specialized appeal of an individual brand as evidenced by the higher degree of consumer insistence. A final type of product advertised extensively over national networks is that of services of mass appeal, such as insurance and amusements. In all cases, however, the elements of mass appeal and mass distribution are present. Whether broadcast advertising necessarily is confined to goods of this type is a matter concerning which there is a considerable difference of opinion. As far as the present investigation is concerned, this is a question the discussion of which will be postponed until the whole process of broadcast advertising has been examined more thoroughly. A word of caution, however, again is added, to the end that the reader be not too readily tempted to assume that, because broadcast advertising has developed primarily in certain directions up to the present time, these necessarily must be the channels which it must follow in its future growth. Much of this development has occurred during highly abnormal conditions, and it remains to be seen what more settled, if not more prosperous, times will bring.

Though no detailed analysis will be presented of the competitive history of broadcast advertising as compared with other media, at least brief mention should be made at this point of the experience of magazines, newspapers, and billboards during the past few years, as against that of radio. The factors operating with respect to the various media are so many, and to date often so obscure in their operation, as to make this a fit subject for a research in itself. All that will be attempted, therefore, will be to outline briefly the major trends with respect to competing media, especially as they have developed since the year of 1929.[19]

Since 1929 all advertising media other than radio have experienced a sharp decline in revenue. In the case of newspapers this decline totaled $55,000,000 between the years of 1929 and 1931, and amounted to approximately 22 per cent of the 1929 receipts. During the same period national magazines lost approximately $37,000,000 or 18 per cent of their 1929 revenue. This was primarily during the period 1930-31, since the loss in receipts from 1929 to 1930 was but 1 per cent. The fact that, between 1930 and 1931, 34 per cent of the advertisers in magazines discontinued their advertising completely, while at the same time the average advertising appropriation rose 26 per cent during the period, indicates that the magazine loss has been largely in the small marginal advertiser. This is also largely true of the newspaper, though here such a variety of causes tend to operate that any broad, general conclusion is inadvisable without a great deal of careful and detailed investigation. Outdoor advertising likewise lost $50,000,000 during the period of 1929-31, again primarily due to the general forces of depression, while car card revenue was cut 50 per cent during the period in ques-

[19] Most of the data for this brief discussion have been taken from an excellent analysis made of the question by Howard Henderson of the J. Walter Thompson Agency, and presented before the National Association of the Teachers of Marketing at their 1932 meeting. It has been reprinted in *Broadcasting*, January 15, 1933.

tion. Radio broadcast advertising alone gained, which, in the writer's estimation, is due to the fact that, as a new medium, it was necessary for broadcast advertising to find its logical place in the advertising media structure before becoming subject to all of the competitive forces operative in the media field as a whole. Now that radio broadcasting seems to have outgrown this stage, one may expect broadcast advertising to face at least some of the difficulties which have been the lot of the older media during the past several years. Then, much better than today, will it be possible to discover the real vitality of this new medium.

Advertising expenditures by national advertisers for various media were estimated in 1931 to be as follows:[20] newspapers, $205,000,000; magazines, $167,000,000; radio broadcasting, approximately $36,000,000; outdoor advertising, $30,000,000; and car cards, $4,500,000, amounting in all to $442,500,000. Of the total amount, therefore, radio broadcasting constituted less than one-tenth. This, of course, is merely taking network time expenditures, total national advertising revenue from both network and spot broadcasting undoubtedly reaching a somewhat higher figure.

A final factor in the field of network advertising is the amount and nature of the broadcast advertising effort carried on over regional networks. As stated earlier in the chapter, advertising over the two principal regional networks, the Yankee and the Don Lee networks, amounted in 1931 to $1,779,362.73. This is the only figure available in the field, and probably includes the great majority of expenditures on regional networks. With regard to the type of industries sponsoring programs over regional networks, a great similarity exists between them and national network advertisers. Thus in July, 1932, 27 per cent of the Yankee Network advertising was by the food industry, 14 per cent by the drug and toilet goods group, and 12 per cent by the tobacco companies, comprising in all 53 per cent of the total regional business. Out of 131 companies broadcasting over the network during the year of 1931, 54.9 per cent were manufacturers with national distribution, and 45.1 per cent regional or local distributors. There was a wide variety of business represented among the companies in question, though the general types

[20] Bureau of Advertising, American Newspaper Publishers' Association.

followed the national sponsors very closely. From an examination of the commercial sponsor lists of the Yankee Network and from conversation with the officials of that organization, the principal uses to which the network is put are as follows: (1) as a trial region for national distributors either introducing a new product or trying out broadcast advertising itself; (2) as a means of applying special pressure to the sale of the product in question in the New England area; (3) as a medium for the small regional manufacturer or distributor, who can take two or three stations at the start and enlarge his broadcast advertising effort as the number and territory covered by his outlets increase; and (4) as a medium for the established regional distributor such as a retail chain, wholesaler, or regional manufacturer. An examination of the Don Lee program sheets reveals the same general type of sponsor as found on the Yankee Network.

CHAPTER VII

THE USE OF SPOT BROADCAST ADVERTISING

Though broadcast advertising originated over individual stations, its growth in that field was much slower than with respect to the utilization of national network facilities for that purpose. The individual station was hampered in securing broadcast advertising in a number of ways. After the first novelty of broadcasting had worn away and programs of higher entertainment standard were being developed to meet the demands of a more discriminating public, all except the most enterprising and financially strong stations in important metropolitan centers, such as New York and Chicago, found it impossible to develop local programs that could compete successfully with the productions of the networks. For this task neither the talent, managerial ability, nor the financial resources were available to the small local station. Consequently, those stations which could do so affiliated themselves with the networks, both for the programs they could secure and the revenue which was possible from broadcasting network commercial programs.

Revenue and program service were of equal importance in turning the stations toward the networks. Broadcast advertising was a new thing, and the local merchant or small manufacturer, usually more conservative than the national distributor by reason both of his ability and his proportionately smaller financial resources, was loath to experiment with the new medium. Rather, he preferred to wait until it had proved itself at someone else's expense. Moreover, the necessity of continuous effort week after week, as compared with the possibility of sporadic inserts on the part of the small local retailer in the community press, made broadcasting a more expensive medium as far as initial outlay was concerned. Finally, the larger and more important retailers, department stores especially, were convinced that the direct selling possible in the local newspapers was of greater value than the mere good-will effect, then believed to be the only result which could be obtained from the use of broadcasting; an opinion which was strengthened by the unfortunate experience of many department-store-owned stations in the early days.[1]

From the viewpoint of securing national advertising business the individual station was limited, as has been mentioned previously, by having little to offer the advertiser in most cases, and, in addition, by the fact that practically no means existed for contacting either the potential advertiser or his agency. Moreover, had the middleman structure, now used largely for that purpose, then existed, there still would have remained the problem of selling the agency and its client, neither of whom possessed the slightest experience in broadcast advertising, and who consequently leaned inordinately much upon network advice and assistance. Finally, the national advertiser was more interested in securing facilities which would cover the entire country than in reaching localized districts; and neither he nor the agency had yet learned the possibility of shaping their broadcasting effort to fit the configuration of their market by the use of individual stations, or even, to any great extent at that time, by the careful purchase of network facilities. For these reasons, then, individual station business grew slowly.

By 1929 there were indications that both networks and individual stations eventually would constitute important factors in the broadcast advertising structure of the country. Some of the larger metropolitan stations were developing, over and above their network programs and business, a distinct personality which gave them widespread circulation in the area covered by their transmitter; and, since that coverage lay primarily in the great buying centers of the nation, it made these stations worthwhile media for both the important local retailers and manufacturers, and the national advertisers as well. Stations of this type were to be found in WOR, Newark, WLW, Cincinnati, WMAQ, Chicago, and WNAC, Boston. In addition to this development, which after all, was highly restricted in extent, enterprising advertisers were discovering that splendid results

---

[1] It seems that this failure of many department store stations was due largely to poor and unenterprising management, as well as to an ignorance and lack of appreciation on the part of the higher executives as to the potential function of the station in merchandising the store. This will be discussed in somewhat greater detail when local broadcast advertising is analyzed.

could be attained by sponsoring time, weather, news, and market reports over large groups of stations scattered throughout the country. Such programs did not necessitate the use of network facilities. A standard form of announcement was prepared, into which the time, weather, market, or news report could be inserted, and time was contracted for directly from the station in question, the station's own announcer reading the advertisement, and its own staff securing the necessary information for the program. Thus programs such as the Longine correct time came into being. Moreover, the local station had conceived the idea some years earlier, and now began to push with vigor the broadcasting of programs at certain hours of the day wherein the announcements of local retailers were permitted to be read between numbers by the staff announcer. These were sold at a nominal charge in most instances, and corresponded to the classified advertisements in a newspaper.

Thus a number of new avenues of potential use were being opened to both the local and national advertiser as far as the individual station was concerned. The larger metropolitan stations were developing personalities which made them important media to local and national advertisers in the principal buying centers. The practice of so-called spot announcements, by which name the trade came to designate both the national announcements sponsored over a large number of stations and those of the small local retailer, inserted, in all probability, between phonograph records, was growing. Moreover, individual station technique in many cases was achieving a level where an increasing number of them were capable of producing satisfactory programs in their own studios; and though the total was small, the trend was significant.

By 1929, also, the more enterprising advertising agencies began to build up, by experience, a sufficient knowledge of broadcasting to be able to visualize a wider extension of its possibilities as a medium than merely a network proposition. It is probable that these potentialities were addressed to them largely by necessity. During that period, especially, network requirements, as to contracts and the number of stations taken, were especially rigid. Moreover, broadcasting was the new vogue in advertising, and the small client, unable to meet the financial demands of national network broadcasting, was attempting to find some means of getting on the air. For him, the "spotting" of time or other announcements over the territory wherein his principal market was located, or the sponsorship of a locally produced program over one or two stations in the leading cities of that territory, constituted a partial solution of the problem. Finally, the agency began to discover that important local markets sometimes remained out of the range of network influence, so that other means were necessary to reach the listeners in this area. Again the possibility of "spotting" a special program in this section presented itself.

In response to the demand for this type of facility, a new middleman structure arose, designed to furnish a point of contact between the agency, which for the most part knew absolutely nothing about the station, and the station itself, which possessed no means of contacting the agency, situated as was the latter either in Chicago or New York, thousands of miles from Brownsville, Texas; or Kalamazoo, Michigan. Thus there came into existence the time broker, and from him, in turn, developed both the spot specialist of the Scott Howe Bowen type and the station representative.

In this manner the gap between the station and the agency was bridged, and a means was provided for securing the new "spot" business, as it came to be called.

The final and most important addition to the structure of spot broadcasting, and the development of the individual station broadcast advertising business, came in the form of the electrical transcription, a type of program reproduced from records made especially for broadcasting purposes. This type made its début in 1929. This provided the advertiser with a means whereby he could produce a program in one place, give it permanent form on records, and broadcast it over any station he pleased, at any time, irrespective of when it was broadcast on some other station, and without the stations in question being linked together by telephone wires into a network. This made it possible to broadcast over groups of stations either greater or less in number than the average network, and to concentrate the broadcast advertising effort in the specific areas which comprised the manufacturer's potential market.

Thus by the following year, 1930, the necessary structure and practice had developed in the field of broadcast advertising to give the individual station two important sources of business, over and above that secured by a network affiliate from acting as an outlet for the network's own commercial programs. The first of these was national spot business, as it was known in broadcasting circles, comprising business placed by national or regional manufacturers or distributors over an individual station either directly or through their local retail representatives.[2] The second was an increasing volume of business being placed by local retailers and small manufacturers such as bakeries and similar concerns broadcasting in their own interest. Since spot broadcasting[3] was seldom carried on over merely one station, it possessed the added characteristic that it almost invariably involved the broadcasting of a program over a number of stations, with the program transmitted from the studio of each station rather than emanating from a central or key station connected with the other broadcasting outlets in the group by means of telephone circuits. The program itself might be either a spot announcement, a so-called "live talent" program, or an electrical transcription.

By 1931 the total of these two forms of individual station business had grown to an estimated sum of $32,493,464.52, comprising 46.4 per cent of the broadcast advertising expenditures for that year. In point of commercial hours broadcast for all forms of advertising over the radio, individual station programs comprised 78.13 per cent of the total commercially sponsored hours presented during the second week of November of the year in question. With regard to the total individual station business, it is impossible to secure any data regarding the probable proportion of national spot business, and of broadcast advertising carried on by local sponsors. Those conversant with the field seem to agree, however, that national spot business is from one-quarter to one-third of the total individual station revenue

[2] This division of business was recommended as a basis for station rates by the Commercial Committee of the National Association of Broadcasters at their Ninth Annual Convention, October 26–28, 1931, in recommending the application of "local" and "general" rates to the two types of business, as is the practice of the American Newspaper Publishers Association. It seems to be followed to an increasing extent, though by no means completely. The word "spot" is trade terminology and not part of the resolution (*Proceedings*, p. 34).

[3] "Spot" announcements and "spot" broadcasting are a trade ambiguity.

derived from other than network sources.[4] That there has been a steady growth of this type of business seems to be indicated by the fact that of 75 stations either interviewed or answering a questionnaire regarding broadcast advertising trends sent them by the writer,[5] 68 per cent reported a steady growth in revenue derived from national advertisers spotting programs over their respective stations during the past several years. Likewise, there is no information existing as to how much of the spot business is comprised of time and other announcements, electrical transcription programs, or live talent broadcasts. The trend regarding the relative importance of these three forms, however, is fairly clear cut. Whereas announcements constituted by far the great preponderance of spot business in 1929, with live talent programs a very poor second, the emphasis has shifted, so that today the electrically transcribed program is the most important part of the spot business, with announcements a fairly strong second, and live talent ranking a rather poor third in spite of its very decided relative growth during the past year.[6]

With the foregoing brief discussion as a general background with respect to the development of broadcast advertising over individual stations, it becomes possible to analyze in greater detail the various elements comprising this type of broadcasting endeavor. Since spot broadcasting is so closely related to the use of national and regional networks as advertising media, it will be considered first; and since electrical transcriptions, in turn, constitute the most important form of spot broadcasting, they likewise will receive precedence in discussion.

In so far as the electrical transcription business is so new, and so little understood, it will be well to discuss its major technical aspects before entering upon any analysis regarding the trend as to its use.

Recorded programs are not new to broadcasting, which, in-

[4] Philip G. Loucks in interview.

[5] The question asked was "To what extent, if any, have national advertisers been spotting programs over your station in recent years? Has this been on the increase or not? Has it been largely transcription or live talent business?" For complete questionnaire see Appendix C, of which this is Question 2 under questions as to "Who Are the Sponsors of Radio Advertising over Your Station?" It was sent to 165 stations mentioned in the Introduction. Stations interviewed by the writer personally were asked the same question.

[6] Howard S. Meighan in interview.

deed, is part of the difficulty involved in securing public appreciation of the nature of the modern electrical transcription. Most of the first programs broadcast were phonograph records, while, following the brief period when volunteer talent filled the anterooms of broadcasting stations, many of the smaller stations were obliged to return to this form of entertainment to a larger degree than probably was desirable. With the elevation of the production of broadcasting programs to a definitely professional level, and the general growth of technical knowledge with regard to the recording of programs—developed jointly through broadcasting, the talking picture, and the orthophonic victrola—there was developed a body of knowledge which made possible the production and recording of programs, especially for broadcasting purposes, far superior to the old-fashioned victrola record; and, which in the case of a good transcription, correctly broadcast, hardly could be discerned from a live talent program except by the most expert ear. This form of program production, introduced in 1929, was seized upon by advertisers as a new and important aid to spot broadcasting.

Technically, an electrically transcribed program differs much less from a live talent broadcast than is commonly supposed. The chief difference is that the one is recorded and then translated into electrical energy and broadcast at a later date, while the live talent program is picked up by the microphone in the studio, turned into electrical impulses, and broadcast immediately. This becomes more clear when the process whereby electrical transcriptions are made is examined in detail, and their characteristics analyzed.

Assuming that a program sponsor or his advertising agency desires to have a number of electrical transcriptions made for use in broadcast advertising, the procedure involved in creating the actual program which they desire will be as follows:[7] The recording of the program will take place in a studio especially constructed for that purpose and acoustically adapted to the production of transcriptions. Two waxes are set on slow speed turntables, similar in principle to that of the ordinary household vic-

[7] Many of the details in the description of making an electrically transcribed program appearing herein have been taken from "Some Practical Facts about Transcription," by J. R. Poppele, chief engineer, Station WOR, published in *Broadcasting*, October 15, 1932. These have been supplemented where necessary with additional data.

trola, the turntables carefully synchronized so as both to revolve at the same rate. Turntables revolving either at the speed of 78 revolutions per minute, the rate of the ordinary victrola (used for shorter programs primarily), or at $33\frac{1}{3}$ revolutions per minute are employed, the trend being toward the latter type of transcription. These waxes record the program simultaneously so that two original records of the performance are later available for use. Following the rehearsals of the program, and when everything is in readiness for recording it, the motor running the turntables, carefully adjusted so as to insure the even revolution of the waxes, is turned on, and the signal is given to begin.

The theme song is played, the opening announcement read, and the program proceeds upon its normal course. The microphones pick up the sound, which is turned into electrical impulses, amplified, and recorded on the waxes. During the recording, one technician watches the volume and the mixing of the sounds picked up by the various microphones used for the different parts of the program, in the same manner as this occurs in the control booth of a broadcasting station. A second technician attends to the amplification, which corresponds to the broadcasting of the program over the station, and the third supervises the room where the waxes themselves are cut.

The cutting of the waxes differs greatly from the days of mechanical reproduction, when the stylus vibrated directly from the sound impulses, and when, as a result, it was either too strongly affected by great volume or too little by soft notes, and missed the higher and lower tones of the scale completely. In the modern transcription, the stylus is electrically impelled by means of the process described above, and thus insures better recording of both tonal range and volume. Evenness of reproduction likewise is secured by the careful regulation of the motor driving the turntables, to an extent not possible under previous methods.

There are two ways of cutting the waxes: the "lateral" and the "vertical" or "hill-and-dale" method. In the case of the former the stylus vibrates from side to side, cutting laterally, and making its imprint on the side walls of the groove. This was the method employed in the phonograph recordings of earlier years, and, until recently, in the great majority of electrically transcribed programs. Today, however, it is being replaced to a considerable degree by the vertically cut recording, which seems to be superior from the viewpoint of both the tonal range and volume that can be secured.

This, then, is the process involved in cutting the waxes. If the program is longer than ten or fifteen minutes, a second set of waxes will be made carrying the latter portion of the program, the shift being timed carefully so as to insure a perfect dovetailing of the two transcriptions.

When the work of transcribing the program is completed, one wax is played back to the interested parties, comprising the transcription company executives, the agency representative, and the program sponsor's own representatives, and the program is edited. The other wax, however, is not played, but goes into an electrical bath where it is plated and a negative made. This negative, which is called the "master," is then used in making two test pressings, manufactured from an earth shellac substance which is heated to a consistency similar to kneaded dough, and following which it is pressed under terrific pressure, still further heated, and baked. These test pressings are then played and approved.

Following the approval of the test pressings, another imprint is made from the master record. This imprint is called the "mother," and from it, in turn, is produced again by electroplating the "stamper" or negative from which the recordings used in broadcasting finally are manufactured. In case any large number of disks are to be produced, more than one stamper is made, the better sound-recording studios definitely limiting the number of pressings made from a given stamper. The original "master" by now has been put carefully away, as an original record of the program.

The transcription is now ready to be sent to the various stations for broadcasting. When this occurs the record is placed on a turntable similar to the one used in recording the program, and is played. However, no microphone picks up the sound waves. Rather, the transcription is immediately translated into the form of electrical impulses, amplified, and broadcast, thus insuring a faithful reproduction of what originally was recorded. In the playing of the transcription, however, the station must exercise considerable care if the best results are to be attained. One of the great difficulties in the early days of electrical tran-

scriptions was that station managers failed to realize the necessity of careful attention to detail in the broadcasting of recorded
programs. To them it was just one more record, no different
from the old victrola record. Often the transcriptions were
played in the wrong order, and even more often without rehears-
al or preliminary inspection, in rooms of any temperature and
under similarly unfavorable conditions. Today the better station will first rehearse the transcription to make certain that the
disk is all right, and the grooves smooth. It will also see to it
that no dust or dirt is on the record, that the turntables are
operating at the correct speed—which is done in part by testing
the notes against those of a piano—that everything is in order
for switching from one disk to the other, and that the room temperature is correct to eliminate the danger of contraction or expansion of the disk and consequent distortion of tone. When
these conditions are observed, and when the original transcription has been made with equal care, it is impossible for any but a
technician to distinguish the transcription from the live talent
program.

The transcription itself, however, should be carefully distinguished from the so-called "dubbed" program, which is a transcription made either from another transcription or more likely
from victrola records, and which is a decidedly inferior product.
The manufacture and distribution of dubbed programs has been
a constant source of annoyance to the reputable transcription
companies, and has affected adversely the public acceptance of
transcriptions as a whole.

Compared to the live talent program of a modern broadcasting station, the electrical transcription possesses the following
characteristics. With regard to tonal range, the vertically cut
transcription can reproduce from 30 to 10,000 cycles, equal to
the best broadcast transmitter, and superior to many; likewise,
far superior to the receiving ability of the average well-constructed modern receiving set with dynamic speaker.[8] The laterally cut $33\frac{1}{3}$ r.p.m. transcription can reproduce tones ranging
from 60 to 6,000 cycles. Compared to this the modern home
phonograph can reproduce from 60 to 5,000 cycles; the average
high-class telephone circuit used in network broadcasting, 50–
8,000 cycles; the ordinary network circuit, 50–5,000 cycles; the

[8] *Radio Retailing*, August, 1931, p. 13.

average modern transmitter, 30–7,500 cycles; and the high-quality modern radio set, 50–5,500 cycles. The volume variation on the best transcriptions also is supposed to be equal to that on network programs.

As to the facilities existing for the broadcasting of electrically transcribed programs, they can be said to include practically all commercial stations of any importance other than the key outlets of the national network companies.[9] The installation of electrical transcription equipment began in 1929 with WOR, Newark, being one of the first stations to announce formally that it was experimenting with this type of business. By May, 1931, approximately 120 stations, or about one-fifth of the stations of the country, were equipped to handle transcription programs.[10] It is especially interesting to note that this included 65 per cent of the stations of 5,000 or more watts in power.

The impossibility of securing conclusive data regarding the amount spent by advertisers for spot broadcasting, and for electrically transcribed programs in particular, has been mentioned previously during the course of this discussion. However, from the experience of station managers and others versed in the transcription business as revealed by questionnaire studies, and by similar means, it is possible to piece together a fairly accurate picture of the trends which have occurred in the field.

Electrical transcriptions first began to be used for advertising purposes to any important degree during the latter half of 1929. During the following year their use increased rapidly, and seemed to reach its peak in 1931. In the course of that season seventy-five commercially sponsored electrical transcription programs were broadcast, representing an increase of 175 per cent over the number of similar programs on the air on January 1, 1930.[11] During the past year the trend, as with all broadcasting, has been more or less uncertain. There is reason to believe that, especially during the latter half of the year, a decline in the electrical transcription business set in, due, in turn, to a number of reasons. Poor management of some of the concerns operating in the field and the eventual failure of one of the leading com-

[9] Howard S. Meighan in interview.

[10] *Present and Impending Applications to Education of Radio and Allied Arts*, National Advisory Council on Radio in Education, p. 42.

[11] *New York Times*, Radio Section, January 24, 1932.

panies in the spring of 1932 were partly contributive to this result. Cut-throat competition by small fly-by-night recorders assisted in the same direction. The most important reason, however, undoubtedly was the general adverse business situation, affecting with especial severity, as it did, the advertising appropriations of the smaller companies, which companies in turn were the principal users of electrical transcriptions.

These general conclusions find confirmation in the experience of the managers of fifty-eight stations scattered throughout the country and representing all classes of power and facilities, as revealed in a questionnaire study made in October, 1932, the answers being as of November of that year.[12] In response to a question as to whether there had been an increase or decrease in their electrical transcription business during the preceding twelve months period, 51.7 per cent stations reported an increase, and 42.8 per cent a decrease.[13] The remaining 5.5 per cent reported no change in the volume of business of this type during the period. Most of the decreases were reported to have taken place during the spring of 1932. It is interesting to compare these results with the replies received from sixty-four stations to a similar question sent out by one investigator in March of the same year.[14] In response to the same question, 64 per cent of the stations reported a growth in electrical transcription business, 49 per cent stating that the rate of increase over the period in question had been rapid. A decrease in the volume of business of this type was reported by 18 per cent of the stations, another 18 per cent stating that there had been no appreciable change.

Much more interesting than the general trend is that evidenced with regard to stations of various classes of power. Thus,

[12] The study referred to is the one mentioned in the Introduction. The list of stations answering the questionnaire are found in the forepart of Appendix A, and the questions in the section of Appendix C entitled "Questions Regarding Electrical Transcriptions." The 58 stations replying constitute an approximate 10 per cent sample of broadcasters equipped to handle this type of business. The results presented above were confirmed in general by the writer's interviews with station executives, not included in the present tabulation.

[13] The question was: Has there been an increase or decrease in your electrical transcription business during the past year? Approximately how much?

[14] Senior Research entitled "The Potentialities of Electrically Transcribed Radio Broadcasting," by Barry Z. Golden, in *Broadcasting*, September 1, 1932.

out of thirteen small stations ranging in power from 100 to 250 watts, all but one of which were non-chain stations, eleven reported increasing revenue from electrically transcribed broadcast advertising programs, and only two stated that their volume of business from this source had declined. Estimated percentages of increase ranged from 10 per cent to 80 per cent for individual stations, with both the median and modal figure being a 20 per cent gain. On the other hand, with regard to thirty stations ranging from 500 to 1000 watts in power, eleven reported increased business in electrical transcriptions, eighteen reported declining business of this type, while one reported no change in volume of revenue from this source. The trend is similarly confused with respect to stations of 5,000 watts and more in power, where seven reported increases, five decreases, and three no change. In the case of the 500–1,000-watt stations increases ranged from 10 per cent to 100 per cent, centering about a mode and median of 20 per cent; while decreases ranged from 10 per cent to 70 per cent with a median of 25 per cent and a mode of 15 per cent. In the high-powered stations the range of increase likewise was from 10 per cent to 100 per cent and the range of decrease was from 20 per cent to 75 per cent, the totals being too small to make possible the striking of averages possessing even the slightest significance.

Though the small number of stations in any one class admittedly makes the preceding data indicative of only the barest trends, and even here open to certain question, the unanimity with respect to the increase in the electrical transcription business of the smaller stations is of especial interest. A number of factors might explain such a trend, among them a shift in the type of program sponsor to smaller retailers and manufacturers; a seeking on the part of the sponsor of the cheapest station over which to broadcast, in terms of cost versus circulation, though not necessarily the station giving the maximum circulation; and finally, the possibility that the electrical transcription sponsor has not been able to get the desired larger stations at the appropriate time. Though any conclusions in this field are conjectures, it seems that the two latter reasons probably explain the situation. The former is quite plausible, while the difficulty of securing larger stations should have been increased during most of the period in question by the lack of enthusiasm, if not always positive discouragement, with which the National Broadcasting Company greeted the broadcasting of electrically transcribed programs over any stations wholly or partially controlled by it, and by a similar result emanating from the Columbia Broadcasting System's control of time on its various member stations.[15] That it was not a case of a shift in type of sponsor will be seen in the following paragraphs. Other than the trend toward increased business on the part of some of the smaller stations, which may or may not have survived the winter, the experience of stations of varying power indicates the same situation as depicted with regard to the field in general.

The trend in the type of concerns sponsoring electrically transcribed programs, as revealed by the replies of the station managers to the question as to whether this business centered principally in local concerns, national advertisers spotting programs on local stations of their own accord, or local dealers advertising national products, also is of interest.[16] In this instance 72.9 per cent of the station managers reported their business to be primarily national accounts placed directly, 8.3 per cent mentioned local sponsorship as most important, while 12.5 per cent stated that their electrical transcription accounts were mostly those of local dealers advertising nationally distributed products. The last-mentioned type of endeavor is usually a co-operative undertaking where the local dealer may stand 50 per cent of the cost, the wholesaler 25 per cent, and the manufacturer 25 per cent, or may purchase the transcriptions from the manufacturer, in addition paying for the broadcasting time itself. There probably are other types of arrangements lying between these two extremes. It is interesting to note in this respect that 20 per cent of the broadcasting stations reporting that their business was made up principally of national advertisers spotting their programs direct also mentioned a trend toward an increasing proportion of transcriptions being placed through the local distributors, either in an attempt to get the local rate for station

[15] *Variety*, April 5, 1932, reports a trend toward the small station, giving as the reason the network domination of affiliated stations.

[16] The question was: Has commercial sponsorship of electrical transcription programs been principally by local concerns, national advertisers spotting programs on local stations of their own accord, or local dealers advertising national products? Has there been any trend in one direction or another in the past year or so? If so what?

time or else to secure dealer co-operation in financing the broadcasts. The latter reason seemed the more important.

An examination of the types of industries represented among the sponsors of electrically transcribed programs does not reveal any marked difference from those employing national networks as advertising media. The principal difference lies in the size of the concern, or of the market to be covered. It is quite true that at times some of the largest concerns in the country have sponsored ambitious programs of electrical transcriptions. Examples of this are the "Chevrolet Chronicles" which made so great a stir in 1931, and the Beechnut Packing Company's "Chandu the Magician" which likewise has experienced almost phenomenal success. Efforts of this type, however, are the exceptions rather than the rule. Most of the large companies employ network advertising, or, if they do use electrical transcriptions, make these subsidiary to their main network effort. Thus for a number of years Philco has used transcriptions either to reach outlying districts, which could not be covered by the regular network broadcasts, or else as a means of special pressure over short periods of time, as in the case of a series of broadcasts over 123 stations for five nights during the week of August 15, 1932, for the purpose of introducing its new model and of conducting a word-building contest which was part of the general sales promotion plan.[17]

More important to the electrical transcription business is the smaller national or regional manufacturer or distributor with too limited resources or too restricted a market to make possible network broadcasting, but who is still a logical prospect for spot advertising. Though no very concrete data are available on this point, it seems, both from an examination of the program sheets of numerous stations and from conversations with executives in the field, that it is this type of concern which constitutes the backbone of the electrically transcribed broadcast advertising program business.

The purposes for which electrical transcriptions are used tend to fall into two general classes. In the majority of cases it is employed instead of a network. Thus out of twenty-seven transcription sponsors who were asked whether they used their spot broadcasting instead of, or supplementary to, network broad-

---

[17] *Broadcast Advertising*, September, 1932, p. 18.

casting, 89 per cent replied that they resorted exclusively to recorded programs.[18] In such cases electrical transcriptions are used in favor of networks for a number of reasons: (1) as stated before, the company's resources may make network broadcasting too expensive an undertaking; (2) because the market for the product or brand in question is concentrated in areas which either cannot be reached by networks or with respect to which the utilization of network facilities would entail too much waste circulation; (3) because of certain seasonal aspects regarding the product advertised which make it advisable to start broadcasting in one part of the country at an earlier date or different season from another, as in the case of tire chains or brake linings; (4) in order to overcome time differences, especially with respect to broadcasts such as children's programs where an hour's difference one way or the other is of utmost consequence;[19] and (5) in order to secure dealer assistance in the financing of the broadcasts, a reason which is equally operative with regard to the supplementary use of electrical transcriptions, but which cannot be relied upon in the case of exclusive use of national networks.

With regard to the 11 per cent of the concerns utilizing electrical transcriptions as supplements to networks, only two reasons were stated: (1) that the use of electrical transcriptions was cheaper in some cases, as a means of reaching certain outlying areas, than the cost of taking the station offered by the network; and (2) to reach certain dead spots in network coverage. It is believed that a third reason, that of using electrical transcriptions as means of special pressure advertising in given areas, will increase. Another factor which may facilitate the increased supplementary use of electrical transcriptions is that now both network companies allow the recording of network broadcasts for additional spotting by electrical transcription direct from their own studios. In the case of the National Broadcasting Company, it is reported, however, that this is allowed only if the re-

---

[18] Barry Golden, *op. cit.*, p. 28.

[19] In a broadcast such as "Just Willie," sponsored by Keds and designed for young boys of about twelve to fourteen years of age, this matter would be of great importance. In the network broadcast in this case, 7:30 was selected as the hour, since it was believed that either earlier or later would miss the market the sponsor wished to reach. Thus 4:30 on the Coast would have been useless. Programs such as "Skippy" face a similar problem. It is possible, also, that programs after eight o'clock at night are much less affected than those at earlier hours.

cording is done by the RCA Victor Company. On the other hand, a reported tendency of the network companies to make concessions as to the number of stations which must be taken by the broadcast advertiser is said by some executives in the field to be the greatest difficulty that electrically transcribed programs face today. However, it is impossible to confirm this with any degree of certainty.

In addition to the general business situation and the type of concern sponsoring electrically transcribed programs, there is another factor of importance in determining the future of the electrical transcription in the broadcasting field. This is the degree to which programs of this sort have won public acceptance. There is no doubt that, at the outset, the public attitude toward electrical transcriptions was unfavorable. The phonograph broadcasts of the early days of radio, the poor handling of the transcribed programs by stations, the inexpert production of transcriptions, and the prevalence of dubbed recordings—all assisted in this direction. Public ignorance of what was meant by the term electrical transcription constituted another difficulty which had to be overcome. To the average mind, this suggested something inferior, "canned" music of a new variety, and, therefore, not as desirable as a first-class live talent broadcast.

Gradually the public opinion shifted from one of distaste to one of nominal acceptance. With the rise of better transcriptions, they began to be preferred to live talent broadcasts of inferior quality, especially over the smaller stations. It is doubtful if the electrical transcription ever will meet with the same public acceptance as the live talent program, since, with respect to the former, the thrill of timeliness is missing. This is still and probably always will be an important factor in radio. However, the fact that "Chandu the Magician," an electrically transcribed program, ranked first in audience mail over station WOR, Newark, during the early fall of 1932, with an average of 8,000 letters a week,[20] and that it achieved sufficiently widespread popularity throughout the entire country to warrant its production in motion-picture form is ample proof that a well-done recording finds public acceptance.

The general conclusions in this respect are confirmed by the testimony of fifty station managers who answered questions

[20] *Broadcast Advertising*, October, 1932, p. 31.

concerning their experience in the matter of public reaction to electrical transcriptions: whether the public was as favorable to them as to live talent broadcasts, and what changes had taken place in the public viewpoint in this field during the past year.[21] Of the entire group 84 per cent responded that the public seemed to accept electrical transcriptions favorably, though 40 per cent of the group were specifically of the opinion that programs of this sort ranked decidedly second in public preference to good live talent broadcasts. It is interesting to note that it was the opinion of 50 per cent of the group that the public attitude had improved over the previous year. Practically all of these gave the improved quality of the transcriptions as the principal reason for the change. Only 10 per cent noted any perceptible public disfavor, as far as recorded programs were concerned, while several small stations were frank in saying that they were preferred to the live talent programs which they themselves could offer. The manager of one small far-western station wrote as follows: "Our experience has shown that electrical transcription programs are rating better than the average live talent programs. There has been a decided increase in favor during the past year. The big drawback is in an adequate supply of electrical transcriptions." In so far as the supply of electrically transcribed programs of high quality which can be bought for local sponsorship or sustaining use is still rather small, this station undoubtedly is facing a problem in securing the supply which it desires. It would be interesting to know how many other small stations are similarly situated.

To what extent does the electrical transcription compete with the network? This is a question which in 1930 and 1931 caused no little concern in network circles, but since then seems to have faded into the background. Though it is stated that it never officially took a position on the question, the attitude of the National Broadcasting Company was decidedly antagonistic to transcriptions when they first appeared on the market. In a public address during the winter of 1930,[22] M. H. Aylesworth,

[21] The question was: What in your experience is the public reaction to electrical transcriptions? Is it as favorable as to live talent programs? Has there been any change in its reaction over the past year or so? If so what? See Appendix C for full list of questions in this field.

[22] *Broadcast Advertising*, December, 1930, p. 7.

president of the National Broadcasting Company, asserted in
no uncertain terms that "If radio is to become a self-winding
phonograph, it would be better to discard radio entirely and go
back to phonographs and records, than to waste the all too few
wave lengths available for living speakers."

Later, concessions seem to have been made in this attitude.
In May, 1932, when the National Broadcasting Company assumed control of station WMAQ, Chicago, the electrical transcription business running on that station was retained. In August of that year "Philco Frolickers," an electrically transcribed
program, was booked for a number of NBC Pacific Coast outlets. Moreover, it was reported in September that the S. S.
Kresge Company had arranged for a series of thirteen electrical
transcription broadcasts over station WGY, Schenectady.[23] Finally, there has come the announcement by the RCA Victor
Company of a new transmitter turntable, which, the advertisement states, was "developed for the National Broadcasting
Company" and was "ordered by them for all the stations which
they operate."[24] It seems therefore that this network, at least,
has accepted the electrical transcription as an important and
permanent part of the broadcast advertising structure. The
Columbia Broadcasting System has always been noncommittal
on the subject of transcriptions, and its attitude therefore has
not presented the same problem as has that of the other network.

The rise of the electrically transcribed program also raised
important problems for the Federal Radio Commission in the
field of program regulation. The new form of program production certainly was not the usual phonograph record; neither was
it a live talent program. The question therefore was as to what
it should be called, and how it should be announced over the air.
Therefore, in its *Third Annual Report* the Commission went to
considerable lengths to say that, though some announcement
should be made to the extent that the program broadcast was
not a live talent production, the Commission did not "feel called
upon to provide stations with an exact form of announcement."
It was stated that it realized that great ingenuity was being exercised in the preparation of these programs, and placed the bur-

[23] *Variety*, September 6, 1932, p. 44.

[24] Advertisement appearing on the back cover of *Broadcasting*, January 15, 1933.

den squarely upon the individual station "of so announcing such programs that no one can possibly be deceived or led to think that they represent an actual rendition by present artists."[25] Shortly afterward the commissioners came to believe that a set form of announcement was necessary after all. Accordingly, General Order 78 was promulgated, requiring the announcement that "This program is an electrical transcription made exclusively for broadcast purposes."[26] In the early part of 1932 this requirement was made less severe by allowing it to be announced in other than the stereotyped form, which, during the intervening period, had become extremely unpleasant to hear over the radio.[27] However, in June of that year, the order again was made more severe and Rule 176 of the Commission was revised to read "The exact form of announcement is not prescribed, but the language shall be clear and in terms commonly used and understood."[28]

Because of their importance in the total field of spot broadcasting, electrical transcriptions have been discussed at some length. However, there are two other forms of spot broadcasting: the so-called spot announcement and the live talent spot program. Though the spot announcement has declined greatly in relative importance in the field of spot broadcast advertising, it nevertheless still constitutes an important part of the total business placed over individual stations by national or regional distributors. Its use has been confined primarily to the distributors of convenience goods such as Rem and Pertussin—both of whom use weather reports—several brands of radio glycerine and other anti-freezes, which likewise sponsor weather and temperature reports; or to articles, such as watches, where there is a natural tie-in between the product and the subject matter of the announcement. One of the most successful users of this latter form of spot announcement has been the makers of Bulova watches. Another use of spot announcements is where a new model of a specialty good such as a radio or automobile is being introduced, and where added pressure is being applied either throughout the country as a whole or in certain special terri-

[25] *Third Annual Report of the Federal Radio Commission* (1929), p. 18.
[26] *Fourth Annual Report of the Federal Radio Commission* (1930), p. 12.
[27] *National Association of Broadcasters News Bulletin*, April 23, 1932, p. 3.
[28] *Broadcasting*, June 1, 1932, p. 12.

tories. Likewise, spot announcements are employed by a number of companies to whom a talent program of any sort would constitute too great an expense. This is more true, however, of the local spot announcement than of the nationally sponsored one discussed here.

Spot broadcasting by means of live talent programs is a comparatively new development. As to its period of origin, however, it antedates the electrical transcription, though it did not grow to any extent until the latter half of 1931 and thereafter. Since then there has been a marked trend in this direction, so that, though live talent spot business still constitutes a negligible proportion of total spot broadcasting, its relative development has been rapid. This growth has been confined largely, though not exclusively, to the more powerful and better-equipped stations such as WLW, Cincinnati; WTAM, Cleveland; WBT, Charlotte; and WOR, Newark. Stations WJR, Detroit, and WCAU, Philadelphia, also report increased inquiries in this direction, while a large number of the radio executives of advertising agencies have mentioned local station programs available for sponsorship as being one of the items of information desired from the individual broadcasters soliciting agency business. This information probably is of value to the agency as a source not only of potential spot talent but of numbers which can be bought cheaply and built into programs of national proportions.

The users of live talent spot broadcasting are primarily the following groups: (1) national advertisers who wish to supplement their network programs in a weak city or territory, or to put on additional pressure in a given district; (2) regional companies distributing their product largely in a few metropolitan centers or restricted to limited areas which can be covered with a few high-powered stations;[29] and (3) national advertisers instituting a test campaign of the effectiveness of broadcasting as an advertising medium, of a particular type of program, or of a new product or package which they wish later to distribute nationally. The programs sponsored are usually local ones which have achieved success over the station and which have already won an audience for themselves. A recent example of this

[29] Thus the more important markets in Ohio might be covered, for instance, by WLW, Cincinnati, and WTAM, Cleveland, both 50,000-watt stations.

type of program is a series of live talent spot programs broadcast by the manufacturers of Pebeco Toothpaste over a group of ten stations, the program being different in the case of each station.

It is quite probably true that, in spite of its recent rapid growth, live talent spot broadcasting will continue to be highly restricted in volume for some time to come. In the first place, the number of stations possessing the requisite facilities for handling such programs is still limited—not always, however, to broadcasters with high-wattage transmitters. Moreover, the cost of a series of live talent programs over any large number of stations tends to mount rapidly because of the necessarily heavy total expenditures for talent. Finally, the cost of production and servicing such a program series tends to be high from the agency viewpoint, while the details of building a series of live talent broadcasts are exceptionally trying in many instances. In spite of these limitations and a small total volume, live talent spot programs should continue to increase in importance, especially as they relate to broadcast advertising in metropolitan centers where program, station, and agency facilities are at their best.

The final question which remains is as to the future of spot broadcasting as a whole. Because of the many conflicting trends in broadcast advertising, a conclusive answer is impossible. In the long run, spot broadcasting *should* show continued growth, since it is doubtful whether it has been employed as yet by all the concerns who profitably could use it.

One interesting development in the spot broadcasting field has been the formation of a special spot broadcasting service by both national network companies for the purpose of soliciting this type of business for the stations owned or financially controlled by them. In September, 1932, the opening of the National Broadcasting Company Local Service Bureau was announced. This bureau was designed to represent seventeen stations in the spot broadcasting field, including those owned or controlled by NBC, the Westinghouse owned stations, and WGY, Schenectady, owned by the General Electric Company. In January of the following year the Columbia Broadcasting System announced the establishment of Radio Sales, Inc.,[30] to fill a similar

---

[30] *Broadcasting*, January 15, 1933, p. 6.

capacity with respect to the Columbia owned and controlled stations. The formation of these subsidiaries, the solicitation of electrical transcription business on National Broadcasting Company owned and controlled stations, and the rumored increase in split-network concessions by the network companies—all seem to indicate a recognition of the importance of spot broadcasting on the part of these organizations, especially in view of the declining rate of increase in the growth of broadcast advertising, as a whole, experienced during the 1932 season. This concern on the part of the network is further accentuated by the fact that they seem to have found it necessary to secure spot business for their owned and controlled outlets, if these stations are to be made to pay. It will be especially interesting to see what effect this development will have upon the future structure of both network and spot broadcasting.

CHAPTER VIII

MIDDLEMEN AVAILABLE FOR SPOT BROADCASTING[1]

The rise of spot broadcasting brought with it some new and perplexing problems for the company employing this form of broadcast advertising as well as for the agency servicing its account. With the purchase of time from a large number of individual stations rather than on the basis of a complete network group, and with the ultimate broadcasting of the program on the same basis, questions arose regarding procedure and available structure which, prior to that time, had not occurred to anyone. The problem arose as to which station to use in a given territory. Was that station available at the time and for the period desired, and was its rate reasonable for the listener circulation which it commanded? Where and how could information be secured regarding available stations and hours on individual stations, and how could the great number of these be contacted most efficiently? Where could talent be secured, now that complete reliance no longer could be placed upon the network program departments? Moreover, what type of program should be produced and who should be secured to produce it? The solution of these, and similar trying problems, necessitated the development of an entirely different structure from that employed in national network broadcasting. The present discussion will, therefore, center about the nature and operation of this structure.

In addition to the individual stations, previously analyzed in considerable detail, the spot broadcasting structure of today includes the following elements: (1) the time broker; (2) the electrical transcription company; (3) the so-called spot specialist; and (4) the special station representative. All of these agencies

[1] Philip G. Loucks, managing director of the National Association of Broadcasters, Fred W. Gamble, executive secretary of the American Association of Advertising Agencies, Howard S. Meighan, of Scott Howe Bowen, Inc., and William Rambeau, special station representative, have helped materially in securing the information necessary for the present chapter.

exist to a greater or less degree, for the purpose of producing the spot program itself and of acting as a contact between the station and the program sponsor or advertising agency. The structure itself is so new, and the line of demarcation between the various elements so vague, that it is impossible to attribute a special function to any one of the organizations mentioned above, except to state that, for the most part, the middleman function of assisting in the smooth flow of broadcast advertising business from agency to station is the most important phase of their activity.

Because of this confused situation, the best approach to an investigation of the middlemen available for spot broadcasting will be an historical one, wherein each agency will be treated in the order in which it developed. Since the time broker was the first spot middleman on the field, his service will be the first to be considered.

The early time broker arose out of the dual need of the agency to secure information and possess a point of contact with the various stations scattered throughout the country, and of the stations to have a means whereby they, in turn, could contact the agency. Thus the time broker fulfilled two important rôles. It was he who secured station information for the agency regarding matters such as rates, station facilities, reputed listener circulation, available hours during the week, contract terms, and similar items. In the second place, he actively solicited business for individual stations from the agencies, and called the attention of the radio executives to the advantages that were to be derived from broadcasting over the stations which he represented. Moreover, because of the relative inexperience of the agencies in the production of broadcast advertising programs and in the servicing of the actual broadcasts of these programs, the time broker tended to assume additional functions. He became a source of program advice, a medium through whom talent could be secured, and at times almost usurped the entire function of an agency radio department. Sometimes he fulfilled these various duties in a most satisfactory manner, and many times he did not.

At that time the industry was in a raw and disorganized state. The multiplicity of functions which developed upon the time broker in the years of 1929 and 1930 opened his position to the possibility of serious abuses, which, indeed, did not take long in springing up. The agency itself was still so much of a newcomer in the field of broadcast advertising that very few, except the organizations which had pioneered in the radio field, knew when the broker was rendering satisfactory service and when he was not. Moreover, the question of broker and agency commissions soon arose and came to constitute one of the most difficult problems of commercial practice in the spot broadcasting field. Under the prevailing practice in this country, the advertising agency receives from the medium in which it places the advertising a commission of 15 per cent, which constitutes its principal revenue. In the case of spot broadcasting, both the agency and the time broker received a commission equaling this amount. This, of course, raised the cost of spot broadcast advertising to the agency's client, which the agency was forced to explain. Many agencies objected strenuously to this increased cost of doing business, especially when their own program and time-buying departments began to function satisfactorily and when costly experience revealed to them some of the inadequacies of the less reputable time brokers.

Had the industry been well organized and the function and activities of the time broker fairly standardized, it is doubtful whether much objection would have been raised to the double commission. The great source of difficulty lay in the fact that the conditions which made necessary the double commission also made possible serious abuses of the time broker's relationship to the station and agency. Business was very difficult to secure, especially for the small local station situated far from the more important centers of trade. Moreover, even with respect to the larger stations, the problem of a large overhead expense loomed continually before the manager's eyes. Consequently there often was a great temptation to secure business at any cost. The station card rates were observed only when special concessions were not necessary to secure the business. This situation still exists to a sufficient extent to imperil seriously the economic stability of the industry.

More important, however, was the fact that, because of the loose relations existing between the time broker and the station, the former at times charged any amount he could secure for the station time, and after paying the station the agreed amount, appropriated the remainder for his own use. In addition, 15 per cent was by no means the uniform time-broker commission. Indeed, it often mounted to 25 per cent and even 50 per cent. It should be noted in this respect that, in the small country newspaper field, a commission of 50 per cent to the newspaper representative is not uncommon, it is said. In some instances the broker even went so far as to attempt to charge a commission from both the agency and the station. This did not last long, though all types of split commission arrangements undoubtedly were tolerated.

Quantitatively, unethical practices of the type mentioned probably were indulged in by a very small portion of time brokers, but they served to make the time broker as a class extremely unpopular with all advertising agencies. In fact, they were not much more welcome among the progressive broadcasting stations. This feeling of dissatisfaction was further increased when the failure of several time brokers precipitated a serious credit problem. The agency had paid the time broker for the station facilities, but had contracted with the station itself for the time. The time broker now failed, and the station remained unpaid. There now arose the question as to who should be held liable for the time costs of the broadcasts and as to what constituted the specific financial responsibility of each party. The net result of this situation was that the agencies tended to place more and more spot business directly with stations, the larger stations soliciting directly where possible, though this was somewhat limited; so the business of the time broker declined considerably. This tendency was given additional impetus by the rise of some of the other elements in the spot broadcasting structure during the year 1931.

Though the time broker, as a class, deserved at least some of the criticism which was leveled at him during the years of 1930 and 1931, it is true that he fulfilled a definite and necessary function in the spot broadcasting field. He served to bring together the station and the agency. At the time he was in the ascendancy, neither were capable of doing this by themselves. Likewise, his lesser functions arose out of the necessity of their being delegated to someone. This does not excuse the lax practices which were indulged in by some of the brokers; though what has aptly been termed "chiseling" is always most prevalent where an industry is in a chaotic and formative period, as was spot broadcasting at that time. It should also be noted that, even though the time broker is no longer as important as he was in the early days of spot broadcasting, problems such as uniform station rates, with which he was largely blamed, still exist to a disquieting degree.

Following the time broker, who originated when spot broadcasting was confined almost exclusively to spot announcements and a very little live talent business, the next element to develop in the spot broadcasting structure was the electric transcription company. When this agency first came into any prominence in the early part of 1930, it confined its activities exclusively to the preparation and sale of electrically transcribed programs. It was soon discovered, however, that this was not enough. Unless some means existed for servicing the program, and for assisting the agency in contacting the stations over which the transcriptions were to be broadcast, there was little hope of developing the electrical transcription business to any great proportions. As a result, in the case of the World Broadcasting System, the problems of selling the transcription, contacting the agencies, servicing the accounts, developing station relations, and similar matters were relegated to the company proper, while a subsidiary, Sound Studios, was formed for the purpose of actually recording the programs. Thus the transcription company came to take over many of the functions of the time broker and to execute them with greater efficiency than usually had been the case on the part of the former middleman.

While the transcription company was usurping part of the field previously served by the time broker, and the agency itself was appropriating another segment, at least one of the pioneers in the field was developing a new type of integrated spot broadcast advertising service, which might be given the name of "spot specialist." The Scott Howe Bowen organization of today constitutes an interesting example of this form of middleman. It takes care of the selection and securing of stations for the advertiser. It also is equipped to undertake production and servicing of spot announcements, live talent broadcasts, or electrical transcriptions, possessing its own subsidiary company for the latter purpose. Recently it has entered the special representative field, acting in this capacity for the Yankee Network and a number of stations. An organization of this type, therefore, is capable of rendering complete spot service to an agency or program sponsor, and is especially well equipped to fulfil the functions attendant to spot broadcasting.

A new development during the past year has been the trend toward the special representative. This had been tried previously, but, largely due to a misunderstanding of what was involved in the situation, the attempt failed. During the summer of 1932 a number of special representatives entered the field, thus constituting a new and interesting type of spot broadcasting middleman. The theory underlying the special station representative is the same as that of the newspaper representative. Few periodicals can support an exclusive representative or maintain their own office in the advertising centers of the country, from which the space buyers of the agency can be approached. Consequently, an individual or organization is appointed as that periodical's special representative in the territory in question. His task then is to secure as much business as possible for his periodical and he usually is paid a certain percentage on all business secured by his paper from companies located in the territory wherein he represents it. The arrangement is a logical one, and, since the question of station representation is a very similar one, there are sound reasons for the entrance of the new middleman. Moreover, the step seems to have the sympathy of the advertising agencies, which should be of material assistance, in the long run.

The position of the special station representative is not as simple as it appears at first glance. The production and execution of a spot broadcasting program is a more complicated problem than the production of a printed advertisement and the sending of the mat to the local newspaper. Though stations are bought separately, they are planned in groups to an even larger extent than probably are newspapers, because of the technical aspects of station coverage. In addition, the program must be produced and its broadcasting serviced. In case the program is an electrical transcription, a company operating in that field is in a position to render most of the services of the special station representative without recourse to him. Moreover, because of the close relations it has built up with large numbers of stations, it may be in a better position to secure the desired time over the entire area in question, thus partially relieving the agency of this burden. The same advantages rest with the spot specialist. Consequently the special representative faces severe competition from the larger and more important middleman organization in the field.

To this is added the difficulty of compensation. During the summer of 1932, commission was paid only on programs actually secured, rather than on all business originating in the territory. Under this form of financial arrangement, the situation may arise where the station representative has expended a great deal of effort in an attempt to secure a certain account, but has failed in achieving his purpose. However, as a result of his activities the company in question later reconsiders its decision and contracts for time directly with the station. Since the business has not been placed through him, the station representative receives no compensation for the program, even though he has been largely responsible for the station getting the business. Because of the possibility of contingencies of this sort, an arrangement providing for compensation to the station representative on all business originating in his territory is the more desirable. This is true in spite of the fact that, under it, a mediocre representative may be unduly compensated for business which he has done little to secure.

Another factor which seriously threatens the future development of the station representative is the so-called associated group plan, sponsored in recent months by Scott Howe Bowen, Inc. Under the plan certain of the stations represented by this company have agreed to sell their time to program sponsors at the same rate as is charged for their facilities by the national network with which they are respectively affiliated. The plan is to be operative only in case that time is contracted for on at least ten stations. Since the network charge for a given station is considerably lower than the station's own card rate, the associated group plan presents the possibility of important savings to the spot broadcaster. It also increases the ability of spot broadcasting to compete successfully with the national networks.

What will be the future of spot broadcasting structure is almost impossible to say. The conflicting tendencies in the field are such as to afford little opportunity even for speculation. Several tendencies seem to be fairly certain. One of these is that the advertising agency will continue to take an increasing part in the preparation and execution of broadcast advertising. A second conclusion is that, as long as spot broadcasting exists, the functions originally performed by the time broker will have to be carried on by some form of organization. Whether this organization will be an integrated one, such as the World Broadcasting System or Scott Howe Bowen, Inc., or whether the special station representative will play an important part in the ultimate middleman structure, is difficult to say. A trend toward integration is to be noted both in the establishment of the associated group plan and in the setting up of spot broadcasting services by the two national networks for the stations owned or controlled by them.

Another interesting possibility which has been suggested is the formation of a co-operative group of stations which would sell time through a central office, engaged in joint promotional effort, and maintain a co-operative source of talent and program material. In brief, they would function much in the same manner as does the "Hundred Thousand Group" in the periodical field, except that, in the case of the radio stations, the scope would be widened to permit an effective adaptation of the organization to the complicated problems of spot broadcast advertising. This suggestion is very similar to the one made regarding a co-operatively owned and operated national network. Indeed, the two ideas are not antagonistic and it may be possible to incorporate both of them into the same general plan. Whether either of them will turn out to be practical, or whether they are merely visionary, only the future can tell. They constitute an interesting possibility, and one which the student of broadcasting will do well to consider seriously before rejecting entirely.

In addition to the problems of structure originating out of the rise of spot broadcasting, new questions of commercial practice have also come into existence. A number of these, such as the question of time broker, already have been discussed in sufficient detail. Others demand additional consideration, if the problems of commercial practice in the spot broadcasting field are to be appreciated.

One of the most important questions facing the broadcasting stations of the country at the present time is the maintenance of published card rates. The practice of accepting business at less than the published time charge originated in the early days of spot broadcasting. Its evils were accentuated by the general laxity which characterized the relations between broadcasting station and time broker. The greater clarification of the middleman problem of the industry, however, has not lessened the station rate problem to any appreciable extent. Many small stations are faced with declining local business due to the protracted business depression, and are willing to accept accounts at any rate which the sponsor is willing to pay. A number of large stations are beginning to find it very difficult to secure the volume of business necessary to meet the operating costs entailed by high power. As a result there is a widespread tendency to accept business at less than the card rate, in spite of the fact that the card rate, itself, may be so low as to provide no more than a fair margin of return over and above station expenses. The introduction of a price-cutting element of this sort into broadcast advertising is a step which imperils the stability of the entire industry. Not only does it adversely affect station revenue, but it also increases the temptation on the part of the station to make up its lost advertising volume by accepting business of lower quality and of doubtful public interest. Unfortunately, the problem is one with regard to which effective joint action is extremely difficult. However, it is earnestly hoped that something will be done to meet the situation before too much damage has been wrought.

Within recent months several new variations of price-cutting have entered the broadcast advertising field. One of these is the rendering of excessive merchandising service on the part of the station. In this case the station will assist the agency or program sponsor in contacting dealers in the territory, setting up displays, making reports on the progress of sales in the district during the broadcast advertising campaign, and will perform numerous other functions entailing considerable expense belonging logically to the company or its advertising agency. The excessive furnishing of free service of this type constitutes a form of price-cutting just as much as does the acceptance of business at less than the published card rate.

Another form of business which is raising a serious problem of rate charges, especially among the smaller stations, is the rise of the so-called payment "per inquiry" or by granting "commission." Under the former method the station is paid a flat rate per inquiry received and forwarded to the advertiser. The latter method provides for payment of the station by means of a commission of a specified amount on each unit of goods sold by it.

An example of the "per inquiry" method is found in the offer of one advertising agency to pay the broadcasting station ten cents for each inquiry received regarding a fat-reducing tea, whose sale the agency is promoting. The letter addressed to the station says in part: "You know your station—we don't. If you have faith in your ability to produce inquiries, we are ready to go ahead with you on the above-mentioned basis. If you haven't faith in your station, then, of course, we could not be expected to have either! That's putting it up to you 'cold turkey,' but we prefer to deal on an open and above-board basis."[2] Another concern[3] writes the station that it has been "fortunate" enough to be able to sign up a company for "a large amount of broadcast-advertising." It states that the advertiser carries regular schedules with "important publications," but asks the stations to read wordy announcements free, except that "this account pays your station 15c net per inquiry." In this manner, not only is the station card rate completely nullified, but the station and not the advertiser is forced to bear the brunt of poorly constructed announcements, badly conceived sales programs, and products of doubtful value.

The commission method of station payment has the effect of putting the broadcaster into the retailing business. Thus one advertiser offers a magic water[4] which is "the most effective in the correction of constipation and most of all, kidney, liver, stomach and bladder disorders" as well as other diseases "resulting from bad blood and faulty elimination." The product costs one dollar a pound, "allowing your station 28c net." Similar propositions have been presented to stations to secure their co-operation in the sale of books, guitar lessons at one dollar with a money back guaranty, as well as various patent medicines. Not only is the method of payment economically unjusti-

[2] *Broadcasters' News Bulletin*, National Association of Broadcasters, February 11, 1933.

[3] *Ibid.*, February 11, 1933.   [4] *Ibid.*, February 11, 1933.

fiable, but the questionable value of many of the products which companies are attempting to sell in this fashion raises a serious problem of public interest. Should any large number of stations accept business of this order, it might become necessary to enforce stringent regulations in this field.

Another problem which arose early in 1930 was the question of whether commission should be paid on talent. This problem was debated at length at the National Association of Broadcasters' Convention[5] of that year. This is a much more important consideration in broadcast advertising than is the corresponding problem of commission on art work, engravings, and similar items in the case of printed advertising. In the case of talent, the cost per program averages from 25 per cent to 50 per cent of the time charge, and sometimes even exceeds it. Art and production charges in the periodical field, on the other hand, seldom exceed from 5 per cent to 10 per cent of the cost of the space. At the National Association of Broadcasters' Convention the sentiment was mostly in favor of granting 15 per cent commission on talent furnished by the station, provided that the agency had done something to earn the commission by preparing the program and rehearsing the talent. The question was largely settled in the negative in the early part of 1931, when the American Association of Advertising Agencies declined the offer of one of the national networks to grant a 15 per cent commission on talent secured through it.[6]

This decision was reached because many of the agencies believed that a commission on talent, though justifiable in theory, was open to much abuse. If anything in the nature of standardized rates had been possible in the talent field, the question might have been decided differently. The cost of talent is subject to individual bidding, and there is such a wide fluctuation in charges, that it was believed a commission on such a variable would have harmed the agency more than it would have helped it.

The preceding have been but a few of the problems of commercial practice which face the broadcasting industry today. A satisfactory solution still remains to be worked out with regard

[5] *Proceedings, Eighth Annual Convention*, National Association of Broadcasters, pp. 45–50.

[6] Mr. F. W. Gamble, in interview.

to the question of agency recognition and the payment of commissions only to agencies and organizations which have been accorded recognition. The problem of the establishment of a bureau of credit information is a pressing one, in order that the annual losses suffered by stations and agencies in the spot broadcasting field may be materially reduced. There is a great need for the development of standard station accounting so that executives in the field may know what are the real costs of station operation. The development and adoption of scientific bases for the measurement of station coverage and popularity, and of standard promotional practice by the industry, is another highly important problem remaining to be solved. These and numerous minor questions require a joint attack on the part of the broadcasting industry as a whole in the near future, if it is to continue to progress in the future.

In addition to problems of commercial practice within the industry itself, several important questions face broadcasting from outside its own borders. The most pressing of these is the urgent necessity of effecting an economically justifiable arrangement with the American Society of Composers, Authors, and Publishers regarding the fees to be paid for the privilege of broadcasting music controlled by that organization. Since this includes a great deal of the broadcasting repertory, the problem is a very serious one. In so far as the question is outside the main scope of the present investigation, and because the bitter controversy of recent months has tended to confuse the issue very greatly, no attempt will be made to discuss the details of the problem at this time. However, it is difficult to see how the broadcasters can be expected to pay a threefold increase in music fees; these fees, in turn, being levied on the basis of a percentage of gross station revenue, regardless of whether the programs in question contain any music, or whether they are confined to talks and dramatic presentations. The only exception made to date has been the exclusion of the political broadcasts of the presidential campaign, from the operation of the copyright fee. Not only is the basis for their collection economically unjustifiable, but, in view of the present condition of the broadcasting industry, it is questionable whether a substantial number of stations could successfully bear the additional expense.

Important problems also exist in the legislative field, which, though they relate largely to taxation and station regulation, indirectly affect the matter of broadcast advertising. Broadcasting is a new, dramatic, and potent influence in the community. Its introduction has raised many perplexing problems in the legal and government fields, as well as economically and socially. Consequently there has been a great temptation to legislate on the matter, and the number of bills introduced with respect to radio is tending to mount annually. This is all the more the case, now that state legislatures are joining Congress in their interest in broadcasting. Undoubtedly some of the legislation has been well conceived and highly beneficial. Other enactments have had less to recommend them. Because of the comparatively inadequate knowledge of legislators and public alike regarding the problems of radio broadcasting, as well as by reason of the efforts of certain special interests to turn radio legislation to their own advantage, this aspect of broadcasting must be followed with great care by the industry for some time to come.

CHAPTER IX

THE USE OF RADIO BROADCASTING IN LOCAL ADVERTISING

Radio broadcasting has always been closely allied with local retail advertising endeavor. Indeed, most of the small stations that grew up like mushrooms during the first years of broadcasting were in the nature of advertising ventures. Manufacturers and retailers saw in this new invention a means of attracting public attention and establishing goodwill for their own products and institutions. The operation of the broadcasting station of 1922 and 1923 was a relatively inexpensive matter, while the publicity value derived therefrom was great. This value was confined principally to the community and its environs in spite of the fan mail which was received from far and wide.

It was this publicity and goodwill value arising out of the ownership of a broadcasting station which later caused L. Bamberger and Company, Newark department store, and owners of WOR, to estimate the publicity value of their station during the period 1924–28 at $1,000,000, a figure more than double the cost of its operation.[1] Since the transfer of the ownership of the store to R. H. Macy and Company, the station has produced sufficient sales results to impel the present management to spend 10 per cent of the store's "space" dollar appropriation for radio broadcasting.[2]

In 1923, a total of 180 of the 573 stations were owned and operated either by electrical shops or radio stores, comprising 31.4 per cent of all of the stations in operation. In the same year 22 department stores and dry goods establishments were among the owners of broadcasting stations.[3] Other similar establishments owning stations in these early years included music shops, garages, banks, theaters and amusements, newspapers, together

[1] *The Use of Radio in Sales Promotion*, by Edgar Felix (McGraw-Hill), p. 16.

[2] "Making Retail Radio Advertising Produce," by Kenneth Collins, executive vice-president, R. H. Macy & Co., Inc., in *Broadcasting*, October 15, 1932, p. 5.

[3] *Commercial and Government Radio Stations of the United States* (1923).

173

with a large number of stations operated under the names of the individual owners, many of whom are certain to have been associated with retail distributive enterprises in their own localities. Indeed, other than churches and schools, this seemed to be the only form of station ownership.

The early rush of retail distributors into the field of radio broadcasting, however, was short-lived. By 1925 the number of electrical and radio stores operating stations had decreased to half the figure of two years previous, while other types of retail ownership also were declining. In the meantime the broadcasting company, devoted exclusively to this business, was coming into the ascendancy. By 1932, electrical- and radio-shop ownership of stations had decreased to 46, while the number of department stores and dry goods establishments owning broadcasting stations had declined from 22 to 10 establishments. For the time being at least, the use of radio broadcasting in local advertising was forced into the background by its development as a national medium.

The slow growth of the local aspects of broadcast advertising was due to a number of reasons. The small shops originally setting up the low-powered stations of the early days[4] were unable to meet the financial requirements of larger stations and more ambitious programs. The larger stores themselves showed little or no appreciation of the potentialities of the new medium, and, as a result, either paid scant attention to it or abandoned it entirely. On the other hand, department-store stations such as WOR, Newark, and WNAC, Boston, became community institutions. The former station broadcast the New York Philharmonic Symphony Orchestra for several years prior to the taking over of that program by the Columbia Broadcasting System. It pioneered in various kinds of programs, such as the "Choir Invisible," broadcast every Sunday night in the interests of *Charm*, the Bamberger house organ. Finally it took an active part in all community events, so that the station created for itself a personality in keeping with that part of its identification announcement which stated that it was owned and operated by "one of America's fine stores, located in Newark, N.J." The story of

[4] A power of 25 or 50 watts was relatively high in 1922, while 100 watts corresponded to the high-power station of today.

WNAC, Boston, owned by the Shepard store of that city, is similar to Bamberger's.

With regard to the failure of the small retailer to enter upon a program of broadcast advertising over local stations, a number of reasons have been operative. The most important of these have been the limited financial resources of the average retailer; his relative lack of merchandising ability and consequent conservatism as compared to the national distributor; and, finally, the misuse which many retailers made of the broadcasting which they did carry on. Regarding the last of these reasons the situation is summed up by Mr. Collins as follows:

Radio advertising has failed to produce for most retailers. That's not the fault of the medium. It's because of the stupidity of the retailers. Stores have repeatedly bought radio time with no notion what they could do with it and have put on different broadcasts for a period of a few weeks or months— and then, failing to get their money's worth, have loudly complained about the deficiencies of this form of advertising.[5]

This situation is not surprising. Retail advertisers, except in the larger centers, have always been relatively unskilled in the art of presenting their sales messages. Broadcast advertising, in turn, is vastly more complicated than is newspaper advertising, and, though it pays high rewards to the enterprising and skilful advertiser, it, in all probability, penalizes severely the mediocre presentation. Finally, the retailer who did summon up the courage to attempt broadcasting had little in the way of a model to copy, while the station, in many cases, could not offer much constructive assistance.

Despite these early handicaps, it is quite probable that the local use of radio broadcasting for advertising purposes by the retailers of the community and small local manufacturers constituted the backbone of more than one station's revenue and comprised an important part of the total expenditure for broadcast advertising. Many stations literally were kept alive by the short spot announcements read between phonograph records during the morning and afternoon periods reserved for this type of broadcast, and for which rates from two dollars and up were charged for each piece of copy.

Though it is impossible to present any statistical data on the subject, it seems fairly certain that there has been a steady

[5] Kenneth Collins, *op. cit.*

growth in the use of radio broadcasting by local advertisers during the past several years. It is equally probable that there has been an actual decline in this type of business during the current season, due to the generally adverse business conditions. Station managers seem to agree that the most important growth in local broadcast advertising has come since 1928 or 1929, and that the reasons for this development lie chiefly in the following factors: (1) the local retailer, having seen the success attained by the national broadcast advertiser, decided to follow the latter's example and at least try the new medium; (2) the satisfactory results attained by the local pioneers in broadcast advertising caused their colleagues and competitors to emulate them; and (3) stations were beginning to offer intelligent broadcasting service to the retailer, both with respect to program service and the actual broadcasting of the sponsor's presentation. From the estimated total broadcast advertising expenditures for the year 1931[6] it seems reasonable to assume that local advertisers spent in excess of $15,000,000 for radio broadcasting during that period.

In connection with the analysis of the trend regarding local broadcast advertising, it is interesting to note the replies of the managers of 30 network stations to the question as to whether their local or chain business had increased most rapidly during the past four or five years.[7] Of the number mentioned, 15 reported a greater increase in local than in network business; 13 indicated the opposite situation to pertain to their station, while 2 stations stated that they did not encourage local business. Of the 13 stations reporting a relatively greater network growth, 5 had been on the chain for less than two years, and in all probability were just beginning to receive their normal proportion of business of this type. It may be that, because of the wording of the question, a certain amount of national spot business was included in the estimates of various managers. However, the answers as to why the local business had increased more rapidly than network advertising seem to indicate this factor to be of relatively small importance. In this respect, the fifteen station

[6] See chap. vi.

[7] The question was: In your opinion or experience, has your local or chain business increased the most rapidly during the past four or five years? What reasons do you believe explain this trend? See Appendix C for other questions.

managers reporting increased local business were practically unanimous in attributing this trend to the following reasons: (1) that broadcast advertising was beginning to attract the better types of local business; (2) that local retailers as a whole were beginning to copy national advertisers; (3) that their own improved facilities made broadcast advertising more attractive to the prospective program sponsor; and (4) that it was vitally necessary for the station to secure local as well as national business.

Though it is impossible to make any detailed tabulations regarding the proportion of various types of local business employing radio broadcasting as an advertising medium, an examination of the sponsor lists of a group of the stations supplying detailed information on this subject indicates the following to be the most important types of local sponsors: (1) local department stores—reported by almost every station; (2) specialty shops, especially those selling shoes, clothing, jewelry, and furs; (3) other larger retail establishments including restaurants, hotels, and a few banks and brokerage houses; (4) local manufacturer-distributors such as bakeries, meat producers, ice companies, lumber dealers, dairies, public utilities, and wholesale-grocery establishments distributing their own brands; and (5) local distributors of nationally advertised products such as refrigerators and automobiles placing their own programs either in co-operation with the manufacturer or completely on their own initiative. In the former instance this form of local advertising impinges upon the spot broadcasting field.

It is interesting to note that, in the foregoing list, some of the most important users of national broadcast advertising—nationally branded food products, cosmetics, cigarettes and tobacco, and similar convenience goods—are missing. Local broadcast advertising, therefore, seems limited chiefly to local brands, local supplementary advertising of national brands, and principally to retail advertising, where the important element is that of creating a loyalty to the store itself. However, it should not be assumed that the potential users of this sort of broadcast advertising constitute a small and closely circumscribed group of establishments. On the contrary, the widest possible variety exists in the types of concerns sponsoring programs over local stations. Included among the types not mentioned previously are building and loan associations, dairies, wholesale-grocery establishments, taxicab companies, real estate brokers, morticians, memorial parks, loan and finance companies, carpet cleaners, meat packers, opticians, theaters, public utility companies, fraternal orders, churches and religious organizations, gasoline service stations, and similar types of business.

The prevalence of morticians and memorial parks on broadcasting stations, and their almost uniform success with this type of advertising, constitutes an interesting if somewhat ironical sidelight upon the functioning of broadcast advertising. Services of this sort can be sold much better through the medium of music and a quiet friendly voice, where the emotional connotation can be expressed in a tactful fashion superior to that possible in cold print. Of course, it is not necessary to go as far as the program on a West Coast station, which was one of the most popular and successful broadcasts on the station, but which, by an incongruity seldom possible outside the realm of Gilbert and Sullivan, had for its theme song "The End of a Perfect Day."

As to the trend in business on the part of stations of various size, no conclusive evidence is possible.[8] There seems, however, to be some slight tendency for the better-class retail trade to look more favorably upon the 100- and 250-watt stations than in earlier years, though this type of business concentrates mostly upon the stations of more than 1,000 watts in power. It is the most powerful stations which seem to secure the largest share of the national spot business, however.

Another question which arises regarding local broadcast advertising is the relative proportion of spot announcements, electrically transcribed programs, and live talent broadcasts sponsored by the local advertisers. As has been mentioned previously, the spot announcement, concentrated largely in one morning and one afternoon period especially devoted to broadcast advertising of this type, is an integral part of the broadcast advertising facilities of the great majority of stations, and often constitutes one of their most important sources of revenue.

---

[8] The conclusions presented in this respect are based on the answers of 58 station managers to the question "Have there been any marked trends or changes in the types of industries or companies sponsoring programs over your station in the past four or five years?" The answers, however, were so variegated in form of presentation that tabular presentation was impossible.

Some of the better announcements have been extremely successful, especially in cases such as department stores, where shopping notices can be broadcast to the housewife prior to her
starting on her morning buying tour, and where information of
this type constitutes a distinct service to many listeners. As far
as can be determined, department stores are tending to add this
form of broadcast to their live talent institutional programs to
an increasing degree.

On the other hand, the electrically transcribed program has
not made much headway among local advertisers. The principal
reason for this has probably been the difficulty of securing desirable transcriptions for local programs, and the fear on the
part of the advertiser that the public reaction might be unfavorable to the recorded program. Finally, the live talent program is
meeting with increasing favor on the part of the better class of
retailers. This type of program assists the store to create a
definite radio personality for itself. Moreover, its personal
touch assists greatly in building goodwill, upon which store
patronage to a large degree is predicated. It also creates a foundation of listener interest which later in the series makes possible
an increased amount of direct selling, providing the latter is tact-
fully done. The trend over the past several years seems to have
been in the direction of this form of program as far as the local
advertiser is concerned, though, within recent months, the continued severity of the depression has brought with it an increased retail demand for the cheaper spot announcement.

In discussing the broadcasting structure, a specialization of
stations with regard to certain types of audience was noted.
This specialization, in turn, is important to the local broadcaster, in that it determines to a very large degree which station
he will employ in a given community. In this respect there is a
tendency for the better class of trade to concentrate upon the
larger and more important stations, while the smaller retailer
eventually seeks the smaller station. The economic and cultural
groups which a station elects to serve also will affect the choice
of the broadcasting outlet on the part of the retailer. Thus a
station such as WLS, Chicago, will be especially well adapted to
any establishment interested in attracting the outlying farm
population who may do part of their trading in that city. Recently, the foreign-language station also has come into promi-

nence in the larger cities, and in turn opens important sales opportunities to certain types of retailers.

A final question which arises with regard to the local use of broadcasting as an advertising medium centers about the problem of selling broadcast advertising to the local retailer. From the practices which he has observed in operation or which have been told to him by station managers, station sales policy seems to have been one of the important contributing factors to the slow growth of retail advertising over radio stations in past years. The entire matter of solicitation often has been pursued in haphazard fashion, without prospect lists of any real value, with little follow-up on potential customers, and with inadequate supervision of the individual salesmen. Thus the sales manager of one station reported that, prior to his assuming the position, the station had had as high as twenty salesmen operating in the city at one time, with the result that hardly any of them were making a living wage. Since then the sale force has been greatly reduced and its efficiency commensurately increased.

Another factor necessary in the sale of local broadcast advertising is the proper servicing of the retail accounts by the station. In the opinion of J. Thomas Lyons, executive vice-president of WCAO, Baltimore, one of the most successful smaller stations on the eastern seaboard, this is one of the most important of all factors in successful station operation. To this end a knowledge of retailing is necessary on the part of the broadcaster so that he may be able to advise the merchant as to the best manner in which to co-ordinate his broadcast advertising with the rest of his sales program. In the case of the station in question, a retailer is not advised to begin broadcasting until the station executives have assured themselves that he is in a position to secure a definite number of permanent customers from the initial sales brought him by broadcasting. To this end the station analyzes carefully factors such as the dealer's inventory, window and interior display, and advises him regarding them. Following this, it attempts to adapt its entire broadcasting policy to meet his special needs. If the dealer is situated away from the main shopping centers, the station announcement will emphasize his location, pointing out its convenience and general accessibility. Moreover, all programs are carefully checked as to results at the end of every fourth week, and those which have failed to produce satisfactory returns during that period are changed immediately. Through methods such as these, ideally adapted to making broadcasting an effective medium for retail advertising, a highly successful business has been created.

PART III
CURRENT PRACTICE IN BROADCAST ADVERTISING

CHAPTER X

VARIATIONS IN THE USE OF BROADCAST ADVERTISING AS TO DIFFERENT SEASONS, DAYS OF THE WEEK, AND HOURS OF THE DAY

The elements underlying the utility of radio to the listener, the adaptability of broadcasting effectively to convey the advertising message, the listening audience available to the broadcast advertiser, the station and network structure through which that audience may be reached, and the extent to which broadcasting facilities are being used by advertisers thus far have been discussed. The next phase of the subject requiring attention is the matter of current broadcast advertising technique. This involves a discussion of such matters as the time of the year, week, and day when radio is employed by advertisers, current practice regarding program construction, commercial announcement technique, the question of contests, special offers,[1] and similar problems.

In so far as the question of the variations in the use of broadcast advertising at different seasons, on different days of the week and hours of the day, affords the best transition from an analysis of the extent of broadcast advertising to the specific problems of its technique, it will be discussed first. The approach will be primarily from the viewpoint of the national networks, with regard to which comparatively detailed information is available.[2] Supplementary data, representing the individual station phase of this problem, will be presented in the form of summations of station executive experience.

The seasonal variation in the expenditures over national net-

[1] This latter field has grown rapidly within the past two years and involves the whole problem of correlating the broadcaster's program with the rest of the advertising campaign.

[2] *National Advertising Records*, published by the Advertising Records Company, constitutes the source of money expenditures over networks. The proportion of commercial to total hours broadcast at different seasons, which constitutes the "time" measure in the chapter, has been secured from original network records.

185

works is presented graphically in Charts X to XII, both for advertisers as a whole and for those industrial groups whose expenditures have been large enough and whose efforts have been sufficiently continuous to make possible the computation of a seasonal pattern.[3] No attempt has been made to indicate the trend in the amplitude of the seasonal fluctuations, since the short span of years during which broadcasting networks have been in existence makes this impracticable. For the same reason, the seasonal pattern for the total network advertising, as well as for industrial groups, should be interpreted chiefly as being representative of the situation to date. This is necessary since it is difficult to determine the probable extent of their bearing on future trends in the field.

The low ebb of broadcast advertising over networks occurs in August following which there is a rapid increase in business until October. From then until January, conditions remain comparatively static. During that month, however, there is a slight rise in network advertising expenditures. In March a much sharper rise occurs, following which there is a gradual decline until the low point is reached in the ensuing August.

The general contour of the seasonal pattern closely follows accepted broadcast advertising practice. Network contracts are usually placed as of the beginning of October and continue in force until the following April or May. The minor variations are more difficult to explain. The slight decline in November, as compared to October, undoubtedly is due to a small number of experimenters dropping out at the end of the first month, a tendency which was more pronounced in the early years of broadcast advertising than at the present time. Network records indicate that the rise in January is due to an increase in number of advertisers occurring annually during that month.

The sharp increase in network advertising expenditures in March is more difficult to explain. At first glance it would seem

[3] The method employed in determining the seasonal pattern was that of relating the data to a 2 over 12 moving average, and taking the means of these values for each month and imposing those values on the average for the year. No attempt has been made to correct for secular trend because of the very short period of years involved. Likewise, the extreme variations in monthly expenditures for certain industrial groups, the capricious manner in which they tended to fluctuate especially in the early years, and at times the small expenditures involved have made impossible the calculation of a seasonal pattern for all of the industrial groups employing national network advertising.

CHART X

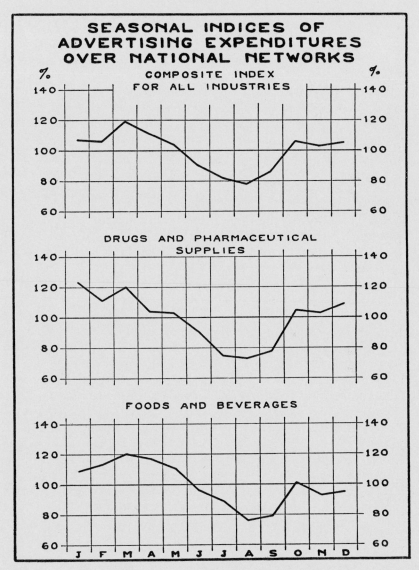

SEASONAL INDICES OF
ADVERTISING EXPENDITURES
OVER NATIONAL NETWORKS

COMPOSITE INDEX
FOR ALL INDUSTRIES

DRUGS AND PHARMACEUTICAL
SUPPLIES

FOODS AND BEVERAGES

CHART XI

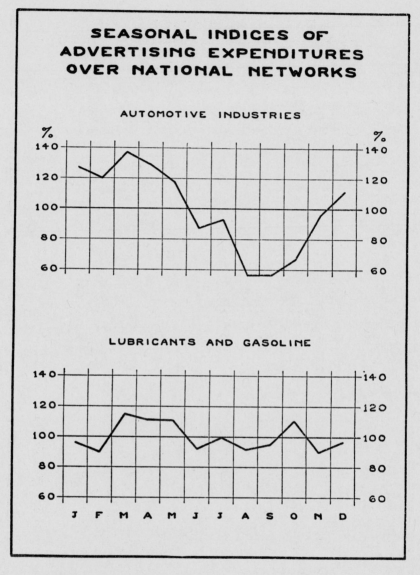

SEASONAL INDICES OF
ADVERTISING EXPENDITURES
OVER NATIONAL NETWORKS

AUTOMOTIVE INDUSTRIES

LUBRICANTS AND GASOLINE

CHART XII

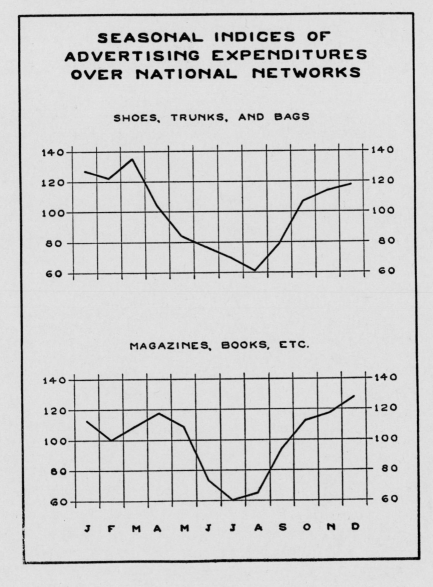

SEASONAL INDICES OF
ADVERTISING EXPENDITURES
OVER NATIONAL NETWORKS

SHOES, TRUNKS, AND BAGS

MAGAZINES, BOOKS, ETC.

that this rise merely indicated that advertisers were putting on pressure in anticipation of spring business. Broadcast advertising, especially over national networks, is not that elastic. It must be remembered that from 75 per cent to 80 per cent of network programs remain on the air[4] at least three months. Moreover, it is not possible to increase the amount of space or the frequency of the inserts for the brief span of a few weeks, as may be done in the case of printed advertising. Network programs require time for their construction and for the building of a habitual audience, so that the best results are attained from continuous effort over a comparatively long period of time. Therefore, if broadcasters were making a practice of placing additional programs in March, this increased business should be reflected in both April and May advertising volume, with resultant modifications in the seasonal pattern.

Though it is not a complete explanation of what occurs, the desire on the part of certain groups of advertisers for additional sales effort during the spring period is at least partially responsible for the March increase in business. Instead of consisting of business placed by regular advertisers, the March increase has been confined largely to experimental broadcasters, most of whom have remained on the air no more than a few weeks. Most of the companies in question have been small concerns. Quite probably many of them faced a situation where the pre-Christmas business has not been nearly as much as anticipated. In an attempt to recoup their losses, they sought some method of further increasing spring sales. Radio broadcasting was a new medium which had produced spectacular results for a number of companies. The small advertiser therefore sought it as a possible solution of his difficulties. After a short period of broadcasting, he found that the expected phenomenal increase in sales had not occurred, and that, in addition, radio was a highly expensive medium. Therefore he discontinued his network effort shortly after he had undertaken it.

An examination of network records indicates that a large number of these small companies have begun advertising either toward the end of February or the beginning of March, and have discontinued advertising shortly thereafter. In so far as they are not concentrated in any one industry, to whom such a

[4] For details, see Table XXIV, chap. vi.

practice conceivably might be an attempted solution of a seasonal problem, it seems probable that the preceding explanation is correct. It should be noted that the number of such concerns has shown a marked decrease over the past two seasons. Only 17.9 per cent of the network program sponsors broadcast for periods of less than three months during the 1931–32 season.[5]

The seasonal pattern of the food industry shows interesting variations from that of the general curve, rising to greater heights in the spring than does broadcast advertising as a whole, and declining later in the year. In addition, it experiences a somewhat slower growth in the fall. A number of factors enter into this situation. Part of the large expenditures during the first five months of the year are due to the concentration of a number of smaller companies on this period, when the demand for packaged food should be at its height. The experimental broadcaster also is responsible for this condition to a slight degree. Finally, the average duration of the broadcasting series of food companies is generally longer than that of concerns in other fields. As in the case of network advertising as a whole, the explanation of the seasonal curve lies principally in the period during which advertisers are on the air, rather than in any increase or decrease in the monthly expenditures of a given company, as might be the case in printed advertising.

The fluctuations in the seasonal curve for the drug industry are somewhat more irregular than those of the food group, and follow closely the trend of business activity in that industry. The only explanation which can be ventured for the monthly fluctuations again is the influence of the experimental broadcaster, who is on the air today and gone tomorrow. The major aspects of the seasonal pattern, however, tend to follow the contract periods of the principal advertisers in this field.

Two factors explain the seasonal variations found in the automotive field. The first of these is that most of the automobile advertising which has been done by different companies has come either at the time of the introduction of new models or else in anticipation of the spring buying season. The second factor is that the General Motors Corporation, the only consistent broadcast advertiser in the industry, has tended to apply pressure at these periods by putting on programs for individual

[5] For details, see Table XXIV, chap. vi.

makes of cars, and has discontinued all except its institutional broadcasting during the summer months. Lubricants and gasoline likewise show a definite correlation between the seasonal fluctuations in business and those of their broadcast advertising expenditures. Since the industry is a comparative newcomer on the air, as far as any large volume of advertising is concerned, it is difficult to present any conclusive evaluation of the significance of its seasonal pattern.

The explanation of the seasonal fluctuations of the shoe industry's broadcast advertising appropriations over national networks is the same as that presented for network broadcasting as a whole. Because of the very serious economic difficulties faced by the industry, its seasonal fluctuations have been especially severe. Though the seasonal pattern with regard to the advertising of magazines over the radio is definite enough in its characteristics, its significance is doubtful. The number of magazines on the air has always been very small. Until recently when they discontinued broadcasting—leaving *Time* the only magazine of importance remaining—*Collier's* and *True Story* were the only consistent broadcast advertisers among the periodicals. The other magazines tended to go on and off the networks in a capricious fashion, so that the peculiar drop in February is probably due almost exclusively to them.

Brief mention should be made of the more important industrial groups for which no pattern of seasonal fluctuation has been presented. In the case of cigarettes, the small number of companies and the irregular policy of several of the advertisers made impossible the determination of a definite seasonal trend. The comparative newness of soaps and household supplies as network advertisers and the varying policies followed by different companies caused the computation of the seasonal pattern in that industry to be impracticable. Insurance and financial advertising constituted the only other industrial group whose advertising expenditures were large enough to make possible a satisfactory calculation of seasonal trend. In this case it was found that practically no seasonal fluctuations existed, advertising continuing without cessation during the entire year.

The relative proportion of time devoted to commercial programs by national networks at different periods of the year also is of interest. This is found in Table XXVI for the key stations of the National Broadcasting Company Red and Blue and the Columbia Broadcasting System as of the second week of February, May, August, and November, annually.

An examination of the table indicates a tendency for the seasonal decline in the proportion of commercial to total hours broadcast to be greater in amplitude than is that of money expenditures for network advertising. This is even more apparent when a comparison is made of the proportion of commercial to total hours broadcast during the second week in August with that of the average of the second weeks of the

TABLE XXVI

PERCENTAGE OF COMMERCIAL TO TOTAL HOURS BROADCAST OVER THE KEY STATIONS OF THE NBC RED AND BLUE AND COLUMBIA NETWORKS DURING THE SECOND WEEK OF FEBRUARY, MAY, AUGUST, AND NOVEMBER, ANNUALLY, 1927–32

| YEAR | PERCENTAGE OF COMMERCIAL TO TOTAL HOURS | | | |
	February	May	August	November
1927............	15.8	19.0	12.2	20.5
1928............	20.6	17.7	13.3	27.7
1929............	28.3	24.6	18.8	24.7
1930............	22.2	21.8	18.9	29.2
1931............	27.5	33.0	25.3	36.5
1932............	33.3	27.4	....	....

preceding November and February.[6] This is found in Table XXVII.

From an analysis of the fluctuations in money expenditures and of the two preceding tables, it seems that it is the larger company, employing widespread network facilities, which tends to remain on the air during the summer months.

Lack of adequate data makes it impossible to present any conclusions regarding the seasonal fluctuations of either regional network advertising or spot broadcasting. Because of the greater elasticity of the latter, it is probable that a greater num-

[6] Because of the pronounced secular trend existing in these figures, which it is impossible to eliminate, the preceding November and February have been taken in preference to those following. This also is more logical from the viewpoint of broadcast advertising practice, since August of any year constitutes the end of a season's broadcast, which began with the preceding September.

ber of minor fluctuations may occur from month to month in this instance.

An indication of the situation with regard to seasonal fluctuations in local broadcast advertising may be secured from the replies of managers of 50 radio stations to the question as to approximately what proportion of their local business remained on the air during the summer.[7] The results of the question are found in Table XXVIII.

It appears that between 70 per cent and 75 per cent of local station business remains on the air during the summer months,

TABLE XXVII

PERCENTAGE OF COMMERCIAL TO TOTAL HOURS
BROADCAST BY THE KEY STATIONS OF THE NBC
RED AND BLUE AND COLUMBIA NETWORKS DUR-
ING THE SECOND WEEK OF AUGUST AS COMPARED
WITH THE AVERAGE OF THE SECOND WEEKS OF THE
PRECEDING NOVEMBER AND FEBRUARY

Year	Percentage of August Commercial Broadcasting to Preceding Winter
1927	59.2
1928	47.5
1929	80.0*
1930	66.2
1931	72.5

* Entrance of CBS on a part-time basis as far as network sustaining service is concerned unduly raises this figure.

the median for the group being 71 per cent and the arithmetic average 75 per cent. The 5 stations reporting no seasonal decline are of especial interest. For the most part, they comprise small local broadcasters with a steady retail trade, and with regard to which increased advertising by typically summer undertakings such as ice and ice cream manufacturers may offset such small decline as has occurred among the regular winter clientèle of the station. In the case of the fiftieth station replying to the question, which does not appear in the table, the seasonal trend was reversed. The volume of summer broadcast advertising was consistently greater than that during other periods of the

[7] The specific question asked was: "Approximately what proportion of your local business remains on the air during the summer? Has the amount of summer radio advertising decreased or remained the same since 1929? If increased, has it done so faster than winter business?" See Appendix B.

year. This was due to the fact that the station was located in an important resort district of a far-western state.

The varying degree to which different days of the week are used for the broadcasting of commercially sponsored programs requires consideration along with the question of seasonal trends. Practice in this respect is indicated in Table XXIX with regard to the key stations of the national networks.

The outstanding feature of the table is the uniform manner in which the amount of broadcast advertising on Saturday lags behind that of other days of the week. The smaller volume of

TABLE XXVIII

PROPORTION OF LOCAL BUSINESS REMAINING ON STA-
TION DURING SUMMER MONTHS, AS ESTI-
MATED BY STATION MANAGERS

Proportion of Business Remaining on Station (Per Cent)	Number of Stations Reporting Same
Under 50	2
50–59	9
60–69	11
70–79	10
80–89	11
90–99	1
100	5
Total	49

Saturday advertising applies to all portions of the day. Morning advertising is from 50 per cent to 80 per cent as much as on other week days, afternoon volume from 25 per cent to 50 per cent as large, and evening commercial broadcasting from 75 per cent to 80 per cent as great. There are two reasons underlying the small volume of Saturday broadcast advertising. The first and most cogent of these is the fact that, the next day being Sunday, more than twenty-four hours must elapse before the listener can act upon the advertiser's suggestion to purchase the article in question. A second reason is the belief on the part of many program sponsors that the potential radio audience is considerably smaller on Saturday than on other days, due to the prevalence of entertaining on Saturday night, and the greater competition experienced from other forms of amusement, such as the motion picture. It is extremely doubtful whether this psychology is true of a sufficient number of people to affect seriously the total size of the Saturday evening audience, though it may possess decided significance with regard to specific classes of listeners.[8]

Outside of the Saturday lag in advertising volume, the only other variation in the daily use of network facilities by program sponsors occurs on Sunday. Here again the volume of advertising tends to be less than that of other days, with the exception of Saturday, which constitutes the low ebb for the entire week.

TABLE XXIX

PROPORTION OF COMMERCIAL TO TOTAL HOURS BROADCAST ON VARIOUS DAYS OF THE WEEK BY THE KEY STATIONS OF THE NBC RED AND BLUE AND COLUMBIA NETWORKS DURING THE SECOND WEEK OF NOVEMBER, 1927-31*

DAY OF WEEK	PERCENTAGE OF COMMERCIAL TO TOTAL HOURS BROADCAST				
	1927	1928	1929	1930	1931
Sunday................	20.4	26.8	28.3	24.6	25.3
Monday...............	18.1	24.6	18.3	26.6	37.5
Tuesday...............	21.6	22.4	28.9	34.7	40.9
Wednesday............	28.2	37.7	24.5	29.9	42.3
Thursday..............	25.2	24.9	22.3	32.8	40.9
Friday................	15.4	37.9	29.6	32.3	41.5
Saturday..............	14.6	19.6	21.0	23.5	27.0
Entire week........	20.5	27.7	24.7	29.2	36.5

* Source: Network program records.

This tendency is especially true of the past several years, the Sunday advertising volume prior to 1930 comparing favorably to that of other days. The principal reason for the slightly poorer showing of Sunday is the fact that there is practically no advertising on Sunday morning. Until a few years ago Sunday morning was devoid of commercial broadcasting, but recently several advertising programs have been scheduled for that time. Even at present the volume of commercial programs on Sunday morning seldom exceeds 6 per cent of the total programs broadcast during that period by the three basic networks. This is undoubtedly due to a reluctance on the part of advertisers to

[8] See chap. iii for a discussion of the size of the listening audience on different days of the week.

run competition with church services for fear of antagonizing important segments of the listening public; and to an apathy on the part of the networks themselves—inspired by the same reason—with respect to the sale of Sunday morning time. Sunday afternoon broadcast advertising, on the other hand, is somewhat greater than that of other days of the week. In November 1930, it totaled 16.6 per cent of the hours broadcast by the key stations of the NBC Red and Blue, and the Columbia networks, as compared with an average of 11.0 per cent for the entire week. In November of the following year the proportion of commercial to total hours on Sunday afternoon was 41.6 per cent as compared with a weekly average of 21.3 per cent. With regard to volume of commercially sponsored programs, Sunday night has always been similar to any other evening in the week.

Seasonal variations with respect to the utilization of various days of the week by broadcast advertisers are of interest. A graphic representation of the proportion of commercial to total hours broadcast during the second week of February, May, August, and November, 1927-31, by the key stations of the three basic networks, as compared with Saturday and Sunday of each week, is found in Chart XIII, the actual percentages being presented in Table XXX.

It will be noted in this respect that Sunday shows the greatest seasonal variation, while the Saturday volume of broadcast advertising tends to decline less in the summertime than does that of the week as a whole. This probably is due to the high proportion of Saturday advertising made up of large companies, sponsoring programs several times a week, who are more prone to remain on the air during the summer than are most advertisers. These companies consist mostly of the more important manufacturers of convenience goods, who financially are best equipped for continuous broadcast advertising and who, in addition are capable of deriving the maximum benefit from such broadcasts by reason of their comparatively steady volume of sales at all periods of the year. The marked decline in the volume of Sunday advertising during the summer months is due to the fact that the listening audience is probably smaller at that time than at any other period of the year.[9]

Differences in the use of various days of the week for broad-

[9] See chap. iii for details regarding this aspect of listener behavior.

CHART XIII

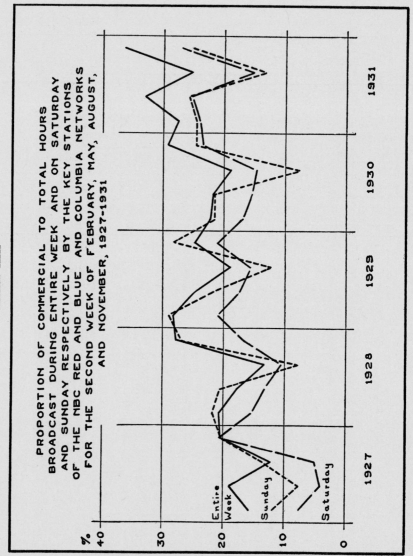

PROPORTION OF COMMERCIAL TO TOTAL HOURS
BROADCAST DURING ENTIRE WEEK AND ON SATURDAY
AND SUNDAY RESPECTIVELY BY THE KEY STATIONS
OF THE NBC RED AND BLUE AND COLUMBIA NETWORKS
FOR THE SECOND WEEK OF FEBRUARY, MAY, AUGUST,
AND NOVEMBER, 1927-1931

cast advertising over individual stations show somewhat greater variations than in the case of the networks. Friday tends to be the best day of the week to an even greater degree than in the case of the networks, while Saturday again is the poorest day, with Sunday ranking a close second. The latter is especially

TABLE XXX

PROPORTION OF COMMERCIAL TO TOTAL HOURS BROADCAST DURING THE ENTIRE WEEK AND ON SATURDAY AND SUNDAY, RESPEC- TIVELY, OVER THE KEY STATIONS OF THE NBC RED AND BLUE AND COLUMBIA NETWORKS DURING THE SECOND WEEK OF FEBRUARY, MAY, AUGUST, AND NOVEMBER, 1927–31

MONTH AND YEAR	PERCENTAGE OF COMMERCIAL TO TOTAL HOURS		
	Saturday	Sunday	Entire Week
1927 February	7.7	11.8	15.8
May	4.0	7.6	19.0
August	5.0	13.5	12.2
November	20.6	20.4	20.5
1928 February	15.4	21.7	20.6
May	13.3	20.5	17.7
August	10.5	7.6	13.3
November	16.6	26.8	27.7
1929 February	21.0	29.0	28.3
May	17.3	21.5	24.6
August	15.6	12.3	18.8
November	21.0	28.3	24.7
1930 February	16.9	21.5	22.2
May	15.4	21.5	21.8
August	14.7	7.6	18.9
November	23.5	24.6	29.2
1931 February	24.0	24.6	27.5
May	25.3	25.7	33.0
August	15.2	13.2	25.3
November	27.0	25.3	36.5

true in agricultural districts and in the South. The trends are confirmed by the replies of fifty station managers to the question[10] as to which were their best and poorest days of the week, respectively, with regard to the amount of commercially sponsored programs broadcast by their stations. Friday was stated to be the best day by 50 per cent of the station executives, Mon-

[10] The question asked was: "What is your best day of the week as far as volume of advertising is concerned? Your poorest? Has there been any shift in the use of broadcasting for advertising on different days of the week that you have noticed since 1929? If so, what?"

day by 12 per cent, and Thursday by 10 per cent, of the group. Another 10 per cent of those replying scattered their answers among the remaining days of the week, while 18 per cent of the managers stated that, other than Saturday and Sunday, all days were of equal value as far as the question of advertising revenue was concerned. Seven stations, most of them located in urban districts reported a trend toward increased Sunday business.

With regard to the question of which was the poorest day of the week, 60 per cent of the station managers specified Saturday, and 26 per cent Sunday. The remaining 14 per cent of the replies were scattered among the other days of the week, with the exception of Friday. Variations with regard to both the best and poorest days tended closely to follow local retail buying habits in all instances.

Of greater importance than either seasonal fluctuations or the varying degree to which different days of the week are used by advertisers, is the question of the degree to which different parts of the day are devoted to the broadcasting of commercially sponsored programs. The trends in this field, with respect to network broadcasting, are found in Table XXXI and Chart XIV.

Evening hours have always been the most popular period of the day for broadcasting commercially sponsored programs, the greater size of the evening audience being the dominating consideration in this respect. Morning ranks next in preference, while the afternoon hours have still to win favor with the broadcast advertiser. With regard to trends during the period under consideration, there has been little change in the proportion of evening hours devoted to commercial programs by network key stations since the formation of chain broadcasting systems. Such increase as there has been in this regard was experienced principally on the part of affiliated stations, which have gained in evening volume of network advertising through the wider use of network facilities by the sponsor companies.[11]

The volume of morning advertising showed no appreciable permanent increase until the fall of 1929, since which time it has grown slowly but with considerable regularity. Advertising by food and cosmetic concerns has chiefly been responsible for

[11] See chap. vi for details regarding the trend toward an increasing use of total network facilities.

this trend. With the exception of the recent sudden rise in popularity of commercially sponsored programs directed to the children, most of which are concentrated between half-past four and six o'clock, the volume of afternoon broadcast advertising still is negligible. As was noted previously, Sunday afternoon com-

TABLE XXXI

PROPORTION OF COMMERCIAL TO TOTAL HOURS BROADCAST AT DIFFERENT TIMES OF THE DAY BY THE KEY STATIONS OF THE NBC RED AND BLUE AND COLUMBIA NETWORKS DURING THE SECOND WEEK OF FEBRUARY, MAY, AUGUST, AND NOVEMBER, 1927–31, AND FEBRUARY AND MAY, 1932

Month and Year	Before Noon (Per Cent)	Noon to Six P.M. (Per Cent)	After Six P.M. (Per Cent)	Entire Day (Per Cent)
1927 February............	11.1	13.9	24.6	15.8
May................	....	0.9	33.7	19.0
August..............	15.8	....	19.4	12.2
November...........	21.3	0.9	33.9	20.5
1928 February............	37.2	1.8	33.9	20.6
May................	11.7	1.2	33.7	17.7
August..............	6.9	1.2	25.4	13.3
November...........	53.5	4.5	40.3	27.7
1929 February............	24.9	6.8	47.3	28.3
May................	21.8	4.8	41.3	24.6
August..............	17.5	5.4	29.5	18.8
November...........	24.7	6.5	41.0	24.7
1930 February............	24.3	4.2	37.0	22.2
May................	23.0	3.3	36.9	21.8
August..............	23.9	0.2	31.2	18.9
November...........	34.2	11.0	42.8	29.2
1931 February............	31.4	9.4	42.4	27.5
May................	35.3	11.4	48.5	33.0
August..............	29.8	9.5	35.5	25.3
November...........	34.2	21.3	49.0	36.5
1932 February............	31.7	15.6	48.9	33.3
May................	29.5	11.8	38.9	27.4

mercial programs have constituted a satisfactorily large volume of business for a number of years, but their effect on the weekly total is nullified by the almost complete lack of broadcast advertising on other afternoons of the week. Recently there has been a slight increase in sponsored programs at this time of the day, though not enough to change appreciably the total volume of this type of business.

Brief mention should be made of the relative concentration of broadcast advertising at various parts of the morning, after-

CHART XIV

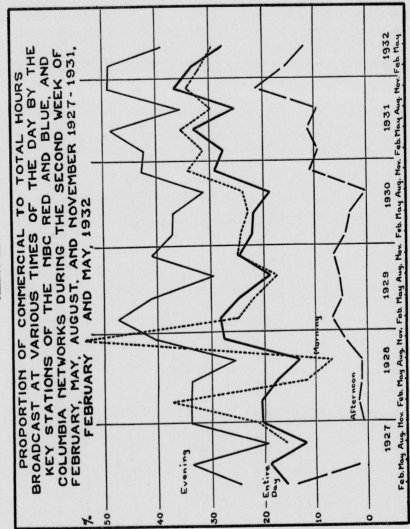

PROPORTION OF COMMERCIAL TO TOTAL HOURS
BROADCAST AT VARIOUS TIMES OF THE DAY BY THE
KEY STATIONS OF THE NBC RED AND BLUE, AND
COLUMBIA NETWORKS DURING THE SECOND WEEK OF
FEBRUARY, MAY, AUGUST, AND NOVEMBER 1927-1931,
FEBRUARY AND MAY, 1932

noon, and evening. The earliest commercial program in the morning is the Metropolitan Life Insurance Company's Tower Health exercises, broadcast over the NBC Red network from 6:45 to 8:00 A.M. every weekday. Following this period, commercial programs are scattered throughout the morning hours, with a slight concentration in the neighborhood of eleven o'clock. Other than the concentration of children's programs in the late afternoon, there seems to be little in the way of a definite trend with regard to this period of the day. Evening broadcasting has undergone an interesting change since the early days of the networks. Originally, broadcast advertising tended to concentrate between the hours of eight and ten o'clock. Gradually sponsored programs began to be broadcast earlier in the evening, until the phenomenal success of "Amos 'n' Andy" in the fall of 1929 convinced advertisers of the value of the supper hours and those immediately following them. Since then commercial broadcasting time has continued to move toward the earlier hours, until, at the present time, the children's and grown-ups' program periods merge with each other at six o'clock. With the exception of full-hour broadcasts, such as the Lucky Strike program, few commercially sponsored broadcasts are scheduled to last later than half-past ten at night.

With regard to the seasonal variations in the use of morning, afternoon, and evening hours for broadcast advertising, the last-mentioned period shows the greatest degree of fluctuation. Afternoon shows the least seasonal variation, due primarily to the very small volume of advertising on the air at that time. Morning also presents less in the way of seasonal fluctuation than does evening. This is explained by the concentration of food, household supply, and cosmetic accounts in the morning hours, all of which are especially regular broadcasters.

Individual station experience with regard to the degree to which morning, afternoon, and evening hours are used for broadcast advertising tends closely to approximate the network situation. Evening presents the greatest volume, morning is second, and afternoon a very poor third. Of forty-five station managers furnishing data regarding the relative degree to which morning and afternoon hours were used for broadcast advertising,[12] 82.2 per cent specified the former as possessing the greatest amount of commercially sponsored hours, 13.3 per cent the afternoon, while 4.5 per cent stated that there was no appreciable difference between the two periods. The degree to which morning business exceeded that of the afternoon varied greatly between stations, though the general tendency seemed for the morning volume to be approximately two-thirds greater. The median for the degree of morning superiority of advertising volume was 67.5 per cent and the arithmetic average 64.2 per cent for the twenty-six stations furnishing information on this point.

Though no definite trend was noted by station executives with regard to the relative rate of growth of daytime and nighttime business, a number of interesting individual variations were revealed,[13] indicating clearly that the trend in this respect depends upon factors such as the type of station—whether large or small, network, or non-network—local reception conditions, and similar matters. Most of the 5,000-watt stations stated that, within recent years, daytime business had increased more rapidly than had evening advertising volume. The chief reason mentioned for this trend was the fact that the evening hours had been sold previously and that no desirable ones were available any longer. The same general tendency was indicated by the 500- and 1,000-watt stations, though here the comparative recency with which they had joined the network possessed considerable bearing upon the trends taken by their business. In the case of the more recent affiliates, the volume of evening business tended to rise faster than daytime advertising, largely due to the fact that network advertisers were just beginning to use the station as one of their outlets. A number of small nonnetwork stations not only experienced a greater proportionate daytime growth in advertising volume but found these hours actually preferred by local sponsors because they were unwilling to have their programs compete with the more spectacular network evening presentations.

[12] The question asked was: "Which is the greater and by approximately how much, your volume of morning or afternoon commercial broadcasting time? Which of the two has increased the most rapidly during the past year?" See Appendix B.

[13] "Which has increased the more rapidly during the past year, your day or night business? Why in your opinion?" See Appendix B.

A discussion of the principal trends regarding the use of radio broadcasting for advertising purposes at different seasons and on different days and hours having been presented, it remains to evaluate the soundness of current practice in this respect. It seems doubtful that broadcast advertisers have made full use of the various times at which radio broadcasting facilities could be used profitably for conveying their sales message to the listening public. Summer broadcast advertising has not been engaged in to the full limit of its potentialities. This is due partly to the normal seasonal decline in all advertising, partly to the belief that the summer listening audience is sufficiently smaller than the winter one to warrant the discontinuance of the broadcast advertising program, and partly to a memory of the unsatisfactory reception experienced by summer listeners during the early years of broadcasting.

Several observations may be presented counter to these opinions. In the first place, there is reason to believe that the summer decline in the size of the listening audience is by no means as great as usually believed. Field studies in the Philadelphia area have indicated that the summer audience is, on the average about 90 per cent as large as that of other seasons; and that even during a late July or early August week-end—when the audience reaches its lowest point of the year—there are approximately 80 per cent of the set owners remaining as a potential audience for the commercial sponsor's presentation.[14] This same tendency is confirmed by studies made in other areas. It must also be remembered that the summertime is one of the best seasons for reaching the farm population of the country, both from the viewpoint of accessibility and because it immediately antedates the post-harvest buying season. It also is doubtful whether the practice of taking vacations away from home is as prevalent in small towns as it is in the larger urban centers, so that this portion of the radio audience will tend to shrink less in the summertime than will that of a city such as Philadelphia.

In addition to the question of the size of the audience, it should be remembered that the discount received by the advertiser on a 52-week contract is sufficient to pay for a large

---

[14] See chap. iii for details regarding the summer audience.

portion of his summer broadcasting time charges.[15] It is true
that the talent still has to be paid for the additional programs
and that this may amount to more than half of the total broadcasting expense. Nevertheless, the time-discount factor looms
sufficiently large in number of dollars to be worthy of careful
consideration. A counter-argument might be presented in the
fact that continued broadcasting throughout the entire year
will tend to burn out the talent and cause the program to lose
its appeal at an early date. With regard to certain types of
broadcasts this factor may possess some validity. However, it
can be overcome without too great difficulty by the presentation
of a special program, designed particularly for the summer audience. Not only would this ease the strain on the regular talent,
but it might allow important savings by the substitution of
lesser-known artists.

Moreover, there are certain types of industries, many of them
important users of broadcast advertising, to whom continuity
of effort during the summer months is of especial importance.
Chief among these is the convenience goods field, including
articles such as groceries and foodstuffs, cigarettes, and cosmetics, which enjoy comparatively steady sales at all seasons,
and with respect to which the relatively low degree of consumer
insistence regarding particular brands necessitates continuous
sales and advertising effort. Another similar class of goods includes articles whose consumption increases in the summer
months. Ice cream, soft drinks, sunburn lotion, and other summer pharmaceuticals, sporting goods, resorts, hotels, and trans-
portation services—all experience increased volume of business
during the summer, and can therefore benefit by broadcast and
other advertising during that period. A third category of goods
to which continued broadcast advertising during the summer is
of importance includes the larger and more expensive specialty
goods, such as automobiles, where the final purchase is the result of long deliberation rather than sudden impulse. Here the
manufacturer's advertising must ever be at hand to direct the
prospective buyer's thoughts toward his own product and brand.
Likewise, retail institutions, to whom continuity of effort is of

---

[15] The time discount on a 52-week contract is 15 per cent, while a 26-week contract
on NBC carries 5 per cent discount. Extending the broadcast through June, July, and
August will cost merely half of the normal additional time charges.

great importance because of the necessity of building up and holding consumer loyalty, should find the continuation of summer broadcast advertising especially helpful.

Finally, since it takes a number of weeks before an audience can be built up for a new program, summer broadcasting lays the groundwork for the winter listening group and, by so doing, adds greatly to the effectiveness of the main sales effort.

A question also may be raised as to whether the broadcast advertiser is making the most of his opportunities on Saturday and Sunday. Here the problem is more involved than in the case of summer broadcasting, the final solution varying with individual localities and depending upon factors such as the season, the area to be covered, and the portion of the public to be appealed to. There also is the problem of whether the broadcast advertiser wishes to compete with programs such as the broadcasts of the New York Philharmonic Orchestra and the religious services which are broadcast over many individual stations on Sunday morning. It is probable that it may be well to refrain from commercial effort on Sunday morning, and not to compete too strongly with the outstanding sustaining broadcasts in the afternoon. The final answer to this question depends largely upon the type of program broadcast; and it may be that, by the exercising of ingenuity in this field, new commercial program forms may be produced that will be especially appropriate to Sunday daytime broadcasting.

Saturday broadcast advertising permits an even less definite answer than in the case of Sunday. Where immediacy of response is desired, the Sunday interruption to retail activity constitutes a definite handicap. On the other hand, there is reason to question the opinion that the Saturday audience is so much smaller than that of other days, field studies tending to indicate a very small decline in number of listeners as compared with the rest of the week. There may be a question as to the best type of program for Saturday night, especially in view of the prevalence of entertaining at home. Under such conditions a broadcast which will constitute a pleasant background for conversation or bridge, or which will make possible dancing, may be the most desirable. A well-constructed, short, and vivid commercial announcement will serve to give sales value to a program of this type. It is quite probable that Saturday night is not quite as satisfactory a time as other evenings, but it is still sufficiently so to be worthy of serious consideration on the part of the broadcast advertiser.

With regard to the time of the day, the afternoon hours constitute an almost unlimited field of development for the broadcast advertiser who is interested in the female listening audience. Research shows that the afternoon audience is generally comparable in size to that of the morning hours, so that there is no problem in this respect. Moreover, there is not as much distraction afforded by housework in the afternoon as in the morning. The heavier duties have been completed, lunch is over, and the housewife desires relaxation. Though she probably is completely uninterested in hearing any more concerning recipes and household hints, the average woman may be highly desirous of entertainment at this period of the day. Consequently, a restful semi-classical concert, popular music done in recital rather than dance style, or an interesting dramatic sketch with sufficient romantic appeal should be very well received. In the rare cases where this reasoning has been followed, the results attained have been uniformly successful. The program in one instance accomplished even more satisfactory results than it had when broadcast over the same stations during the evening hours. Careful study as to the most desirable types of programs for afternoon broadcasting is required before the potentialities of this period of the day can fully be utilized. Until any great volume of afternoon advertising has been built up, the pioneer in this field will have the added advantage of having little competition from the programs of other products or brands.

Likewise, a great deal remains to be done with regard to the most effective utilization of the morning hours for broadcast advertising. The latest development in this field is an increasing appreciation of the advertising value of the early morning hours, especially from 7:45 to 8:30 o'clock. This period lends itself to news broadcasts, shopping periods, and entertainment. In the case of one station, a coal company, broadcasting from seven to eight o'clock in the morning, with inferior talent, secured enough orders in the first six days to pay for its entire 26-week radio contract. Educational programs have been found to be very successful during the eight to half-past eight period by station WMAQ, Chicago.[16] These programs were broadcast directly from classrooms at the University of Chicago, and were accorded a splendid reception by the more cultured listeners, who tuned in on them prior to leaving for work. This again indicates the potentialities of the early morning period if the right kind of program is presented.

There still is a great deal of reluctance on the part of broadcast advertisers to experiment in daytime broadcasting. This is especially true with regard to the afternoon, most agencies admitting quite willingly the possibilities of that period of the day, but confessing a reluctance to recommend an afternoon broadcast to their clients. There are other agency executives who are skeptical as to the value of all daytime broadcast advertising, claiming that the number of women listeners is greater at night than in the day, and that, in the case of many articles, both the husband and wife must be won to the purchase. However, there are many other products with respect to which it is necessary only to reach the woman listener. Here the possibility of a specialized appeal, as well as less stringent program competition during the morning and afternoon hours, constitute added inducements to daytime broadcast advertising. A great deal of experimentation is still necessary with regard to the most effective use of daytime broadcasting by advertisers. Its potentialities, however, seem to be well worth the effort.

In addition to the fundamental question of the variations in the amount of broadcast advertising during different seasons, days of the week, and hours of the day, two minor problems, closely related to these broader aspects, require consideration. The first of them is the degree to which the same program is broadcast more than once during the day, while the second relates to the practice of broadcasting on more than one day during the week.

The repetition of the same program at a second hour was introduced to broadcasting by the Pepsodent Company in the fall of 1929. Originally this concern had broadcast "Amos 'n' Andy" at eleven o'clock at night. The program later was shifted to seven o'clock in order to reach a larger portion of the eastern

---

[16] Miss Judith Waller, educational director, Mid-western Division NBC; also vice-president and general manager Station WMAQ, Chicago.

audience. This move, however, aroused a tremendous storm of protest from middle-western listeners, who now were prohibited from following the doings of their favorite comedy pair by reason of the difference in time between the east and their own part of the country. As a result of this protest, it was decided to present the program twice during the same night, broadcasts being scheduled for seven and half-past ten o'clock, respectively. The later period was finally shifted to eleven o'clock, where it has remained ever since then.

The success of the Pepsodent venture in overcoming the time differences existing between various sections of the country prompted other companies to follow its example. In November, 1932, thirteen concerns were repeating their programs at different hours of the day. Five of them were broadcasting their original morning program, either at a later morning hour or during the afternoon, while four companies were following a similar practice with regard to afternoon programs. Four other companies, broadcasting their programs between seven and nine o'clock at night, repeated their presentations usually at eleven o'clock or just preceding that hour. In all cases the companies engaging in this double broadcast advertising effort were large manufacturers of convenience goods enjoying nation-wide distribution.

The trend toward the presentation of a program on more than one night a week first came into evidence in the latter part of 1929 and early months of 1930. It rose to prominence during the fall of that year and increased rapidly throughout 1931, receiving considerable impetus from the growing popularity of the so-called comedy and dramatic strip, which was ideally suited for daily broadcasting. In November, 1932, a total of forty-five companies, comprising approximately 15 per cent of all program sponsors, were broadcasting programs which were presented on more than one night of the week. Eleven of the companies were broadcasting twice a week, eleven others three times a week, while three concerns were presenting programs four times a week. Fourteen companies were broadcasting five times a week, and six others were offering their presentations six nights weekly. Dramatic programs, either for children or adults, including both comedy sketches and straight dramatic presentations, comprised approximately one-half of the programs broadcast in this fashion. Fifteen of the programs were presented prior to twelve o'clock noon; eleven in the afternoon, especially after half-past four o'clock; and nineteen after six o'clock at night. The advantage of this type of program lies in its repetition, which serves to impress the advertising message more firmly upon the consciousness of the listener, as well as to build up a more loyal audience than that commanded by the average weekly broadcast. However, its use raises other important program problems, which lie primarily in the field of program technique.

CHAPTER XI

PROGRAM PRACTICE: TYPES OF PROGRAMS BROADCAST OVER NETWORK KEY STATIONS

The question of the types of programs broadcast by networks and individual stations is of fundamental importance to an understanding of the use of radio broadcasting as an advertising medium in the United States. The entertainment and helpful information derived from hearing programs is the basis of the utility of radio to the listener. With reception problems mastered to a degree sufficient to insure satisfactory listening conditions to the great majority of the public, the program becomes the most important single factor in building listener circulation. Because of its direct bearing upon the size of the audience and listener response received, the program is a matter of greatest interest to the advertiser. Moreover, since the program service rendered by a broadcasting system is the only justification for its existence, an analysis of the types of programs furnished the listener is necessary to an evaluation of the extent to which American broadcasting is fulfilling the public interest.

The approach to this question will be primarily from the viewpoint of the national networks. Moreover, since the network key stations[1] are representative of the highest level of general program development in this country, special attention will be given to their program practice. Both commercial and sustaining programs[2] will be considered because of the close relationship which exists between them. Programs broadcast during the second weeks of February, May, August, and November[3] have been selected for analysis in so far as they have

---

[1] The key station of the NBC Red network is WEAF, New York; of the NBC Blue network, WJZ, New York; and of the Columbia System, WABC, New York.

[2] A commercial program is one sponsored and paid for by an advertiser, while a sustaining program is presented under the auspices of the network or station itself, and for which it bears the cost.

[3] November and February are typical of the winter broadcasting season, May of the spring decline, and August of the seasonal low ebb of commercial broadcasting.

been deemed most typical of the broadcasting year. Key station data will be supplemented with information regarding the degree to which network programs are broadcast by the various affiliated stations, as well as by studies of regional network and individual station program practice. Program analyses have been given for combined networks only, so as to present trends in simple summarized form and to avoid the inclusion of competitive data which would have required lengthy explanation to insure its proper evaluation and would have added little of practical value to the discussion.

Any classification of programs is necessarily arbitrary, since programs do not group themselves into distinct and mutually exclusive categories with ease and simplicity. Many programs are hybrid in nature. The question therefore arises as to what basis can be employed in classifying them, especially where one program contains several types of entertainment. Here two alternatives present themselves. The first is to break programs into their component parts and to tabulate the proportion of time devoted to each kind of entertainment contained within it. The final summation therefore represents the proportion of time devoted to various kinds of entertainment, regardless of whether the items tabulated comprised a complete program entity or merely a portion of a program. The second method is to classify programs as to their dominant characteristics—dance music, drama, or whatever it may be—and to tabulate the number of hours devoted to various types of programs. The latter method has been employed in the present instance in so far as it is believed to be the most logical one, where the data are to be used in an evaluation of program service to the listener. After all, the listener tends to tune in on programs as a whole, and not merely to seek out certain parts, shifting from one program and station to another in most rapid succession.

The classification of programs which has been used as the basis for analysis is as follows: (1) classical music, (2) semi-classical music, (3) folk music and ballads, (4) variety music, (5) popular music, (6) a summation of the total proportion of time devoted to music programs, (7) children's programs, (8) comedy broadcasts, (9) other dramatic programs, (10) children's educational programs, (11) adult educational programs, (12) news, market, and weather reports, (13) religious broadcasts,

(14) sports broadcasts, (15) special features of public interest, (16) international broadcasts, (17) women's feature programs, (18) variety programs, and (19) farm programs. This classification was based upon a careful analysis of similar classifications used in previous investigations,[4] and finally was decided upon as the most satisfactory one which could be used in depicting American conditions.

The exact construction which has been placed upon the various classes of programs is of interest. Classical music has been strictly interpreted on the basis of the inherent value of the compositions as accepted in musical circles. Inclusion has been made of popular classics, which, though hackneyed from constant repetition, nevertheless possess sound musical value. Examples of these are Rachmaninoff's "C Sharp Minor Prelude," and the overtures of Rossini. Semi-classical programs have been interpreted as those made up of music of the Victor Herbert type. Folk music and ballads include only American folk tunes, such as cowboy songs, hill-billy tunes, and the melodies of Stephen Foster. Foreign folk music has been placed in the semi-classical group. A Hungarian gypsy dance is viewed as being either classical or semi-classical music by an American listener rather than as folk music. World War melodies, such as "Keep the Home Fires Burning" also have been included in the folk music group.

Variety music is less definite as a classification. It is made up primarily of programs wherein varying types of music have appeared to such a degree as to make it impossible to classify the program as belonging to any one of the other types. Combinations of classical and popular music constitute an example in point. Popular music includes current dance tunes and song hits, and requires no discussion at this point.

Children's programs comprise broadcasts directed principally to child listeners. They are almost entirely dramatic presentations, and include programs such as "Skippy," the "Lone Wolf Tribe," and the "Kellogg Singing Lady." Comedy programs

[4] Program classifications used by Hettinger, Riegel, and Starch in their radio research, as well as the classification used by the International Radio Union, Geneva, Switzerland, were used as the basis for the present classification. Network research executives likewise were consulted. The satisfactoriness of the classification is witnessed by the closely comparable results derived by it as against the few existing network tabulations.

comprise periods such as "Amos 'n' Andy," the gossip of "Clara, Lu 'n Em," and the tomfoolery of the "Sisters of the Skillet." They, also, are almost entirely dramatic in nature, though inclining at times toward the vaudeville patter type of act. Dramatic programs include all types of drama other than those mentioned previously. The classification of children's educational programs consists primarily of presentations such as those of the American School of the Air. The Damrosch Friday morning concerts have not been included in this category, since their following is so much wider than merely in the schools and among young people. They therefore have been considered as part of the classical music broadcasts of the networks. Adult educational programs consist primarily of short talks on interesting subjects. Series of talks such as "Devils, Drugs and Doctors," by Dr. Howard W. Haggard, well-known medical authority, the political analyses of William Hard and Frederick William Wile, and broadcasts of the National Advisory Council on Radio in Education are included in this category.

News, market, and weather reports require no comment. Religious programs mostly comprise devotional periods, the broadcasts of Dr. Harry Emerson Fosdick and the Rev. S. Parkes Cadman, and the programs of the Columbia Church of the Air, constituting examples of this type of endeavor. Sports broadcasts are either actual eye-witness accounts or reports and analyses of contests. Special features of public interest include items such as the broadcasts of the President of the United States, pick-ups of public meetings and important public gatherings, special programs by visiting foreign dignitaries, and stunt broadcasts such as those made from a moving train or the broadcasting of the sounds created by electrons.

International rebroadcasts include all programs received in this country from overseas by means of short-wave transmission and rebroadcast to American listeners. Women's features include programs addressed particularly to women listeners and largely comprise matters such as recipes, beauty helps, and household suggestions. Variety programs are primarily novelty programs where several forms of entertainment, musical and non-musical, have been combined in one period in such proportions as to make it impossible to classify the program under any other category. Programs of the Ed Wynn and Eddie Cantor type are examples in point. Farm programs are those addressed primarily to rural audiences, the only one of these broadcast over a New York key station being the National Farm and Home Hour on WJZ.

Before entering into a discussion of program trends in recent years, brief mention should be made of the types of programs broadcast in the early years of radio. The first program broadcast over a station regularly in operation was the Harding election news, sent out by KDKA, Pittsburgh, on the night of November 2, 1920. Later in the year KDKA began the regular broadcasting of Arlington time. It also carried the first church service to be sent out on the air. This program was broadcast from the Calvary Episcopal Church, Pittsburgh, in 1920, and, in addition to being the first church service presented by a radio station, was also the first program broadcast from a point other than the station's own studios. In 1921 KDKA added to its list of attractions addresses by members of Congress, market and weather reports, and, in August of that year, broadcast the Davis Cup tennis matches held at the Sewickley Country Club. In the same year, station WJZ, New York, presented the first broadcast of the World's Series baseball games, and KYW, Chicago, the first radio pick-up of the Chicago Civic Opera Company.[5]

It is interesting to note some of the programs which were broadcast over station WJZ during the period May 15—December 31, 1923. Out of 3,426 programs, 670 were vocal solos, 391 instrumental solos, 723 talks, 205 bedtime stories, 7 operas, 67 church services, 14 Philharmonic Stadium concerts, 49 programs broadcast direct from theater stages, 106 concerts from the Wanamaker store, and 21 athletic contests, in addition to numerous other types of programs.[6]

The rise of the national network companies provided the necessary financial and technical resources for the construction of programs of higher quality and greater variety. Moreover, this same development made it possible to carry to the American public presentation originating in the great talent centers of the country. Thus the rise of the national network lent great impetus to program development. The trend in network program

---

[5] *This Thing Called Broadcasting*, by Goldsmith and Lescaboura (Holt), pp. 99–101.
[6] *Ibid.*

service, as reflected in the proportion of hours devoted to various types of programs broadcast over the key stations of the National Broadcasting Company Red and Blue networks, and the Columbia Broadcasting System during the second weeks of February, May, August, and November, 1927–32, is found in Table XXXII.

The proportion of hours devoted to the broadcasting of classical music has varied only slightly since the beginning of the networks. In so far as the number of hours broadcast by network key stations has increased appreciably since 1927, the percentage of time devoted to music of this type today represents a larger absolute number of hours than it did in the early years of radio. This is especially true prior to 1929, since which time there has been relatively little change as to the number of hours per week during which programs are presented.[7] The result of this factor has been that, in the spring of 1932, approximately eight and one-half hours of classical music were broadcast each week as compared to about five and one-half hours in November, 1929. Moreover, the quality of the classical music broadcast has increased appreciably. Today, for the first time, the four greatest musical organizations in the country are on the air with a reasonable degree of regularity: the Metropolitan Opera Company, the New York Philharmonic Symphony Orchestra, the Philadelphia Orchestra, and the Boston Symphony Orchestra. With the exception of the Philadelphia Orchestra, all of them broadcast on a regular weekly schedule.

The low proportion of classical music broadcast in the second week of November, 1932, should be interpreted with care, since it probably is not representative of the situation during the 1932–33 season. Due to the disturbing factor of the Presidential campaign, the network program schedule was considerably upset and the completion of the normal weekly program structure delayed. Consequently a higher percentage of classical music quite probably would be revealed if an analysis were made of programs broadcast during February, 1933.

There has been a marked decline in the proportion of semi-classical music broadcast over the network key stations ever

---

[7] Prior to November, 1929, the average number of hours broadcast per week by key stations was in the neighborhood of 80, increasing to 119 in November, 1929. Since then there has been little change, the number of hours ranging between 119 and 126.

TABLE XXXII

PROPORTION OF VARIOUS TYPES OF PROGRAMS BROADCAST OVER KEY STATIONS OF NATIONAL NETWORKS DURING THE SECOND WEEK OF FEBRUARY, MAY, AUGUST, AND NOVEMBER, ANNUALLY, 1927–32

(Average NBC Red, Blue, and the Columbia Broadcasting System networks)*

PERCENTAGE OF HOURS OF VARIOUS TYPES OF PROGRAMS

Type of Program	1927				1928				1929				1930				1931				1932†		
	Feb	May	Aug	Nov	Feb	May	Aug	Nov	Feb	May	Aug	Nov	Feb	May	Aug	Nov	Feb	May	Aug	Nov	Feb	May	Nov
Classical music	9.4	5.2	6.4	7.0	9.3	10.3	11.1	8.0	3.0	10.1	7.6	4.6	8.4	8.5	7.7	9.3	10.0	7.1	10.0	7.7	6.6	7.5	4.9
Semi-classical music	24.2	21.9	18.9	25.2	21.4	24.4	24.5	17.0	21.8	19.3	15.3	14.2	17.8	16.5	18.9	14.6	12.6	15.4	13.4	12.0	14.4	12.3	10.6
Folk music and ballads	0.9	5.2	6.8	5.1	6.6	4.5	7.9	7.5	9.1	6.4	4.6	3.9	1.3	2.3	3.0	3.7	2.8	3.6	3.9	3.0	3.4	5.3	1.0
Variety music	0.3	8.5	5.2	9.1	5.0	4.7	5.4	3.6	8.2	3.7	4.9	5.5	4.8	4.6	5.3	5.0	7.2	5.9	4.5	4.2	3.1	5.3	2.0
Popular music	36.5	32.8	38.8	25.1	29.5	22.0	23.3	21.2	28.5	32.9	36.1	36.7	31.5	31.5	32.7	27.6	28.1	29.5	37.3	33.8	39.3	37.2	42.9
Total music	71.3	73.6	76.1	71.5	71.8	65.9	72.2	57.3	70.6	72.4	68.5	64.9	63.8	63.4	67.2	60.2	60.7	61.5	69.1	60.7	66.8	67.6	61.4
Children's programs		2.1	0.2	0.7	0.6	1.2	1.0	1.9	1.6	0.1	0.4	0.4	1.8	1.7	1.8	1.4	1.8	1.5	1.4	2.7	2.9	2.4	3.4
Comedy broadcasts										1.3	1.6	1.3	1.4	1.7	1.7	1.4	3.3	3.2	3.7	4.7	3.4	3.6	4.1
Other dramatic programs	1.9	2.4	1.4	0.7	2.1	2.2	3.4	3.9	3.2	3.6	4.6	4.9	5.1	5.3	6.0	5.5	5.8	7.4	5.2	5.5	5.1	5.0	4.9
Adult educational programs	10.2	5.9	7.0	9.7	9.9	13.9	9.8	11.8	8.5	9.6	6.9	7.1	8.5	7.4	5.7	6.3	6.9	4.8	4.1	5.0	5.4	5.7	3.6
Children's educational programs	0.9	0.7	0.8		0.8	1.8	2.1	2.2	2.5	1.7	1.1	1.7	0.4	0.3	1.3	0.9	0.7	1.6		0.7	0.6	1.6	0.8
Farm programs	0.2												1.3	1.2	1.3	1.7	1.8		1.7	1.7	1.8	1.6	
International rebroadcasts													0.1	0.1	0.3	0.4	0.1	0.1	0.1	0.1	0.7	0.4	0.3
News, market and weather reports	5.2	1.8	2.5	3.3	1.9	3.2	2.0	1.6	1.6	2.1	1.9	1.7	1.6	3.7	3.4	2.5	2.2	2.0	1.5	1.4	1.3	1.8	1.5
Religious broadcasts	4.2	5.2	2.9	2.8	3.9	3.4	2.1	3.4	2.9	2.6	2.9	3.4	2.6	3.1	2.6	3.3	3.7	2.4	2.5	1.9	1.2	1.3	0.5
Sports broadcasts	0.3	2.4	3.4	3.9		0.2	0.1	3.7	0.6	0.1		2.6	0.1	0.3	0.2	2.4		0.1	0.2	2.7	0.1		2.6
Special features of public interest	0.3	1.6		3.7	3.2	3.3	2.4	8.9	2.5	1.3	0.4	1.2	0.9	1.0	0.2	2.3	0.7	0.3	0.3	0.8	0.3	0.1	2.7
Women's feature programs	1.5	1.6	1.5	0.8	1.9	1.6	2.5	3.0	5.0	3.6	5.5	6.1	5.8	4.5	4.1	5.6	4.9	6.2	5.6	5.3	3.4	4.1	2.7
Variety programs	4.0	2.7	4.2	2.9	3.9	3.3	1.8	2.3	1.0	1.6	6.2	4.7	6.6	6.8	5.8	6.1	7.4	8.9	4.9	6.8	7.0	7.0	9.6
Total programs	100.0	100.0	100.0	100.0	100.0	100.0	100.0	100.0	100.0	100.0	100.0	100.0	100.0	100.0	100.0	100.0	100.0	100.0	100.0	100.0	100.0	100.0	100.0

* Source: NBC and CBS program records.
† August, 1932, is missing because of limitation of time with respect to the tabulation of the data.

since 1929. Though this type of music still ranks second in the amount broadcast, it comprises no more than half of the proportion of total hours broadcast as compared with 1927 and 1928. No definite trend is indicated with respect to folk music and ballads. This type of entertainment reached its peak in the winter of 1928 and spring of 1929, following which it declined until the spring of 1932. At that time there was a brief increase, which soon died out. This latter rise in folk music differed from that broadcast in the earlier period, in that it consisted almost exclusively of cowboy and hill-billy tunes, whereas the earlier programs in this field were comprised of the old songs familiar to everyone.

Variety music not only is difficult to classify but also requires great care in its interpretation. Though the proportion of such music has remained comparatively the same during the period under consideration, the type of variety music has changed radically. The variety program of the early days of network broadcasting was made up largely of classical and semi-classical music with an occasional popular ballad thrown in. This type of program began to pass from the picture about 1930. Since then it has been supplanted almost completely by a form of program which consists primarily of popular music rendered in concert fashion, combined with occasional classical numbers.

The proportion of popular music has increased less in comparison with other forms of programs than might be expected. With the exception of 1928, when it was at low ebb, there has been little change in the percentage of hours devoted to popular programs, until quite recently, when a slight increase has occurred. It is interesting to note that the 1928 low point in popular music broadcasts coincided with the period during which advertisers were convinced that goodwill engendered from classical concerts was the factor in radio from which the greatest benefit could be derived.

It also must be remembered that, during the period under consideration, popular music itself changed greatly. Early programs in this field consisted entirely of music played for dancing purposes. Later, orchestras began to develop distinctive tempos and forms of presentation in an endeavor to win the interest of the listener who was not concerned with dancing. Orchestras, such as that of B. A. Rolfe and the banjo ensemble of the "Cliquot Club Eskimos," came to be known throughout the country and to be among the most popular programs broadcast.[8] Continually greater novelty was introduced in the presentation of popular music. Orchestration and distinctive arrangements became increasingly important, with the result that new aspects of melodic and harmonic development found their way into popular music. Soloists also were added to the dance band itself. By 1931 the popular music program presented a vastly more sophisticated and musically superior presentation than did that of the first years of network broadcasting.

In this development, radio benefited greatly from the general trend which was taking place in the field of popular music. The extreme rhythms of the immediate post-war period were being discarded in favor of better melody and more subtle rhythm. This trend was given added impetus by the return in popularity of the costume operetta, such as "Blossom Time" and "The Student Prince"; the vogue for a concert rendition of popular music established about that time by Paul Whiteman; and the compositions of George Gershwin, which served to lend an aura of musical respectability to certain aspects of popular music.

However, radio not only benefited from the general trend in popular music but also probably exerted an important influence on the rate and extent of its development. The necessity for introducing distinctiveness and novelty into popular programs broadcast over the radio undoubtedly caused many musicians in the field to devote greater attention to questions of presentation and arrangement than otherwise would have been the case. The reward for distinctiveness was greatly increased by the advent of broadcasting, while the penalty imposed in the way of reduced acceptance of both compositions and orchestras where distinctiveness was missing likewise was made more severe. Thus it seems that radio broadcasting, while dependent upon popular music for at least some measure of its public acceptance, has also exerted a beneficial constructive influence upon the quality of that form of music.

This influence has not been without some drawbacks, for it

[8] In December, 1928, "Cliquot Club Eskimos" ranked third, and B. A. Rolfe, fifth, in popularity among Philadelphia audiences (*A Merchandising Interpretation of Listener Reactions and Habits with Respect to Radio Broadcasting*, by Herman S. Hettinger, p. 39).

has included, among other items, the development of the crooner. Since crooning technique has its foundations in musical im-
perfection—that of sliding into a note rather than striking it
true on the first attack—it can hardly be said to be an improvement in the art of singing. The real success of crooning has been
not in its musical aspects, but in the personal touch and atmosphere of romantic intimacy which the crooner has been able to
build up through his distinctive delivery. It is quite possible
that the same intimacy can be achieved by other artists without
a wholesale distortion of the musical scale. Another difficulty of
popular music, namely, the tendency for it to concentrate at the
hours of the day when the greatest audience is available—sometimes at the expense of other types of programs—will be discussed when the question of variations in program service during the morning, afternoon, and evening periods is considered in
detail.

The proportion of total program hours devoted to strictly musical presentations is approximately 15 per cent less today than
it was in 1927 and 1928. There was a sharp decline in the proportion of hours given over to musical programs in 1929, and,
since then, this has remained comparatively unchanging. The
number of hours actually devoted to musical programs has varied but little since 1929, and averages in the neighborhood of
from 80 to 85 hours out of from 120 to 125 hours broadcast
weekly. The proportion of total hours devoted to musical programs at the present time is slightly in excess of 60 per cent.
This does not include quite all of the music broadcast, since
there is a rather large amount of music to be found among the
variety programs. This factor, however, is not sufficient to
change the general trend to any important degree.

One of the forms of non-musical programs to have experienced the most rapid rise in recent years has been the children's
program. No broadcasts, other than bedtime stories, were presented for children until the spring of 1929, while there was no
marked trend in this direction until the fall of 1931. Since then
there has been a steady growth in this form of program, which
shows no signs of abating. Practically all of the programs in this
field are dramatic offerings which have to do with the exciting,
and often lurid, adventures of some youngster such as Skippy or
Little Orphan Annie, or of boys' heroes, such as Captain Jack,

the aviator. However, several programs, including the "Kellogg Singing Lady," the "Lone Wolf Tribe," and the "Adventures of Helen and Mary," strike a more restrained note.[9]

Comedy programs also are predominantly dramatic in form, though a number of them incline toward the vaudeville dialogue or patter. Amos 'n' Andy are the best example of the former, while Billy Jones and Ernie Hare, the original Happiness Boys, are typical of the latter.[10] The proportion of hours broadcast devoted to comedy programs increased with marked rapidity in 1931, and today stands at approximately twice that of 1930.

Other forms of dramatic programs have experienced a steady increase since the beginning of network broadcasting, and today are more important than either comedy or children's programs. The early programs in this field were straight dramatic presentations, often radio adaptations of well-known stage plays. Later, the homely drama, containing no small measure of humor, came into existence, and reached its greatest vogue in programs such as "Tomkins Corners," "Real Folks," "Seth Parker," and the "Country Doctor." The dramatized sketch, usually based on tales of history and adventure, came into prominence about the same time. Examples of this type of program include "Death Valley Days"—recounting stories of the western mining days and especially of the Death Valley country—"Roses and Drums" and "Great Moments in History," both of which feature dramatizations taken from American history. In the past several years the mystery and melodrama have come to the forefront. This trend was originated by the Sherlock Holmes program, and has come to embrace a large portion of the total dramatic programs broadcast. The "Adventures of Fu Manchu," and the "Eno Crime Club" are typical of this type.

Children's educational programs have tended to show a slight

[9] Skippy and similar programs unvaryingly center about wild adventures with robbers and other villains of the deepest dye, and in the course of whose pursuit seemingly insuperable obstacles are overcome, usually with the assistance of the child hero or heroine. The "Kellogg Singing Lady" presents a vastly different type of program, consisting of songs which she teaches the children and stories which she relates. The "Lone Wolf Tribe" is built along adventure lines, but less in the style of Nick Carter and more of the American boy. The "Adventures of Helen and Mary" are dramatizations of well-known fairy tales.

[10] The Jones and Hare presentation, originally sponsored by the Happiness Candy Stores, and since then by Interwoven Socks, and later Hellman's and Best Foods Mayonnaise, is a typical vaudeville comedian presentation.

decline since 1929, but, on the whole, have maintained a comparatively steady proportion since their inception. Such decline as there has been in this field is due to the increased number of total hours of programs broadcast, rather than any marked decrease in the number of hours devoted to programs of this class. Broadcasts in this category are confined principally to the American School of the Air, though it should be kept in mind that the Damrosch Friday morning concerts, listed with classical music rather than in this group, likewise have a most important educational significance for children and adults alike. It is quite probable that this type of program will neither increase nor decline to any great extent, since network broadcasts of such programs necessarily are limited as to when they can be presented and the degree to which they can be adapted to the needs of varying curricula and methods of instruction.

While adult educational programs have declined considerably in quantity, there has been a marked improvement in the quality and interest value of those remaining on the air. The reason for the large proportion of programs of this type broadcast in the 1927–28 period lies in the fact that talent was scarce and speakers easy to secure. Since then the public has grown weary of mere addresses, and new methods of presentation have had to be devised. The dialogue and dramatized version have been important contributions in this field, as has been the development of a better technique for the delivery of talks themselves. Throughout the entire range of educational programs, a saving measure of informality has been injected.

Especially noteworthy has been the work done in this field by the National Advisory Council on Radio in Education, which at different times has produced series of programs in the fields of psychology, civics and government, economics, vocational guidance, and the labor movement. The most modern methods of presentation have been used in all of the programs, with a corresponding increase in listener interest. Other interesting programs in the same field include the one entitled "Our American Schools" under the direction of Miss Florence Hale, of the National Education Association, broadcast over the National Broadcasting Company's Red network, the Columbia Broadcasting System's Public Affairs Institute, and similar programs. Many progams not listed in this group, especially those appearing under the classification of news, drama, classical music, women's features, international rebroadcasts, and farm programs, also are highly important from an educational viewpoint. The adult educational value of radio broadcasting is extremely broad and cannot be measured by any mere method of classification of programs.

The broadcasts of news, market, and weather reports have decreased materially over network stations since 1927. This has been due to the almost complete deletion of news flashes and stock market reports from the network programs. At the present time network news broadcasting is confined to brief summaries, combined with editorial comments, such as those given by Lowell Thomas and Boake Carter. There is no reason why the network should concern itself in this field, since it enjoys no marked advantage over the individual station in this respect. In addition, the possibility of incurring the ill will of the newspaper profession through too strenuous competition in the dissemination of news would do the network a great deal of harm as far as its publicity was concerned. This may be an additional factor dictating a conservative policy with regard to the broadcasting of news flashes.

The proportion of hours devoted to religious programs remained comparatively steady until 1931 when a decline set in. This seems to have been due primarily to the withdrawal of a number of commercially sponsored religious broadcasts from the air. Likewise, there has been little change with regard to the proportion of time devoted to sports broadcasts. The variety of sports included has tended to increase, so that at the present time accounts of football and baseball games, tennis, polo and boxing matches, golf tournaments, track meets, and horse races are among the programs broadcast. A factor which may affect seriously the future development of this type of program is the attitude of the colleges and baseball leagues to broadcasts of their respective games. There has been a rather widespread opinion that broadcasting has hurt gate receipts in college football and professional baseball. Regardless of whether this has or has not been the case, the existence of such an opinion has given rise to a reluctance to broadcast contests on the part of a number of schools and clubs. At the present time, however, it does not seem as if the objections raised will make much headway. There also is reason to doubt the validity of the premise upon which they are based, in so far as the baseball teams of some cities have experienced marked success with the broadcasting of games.

International broadcasts are one of the most spectacular forms of program service rendered by networks, and have served to link together nations and continents in a manner that would have been inconceivable but a few years ago. International programs were first broadcast in 1930, and since then have increased steadily, though they probably always will remain a small portion of total network programs. Speakers brought to the American public by means of international rebroadcasts have included such distinguished figures as His Holiness Pope Pius XI, King George V of England, Prime Minister Ramsay MacDonald, President Hindenburg of Germany, the presidents of Austria, Switzerland, and the Irish Free State, King Albert of Belgium, former Chancellor von Papen of Germany, Winston Churchill, Guglielmo Marconi, Mahatma Gandhi, George Bernard Shaw, Leon Trotzky, and numerous others of international note. Opera and other musical programs have been rebroadcast from various parts of Europe. The technique and facilities in this field have been developed to a point where regular international rebroadcasting has been made possible. At the present time both national network companies are maintaining comparatively regular schedules of international features.

Special feature broadcasts are another of the particularly interesting categories of American program service, and constitute a feature of distinctive strength in the programs of this country. One of the most important groups of programs coming under this classification are the broadcasts by numerous members of the United States government. In 1931 the two national network companies broadcast approximately 530 hours[11] of speeches by government, state, or city officials. This totaled 478 programs, representing a time value of approximately $2,844,-000. Though some of these appearances must be classified under either adult educational programs or farm broadcasts, the great majority of them fall into the category of special features. They constitute the most direct method thus far devised for bringing the members of the government directly before the people. Dur-

[11] *Commercial Radio Advertising*, Federal Radio Commission, pp. 17, 21.

ing the past year the possibility of broadcasting the debates of
the Senate was seriously considered by both the networks and
the officials of that body, though nothing thus far has transpired
in this direction. It may be that this would constitute too direct
a contact between the people and their representatives.

Other special features of widespread interest and significance
included the broadcasting of the two national political conventions, addresses by distinguished figures in various walks of life,
broadcasts of important public events, and similar occasions.
Though the proportion of this type of program declined in 1931,
it again has increased. Today it is almost as high as it was during 1928 when programs of this kind reached their peak. The
showmanship in current special feature programs is vastly superior to that of previous years, so that those which are presented contain a higher degree of public interest than at any
time in the history of network broadcasting.

Women's features grew slowly during 1927 and 1928, rose
rapidly in 1929, and constituted a relatively important portion
of total program hours until 1932, when they declined. In so far
as these programs are mostly broadcasts of recipes, household
helps, child-care information, suggestions regarding interior dec-
oration, beauty hints, and similar features, their decline may be
due to the fact that American women are tiring of the repetition
of these matters and are demanding more in the way of entertainment. However, it is too early to state whether or not this
is the case.

Variety programs have shown a steady increase, due primarily to the attempt of advertisers to find distinctive ways of presenting programs consisting of dance music and vaudeville or
musical comedy entertainers. The result has been the rise of the
Ed Wynn type of program, which at present is at the height of
its popularity. Whether it will continue in vogue for any protracted length of time, remains to be seen.

Farm programs have constituted a relatively unvarying proportion of program hours broadcast since 1930. Since these
broadcasts are devoted exclusively to the "National Farm and
Home Hour," presented over the National Broadcasting Company's Blue network, the trend regarding this form of program
promises to remain an even one.

The differences which exist between the types of programs

sponsored commercially and presented by networks on a sustaining basis constitute an important question with regard to an evaluation of the American radio program structure. It is claimed at times that it is the commercial program which constitutes the disturbing element in the program service furnished the listening public in this country. Granting the premise that a broadcasting system should furnish the type of program which the people enjoy and desire, this claim seems to be erroneous for the most part. This is indicated in Table XXXIII where it is revealed that the concentration of commercial programs upon certain types has not been enough to have the effect sometimes attributed to it.

In the field of classical music the commercial program has been weak since 1928, the proportion of commercial hours devoted to such presentations declining ever since then. The 1932 figure, however, must be interpreted conservatively—as was the case with regard to total classical music—in so far as some of the most important classical programs of that season were not broadcast until after the second week in November. The proportion of sustaining program hours devoted to classical music rose steadily until 1931, declining slightly during that and the following year.

Commercial broadcasts of semi-classical music have never been more than from one-third to one-half as much as sustaining programs of the same class, and have declined steadily since the outset. Today, only 2.0 per cent of commercial program hours are devoted to programs of this type. Sustaining programs have decreased more slowly in the semi-classical field. In the field of folk music the proportion of commercial hours devoted to entertainment of this sort always has been higher than with regard to sustaining programs. Both have experienced a comparatively steady decline, in spite of a brief return to popularity of commercially sponsored hill-billy music in the spring of 1932. Commercially sponsored variety music programs dropped considerably in 1931 and 1932, largely due to the passing of the classical-popular type of program. Sustaining programs of this sort have been of little importance.

It is interesting to note that the proportion of commercial program hours devoted to the broadcasting of popular music has always tended to be lower than with regard to sustaining pro-

TABLE XXXIII

PROPORTION OF COMMERCIAL AND SUSTAINING HOURS, RESPECTIVELY, DEVOTED TO PROGRAMS OF VARIOUS KINDS DURING THE SECOND WEEK OF NOVEMBER, 1927–32, BY THE KEY STATIONS OF THE NBC RED AND BLUE AND COLUMBIA NETWORKS

PERCENTAGE OF HOURS OF VARIOUS KINDS OF PROGRAMS

TYPE OF PROGRAM	1927			1928			1929			1930			1931			1932		
	Commercial	Sustaining	Total	Commercial	Sustaining	Total	Commercial	Sustaining	Total	Commercial	Sustaining	Total	Commercial	Sustaining	Total	Commercial	Sustaining	Total
Classical music	16.2	4.6	7.0	7.9	8.1	8.0	0.6	5.9	4.6	6.4	10.4	9.3	2.7	10.6	7.7	0.1	6.5	4.9
Semi-classical music	25.7	25.1	25.2	7.9	20.5	17.0	9.6	15.7	14.2	3.5	19.3	14.6	6.9	15.0	12.0	2.0	13.5	10.6
Folk music and ballads	3.4	5.5	5.1	13.0	5.3	7.5	4.5	3.7	3.9	6.9	2.4	3.7	4.3	2.2	3.0	2.6	0.5	1.0
Variety music	18.8	6.6	9.1	8.4	1.8	3.6	6.8	5.1	5.5	9.2	3.3	5.0	4.5	4.0	4.2	3.9	1.4	2.0
Popular music	21.4	26.1	25.1	15.2	23.4	21.2	29.2	39.2	36.7	20.2	30.7	27.6	28.7	36.7	33.8	21.4	50.4	42.9
Total music	85.5	67.9	71.5	52.5	59.1	57.3	50.7	69.6	64.9	46.2	66.1	60.2	47.1	68.5	60.7	30.0	72.3	61.4
Children's programs	1.7	0.5	0.7	4.6	0.8	1.9		0.6	0.4	1.9	1.2	1.4	3.0	2.6	2.7	9.2	1.3	3.4
Comedy broadcasts							3.4	0.6	1.3	4.5	0.1	1.4	8.9	2.3	4.7	10.0	2.1	4.1
Other dramatic programs	0.8	0.8	0.7	8.8	2.1	3.9	7.6	4.1	4.9	11.4	3.1	5.5	9.8	2.9	5.5	13.5	1.9	4.9
Adult educational programs	3.4	11.4	9.7	19.7	8.3	11.8	10.8	6.0	7.1	8.9	4.9	6.3	7.2	3.6	5.0	9.5	1.6	3.6
Children's educational programs				0.8	2.7	2.2	2.3	1.5	1.7	1.9	0.5	0.9	0.1	1.1	0.7		1.1	0.8
Farm programs											2.4	1.7		2.8	1.7		2.4	1.9
International rebroadcasts										0.5	0.3	0.4		0.1	0.1		0.4	0.3

TABLE XXXIII—*Continued*

PERCENTAGE OF HOURS OF VARIOUS KINDS OF PROGRAMS

Type of Program	1927			1928			1929			1930			1931			1932		
	Commercial	Sustaining	Total	Commercial	Sustaining	Total	Commercial	Sustaining	Total	Commercial	Sustaining	Total	Commercial	Sustaining	Total	Commercial	Sustaining	Total
News, market and weather reports		3.9	3.3		2.3	1.6		2.3	1.7	2.4	2.7	2.5	1.6	1.4	1.4	1.9	1.4	1.5
Religious broadcasts		3.5	2.8	0.8	4.4	3.4	0.6	4.3	3.4	0.9	4.3	3.3	0.4	2.7	1.9		1.9	0.5
Sports broadcasts		4.8	3.9	0.4	5.0	3.7	0.6	3.0	2.6		3.4	2.4	0.4	4.1	2.7	0.8	3.2	2.6
Special features of public interest		4.6	3.7		12.6	8.9		1.6	1.2		3.3	2.3		1.3	0.8	1.1	2.4	2.7
Women's feature programs	1.7	0.7	0.8	7.1	1.4	3.0	17.5	2.3	6.1	12.9	2.5	5.6	12.0	1.5	5.3	7.4	1.1	2.7
Variety programs	6.9	1.9	2.9	5.3	1.3	2.3	6.5	4.1	4.7	8.5	5.2	6.1	9.5	5.1	6.8	16.6	6.9	9.6
Total programs	100.0	100.0	100.0	100.0	100.0	100.0	100.0	100.0	100.0	100.0	100.0	100.0	100.0	100.0	100.0	100.0	100.0	100.0

grams. This is offset partly, since 1931, by the rise of the variety program which contains a large measure of popular music. This type of program increased from 9.5 per cent in that year to 16.6 per cent in 1932. Even adding this figure to commercially sponsored popular music still leaves the latter's percentage far behind that of sustaining programs in the same field. With regard to musical programs as a whole, the commercial group again lags behind that of the sustaining. The proportion of commercially sponsored musical programs has been declining steadily, having constituted 85.5 per cent of all hours devoted to commercial programs in 1927, 46.2 per cent in 1930, and 30.0 per cent in 1932. The proportion of sustaining program hours devoted to musical presentations has been increasing steadily in recent years.

Commercial children's programs increased rapidly since 1931, having represented 1.9 per cent of total commercial program hours in 1930 and 9.2 per cent in 1932. Sustaining programs in the same field showed no appreciable change during the period under consideration. Commercially sponsored comedy broadcasts also have increased to a marked degree, rising from 3.4 per cent in 1929 to 10.0 per cent in 1932, while sustaining programs of this type have increased but slightly. Dramatic programs broadcast by advertisers rose rapidly in 1928, increasing tenfold over the previous year, and since then have continued to increase steadily until they represented 13.5 per cent of commercial program hours in November, 1932. Sustaining dramatic programs have dropped gradually since 1929, and at present are but 1.9 per cent of total sustaining hours broadcast by key stations.

Since the withdrawal of the Grigsby Grunow Company from partial sponsorship of the American School of the Air, there have been no commercial programs in this field. Commercially sponsored adult education programs have been consistently higher than sustaining, probably due to the relatively steady number of commercial programs of the "Devils, Drugs and Doctors" and Angelo Patri[12] types, as compared to the small number of total commercial program hours. There were no news broadcasts commercially sponsored prior to 1930, while the pro-

---

[12] The former is an interesting series of discussions on the history of medicine and the latter of child-care problems, especially as they relate to older children of the school age.

portion of such programs has declined steadily since the first year, though not as rapidly as sustaining programs of this type.

Women's programs sponsored by broadcast advertisers constituted a larger proportion of total commercial hours in 1929 than in any other year. Since that time they have dropped from 17.5 per cent to 7.4 per cent in November, 1932. Sustaining programs in this program category have always been less in proportion to total program hours of that type, though their trend has been more steady.

In the field of variety programs, commercial broadcasts have been the most important and have increased to the greater degree. Religious programs which have been commercially sponsored have always been negligible in amount, while sports, special features, international rebroadcasts, and farm programs always have been the particular province of the sustaining program. Thus it seems that broadcast advertising has tended to concentrate more upon the following types of programs than have the networks themselves: folk music, variety programs, children's, comedy, and dramatic programs, adult educational broadcasts, and women's features. However, in terms of the proportion of total commercial hours devoted to various kinds of programs in November, 1932, popular music ranks first with 21.4 per cent; variety second, with 16.6 per cent; drama third, with 13.5 per cent; comedy fourth, with 10.0 per cent; adult educational programs fifth, with 9.5 per cent; children's programs sixth, with 9.2 per cent, and women's features seventh, with 7.4 per cent of the total commercial hours. No other program types are of any importance in the commercial group.

Because of the great differences which exist in the size of the radio audience at various times of the day, program variations in this regard are of especial importance in an evaluation of American broadcasting. General trends in this respect are found for the key stations of the three basic networks in Table XXXIV.

Major tendencies in this field are shown to be as follows: The morning hours are devoted primarily to broadcasts of classical and semi-classical music, comedy, children's educational programs, adult educational programs, religious broadcasts, and women's feature programs. Much of the classical music broadcast in the morning is concentrated on Sunday, though the re-

TABLE XXXIV

PROPORTION OF HOURS OF VARIOUS KINDS OF PROGRAMS BROADCAST DURING THE MORNING, AFTERNOON, AND EVENING HOURS, RESPECTIVELY, OVER THE KEY STATIONS OF THE NBC RED AND BLUE AND COLUMBIA NETWORKS DURING THE SECOND WEEK OF NOVEMBER, 1927-32*

PERCENTAGE OF HOURS OF VARIOUS KINDS OF PROGRAMS

TYPE OF PROGRAM	1927 Morning	1927 Afternoon	1927 Evening	1928 Morning	1928 Afternoon	1928 Evening	1929 Morning	1929 Afternoon	1929 Evening	1930 Morning	1930 Afternoon	1930 Evening	1931 Morning	1931 Afternoon	1931 Evening	1932 Morning	1932 Afternoon	1932 Evening
Classical music	.....	3.5	9.9	4.0	7.4	9.4	2.3	5.8	4.8	5.6	10.0	11.0	7.5	11.8	4.8	4.7	6.6	3.5
Semi-classical music	10.7	22.8	27.6	12.3	18.2	17.2	12.9	10.5	18.5	16.2	18.7	9.6	10.8	16.0	9.8	15.2	12.9	5.7
Folk music and ballads	3.4	3.5	6.2	.....	7.4	9.1	2.0	4.4	4.6	1.9	4.1	4.4	2.7	3.9	2.3	0.5	0.8	1.5
Variety music	14.2	1.7	13.6	.....	1.1	6.5	2.9	4.8	7.9	1.1	5.7	6.7	7.2	2.9	3.5	1.1	2.2	2.4
Popular music	17.9	24.3	26.3	9.2	21.6	23.5	36.9	33.6	39.9	20.2	23.3	36.4	20.8	21.4	51.2	37.5	32.1	55.6
Total music	46.2	55.8	83.6	25.5	55.7	65.7	57.0	59.1	75.7	45.0	61.8	68.1	49.0	56.0	71.6	59.0	54.6	68.7
Children's programs	.....	.....	.....	.....	.....	.....	1.5	.....	.....	1.7	2.5	0.1	4.4	4.6	0.3	3.4	7.3	0.1
Comedy broadcasts	.....	.....	1.2	5.4	.....	2.5	0.5	.....	2.9	2.3	.....	2.0	5.3	0.2	7.6	3.4	5.6	3.2
Other dramatic programs	.....	.....	.....	3.0	0.6	6.8	2.5	2.0	9.2	1.5	2.5	10.9	2.5	4.6	7.9	0.8	2.0	9.6
Adult educational programs	28.4	15.8	4.1	41.3	9.8	5.9	9.5	9.4	3.8	10.9	4.8	4.2	11.1	3.0	2.7	8.4	3.0	1.2
Children's educational programs	.....	.....	.....	4.0	3.8	0.4	2.6	2.4	0.3	.....	2.7	.....	.....	2.3	.....	0.3	2.2	.....
Farm programs	.....	.....	.....	.....	.....	.....	.....	.....	.....	.....	4.7	.....	.....	5.5	.....	.....	5.3	.....
International rebroadcasts	.....	.....	.....	.....	3.2	.....	.....	.....	.....	0.6	0.5	0.4	.....	0.2	.....	.....	0.9	.....

* Source: NBC and CBS program records.

TABLE XXXIV—*Continued*

PERCENTAGE OF HOURS OF VARIOUS KINDS OF PROGRAMS

Type of Program	1927			1928			1929			1930			1931			1932		
	Morning	Afternoon	Evening	Morning	Afternoon	Evening	Morning	Afternoon	Evening	Morning	Afternoon	Evening	Morning	Afternoon	Evening	Morning	Afternoon	Evening
News, market and weather reports		8.8			2.6	1.1		3.8	1.1		3.6	3.0		2.3	1.8		1.2	2.7
Religious broadcasts	14.5	4.6	0.6	5.4	6.5	0.4	4.9	4.8	1.1	5.6	2.7	2.5	3.9	2.4	0.4	2.3	2.0	0.6
Sports broadcasts		9.6	0.3		8.3	0.9		7.5			6.6	0.1		8.6	0.2		7.0	0.4
Special features of public interest		4.6	3.4		9.5	11.4	0.8	2.0	0.6	1.5	4.9	0.7		1.1	0.8	0.2	3.0	2.4
Women's feature programs	10.9	0.8		15.4			13.9	5.0	1.6	21.6	0.8		12.2	5.8		9.5	0.9	
Variety programs			5.6			4.9	6.8	4.0	3.7	9.3	1.9	8.0	10.6	3.4	6.7	12.7	5.0	11.1
Total programs	100.0	100.0	100.0	100.0	100.0	100.0	100.0	100.0	100.0	100.0	100.0	100.0	100.0	100.0	100.0	100.0	100.0	100.0

ligious programs are scattered throughout the week. The adult educational programs broadcast at this time of the day are of especial, though not exclusive, interest to women listeners. The only trends noticeable with regard to morning programs is a slight increase in popular music and decrease in religious broadcasts.

TABLE XXXV

COMPARISON OF THE PROPORTION OF HOURS OF VARIOUS KINDS OF PROGRAMS BROADCAST COMMERCIALLY AND ON A SUSTAINING BASIS OVER THE KEY STATIONS OF THE NBC RED AND BLUE AND COLUMBIA NETWORKS DURING THE MORNING HOURS OF THE SECOND WEEK OF NOVEMBER, 1927–32

TYPE OF PROGRAM	PERCENTAGE OF HOURS OF VARIOUS KINDS OF PROGRAMS											
	1927		1928		1929		1930		1931		1932	
	Commercial	Sustaining	Commercial	Sustaining	Commercial	Sustaining	Commercial	Sustaining	Commercial	Sustaining	Commercial	Sustaining
Classical music			7.6			3.2		8.5		11.5		6.4
Semi-classical music		13.7		26.6		16.9		24.8		16.6		20.7
Folk music and ballads		4.7				2.8	3.2	1.3	0.8	3.8		0.8
Variety music	67.0					3.9	2.5	0.5	5.7	8.1	1.0	1.1
Popular music		22.7		19.9	10.3	45.6	4.9	28.1	9.8	26.8	6.2	49.0
Total music	67.0	41.1	7.6	46.5	10.3	72.4	10.6	63.2	16.3	66.8	7.2	78.0
Children's programs						2.1	4.9		4.9	4.2	6.0	2.8
Comedy broadcasts				11.1		0.7	5.7	0.5	6.6	4.7	10.2	1.1
Other dramatic programs			5.7			3.4	2.5	1.0	4.9	1.3	2.1	0.4
Adult educational programs		36.1	61.8	17.9	36.3	0.7	27.9	2.1	27.1	3.0	31.3	0.4
Children's educational programs				8.7	6.4	1.4						0.4
Farm programs												
International rebroadcasts								1.1				
News, market and weather reports												
Religious broadcasts		18.1		11.1		6.3		8.4		6.0		2.8
Sports broadcasts												
Special features of public interest						1.1		2.1				0.4
Women's feature programs	33.0	4.7	24.9	4.7	47.0	2.8	45.2	9.2	32.0	2.1	28.1	2.8
Variety programs						9.1	3.2	12.4	8.2	11.9	15.1	11.9
Total programs	100.0	100.0	100.0	100.0	100.0	100.0	100.0	100.0	100.0	100.0	100.0	100.0

Afternoon hours show the greatest variety of programs broadcast. It is this time of the day that most classical and semi-classical music is broadcast. In the case of the classical music this is due largely to the afternoon programs of the New York Philharmonic Symphony Orchestra and the Metropolitan Opera Company. Children's programs tend to concentrate in the late afternoon hours. Other programs broadcast in appreciable amounts between twelve o'clock noon and six at night include: adult education, news, religious, sports, special features, international rebroadcasts, and farm programs. Trends in this respect indicate a slight increase in the proportion of afternoon time devoted to drama, semi-classical music, popular music and religious programs, with a small decrease in adult educational broadcasts.

TABLE XXXVI

COMPARISON OF THE PROPORTION OF HOURS OF VARIOUS KINDS OF PROGRAMS BROADCAST COMMERCIALLY AND ON A SUSTAINING BASIS OVER THE KEY STATIONS OF THE NBC RED AND BLUE AND COLUMBIA NETWORKS DURING THE AFTERNOON HOURS OF THE SECOND WEEK OF NOVEMBER, 1927–32

TYPE OF PROGRAM	PERCENTAGE OF HOURS OF VARIOUS KINDS OF PROGRAMS											
	1927		1928		1929		1930		1931		1932	
	Commercial	Sustaining	Commercial	Sustaining	Commercial	Sustaining	Commercial	Sustaining	Commercial	Sustaining	Commercial	Sustaining
Classical music	50.0	3.2		7.8		6.3	10.5	9.9	10.8	12.1		8.1
Semi-classical music	50.0	23.4	13.6	18.4		11.3	6.9	20.2	5.5	18.8		14.7
Folk music and ballads		3.7	13.6	7.2		4.8	3.2	1.3	12.0	1.8	4.2	0.2
Variety music		11.8	26.4		12.4	4.3	22.7	3.7	1.0	2.9	2.8	2.1
Popular music		44.3		22.5	6.3	35.2	5.2	25.6	2.4	19.1	19.3	34.0
Total music	100.0	56.4	53.6	55.9	18.7	61.9	71.6	60.7	53.3	54.7	26.3	59.1
Children's programs							3.5	2.4	7.6	3.8	40.1	1.5
Comedy broadcasts										0.3	22.5	2.5
Other dramatic programs				0.6		2.2	3.5	2.4	7.6	3.8		2.3
Adult educational programs		15.7	6.4	10.0	6.3	9.3		5.4	1.0	5.5	4.2	2.8
Children's educational programs				4.0		2.6	14.4	1.3		2.9		2.5
Farm programs								5.2		7.1		6.4
International rebroadcasts								0.4		0.3		1.0
News, market and weather reports		8.4		2.8		4.1		4.1		2.9		1.3
Religious broadcasts		4.5	13.6	6.3	6.3	6.3	3.5	2.6	2.2	2.4		2.4
Sports broadcasts		9.6		8.7	6.3	7.6		7.6	1.0	10.6		8.6
Special features of public interest		4.5		9.4		2.5		5.4		1.8		3.6
Women's feature programs		0.9	26.4	2.3	56.1	1.5		0.8	23.9	2.4		1.0
Variety programs					6.3	3.8	3.5	1.7	3.4	3.5	6.9	5.0
Total programs	100.0	100.0	100.0	100.0	100.0	100.0	100.0	100.0	100.0	100.0	100.0	100.0

Evening programs tend to concentrate on popular and folk music, drama, comedy, variety programs, and news. Popular music and comedy were increasing in November, 1932, while news was decreasing. A rather large proportion of the popular music broadcast at night comes after half-past ten o'clock at night.

A comparison of the proportion of commercial and sustaining hours devoted to programs of various types at different times of the day is found in Tables XXXV, XXXVI, and XXXVII.

Commercial programs tend to concentrate upon other than musical presentations during the morning hours. Women's features and adult educational broadcasts rank most important, together comprising almost 60.0 per cent of the total programs broadcast. In November, 1932, music comprised only 7.2 per

TABLE XXXVII

COMPARISON OF THE PROPORTION OF HOURS OF VARIOUS KINDS OF PROGRAMS BROADCAST COMMERCIALLY AND ON A SUSTAINING BASIS OVER THE KEY STATIONS OF THE NBC RED AND BLUE AND COLUMBIA NETWORKS DURING THE EVENING HOURS OF THE SECOND WEEK OF NOVEMBER, 1927–32

| TYPE OF PROGRAM | PERCENTAGE OF HOURS OF VARIOUS KINDS OF PROGRAMS | | | | | | | | | | | |
| | 1927 | | 1928 | | 1929 | | 1930 | | 1931 | | 1932 | |
	Com-mer-cial	Sus-tain-ing	Com-mer-cial	Sus-tain-ing	Com-mer-cial	Sus-tain-ing	Com-mer-cial	Sus-tain-ing	Com-mer-cial	Sus-tain-ing	Com-mer-cial	Sus-tain-ing
Classical music	16.5	6.6	8.7	9.8	0.9	7.6	8.6	12.5	1.4	8.2	....	5.2
Semi-classical music	26.6	28.1	9.9	22.1	14.9	21.0	4.5	13.8	10.2	9.5	3.8	6.7
Folk music and ballads	3.6	7.5	16.9	3.9	7.0	3.0	4.1	4.9	3.4	1.3	3.4	0.5
Variety music	16.6	12.2	9.3	4.3	8.7	7.3	9.4	4.9	5.1	2.0	5.9	0.8
Popular music	22.9	28.1	21.2	25.4	40.4	39.0	31.1	39.7	37.9	64.2	21.4	68.7
Total music	86.2	82.5	66.0	65.5	71.9	77.9	57.7	75.7	58.0	85.2	41.8	81.9
Children's programs	....	....	....	....	....	....	0.3	....	0.7	....	0.5	....
Comedy broadcasts	1.6	0.9	6.4	....	5.3	1.2	4.9	....	12.6	2.6	5.4	2.2
Other dramatic programs	0.9	1.4	10.5	4.3	11.8	7.3	17.5	5.8	12.6	3.3	24.4	2.5
Adult educational programs	3.6	4.2	8.2	4.3	0.9	5.8	1.7	6.1	1.0	4.1	0.9	1.2
Children's educational programs	....	....	1.1	....	0.9	....	....	....	....	....	....	....
Farm programs	....	....	....	....	....	....	....	....	....	....	....	....
International rebroadcasts	....	....	....	....	....	....	0.8	....	....	....	....	....
News, market, and weather reports	....	....	....	1.9	....	1.9	4.1	2.1	2.7	0.7	3.4	2.5
Religious broadcasts	....	0.9	....	0.8	....	1.9	0.8	3.7	....	0.7	....	1.0
Sports broadcasts	....	0.5	0.5	1.1	....	....	....	0.3	0.3	....	1.5	....
Special features of public interest	....	5.4	....	18.9	....	1.1	....	1.2	....	1.7	1.7	2.7
Women's feature programs	....	....	....	....	....	2.9	....	....	....	....	....	....
Variety programs	7.5	4.2	7.3	3.2	9.2	....	12.5	4.8	12.1	1.7	20.4	6.0
Total programs	100.0	100.0	100.0	100.0	100.0	100.0	100.0	100.0	100.0	100.0	100.0	100.0

cent of the commercial morning program hours, as compared with 77.0 per cent of the sustaining program time. Popular music consumed 49.0 per cent of sustaining time in the morning, semi-classical music 20.7 per cent, and variety programs 11.9 per cent.

In the afternoon, commercial periods consist primarily of children's programs, comprising 40.1 per cent of all afternoon commercial time; comedy, consisting of 22.5 per cent, and popular music, amounting to 19.3 per cent, of the afternoon hours devoted to sponsored programs. This forms a marked contrast to

1927 when 50.0 per cent of the afternoon commercial programs comprised classical music, and women's features 33.0 per cent of the afternoon hours sold to advertisers. Sustaining programs at this time of the day center in classical, semi-classical, and popular music, which comprised 8.1 per cent, 14.7 per cent, and 34.0 per cent, respectively, to the total afternoon sustaining hours in November, 1932.

The trend in evening commercial programs has been somewhat more complicated. Since 1927 classical music has declined to almost nothing, as has semi-classical music. The proportion of hours devoted to popular music likewise has dropped from 40.4 per cent in 1929 to 21.4 per cent in 1932, while variety programs have risen from 9.2 per cent to 20.4 per cent in the same period. Drama comprises almost one-quarter of all evening broadcasts and has been increasing steadily. Comedy is less important, comprising but 5.4 per cent of evening commercial program hours. With regard to the sustaining field, music comprises 81.9 per cent of total program hours as compared with 41.8 per cent in the case of advertising programs. Of total sustaining time 5.2 per cent is devoted to classical music, 6.7 per cent to semi-classical music, and 68.7 per cent to popular music. Few other program types are represented.

Two other factors remain to be examined before it is possible to evaluate the program service of national network key stations. The first of these is the variations in types of programs broadcast on various days of the week, while the second pertains to the seasonal variations existing with regard to program practice on the part of networks.

Data regarding the first of these questions are found in Table XXXVIII.

Sunday and Wednesday were chosen for comparison in so far as the latter was found to be representative of all week days, while Sunday alone showed any marked variations. These variations are shown to consist of a greater proportion of time devoted to classical music—16.6 per cent in all—folk music, variety music, religious broadcasts, and special features. No children's educational programs, news, or farm programs were broadcast on Sunday.

Seasonal trends with regard to the proportion of various types of programs broadcast seem to show little in the way of a definite pattern. Other than a summer decline in children's educational programs, adult education, special features, and variety programs, and a marked increase in sports broadcasts during the football season in November, there is little in the way of significant variations in programs at different times of the year.

TABLE XXXVIII

PROPORTION OF HOURS OF VARIOUS TYPES OF PROGRAMS BROAD-
CAST OVER THE KEY STATIONS OF THE NBC RED AND BLUE
AND COLUMBIA NETWORKS ON SUNDAY, NOVEMBER 6, AND
WEDNESDAY, NOVEMBER 9, 1932*

TYPE OF PROGRAM	PERCENTAGE OF HOURS OF VARIOUS KINDS OF PROGRAMS	
	Sunday Nov. 6	Wednesday Nov. 9
Classical music.	16.4	6.6
Semi-classical music.	19.0	14.0
Folk music and ballads.	3.0	1.5
Variety music.	3.4	1.5
Popular music.	26.5	37.5
Total music.	68.3	61.1
Children's programs.	2.4	5.5
Comedy broadcasts.	2.0	5.6
Other dramatic programs.	7.4	8.0
Adult educational programs.	3.4	3.6
Children's educational programs.	....	1.0
Farm programs.	....	2.0
International rebroadcasts.	1.0	1.0
News, market and weather reports.	....	1.0
Religious broadcasts.	7.0	0.6
Sports broadcasts.	....	....
Special features of public interest.	1.0	0.6
Women's feature programs.	7.5	10.5
Variety programs.	....	4.5
Total programs.	100.0	100.0

* The two days selected are highly representative of the major variations in available programs on different days of the week. Source: NBC and CBS program records.

The seasonal decline in variety programs is due to the discontinuance of programs featuring popular entertainers during the summer months, while the smaller portion of time devoted to special feature broadcasts is because the speakers are not available at that period. Other summer changes in program structure are due to varying listener interest. The situation in this respect is summarized in Table XXXIX.

TABLE XXXIX

COMPARISON OF THE PROPORTION OF HOURS OF VARIOUS KINDS OF PROGRAMS BROADCAST COMMERCIALLY AND ON A SUSTAINING BASIS OVER THE KEY STATIONS OF THE NBC RED AND BLUE AND COLUMBIA NETWORKS DURING THE SECOND WEEKS OF AUGUST AND NOVEMBER, 1927–31*

PERCENTAGE OF HOURS OF VARIOUS KINDS OF PROGRAMS

Type of Program	1927				1928				1929				1930				1931			
	August		November		August		November		August		November		August		November		August		November	
	Commercial	Sustaining	Commercial	Sustaining	Commercial	Sustaining	Commercial	Sustaining	Commercial	Sustaining	Commercial	Sustaining	Commercial	Sustaining	Commercial	Sustaining	Commercial	Sustaining	Commercial	Sustaining
Classical music	10.2	7.3	16.2	4.6	2.0	12.5	7.9	8.1	5.7	8.0	0.6	5.9	6.7	7.9	6.4	10.4	2.4	12.6	2.7	10.6
Semi-classical music	20.1	20.1	25.7	25.1	20.6	25.1	7.9	20.5	5.4	17.6	9.6	15.7	2.2	22.4	3.5	19.3	6.2	15.8	6.9	12.0
Folk music and ballads	6.4	6.4	3.4	5.5	6.8	8.1	13.0	5.3	2.7	3.7	4.5	3.7	5.2	2.5	6.0	2.4	6.8	2.9	4.3	2.9
Variety music	29.9	1.9	18.8	6.6	19.5	3.3	8.4	1.8	9.9	5.1	6.8	5.1	12.0	3.7	9.2	3.3	4.6	4.5	4.5	4.0
Popular music	37.3	39.0	21.4	26.1	20.7	23.6	15.2	23.4	30.7	37.4	29.2	39.2	18.8	35.9	20.2	30.7	26.9	40.8	28.7	36.7
Total music	86.4	74.7	85.5	67.9	69.6	72.6	52.5	59.1	54.4	71.8	50.7	69.6	44.9	72.4	46.2	66.1	46.9	76.6	47.1	68.5
Children's programs		0.2		0.5		1.2		0.8		0.5		0.6	2.2	1.7	1.9	1.2	2.2	1.1	3.0	2.6
Comedy broadcasts	3.4	1.2	1.7	0.8			4.6	2.4	3.8	1.1	3.4	1.1	7.2	0.4	4.5	0.1	9.7	1.7	8.9	2.3
Other dramatic programs		8.9	0.8	11.4	8.9	11.3	8.8	2.1	6.9	3.9	7.6	4.1	7.2	4.6	11.4	3.1	9.9	8.8	9.8	2.9
Adult educational programs	3.4					2.4	19.7	2.7	13.4	5.7	10.8	6.0	12.0	3.9	8.9	4.9	9.9	2.2	7.3	3.6
Children's educational programs	0.9						0.8	2.7	1.4	1.4	2.3	1.5		1.7	1.9	0.5		0.1		1.1
Farm programs														0.3		0.5		0.1		0.1
International rebroadcasts			0.5					2.3	2.8				1.7		0.5	2.4	1.9	2.2		1.4
News, market and weather reports	2.8			3.9	3.0	3.0		4.4	3.6	3.6		2.3	3.4	0.8	2.4	3.4	1.9	0.1	1.6	1.4
Religious broadcasts	3.2		3.9	3.5	3.5	2.4	0.8	4.0		3.6	0.6	3.0		3.2	0.9	2.7		1.4	1.6	2.7
Sports broadcasts	3.9		4.8	4.0		0.2	0.4	4.5			0.6	1.6	0.4	0.2		4.3		3.4	0.4	4.1
Special features of public interest					3.2	2.2		12.6		0.5				0.3		3.3		0.3		1.3
Women's feature programs	1.7	1.7	1.7	0.7	3.9	1.9	7.1	1.4	18.8	2.4	17.5	2.3	11.2	2.3	12.9	2.5	12.4	3.3	12.2	1.5
Variety programs	6.8	3.9	6.9	1.9	11.7	0.3	5.3	1.3	2.7	6.9	6.5	4.1	6.7	5.6	8.5	5.2	7.6	3.9	9.5	5.1
Total programs	100.0	100.0	100.0	100.0	100.0	100.0	100.0	100.0	100.0	100.0	100.0	100.0	100.0	100.0	100.0	100.0	100.0	100.0	100.0	100.0

* Source: NBC and CBS program records.

CHAPTER XII

PROGRAM PRACTICE: ADDITIONAL PROGRAM CONSIDERATIONS, AND AN EVALUATION OF THE AMERICAN PROGRAM STRUCTURE

Though an analysis of the types of programs broadcast over the key stations of the national networks is of basic importance to an understanding of American program practice, there are a number of additional factors which remain to be considered. Since key station programs are broadcast to a varying degree by the different members of the network, the question arises as to the proportion of various types of network programs which are broadcast by these stations as a group. Regional network and individual station program practice also must be examined. Moreover, the trend regarding the length of program must be investigated since it is a matter closely associated with developments regarding the kinds of programs broadcast. It is these factors which will be discussed next.

The question as to the proportion of various kinds of their own programs broadcast by networks must not be confused with that of the percentage of different types of programs broadcast by all of the affiliated stations of the network. The latter involves an analysis of the local programs of each station, as well as of the network programs broadcast by it, a matter which limitations of data make impossible. What is being studied, therefore, is the degree to which network programs of various kinds are broadcast by the different affiliated stations. The unit which has been developed for effecting this measurement is the station-hour, which is secured by multiplying a program of a given length by the number of stations over which is has been broadcast. The station-hours are then classified and tabulated according to type of program, with the result that a fairly accurate conception may be secured of what the country as a whole receives in the way of network service.

The general trend with regard to the proportion of total network station-hours devoted to various kinds of programs during the second week of November, 1927–32, is found in Table XL. As in the case of key station broadcasts, the data for all networks have been combined to present a picture of American network broadcasting as a whole, and to avoid misleading competitive comparisons.

A comparison of the proportion of network station-hours devoted to programs of different types, with the percentage of program hours devoted to the same types by the key stations, furnishes an interesting approach to the analysis of network program trends. With regard to classical music, the proportion of time devoted to it, measured in terms of station-hours, is higher than in the case of the key station broadcasts, indicating a relatively wider acceptance of classical offerings by affiliated stations. The trend in this respect, however, is toward a slightly decreasing acceptance. Semi-classical music, on the other hand, has always received less widespread circulation over the networks than has classical music, while the trend is toward an even narrower use of this type of program by affiliated stations.

Folk music and variety music show little in the way of definite trends. The proportion of network station-hours devoted to popular music has been appreciably less than the relative amount of time devoted to it by key stations, showing that the member stations have been relying upon their own resources in this field. Recently there has been a tendency toward a wider acceptance of network presentations in the field of popular music. This is probably due to the fact that network broadcasts of dance bands are beginning to achieve a distinctiveness which the individual station finds difficult to match.

The proportion of network station-hours devoted to children's programs is from one-half to one-third as much as the time given over to such programs by the key stations. This is explained by the fact that time differences cause many of the children's programs to be unacceptable to far-western stations. For these stations, the children's programs fall at the wrong period of the day. There is no clearly defined trend with regard to either comedy or dramatic programs, though both seem to receive an average acceptance. Adult educational programs have tended to receive a decreasing measure of acceptance from affiliated stations, though the trend has been reversed during the past year. Children's educational programs, on the other

TABLE XL

PROPORTION OF COMMERCIAL AND SUSTAINING HOURS, RESPECTIVELY, DEVOTED TO CHAIN PROGRAMS OF VARIOUS KINDS DURING THE SECOND WEEK OF NOVEMBER, 1927–32, AND MAY, 1932, OVER THE ENTIRE NBC AND COLUMBIA NETWORKS

PERCENTAGE OF STATION HOURS OF VARIOUS KINDS OF PROGRAMS

TYPE OF PROGRAM	1927 Commercial	1927 Sustaining	1927 Total	1928 Commercial	1928 Sustaining	1928 Total	1929 Commercial	1929 Sustaining	1929 Total	1930 Commercial	1930 Sustaining	1930 Total	1931 Commercial	1931 Sustaining	1931 Total	1932 Commercial	1932 Sustaining	1932 Total
Classical music	25.8	9.7	17.7	9.3	15.1	13.7	5.4	13.0	9.2	8.5	12.7	11.2	6.2	8.0	7.3	0.8	9.2	6.9
Semi-classical music	25.9	16.4	21.2	7.3	16.2	12.1	9.8	18.9	14.3	3.6	16.8	12.5	7.0	14.5	12.0	7.1	14.8	12.8
Folk music and ballads	7.8	4.8	5.8	10.5	6.0	8.3	8.9	3.6	7.7	4.8	2.7	3.4	2.0	4.0	3.3	3.4	2.7	2.9
Variety music	8.3	12.6	10.7	18.0	5.2	11.4	11.7	5.7	8.7	8.5	3.0	4.9	4.3	4.2	4.2	2.6	6.9	5.7
Popular music	13.7	15.0	14.6	23.9	14.4	18.0	25.6	24.4	24.7	25.1	26.0	25.6	39.2	36.5	37.5	41.9	39.7	40.3
Total music	81.5	57.5	70.0	69.0	56.9	63.5	61.4	65.6	64.6	50.5	61.2	57.6	59.5	67.2	64.3	55.4	73.3	68.6
Children's programs		....	....		0.4	0.4		0.1	0.1	0.7	0.7	0.7	2.0	1.5	1.7	3.4	0.9	1.5
Comedy broadcasts	0.6	0.1	0.4	0.9	0.4	0.7	2.8	0.3	1.7	8.2	0.3	2.9	7.4	1.7	3.9	10.6	1.0	3.6
Other dramatic programs		5.4	3.0	9.7	3.8	5.6	6.8	4.6	4.4	8.0	2.6	4.6	7.5	2.9	4.6	8.7	2.8	4.4
Adult educational programs	12.4	7.2	9.7	4.1	8.4	6.4	5.9	5.1	6.4	3.2	4.7	4.2	5.7	3.7	3.8	3.5	4.7	5.0
Children's educational programs		0.2	0.1		0.8	0.4	0.5	1.8	1.1	3.4	1.7	2.3	0.8	1.7	1.3		1.0	0.7
Farm programs		....	....	0.8	....	0.4	4.2	1.1	2.7	4.4	7.3	6.3	0.2	6.0	3.9		5.5	4.1
International rebroadcasts		....	....	....	....	....	....	....	....	0.8	0.4	0.6	0.2	0.2	0.2	0.6	0.5	0.6

TABLE XL—*Continued*

PERCENTAGE OF STATION HOURS OF VARIOUS KINDS OF PROGRAMS

Type of Program	1927			1928			1929			1930			1931			1932		
	Commercial	Sustaining	Total	Commercial	Sustaining	Total	Commercial	Sustaining	Total	Commercial	Sustaining	Total	Commercial	Sustaining	Total	Commercial	Sustaining	Total
News, market and weather reports	.....	1.1	0.6	.....	0.2	0.1	.....	0.8	0.4	2.3	0.4	1.1	0.9	0.4	0.6	0.2	0.2	0.2
Religious broadcasts	.....	3.7	1.8	1.5	5.2	2.8	0.6	6.3	3.6	1.0	5.7	4.1	0.3	5.5	3.5	.....	2.5	1.6
Sports broadcasts	.....	13.4	6.4	1.1	8.3	5.5	0.5	4.9	2.8	.....	3.9	2.4	0.3	2.6	1.7	.....	0.1	0.1
Special features of public interest	.....	8.5	4.3	0.2	10.7	5.3	.....	4.4	2.1	.....	2.6	1.7	.....	1.3	0.8	.....	0.1	0.1
Women's feature programs	3.1	0.7	1.7	7.2	0.6	3.8	10.7	0.7	4.8	12.5	3.5	6.6	11.0	1.6	5.1	7.5	1.2	2.5
Variety programs	2.4	1.2	1.7	5.5	4.7	5.5	5.6	4.3	5.3	5.0	4.0	4.7	6.2	3.7	4.6	10.1	6.2	7.1
Total programs	100.0	100.0	100.0	100.0	100.0	100.0	100.0	100.0	100.0	100.0	100.0	100.0	100.0	100.0	100.0	100.0	100.0	100.0

hand, are more widely accepted, probably due to the fact that, in spite of time differences, they still are available during the school day. Recently there has been a slight increase in the proportion of network station-hours devoted to religious programs. Comparison with key stations in this respect reveals a tendency toward a somewhat wider use of religious programs by the member stations of the network. International rebroadcasts and farm programs always have been very widely used. Features of special interest are tending to be accepted to a much less degree than in earlier years, the same trend being noticeable with regard to sports broadcasts. In the latter case, local programs are supplanting the network presentation. The reason for the trend as to the acceptance of special feature broadcasts cannot be determined from available data. An average acceptance is indicated for news broadcasts and women's feature programs.

An analysis of the proportion of commercial and sustaining network hours devoted to various types of programs confirms the general trends revealed with regard to station acceptance of network programs as a whole. Two general conclusions may be drawn in this respect: (1) The wider acceptance noted in commercial programs of the comedy, drama, and popular music types is due to the fact that advertisers sponsoring programs of this nature tend to buy time over a wider territory than do advertisers employing other forms of programs and, in all probability, seeking more specialized audiences. (2) The trend regarding individual station acceptance of network sustaining programs is based primarily upon the types of programs which it cannot provide for itself and therefore regarding which it requires network assistance. Programs devoted to classical music, international rebroadcasts, adult education programs secured on a sustaining basis, and farm programs are examples in point.

Outside of a slight tendency toward less acceptance of morning, than of afternoon and evening, programs by individual stations, there are no significant trends regarding the proportion of network station-hours devoted to various kinds of programs at different periods of the day. The general conclusion which presents itself regarding this entire question is that, with the exception of a few minor and for the most part readily understandable variations, the proportion of various kinds of network programs broadcast by affiliated stations does not vary greatly from the program structure of the key stations themselves.

Two minor considerations remain before regional network and individual station program practice may be investigated. The first of these is the question of special broadcasts to various small groups of affiliated stations, these broadcasts being in

TABLE XLI

AVERAGE NUMBER OF HOURS OF PROGRAMS BROADCAST OVER THE NBC RED AND BLUE AND COLUMBIA NETWORKS, TO SPECIAL GROUPS OF STATIONS, DURING THE SECOND WEEK OF MAY, AUGUST, AND NOVEMBER, 1928, FEBRUARY, MAY, AUGUST, AND NOVEMBER, 1929–31, AND FEBRUARY AND MAY, 1932*

SECOND WEEK OF	HOURS		
	Commercial	Sustaining	Total
1928 May	0.8	0.5	1.3
August	0.8	0.4	1.2
November	1.0	4.8	5.8
1929 February	2.3	2.1	3.4
May	3.7	3.8	7.5
August	1.6	1.7	3.3
November	1.2	6.4	7.6
1930 February	1.3	4.0	5.3
May	4.4	4.9	9.3
August	3.0	2.6	5.6
November	5.7	3.6	9.3
1931 February	4.2	5.2	9.4
May	2.4	5.8	8.2
August	4.3	3.3	7.6
November	9.3	10.5	19.8
1932 February	9.0	12.2	21.2
May	7.2	15.3	22.5

* Source: NBC and CBS records.

addition to the regular program service of the network, and, though often originating in the key station studios, not being broadcast by it. The second question is the degree to which network broadcasts are originating in other than the New York key stations.

With regard to the former, a definite increase is to be noted, especially within the last year. The increase is revealed in Table XLI and is shown to be more pronounced with regard to sustaining than commercial programs. The broadcasts of commercially sponsored programs to special parts of the network are explained either by the practice of sending the program to the western stations later in the evening than the hour at which it has been broadcast over the key station or by a few special farm programs originating in middle western stations and not being broadcast in the East at all. The former of these two conditions undoubtedly has been the most important. Sustaining program service of this type is explained on the basis of the need for providing program service for stations which have not been included on the commercial broadcast scheduled for the period in question. An increase in this type of service points to the possibility of a like increase in the amount of network business which is being booked on a split-network basis, that is, where less than the complete basic network is purchased by the advertiser. With regard to the type of programs broadcast in this manner, the commercial trend has been toward children's programs, comedy, variety programs, and popular music, while the sustaining trend has been almost exclusively toward popular music.

The trend regarding the number of hours of network programs originating in other than the New York key station is shown in Table XLII. Prior to the latter part of 1929 no programs originated outside of New York, while the total of these broadcasts did not amount to a figure of any significance until the following year. It was not until November, 1931, that any marked increase took place in the number of commercial hours originating elsewhere than in the principal key station of the network, though the number of sustaining hours of this type began to rise as early as May of that year. Even today the total volume of such programs remains small, and, up until the present time, network efforts to make Chicago a second key center have met with only partial success.

Thus far the largest proportion of programs of this sort have consisted of popular music, though recently in the sustaining program field a trend has been noticeable toward the inclusion of semi-classical broadcasts from outside centers. A number of commercially sponsored children's programs and comedy broadcasts are originating outside of New York, principally in Chicago, as are a few programs of other types. As outside program facilities improve, a marked increase may be expected in this direction with regard to both commercial and sustaining programs.

Program trends with regard to regional networks and individual stations form another important aspect of practice in this field which must be investigated. An example of program practice in the case of a regional network is found in Table XLIII, which shows the proportion of various forms of entertainment broadcast by the Yankee Network.

TABLE XLII

AVERAGE NUMBER OF HOURS OF PROGRAMS BROADCAST OVER NBC RED AND BLUE AND COLUMBIA NETWORKS ORIGINATING IN OTHER THAN THE KEY STATION STUDIO DURING THE SECOND WEEK OF FEBRUARY, MAY, AUGUST, AND NOVEMBER, 1930–31, AND FEBRUARY AND MAY, 1932*

SECOND WEEK OF	HOURS		
	Commercial	Sustaining	Total
1930 February	3.4	10.1	13.5
May	6.1	18.3	24.4
August	4.4	17.7	22.1
November	9.1	19.7	28.8
1931 February	6.2	22.7	28.9
May	8.9	25.6	34.5
August	8.4	28.4	36.8
November	12.7	30.9	43.6
1932 February	13.1	33.3	46.4
May	14.2	39.2	53.4

* Source: NBC and CBS program records. Since there was practically no broadcasting of this type prior to 1930, the table begins at this point.

In the case of the regional network there is little variation from the program structure found in the national organizations. There is a tendency to broadcast slightly less classical and semi-classical music than do the national networks. Fewer comedy programs are presented, while the same trend is true with regard to adult education broadcasts, women's features, and variety programs. On the other hand, the regional chain, as exemplified by the Yankee Network, tends to broadcast more religious programs, sports events, children's educational programs, and news flashes than does the national chain. The program structure of the regional network, therefore, is colored, on the one hand, by available program material, which at times restricts it slightly, and on the other hand, by the necessity of adapting itself to the particular section served. The regional network enters more actively into the community life than is possible for the national network. There, therefore, is a marked tendency for the program

TABLE XLIII

PROPORTION OF HOURS OF VARIOUS KINDS OF PROGRAMS BROADCAST OVER WNAC, KEY STATION OF THE YANKEE NETWORK, DURING THE SECOND WEEKS OF MAY AND AUGUST, 1930, AUGUST, 1931, FEBRUARY AND MAY, 1932*

(In Per Cent)

Type of Program	May, 1930	Aug., 1930	Aug., 1931	Feb., 1932	May, 1932
Classical music....................	2.1	3.7	6.0	3.4	4.0
Semi-classical music..............	9.3	9.5	4.8	9.2	14.7
Folk music and ballads............	0.8	....	1.3	0.2	....
Variety music.........	14.1	16.5	22.3	14.8	14.3
Popular music...................	35.9	35.7	34.6	40.4	44.7
Total music................	62.2	65.4	69.0	68.0	77.7
Children's programs..............	0.2	0.9	2.7	0.4	2.1
Comedy broadcasts...............	0.8	0.4	0.6	1.5	0.5
Other dramatic programs...........	3.0	1.7	2.5	2.7	3.1
Adult educational programs........	2.3	1.9	0.8	2.7	2.1
Children's educational programs....	....	....	0.8	0.8	0.2
Farm programs....................	....	....	....	....	....
International rebroadcasts.........	....	....	....	....	....
News, market, and weather reports..	5.3	5.2	4.0	5.3	4.5
Religious broadcasts...............	3.2	1.9	2.2	5.5	2.1
Sports broadcasts.................	12.2	12.2	11.9	5.2	1.2
Special features of public interest....	1.5	0.2	0.5	2.9	1.0
Women's feature programs.........	8.0	9.3	2.7	1.2	2.6
Variety programs.................	1.3	0.9	2.3	3.8	2.9
Total programs..............	100.0	100.0	100.0	100.0	100.0

* Source: Program records of WNAC, Boston, key station of the Yankee Network, and therefore fairly representative of the network's program service. Months given are the only ones for which complete data were available.

policy of the regional network to reflect aspects of both a national network and a local station.

Data regarding individual station program practice have been gathered from several principal sources. The first of these has been detailed program information furnished by 7 individual stations. This comprises too limited a sample for more than merely illustrative purposes. It has been supplemented, therefore, by an analysis of the opinions of 52 station executives to whom questions were addressed regarding program trends, as well as by interviews with managers of other stations. Individual station data are found in Table XLIV.

TABLE XLIV

PROPORTION OF HOURS OF VARIOUS KINDS OF PROGRAMS BROADCAST OVER A NUMBER OF REPRESENTATIVE STATIONS DURING THE SECOND WEEK OF FEBRUARY, 1932*

(In Per Cent)

TYPE OF PROGRAM	WCAU† Philadelphia	WFAA Dallas	WMBD Peoria	KFBB Gt. Falls	KMJ Fresno	KNX Hollywood	KOMO Seattle
Classical music................	2.3	8.1	5.3	1.0	3.4	9.7	6.3
Semi-classical music...........	8.2	5.1	14.6	19.2	2.3	1.0	10.9
Folk music and ballads.........	......	1.5	10.2	6.2	0.7	3.9	0.4
Variety music.................	7.4	5.1	10.5	8.4	6.4	0.8	5.3
Popular music................	37.3	38.6	25.5	24.5	49.3	20.9	30.7
Total music..............	55.2	58.4	66.1	59.3	62.1	36.3	53.5
Children's programs...........	1.7	1.0	2.0	0.6	0.2	......	0.2
Comedy broadcasts............	0.8	6.1	0.6	....	0.7	3.1	6.6
Other dramatic programs.......	4.0	......	0.9	4.0	2.7	2.3	5.6
Adult educational programs....	2.9	2.0	7.9	12.1	4.4	9.9	1.6
Children's educational programs.	......	......	......	......	......	......	......
Farm programs...............	0.2	8.8	......	6.9	4.3	......	3.3
International rebroadcasts......	0.4	......	0.3	......	......	......	1.2
News, market, and weather reports...................	8.7	4.5	4.8	5.6	3.2	5.5	2.9
Religious broadcasts...........	1.5	2.5	5.6	5.3	2.1	8.6	1.9
Sports broadcasts.............	4.7	......	3.2	......	2.7	0.8	1.6
Special features of public interest	5.3	2.0	1.2	1.8	0.4	0.6	2.9
Women's feature programs.....	3.4	8.1	2.0	......	11.7	6.8	8.6
Variety programs.............	11.2	6.6	5.4	4.4	5.5	26.1	10.1
Total programs...........	100.0	100.0	100.0	100.0	100.0	100.0	100.0

* The month of February was selected inasmuch as the greatest number of stations furnished information for this particular month.

† WCAU, Philadelphia, Pennsylvania, 10,000 watts, CBS, recently changed to 50,000 watts; WFAA, Dallas, Texas, 50,000 watts, part-time, NBC; WMBD, Peoria, Illinois, 500 watts, CBS; KFBB, Great Falls Montana, 1,000 watts, independent; KMJ, Fresno, California, 100 watts, independent; KNX, Hollywood, California, 5,000 watts, independent, recently changed to 25,000 watts; KOMO, Seattle, Washington, 1,000 watts, NBC.

Though the sample is an imperfect one, several features eunoticeable. One of these is the tendency for the program stracr ture of the station to vary with its talent facilities, the market upon which it is concentrating, and its network affiliation. Another is the larger proportion of time devoted to news flashes, sports broadcasts, religious programs, and special features, as compared with the networks.

Additional information regarding individual station program practice is found in the replies of 52 station managers to the question as to what had been the chief trends in the kinds and types of programs broadcast over their station since 1929.[1] Of the entire group, 50 per cent reported a trend toward more dramatic programs, 40 per cent toward comedy, 38 per cent in the direction of old-time music, and 28 per cent toward semi-classical programs. Only 4 per cent noted any trend toward classical music, 4 per cent toward news broadcasts, 16 per cent toward popular music, and 14 per cent toward variety programs. The replies of the 18 managers of non-network stations are especially interesting. Of this group 52 per cent indicated a trend toward old-time melodies, hill-billy tunes, and similar forms of music, 35 per cent toward popular music, 28 per cent toward drama and comedy respectively, and 22 per cent toward semi-classical programs. Though this group is limited as to number, it forms a significant contrast to the trends indicated as pertaining to the entire number of individual stations.

With regard to a comparison of the types and quality of commercial and sustaining programs broadcast, 48 per cent of the station managers stated that they could perceive no difference in this respect, while 50 per cent of the group were of the opinion that the sustaining programs possessed the greater variety.

Another question of importance in program practice is the trend regarding the length of the programs broadcast. Data regarding this feature are found in Tables XLV and XLVI.

An examination of the tables reveals that the percentage of programs an hour in length has decreased tremendously. Those of one-half hour duration have increased slightly, while a marked gain has taken place in the proportion of fifteen-minute programs. The gain in the last-mentioned group has been greater in the commercial program field than with respect to sustaining programs. The proportion of commercial programs one-half hour in length has decreased steadily since 1929, but this has been more than offset by the increase in the percentage of sustaining programs of this length.

[1] See Appendix B for detailed questions, p. 325.

TABLE XLV

PROPORTION OF PROGRAMS OF VARIOUS LENGTHS BROADCAST OVER THE KEY STATIONS OF THE NBC RED AND BLUE AND COLUMBIA NETWORKS DURING THE SECOND WEEK OF NOVEMBER, 1927–31, AND THE SECOND WEEK OF MAY, 1932

LENGTH OF PROGRAM	PERCENTAGE OF PROGRAMS OF VARIOUS LENGTHS					
	1927	1928	1929	1930	1931	1932
Under 15 minutes........	17.8	13.9	11.7	6.7	1.5	2.0
15 minutes..............	25.2	27.5	28.8	46.6	61.4	61.7
16–29 minutes...........	3.4	2.5	2.2	1.5	0.2	1.9
30 minutes..............	22.4	31.5	31.9	30.7	30.4	29.8
31–44 minutes...........	0.3	0.5	....	0.7	....	....
45 minutes..............	0.6	2.7	7.9	3.1	2.1	0.7
46–59 minutes...........	3.4	0.5	0.2	1.4	....	....
60 minutes..............	22.4	17.2	15.5	8.1	3.4	3.4
Over 60 minutes.........	4.5	3.7	1.8	1.2	1.0	0.5
Total programs.......	100.0	100.0	100.0	100.0	100.0	100.0

TABLE XLVI

PROPORTION OF COMMERCIAL AND SUSTAINING PROGRAMS OF VARIOUS LENGTHS BROADCAST OVER THE KEY STATIONS OF THE NBC RED AND BLUE AND COLUMBIA NETWORKS DURING THE SECOND WEEK OF NOVEMBER, 1927–31, AND THE SECOND WEEK OF MAY, 1932

LENGTH OF PROGRAM	PERCENTAGE OF PROGRAMS OF VARIOUS LENGTHS											
	1927		1928		1929		1930		1931		1932	
	Commercial	Sustaining	Commercial	Sustaining	Commercial	Sustaining	Commercial	Sustaining	Commercial	Sustaining	Commercial	Sustaining
Under 15 min....	27.1	14.7	19.5	11.6	11.2	11.3	5.9	7.1	.....	2.5	.....	2.8
15 min....	10.0	30.0	8.2	34.5	14.9	33.3	58.9	40.9	73.6	53.8	75.6	55.9
16–29 min.	.....	4.6	.....	3.4	.....	3.1	.....	2.2	.....	0.4	.....	2.5
30 min....	30.0	19.9	43.5	26.6	53.9	24.8	27.8	31.8	20.9	35.9	20.5	33.8
31–44 min.	.....	0.4	.....	0.6	.....	.....	.....	1.1	.....	.....	.....	.....
45 min....	.....	0.9	4.6	2.0	4.4	9.3	0.6	4.3	0.5	3.2	.....	1.1
46–59 min.	1.4	4.1	.....	0.6	.....	0.2	.....	2.1	.....	.....	.....	.....
60 min....	31.5	19.4	18.7	17.7	11.2	17.2	4.8	9.7	3.5	3.5	2.1	3.9
Over 60 min....	.....	6.0	5.5	3.0	4.4	0.8	2.0	0.8	1.5	0.7	1.8	.....
Total programs	100.0	100.0	100.0	100.0	100.0	100.0	100.0	100.0	100.0	100.0	100.0	100.0

With regard to individual station experience as to the trend in the length of programs broadcast, 69.1 per cent of the station executives questioned regarding this feature stated that the quarter-hour programs were increasing. Another 21.1 per cent mentioned the half-hour as increasing, though half of them stated, in addition, that the quarter-hour program was holding its own. The remainder of the station managers noted no appreciable trend in any direction.

Detailed information having been presented regarding the major aspects of program practice, it now becomes possible to evaluate American broadcasting procedure in this regard, both from the viewpoint of the program service rendered the listening public and of the advertising aspects of current methods. The first question to be touched upon is that of the adequacy of the general program structure from the viewpoint of listener service. From data presented, it seems that the program structure of American broadcasting, both network and individual station, is fundamentally sound. It is true that individual station program quality must be raised considerably. However, in view of the difficulties faced by many broadcasters, they have succeeded in making a fairly creditable showing in the matter of programs. Where improvement is most necessary is with regard to the quality of programs rendered, rather than with respect to a greater balance between types.

The national network program structure shows signs of a tendency toward greater diversity in programs offered, which should result in improved listener service. Network program schedules are still weak as far as the proportion of classical and semi-classical music is concerned, and steps should be taken to rectify this situation. This does not mean that any great measure of this type of music need be added to the program schedule. Because of its inherent psychology, popular music always will remain popular. However, a few classical programs, placed at strategic hours during the day and week, would add greatly to the pleasure derived from broadcasting by important minorities among the listening audience, and would go far to quell the criticism often heard of American programs among certain groups of listeners.

Though the proportion of various kinds of programs broadcast throughout the week as a whole is fairly satisfactory, the same cannot be said with regard to the apportionment of these programs on different days, and at various hours of the day. At present there is too great a concentration of classical music on Sunday, with the result that the listener receives a surfeit at this time and is starved for the remainder of the week. Likewise, though the variety of programs offered to afternoon listeners is splendid, and that of the morning generally satisfactory, there tends to be too great a concentration of evening broadcasts upon certain types of entertainment. Consequently, unless a listener enjoys comedy, variety programs, melodrama, or popular music, he will find it difficult to satisfy his taste after six or seven o'clock at night, except in rare instances. Indeed, it seems that this lack of balance with regard to evening programs is what is really at the heart of much of the criticism of American broadcasting which is extant today.

The matter is a simple one to solve, and requires no sweeping change of program policy to rectify the situation. Only a few higher-class programs need or should be added. In a democratized system of broadcasting, it is vitally essential to devote the great majority of the time to the types of programs popular with the great mass of listeners. However, the minority of listeners preferring better music and more cultured programs deserves greater consideration. Though it may constitute no more than 5 per cent or 10 per cent of the total radio audience, it still comprises from 1,000,000 to 2,000,000 radio families. This minority possesses important purchasing power, and is worth the careful consideration on the part of the broadcast advertiser. It is quite true that these listeners may laugh with the remainder of the country at the capers of Eddie Cantor, or the asininities of Gracie Allen. But the number of such programs is definitely limited. It therefore may be well for the advertiser desirous of reaching this important purchasing group to consider some of the better types of programs. A few such broadcasts, placed at times when most listeners will be able to enjoy them, would add tremendously to the service value of American programs, without greatly disturbing the basic structure designed for the great mass of listeners.

The effect of commercial programs upon American broadcasting has often been misunderstood. It is frequently assumed that it is the commercial sponsor who is responsible for the lack of balance which at times exists in the American program structure. This does not seem to be the case, for the commercial sponsor has tended to concentrate less upon forms such as popular music broadcasts than have the executives in charge of network sustaining programs. In addition it has been the commercial sponsor, primarily, who has given impetus to the development of the comedy, dramatic, and children's types of programs. Many of the programs in these categories still are comparatively crude. However, it is doubtful whether radio dramatic technique would have progressed as far as it has, were it not for sponsor demand for programs of this type. On the other hand, the broadcast advertiser is not entirely without blame, for it is he who is largely, though not exclusively, responsible for the endless repetition of certain types of programs on every night of the week. His negative effect on programs, however, has been greatly overrated.

Comparison of the proportion of network station-hours of various kinds of programs with the percentage of the same programs broadcast over the key stations of the networks revealed no significant variations. The same was true with respect to the program practice of regional networks. Individual stations were shown to follow network leadership in program development for the most part, though there was a greater tendency to adapt programs to local conditions and to enter actively into the civic life of the community. Whether this network dominance of program trends is desirable is a matter of question, though until station program departments grow in strength it undoubtedly will continue to exist.

With regard to the potentialities of various kinds of programs, both from the viewpoint of listener service and advertising value several comments are necessary. In the field of music, popular melodies will always be the most acceptable to radio audiences. Popular music is based upon pronounced rhythm and simplicity of melodic line. Consequently it will be appreciated and understood by the most musically naïve intellect, while under the correct conditions its motor aspects may produce beneficial results in the listener. Furthermore, it requires no concentration, and is well-adapted to what may be termed "lazy listening."

On the other hand, the very simplicity of popular music causes the listener to tire quickly of any given number and tends to introduce problems with regard to the maintenance of continued novelty and distinctiveness in the program. As one program manager remarked,[2] "Avoid riding new popular tunes to death. They are short-winded brutes." Moreover, because of the multiplicity of such broadcasts, it becomes necessary to create a distinctive form of presentation in order to have one's program stand out from the general run of similar endeavors. This may be done by securing an outstanding soloist, by achieving a unique rhythm or manner of orchestration, or by including a well-known comedian or musical comedy star in the program. In the latter case script is added to the program and it becomes a variety presentation. This causes the popular music program to be an effective weapon in the hands of the enterprising and ingenious advertiser, though it is weak when used by one of only mediocre ability.

The variety program has gained tremendously in vogue, though it still remains to be seen whether it possesses sufficient vitality to continue its dominant place in the broadcasting field. Comedians, script writers, "gag" artists, and program directors will be hard put to keep these programs running at their present tempo. Developing effective humorous lines for one theatrical performance, where they may be repeated night after night for the run of the show, is a vastly different matter from producing new laughs either nightly or weekly. Radio burns out its artists very swiftly. This is true of comedy broadcasts as well as of variety programs.

Classical and semi-classical programs already have been discussed at some length. However, a consideration of these types raises several additional questions. Though more limited in its appeal than is popular music, the classical program is fundamentally stronger in its interest value, and consequently does not lose its novelty as quickly as does dance music. Moreover, because of the little competition existing in the field today, classical and semi-classical programs have greater possibilities for isolation and distinctiveness than do the more widely sponsored dance melodies. Thus these forms merit the careful consideration of the advertiser.

Another problem relating to musical programs is the size and

[2] *How To Broadcast: The Art of Teaching by Radio*, by Dr. Cline M. Koon, senior specialist in education by radio, U.S. Office of Education.

nature of the performing unit. In the early days of broadcasting, most musical programs consisted either of instrumental or
vocal solos. As time progressed, larger units came into prominence, culminating in the broadcasts of symphony orchestras,
choruses, and large dance bands. This resulted in greatly improved musical rendition. However, what radio gained in versatility and tonal quality, it lost in intimacy. For the most part
the possibilities of intimate music over the radio has been overlooked. A symphony orchestra, turned on loud enough to secure
the proper tonal values, usually has too much volume for the
listener's comfort, except in a large room. This does not nullify
the value of the symphonic broadcasts, but at times arouses the
desire for something less pretentious. Consequently smaller
groups, such as string quartettes, instrumental trios, piano ensembles, woodwind ensembles, and similar groups possess much
greater broadcasting value than thus far seems to have been
realized. With intelligent and enterprising showmanship, new
program forms might be developed out of these possibilities.

In this regard, the development need not be exclusively in the
field of purely classical music. The classical string quartette
stresses form and development too much to be of sustained
interest to other than the musically educated listener. However,
old songs and simple melodies are especially adaptable to performing groups of this type. One of the most splendid renditions of this nature is the record made many years ago of "Drink
to Me Only with Thine Eyes" by the famous Flonzaley Quartette, since disbanded. It is the intimacy inherent in such music
which has been the secret of the success of the crooner and radio
speaker. Why should it not be employed effectively by the radio
musician and broadcast advertiser?

With regard to other forms of programs, the entire field of
education by radio possesses marked potentialities. It need not
be expected that radio will supplant the school to any important
degree, or that it will be taken over by the school system. Its
function in the total educational scheme is too small, and the
cost too great, for such an undertaking on the part of the edu-
cators. However, in the dramatization of history and similar
fields, as well as in other limited aspects, broadcasting can constitute an important supplement to the work of the classroom.
There should be a great development in this field with regard to

individual stations, as their technical and program facilities improve, and as the local school authorities become better acquainted with the possibilities of radio as an educational force. Broadcasting possesses even greater potentialities in the field of adult education, and here it is to be hoped that the numerous endeavors now under way will continue to be carried on with even greater vigor. This latter field has important advertising significance, for, through a well-constructed program such as the broadcasts of Angelo Patri or Dr. Haggard, groups of listeners may be reached and formed into loyal and remunerative audiences.

Drama is the other field of program development which warrants detailed discussion of its potentialities. It is one of the strongest features of radio broadcasting; for it allows untrammeled play of the imagination in a manner impossible to the theater, motion picture, or the printed page. Broadcasting, in the drama, tends to recapture the psychology of ancient story telling. "The fact that nothing can be seen in some ways is not a loss but rather a gain;" states Dr. Koon,[3] "for a given clue—a directing impulse, and the mind's eye will visualize the scenes beyond the physical powers of designers to build or the camera to photograph. . . . . Radio plays fall flat if they fail to create illusions and to affect human emotions."

Next to its ability to transmit music, this is the greatest advantage of radio broadcasting. It is of value, not only in dramatic programs proper, but in educational broadcasts, news reports, and similar types of programs. Through the use of dialogue, or even of more than two characters, and through casting them in definite dramatic form, old types of programs may be invested with new interest by advertiser and network program official alike. Though dramatic programs at present are mostly devoted to melodrama, it is quite probable that this is merely a passing vogue. It should be noted, however, that because of the great freedom of play which broadcasting affords the listener's imagination, it is especially well adapted to the mystery drama form of program. Here no concrete objects exist to question the plausibility of the plot, and the imagination courses untrammeled through its intimacies. The folk drama, presenting

[3] *Ibid.*, pp. 43–44.

daily experiences familiar to all listeners, also possesses great possibilities of development.

The question of drama is closely akin to the problem of the length of the program. The rise of the fifteen-minute program has been closely related to the development of the comedy strip act, repeated several nights a week, and to the increasing popularity of dramatic broadcasts in general. Regarding the value of the fifteen-minute program for general purposes, there is a considerable difference of opinion among experts. Advertising agency and network executives are unanimous in stating that the quarter-hour period is the only one adapted to the comedy or dramatic "strip" program, which is repeated on successive nights. A longer program would require more action than could be created in each episode, so that the program either would burn out at an early date or would become monotonous because of repetitions inserted to use up time.

As to its applicability to other forms of entertainment, the answer is less certain. The fifteen-minute program possesses the advantage of being a small self-contained unit, which enables a quick flow of action and, in the opinion of some experts, a distinct personality. The nightly repetition which usually accompanies its use, however, is a heavy strain upon the originality of the actors and writers, and it is difficult to maintain the tempo of a fifteen-minute broadcast over any long period of time. Moreover, it is impossible to secure much variety in a fifteen-minute program. The time is limited, and, in addition, any great variety of talent on so brief a program raises the cost of broadcast advertising far beyond reasonable limits. Some agency executives believe that contrasting numbers and moods are not necessary to insure color in a program, while others are equally insistent with regard to the opposite opinion.

An important disadvantage of the fifteen-minute program is its comparative lack of isolation. Programs follow upon one another so swiftly that the listener cannot adjust himself to any of them. Consequently, unless it is a dramatic or comedy presentation, possessing sustained interest and repeated daily, the fifteen-minute program will have little opportunity to impress itself upon the mind of the listener. Moreover, since the listener must continually be turning the dial of his set from one station to another, in search of an acceptable program, the prevalence of the fifteen-minute period may be contributive to such dissatisfaction as exists with broadcasting today.

The half-hour period has much greater adaptability than does the fifteen-minute program, and is probably the best length. Except for strip acts, it possesses practically all of the advantages of the fifteen-minute program, without many of its weaknesses. The hour program also is splendid from the viewpoint of broadcast advertising. It gives opportunity for a large-handed procession of talent before the microphone, and, because of its very size, builds prestige. It also possesses a high degree of isolation, by reason of its length. The chief disadvantages of the hour period are the high cost involved in a program of this sort, and the difficulty, at times, of maintaining a continued rapid pace throughout a program of that length. At the present time financial resources, more than advertising logic, will probably determine the length of the average program, so that the fifteen-minute period is almost certain to continue in popularity for some time to come.

More important than the length or basic type of program broadcast is the problem of the similarity of all programs within a given category. This has become more noticeable within recent months, and constitutes a serious challenge to program progress. Agency executives have been especially outspoken on the point, and have been inclined to attribute this similarity of program to the network program departments. They have stated that it was impossible for the agency to carry on the experimentation necessary to the creation of new and more attractive forms of programs. For such a task, the agency has neither the time nor the resources. In contrast to it, the network possessed the requisite staff, facilities, and a much greater need for producing distinctive programs. A radio broadcasting network is selling the advertiser circulation based upon programs. It is programs, therefore, which constitute its stock in trade, not the mere coverage of the stations affiliated with it. Thus far, networks have sold groups of individual stations; not even networks as a whole, to say nothing of their program facilities. As one agency executive remarked, "If the president of either of the national network companies were to give his program department one million dollars with which to produce dis-

tinctive programs, and demand that they do it, he could sell
those programs tomorrow for four times what they cost him."

In view of the fact that network programs seem to have followed, rather than led, commercial program developments,
there seems to be some justification for the agency criticism.
Why triteness and lack of originality should have become so
thoroughly entrenched in sustaining program policy is hard to
say. It undoubtedly was due, at least in part, to the fact that
networks have been engaged in constructing programs for immediate sale rather than in building solidly for the future. It
also may have been partly due to the mushroom growth, and
consequent lost motion, existing in network programs departments. No matter the cause, the problem remains to be faced.
It is the most serious problem in the field of broadcasting technique, for upon the continued virility and novelty of American
programs depends the future of broadcasting and broadcast
advertising in this country.

A minor matter regarding broadcast advertising technique
is the growing practice of companies to sponsor more than one
program. Usually one program is broadcast in the morning or
afternoon for the housewife, another late in the afternoon for
the children of the family, and another in the evening for the
entire family, including the head of the household. This procedure is varied to meet the requirements of the company, but
the principle remains the same in all cases. Thus in the spring
of 1932 the Wrigley Company broadcast "Myrt and Marge" at
seven o'clock at night to reach the adult audience, presented the
"Lone Wolf Tribe" late in the afternoon to secure the attention
of the children, and presented a series of bridge lessons by Ely
Culbertson both during the daytime and again at night in order
to reach the feminine listener. A more recent endeavor along
the same general line has been the "Five Star Theatre of the
Air," which presents five different programs divided over the
two national network companies, on five successive nights during the week. It is sponsored by the concerns marketing Esso
gasoline. In the spring of 1932 there were 38 companies using
two or more periods, and two or more networks to advertise
their product or products.[4]

[4] *Variety*, May 17, 1932, pp. 49, 54.

CHAPTER XIII

COMMERCIAL ANNOUNCEMENT TECHNIQUE

In the radio program of today the principal sales burden is carried by the commercial announcement. It is this part of the program which identifies it as being the offering of a specific company, and which is the chief means by which the desirability of purchasing the sponsor's product is conveyed to the listener. During the ten years in which broadcast advertising has been in existence, the technique of presenting the commercial announcement has changed more than is generally appreciated. These changes will be considered, both from the aspect of their bearing upon broadcast advertising practice and upon the larger problem of the degree to which American broadcasting has been able to fulfil the public interest.

The commercial announcement did not originate immediately upon the advent of broadcast advertising. The first advertising ventures over the new medium consisted of ten-minute talks, during the course of which the advertiser presented his sales message. It was not until some months later, when the so-called sponsored program came into being, that the commercial announcement also sprang into existence. Since the ten-minute sales talk was clearly recognizable as to sponsorship and purpose, it presented no special selling problem. However, when entertainment came to be part of the commercially sponsored program, the question immediately arose as to where and how the advertising material should be inserted.

Early practice regarding the construction and insertion of the commercial announcement in the sponsored program was based upon the theory that the sole value to be derived from broadcast advertising was the listener goodwill which was engendered, and which reflected itself in increased purchases of the sponsor's product by those who had enjoyed the entertainment. Broadcasting was believed to be unadaptable to selling effort of a more direct nature. As a result of this opinion, the first commercial announcements contained little more than the mere mention of sponsorship. An example of this early type of announcement is found in the following one, taken from among the morning programs broadcast over station WEAF, New York, October 15, 1926:

The Washburn Company engaged the facilities of our station to present these home service talks on Monday, Wednesday and Friday. The subject of our lesson this morning is Gold Medal's Orange Pie.

This brief announcement, together with a statement that Betty Crocker, the Gold Medal cooking expert, would be glad to answer any questions addressed to her, constituted the opening announcement for a twenty-minute program. The closing announcement was almost identical as to content and expression. The same type of announcement is illustrated by those employed on the "Happiness" program, sponsored in 1926 by the Happiness Candy Stores of New York City and featuring the famous Jones and Hare combination. As in the previous case, the opening and closing announcements were little more than twenty seconds long and were confined almost exclusively to mentioning the name of the sponsoring company and its product. In the "Happiness" program, however, there was a slightly greater attempt at selling, for the company slogan, "Happiness Is Just Around the Corner," was mentioned frequently during the course of the entertainment.

It must not be assumed that all of the early commercial announcements were of this nature. Indeed, a perusal of network files indicates that the sponsorship type of announcement was always in the minority. One is impressed with the degree to which commercial announcements of the year of 1926 contain the seeds of current practice. Thus a program sponsored in the fall of that year by the LaFrance Company possessed practically all of the elements considered essential in the announcement of today. The program opened with an excerpt of a march, employed in theme-song fashion. Following this, there was an announcement of approximately one minute and a half in length, telling of the qualities of LaFrance Bluing and Cleansing Flakes, and Saturna Starch Tablets. There was another selling announcement, a minute in length, at the mid-point of the half-hour program, and a brief closing announcement offering to send listeners post cards of the LaFrance display at the Philadelphia Sesqui-Centennial Exposition.

A similar precursor of modern practice is to be found in the "Ipana Troubadours" program. Though most of the brief copy was institutional, there was considerable mention of the red and yellow box in which Ipana Toothpaste was packaged. This was skilfully woven into the program by stating that the troubadours themselves were dressed in red and yellow costumes. Cliquot Club Ginger Ale, at the same period, was emphasizing the pronunciation of their name and calling attention to the Eskimo on the label, while the "Whittall Anglo-Persians" were combining semi-classical music with two-minute announcements as to the qualities of domestic replicas of oriental rugs, and offering a booklet entitled *Little Journeys into the Far East* to anyone who would write them. For the most part, early commercial announcements bore a close similarity to present ones in many of their features, though the skill with which they were done was much less than it is today. There was an almost universal request for fan mail in 1926, which is highly reminiscent of the feverish attempts to secure listener response through the use of contests in 1931 and the early part of 1932.

Commercial announcement practice did not change materially during the following season. However, during the latter part of 1928 and the year of 1929, the selling type of announcement began to be developed. The theory that broadcasting possessed value only as a good-will agent was being discarded and advertisers were coming to see that sales messages, similar to those inserted in other media, could be sent out over the air. Though its good-will element was, and always will be, one of its greatest sources of advertising strength, broadcasting was seen to possess wider possibilities.

In the Arch Preserver Shoe program of that year, there was a tendency to use a brief introductory announcement, a long middle announcement telling of the distinctive qualities of the product advertised, and a minute's closing announcement suggesting that the listener visit their local dealer at the earliest possible moment. Firestone, Bond Bread, Coward Shoes, and similar programs all exhibited the same general trend.

A beginning of the use of more indirect forms of approach was to be noticed in a few programs in 1929. Thus on the Chevrolet program of the "General Motors Family Party," which presented John Philip Sousa and his band for the first time over the air, an indirect approach to the advertising message was employed. The program opened with a brief statement regarding the premier radio performance of the famous leader and his band, and then went directly into the entertainment proper with only the briefest mention of sponsorship. Such selling message as there was, was included in the closing announcement. During the same year, Fels Naptha Soap produced one of the first announcements to be presented in dramatized form. The announcement in question recounted briefly, in dramatized version, the story of an uncle who gave his niece a small house where he intended her to learn housekeeping before presenting her the family mansion. Needless to say, the heroine used Fels Naptha Soap and won the right to her uncle's estate.

The announcements of the period 1928–30 were distinctly formal, employing stock phrases, and always appearing at the same points in the program. Even the best of these were more acceptable when read than when heard. Informality and personal appeal were still to be introduced into them. An example of the better type of program of the period is to be found in the closing announcement of a program broadcast over station KOMO, Seattle, June 25, 1929:

You have just listened to a feature brought to you through the courtesy of Cheasty's Incorporated. Mr. Reseburg will address you again, next Saturday evening at 9:30 P.M. discussing various swimming strokes. Cheasty's Incorporated sponsors these talks on swimming every week—Cheasty's—the distributor of Wil White swimming suits. Bathing suits have become swimming suits now,—and the Wil White lines come in all the alluring colors and bewitching styles of the season—their names are as intriguing as the styles—Caprice,—Coquette,—Sun Tan,—Debonaire,—Silhouette and Cameo. Swimming suits have style as well as any other garment,—and it is of utmost importance that they both have style and colors that flatter. So remember the Wil White Line at Cheasty's Incorporated when you look for a new bathing suit.

Another example, taken from station WNAC, Boston, illustrates the same point, and further indicates the universality of the practice at that period of broadcast advertising. The program in question was broadcast on January 5, 1930.

You have been hearing the Salem Cadet Band broadcast by courtesy of the Pequot Mills, makers of Pequot Sheets and Pillow Cases, the most popular brand of sheets and pillow cases in America. Thousands of housewives say "that Pequot Brand" when buying bed linen. Perhaps you yourself know of some instance of the unusual wearing qualities of Pequot. If so, Pequot would be glad to have you write them a letter and tell them about it. But in any case, be sure to drop them a card and say that you have listened to this program. In return for your courtesy, they will send you a fascinating booklet called "The Story of Pequot." This booklet is beautifully illustrated and gives an insight into one of New England's greatest industries. It will help the children in their school work for it gives a new light on history, geography and economics. It is free, of course. Just send a card to the Pequot Mills, Salem, Mass., or to station WNAC.

Both of the foregoing announcements were above the general standard at the time when they were broadcast. However, they form a decided contrast to the commercial announcements of today. When merely read, they are not unpleasing, but when read aloud they tend to become impersonal and less inviting. Careful examination of either announcement will reveal a superfluity of words and a repetition of ideas. The thoughts contained in the announcements have not been expressed in an economical and telling fashion. There is little personal approach to the listener. The "you" and "we," which looks badly in print but sounds well in speech, is almost entirely missing.

The preceding announcements form a marked contrast to those of 1931 and 1932. At that time several radical changes were made in commercial announcement practice. The first of these was the injection of high-pressure selling into the announcement. This was done by a stressing of the personal pronoun "you," and by a free use of imperatives. The high-pressure effect was further stressed by an almost hysterical use of contests. This period was followed in the spring of 1932 by a decline in high-pressure selling and by the greater use of indirect methods of injecting the commercial announcement into the program. The shift undoubtedly was stimulated partly by the vociferous objections raised against commercial announcements by certain groups in the community. More important, however, was the growing recognition that informality, and the presentation of the commercial announcement as part of the entertainment, possessed definite sales value. Since the announcements of the 1931–32 period constitute the basis of current broadcast advertising practice, and since they have been those most criticized as being incompatible with the public interest, they require considerable discussion.

Two aspects of commercial announcements are of interest:

the length of the announcement, and its type. The trend regarding the length of commercial announcements broadcast over the national networks is presented in Table XLVII.

The reliability of the table is confirmed by the fact that in a count of all commercial announcements broadcast over the

TABLE XLVII*

AVERAGE LENGTH OF COMMERCIAL ANNOUNCEMENTS BROADCAST BY THE NBC RED AND BLUE AND COLUMBIA NETWORKS, 1927-32†

YEAR	¼-Hour Program		½-Hour Program		1-Hour Program	
	Length of Time	Percentage of Period	Length of Time	Percentage of Period	Length of Time	Percentage of Period
			Daytime			
1927........	1 min. 40 sec.	11.1	3 min. 54 sec.	13.0	....	......
1928........	3 min. 20 sec.	22.2	3 min.	10.0	3 min. 42 sec.	6.1
1929........	2 min. 40 sec.	17.8	3 min. 24 sec.	11.4	....	......
1930........	1 min. 36 sec.	10.7	2 min. 10 sec.	10.6‡	....	......
1931........	2 min. 15 sec.	15.0	2 min. 35 sec.	11.9	....	......
1932........	2 min. 20 sec.	15.5	2 min. 28 sec.	11.6	....	......
			Nighttime			
1927........	....	......	1 min. 40 sec.	5.6	2 min. 20 sec.	3.9
1928........	....	......	2 min. 7 sec.	7.0	2 min. 45 sec.	4.6
1929........	1 min. 36 sec.	10.7§	2 min. 20 sec.	7.8	3 min. 58 sec.	6.6
1930........	1 min. 40 sec.	11.1	1 min. 45 sec.	5.9	3 min. 45 sec.	6.2†
1931........	1 min. 55 sec.	11.7	2 min. 39 sec.	8.8	3 min. 43 sec.	6.2
1932........	1 min. 50 sec.	11.6	2 min. 39 sec.	8.8	3 min. 41 sec.	6.1

* Average of 75 programs annually chosen at random from network files for one-fourth and one-half hour programs, and 25 annually for hour programs.

† Count based on 150 words a minute, as used by Radio Commission in Commercial Radio Advertising.

‡ Columbia Broadcasting System first appears in summary, due to 1929 announcements being unavailable.

§ First 15-minute nighttime program was "Amos 'n' Andy," August 19, 1929.

national networks during the second week of November, 1931, by the Federal Radio Commission, the proportion of time consumed by commercial announcements on daytime programs was shown to be 11.56 per cent and on nighttime programs 11.07 per cent.[1] Commercial announcements comprised 2.50 per cent

[1] *Commercial Radio Advertising*, Federal Radio Commission, p. 32.

of total daytime broadcasting hours over national networks, and 5.94 per cent of the nighttime hours. The lower proportion of daytime hours consumed by commercial announcements, in spite of the greater average length of the daytime announcement, is due to the smaller number of commercial programs broadcast prior to six o'clock at night. The proportion of direct selling in broadcast advertising is comparable to the ratio of advertising to total space in the periodical field, which usually ranges from 40 per cent to 60 per cent.

There has been surprisingly little increase in the length of the average commercial announcement within recent years, so that the objections of certain groups of listeners on this ground seem to be without foundation. This trend exists in spite of the fact that the widespread introduction of the contest tended to increase the length of the commercial announcement rather than to shorten it. Thus any criticism of broadcast advertising procedure in this field must have its basis in other causes.

It is quite impossible to venture any conclusion as to the real extent to which listeners have been dissatisfied with commercial announcements. It is too easy to assume that the behavior of one's own class is typical of the entire public, whereas it may be exactly the opposite. Educational circles and similar cultural groups may be especially displeased by high-pressure sales announcements. Because of their position in the community and their advantageous situation with regard to winning public hearing, their opinions are more liable to receive wide circulation than are those of other segments of the listening audience. Whether the opinion held by these groups is right or wrong does not alter the fact that there is no basis for believing it to be representative of listeners as a whole. Such agitation as there was of this type received additional impetus from propaganda issued by certain educational groups and by the willingness of the press to publish information of this type concerning their competitors.

Moreover, there were a number of additional factors which may have been at the basis of such legitimate criticism as may have existed. The trend toward the fifteen-minute period brought commercial announcements of adjacent programs closer to each other in point of time and undoubtedly increased their prominence. The imperatives used so freely in the high-pressure announcements at times may have had the effect of arousing listener resistance and consequent dislike for the announcement. An announcement that is disliked invariably will seem longer than one which is enjoyed, if the time actually consumed by either of them is at all comparable to the other. The more efficient use of words, and resulting greater number of ideas that could be expressed in an announcement of given length, may serve to make announcements seem longer than they really are. Whatever may actually have been the case regarding public attitude toward commercial announcements, the fact remains that the great increase in length sometimes attributed to them never occurred. There is little doubt that the positiveness of many announcements in 1931 was of a nature to merit censure,[2] but this difficulty has largely been overcome in the changes in announcement procedure which have been instituted since the beginning of 1932.

The principal trends in commercial announcement practice since the early part of 1932 can be summarized as follows: The commercial announcement of today, as compared with but a few months ago, is more elastic and adaptable than ever before. It is not always inserted at the same point of the program or in the same fashion. It appears at the beginning and end of programs less often than before, in many cases being followed by a short postlude made up of entertainment. The announcement of today is better adapted to the spoken word, thus gaining in directness, conviction, and personal appeal. This personal appeal is further enhanced by a conscious attempt of both writers and announcers to converse with their audience rather than to mount the rostrum and to preach at them. There is a greater entertainment element in all announcements, while in many instances the announcement becomes part of the program itself.

Dramatization of the announcement, such as practiced in the Sherlock Holmes program of G. Washington Coffee and on the Canada Dry Ginger Ale period, is coming to the forefront to an increasing degree. Dialogue between the announcer and other characters is being used generally. In the case of some programs the announcement itself is being held up to mild ridicule,

---

[2] The much-discussed and undoubtedly justifiably criticized Cremo announcement of a short time ago is an example in point. Most of these announcements ran from 45 seconds to 1 minute despite their seemingly greater length. The nature of the copy created the illusion of length.

as in the case of Ed Wynn with Texaco Gasoline and Ben Bernie with Blue Ribbon Malt. In other cases special announcers, not of the broadcasting profession itself, have been employed to achieve informality and conviction. The use of Heywood Broun on the General Electric program during the winter of 1932 was an example of this type of procedure. Quite recently a new form of announcement has appeared in scattered instances. This form capitalized upon consumer goodwill in a concrete and practical fashion. It states specifically that listener purchases of the product make possible the broadcast in question and that unless these continue it may be necessary to withdraw the program. In other cases withdrawal is not threatened though the rest of the approach remains the same. In the case of one hand lotion, an announcement of this type produced a 50 per cent increase in sales during the following week.[3]

An example of a straight selling announcement, presenting a more direct and personal approach than found in the earlier years of broadcasting is found in the following concluding announcement of the Lowell Thomas–Blue Sunoco program of February 15, 1933.

Like inches, pounds and even minutes, gallons too, are measured by rigid regulations and laws. That is why, when we sell you Blue Sunoco we must give you just so much of this brilliant motor fuel, no more or no less. But even if the law is so rigid about the *amount* of motor fuel we sell you, it has nothing to say about the *quality* of that motor fuel. And do you know, that is one of the reasons why over a million motorists use Blue Sunoco? They feel that Blue Sunoco gives them more quality per gallon. Why don't you try it yourself? Drive on Blue Sunoco for just a few weeks. Get your first tankful to-night and by this same time tomorrow evening, when Lowell Thomas will again be heard, you will begin to notice the improvement in the performance of your car.

An example of the dramatized form of commercial announcement is found in the Canada Dry program of January 19, 1933. This company was one of the pioneers in product dramatization, and originally featured the sound of ginger ale being poured into a glass. Later the sales appeal was shifted to that of emphasizing its fountain trade and the fact that five cents would be refunded for every bottle returned to the dealer. In the example in question this is the principal point of selling interest.

[3] Campana's Italian Balm, reported in *Variety*, January 31, 1933, p. 41.

The announcement begins with a brief opening comment by the announcer:

Ladies and gentlemen, a half hour of sparkling entertainment by Canada Dry—the Champagne of Ginger Ales. Canada Dry is now available in the large, as well as the regular size bottles for the home, and made to order by the glass at fountains. This program stars Jack Benny,—the Canada Dry Humorist—and Ted Weems' Orchestra.

Following this there is a brief musical interlude and the program begins. The announcer, a character by the name of Mary and another by the name of Andrea are hunting for Jack Benny. Finally Ted Weems tells them that Benny has been taken to a sanitarium. The scene shifts to the sanitarium where Mary questions Benny as to why he is there. From here they proceed as follows:

MARY

Hello, Jack. Don't you know me? I'm Mary, your secretary.

JACK

Mary! How are you, dear?

MARY

Why . . . . why . . . . don't you know where you are, Jack?

JACK

Yes, Mary, I'm in a sanitarium.

MARY (whispers)

Gee, Paul, he seems perfectly sane. They shouldn't have him in here.

PAUL (whispers)

Wait—I'll find out . . . . how are you feeling, Jack?

JACK

Fine, Paul. I never felt better in my life.

PAUL

Well . . . . well . . . . then why have they got you in here?

JACK

I don't know, Paul. All I know is that I'm in here. . . . . Oh hello, Andrea.

ANDREA

Hello, Jack . . . . I'm awfully sorry to see you here.

JACK

That's all right, Andrea. They'll find out their mistake.

PAUL (*whispers*)

Say, Ted, you ask him a few questions.

TED

Oh Jack, you remember me—don't you?

JACK

Sure, Ted Weems . . . . did you bring that fruit for me, Ted?

TED

Yes.

JACK

Then stop eating it.

TED (*laughs at this*)

There's nothing the matter with you, Jack. What have they got you in here for?

JACK

You're asking me? Say Ted, there are a lot of people here who don't belong.

TED

Yeah?

JACK

Yeah . . . . you see that fellow in the next cell?

TED

Yes, Jack.

JACK

Well, he thinks he's President. He leaves here March the 4th.

(*Everybody laughs at this*)

MARY

But you don't think *you're* somebody else—do you, Jack?

JACK

No, Mary, I'm Jack Benny.

MARY

Well, I'm going to see the superintendent and make him let you out. . . . . I'll be right back.

TED

There must be something wrong, Jack. Did you lose your money in the market?

JACK

Certainly not. I sold before the crash.

TED

Is it a woman?

JACK

Don't make me laugh. . . . . I never have trouble with women.

TED

But you must be here for a reason.

JACK

I tell you—it's all a mistake.

PAUL

But it's not a mistake to buy Canada Dry Ginger Ale made to order by the glass, sold in the 5-glass bottles, with a nickel back on each large bottle . . . . Canada Dry Ginger Ale . . . . Canada Dry Ginger Ale. . . . .

Jack starts to scream
That's it . . . . that's it. Take him away. . . . . Canada Dry Ginger Ale. . . . .

PARKER

Hold him, hold him, hold him.

ANDREA

Jack—Oh Jack . . . .

Another phase of commercial announcement practice which recently has come into prominence is the question of price mention. Until the latter part of 1932, no price mention was allowed over networks, while individual stations limited it largely to the hours before six o'clock at night. During the spring of that year, however, network executives began to consider the possibility of revoking the ban on the quotation of prices. Finally, in July, the National Broadcasting Company announced that it would allow the mention of price on its daytime programs,[4] other than on Sunday, and on September 15 the Columbia System[5] published an even more comprehensive series of regulations regarding the mention of price over its facilities.

The Columbia System regulations allow the mention of price on both day and night programs providing certain requirements are complied with. The first of these is that two price mentions will be allowed on a fifteen-minute program, three on a thirty-minute program, and five on an hour's broadcast, provided that in each case the total "sales talk" shall not exceed 10 per cent of the total program time. Price mentions are construed as any or all price mentions of one or more products on any program.

[4] *Broadcasting*, July 15, 1932, p. 15.

[5] *A Statement to Advertisers and Advertising Agencies*, by William S. Paley, president, Columbia Broadcasting System, Inc.

Competitive and comparative prices are not to be broadcast in any form whatsoever. Time limits set forth in the regulations apply to the direct selling message and not to mere mention of the sponsor's name during the course of the program. The Columbia System also reserves the right to refuse any announcements where more than 150 words have been crowded into a minute's delivery, as well as any others which either violate one or another of the regulations previously mentioned, or which the System deems to be contrary to the best interest of the public and the advertiser.

Shortly after the publication of the Columbia regulations the Yankee Network adopted similar rules for its nighttime programs. The network always had allowed price quotation on its daytime programs within what it termed "reasonable limits," so that its policy in this respect remained unaltered.

The prohibition of price mention originally was placed on broadcast advertisers because network executives were afraid that, if once allowed, it might be carried to undue proportions. This might easily have been the case in the early days of broadcasting. It is interesting to note, therefore, that in December, 1932, no more than 25 per cent of broadcast advertisers over national networks were availing themselves of the privilege of quoting prices. There were 29 companies in all following this practice during the first week of that month.[6] This represented a decline from the number of concerns first taking advantage of the new regulations.

Individual station practice with regard to commercial announcements varies in several respects from that of the networks. In the first place, the announcements are uniformly longer. In November, 1931, commercial announcements totaled 20.74 per cent of the total commercial hours broadcast by individual stations prior to six o'clock at night and 18.26 per cent of nighttime commercial hours. Announcements of this type comprised 7.83 per cent of total daytime and 6.39 per cent of total nighttime hours broadcast by these stations.[7]

In response to a question as to whether commercial announcements had been growing longer or shorter since 1929,[8] 67 per cent

<hr>

[6] *Variety*, December 6, 1932, p. 32.

[7] *Commercial Radio Advertising*, Federal Radio Commission, p. 32.

[8] See Appendix B for detailed questions.

of the managers of 50 stations replied that they had been growing shorter, 17 per cent that the trend was toward longer announcements, while 16 per cent noted no marked difference.
Most of those reporting a trend toward shorter announcements
also stated that there had first been a tendency toward longer
announcements, following which the reverse tendency set in.
It also is interesting to note that 23 per cent of station executives indicated it to be their opinion that the removal of price-
mention restrictions was partly responsible for the trend toward
shorter announcements. Another 28 per cent of the group stated
that they had been making a practice of limiting the length of
announcements, usually to a maximum of 150 words.

The question of the soundness of present commercial announcement practice presents itself at this point. The reading
of large numbers of announcements for the various years during
which network broadcasting has been in existence, as well as
careful listening to current presentations over the air, leads one
to the conclusion that the past eight or ten months have witnessed the greatest progress made thus far in the field of the
commercial announcement. This progress has centered primarily about two features: the introduction of an element of informal
conversation into the broadcast advertising, and the development of various forms of dramatization with respect to it. The
latter course of procedure is not open to all products and programs, though the former presents no such limitations. The informal element probably has the greater potentialities, for it
makes possible the combination of the strong points of both
advertising and salesmanship in the delivery of the commercial
announcement.

Though the progress has been marked in this field, it should
not be assumed that a great deal does not remain to be done.
Some of the criticism of commercial announcements has been
well founded. Numerous announcements have been too long,
and many have been poorly done. Even the present innovations
do not represent anything near perfection in this field. Advertising agency executives have been almost unanimous in their
opinion that, though commercial announcements are improving, much remains to be done before even a point of satisfactory
development is reached.

One of the most interesting and helpful statements of the requirements of effective commercial announcements has been presented by Roy C. Witmer, vice-president in charge of sales, National Broadcasting Company. The requirements, as visualized by Mr. Witmer, are as follows:[9]

1. If straight commercial announcements are used, do they give the listener some interesting and worthwhile information about the product?
2. Do they tell the story in a pleasant manner?
3. Do they ring absolutely true?
4. If actually calling on the listeners personally, would the same story be used in the same way?
5. Are they positive, or do they have a tendency to belittle a competitor's story?
6. Are they sufficiently untechnical, so that the layman understands and is interested?
7. Are they in good taste? Human nature does not like to hear or discuss disagreeable things unless compelled to.
8. Does the commercial part of the program harmonize in spirit and tone with the rest of the program?
9. Is the result of the foregoing checking, *a program*, or *a program* with *commercial credits?* It should be *a program* full of entertainment and interest from first to last.

[9] *Applying the Singularities of Radio*, by Roy C. Witmer (National Broadcasting Company), pp. 11–12.

CHAPTER XIV

CONTESTS, SPECIAL OFFERS, AND RELATED MATTERS

A broadcasting program does not stand alone as an advertising undertaking. In order to secure the maximum value from effort of this sort it is necessary to correlate it closely with other devices and activities in the field. In the early days of broadcasting, practice in this respect was limited to the offer of a small souvenir or useful gift to listeners who would write in to the sponsoring company or the station over which the program was broadcast. Later, free samples were offered either directly or through dealers. More recently, introductory offers have been made, whereby the listener will receive a sample or full package of the new article upon the purchase of one or more units of the company's standard product. In 1931 the offer was replaced in popularity by the contest, while other forms of tie-in with the company's general advertising program began to be devised during that and the preceding year.

The offer has been closely associated with broadcast advertising almost since the beginning of the networks. Booklets and souvenirs were offered to listeners as early as 1926, prior to the formation of the National Broadcasting Company. In the following year the Cities Service Company first offered its budget book, including also a list of their gasoline filling stations in the listener's district. This offer was continued for a number of years, and, in 1931, a total of 182,000 requests were received for the budget book.

The use of this form of sales tie-in continued to grow during 1929 and 1930, though in the following season it was eclipsed temporarily by the contest. Since then the trend has again been reversed, and the special offer is replacing the contest. In December, 1932, approximately one-third of the companies on the air were giving something to listeners, either merely upon receipt of a letter or else requiring the inclusion of a carton top or similar proof of purchase. Among the offers made over the radio during the early part of 1932 were the following: a bath sponge given away by the manufacturer of a household cleaner upon the receipt of a label from the product's container; a refillable toothbrush offered by the manufacturer of a brushless shave upon receipt of a carton top; a bottle of hair tonic upon request; recipes upon request; a lucky piece; copies of talks; instructions for making a cellophane belt; an enlargement suitable for framing of any photograph sent in with four carton tops of a well-known household cleanser; together with similar items. In several other cases, full-size samples of the product were offered to the public, either free or in the form of a combination offer.

Many of the offers have been highly successful in bringing listener response. A brief announcement to the effect that the Standard Oil Company of New York would mail a booklet entitled *Christmas in Soconyland* was made on two succeeding weeks over eight stations early in December, 1931. The combined listener response was 75,000. During the first six months of 1931 the R. B. Davis Company, manufacturers of baking powder, received over 200,000 requests for recipes on their "Mystery Chef" program. In January, 1932, Ovaltine, sponsors of "Little Orphan Annie," distributed 174,000 children's mugs. One of the most successful of all offers was that made by Pepsodent when introducing its new antiseptic. The response to an offer of a free full-sized bottle of the new product to anyone who would turn in the tops of two of the company's toothpaste cartons was so great, that, it is said, the antiseptic was bought by New York City chain stores at a one per cent premium from any wholesaler who was fortunate enough to possess it. By the second week of the offer it was necessary for the company to announce that, due to the unexpected demand, it might be impossible for the listener's local dealer to fill his order immediately, and cautioned the radio audience against accepting substitute brands. It is said that approximately 2,500,000 units of the antiseptic were distributed in this manner.

The contest did not enter the field of broadcast advertising in any direct manner until 1931, when the networks removed their prohibition of this type of sales promotion at the insistence of advertisers. In 1928 and 1929 statements were inserted in the commercial announcements of some companies to the extent that listeners could procure details regarding contests by visiting their nearest dealer or by watching the columns of their local newspaper. This indirect method was unsatisfactory, so that it was necessary to make concessions in the broadcasting of contest information.

Following the removal of network regulations prohibiting the use of contests as part of the advertiser's commercial copy, companies flocked to the new device. The trend toward contests was not uniform throughout all industrial groups, since not every company possessed a product or market to which this form of promotion was adaptable. It was primarily in the convenience goods field that the contest was utilized, it being estimated that, at the peak of the vogue, approximately 20 per cent of concerns of this type were making use of tests of this sort.[1] It also is estimated that at no time did more than 10–12 per cent of the total broadcast advertisers over national networks resort to contests. By December, 1932, the vogue had passed and the number of contests continuing on the air had been greatly reduced.

The contests broadcast were principally of several types: the word-building contest; the contest wherein the listener was required to write a letter regarding the points of superiority in the sponsor's product; the limerick contest and the puzzle or riddle. The letter type of contest was the first to win prominence. This form is exemplified by the contest sponsored by the Cudahy Packing Company in the spring of 1932 for one of their products, Old Dutch Cleanser. In this instance an 18-carat white-gold diamond ring with a $\frac{1}{2}$-carat diamond was given out each week for the best letter on the subject of "Why Old Dutch Cleanser Is the Only Cleanser I Need in My House." There was no prerequisite to entering the contest.

The word-building contest almost invariably follows one formula. The contestant is given either the name of the company or its slogan, and is instructed to make from it the longest possible list of standard English words, the longest list being adjudged the winner. In more recent contests the listener has been confined to three-letter English words, probably because of the difficulty involved in counting and checking the longer lists resulting from a freer choice of words. In most cases the

[1] E. P. H. James, manager of sales promotion, National Broadcasting Company.

list must be accompanied by one or more tops of cartons containing the sponsor's product, or a like number of facsimile drawings of the same. The latter is introduced so that the contest may not fall within the provisions of the lottery laws. To be legal a contest must not have a price of admission as a requirement for entry, nor can any prize be awarded on chance alone. Some element of skill or merit must be involved. The announcement regarding the facsimile drawing meets the former of the two provisions, while the test of skill involved either in word-building or the writing of a letter meets the other.

Contests have been much less prevalent on local broadcast advertising programs. Of a group of 52 station managers giving their experience regarding contests, 37.5 per cent stated that they had not had any of them on local periods.[2] Other than this there seems to be no difference between network and individual station experience in this field.

The value of contests is a mooted question. To the sponsor seeking fan mail, they are an effective means of meeting his wish. Likewise, they temporarily increase the sale of the product, due to the fact that the average listener will buy a package of the sponsor's brand in order to secure the necessary carton top, rather than go to the trouble of drawing a facsimile. On the other hand, the mail response received by a contest is hardly an indication either of the popularity or the selling value of the program. It is merely a measure of the popularity of the specific contest among the listeners who have heard the program. If the contest is difficult or the prizes small, the response will be slight. If the prizes are attractive and the requirements reasonable, the listener interest should be relatively large. Experienced agency executives are mostly of the opinion that contest mail is at least partially controllable in quantity by means of the requirements laid down for entry. Moreover, at the height of the contest craze, there was reason to doubt whether the listener response came principally from the regular audience or from the professional contestant, of whom there were a large number. Contest magazines even flourished for a brief period.

The temporary increase in the sale of the article connected with the contest is gratifying while it lasts. However, there are grave questions as to its ultimate value. In a sense, the contest

[2] See Appendix B for detailed questions.

acts as an introductory offer. But it is an introductory offer based upon an incentive other than the inherent value of the product itself. Rather, it is associated with the hope of receiving something for nothing. The purchaser has never been sold on the merits of the article and consequently the basis for a continued purchasing habit has not been set up within him. The contest over, he may never buy another box of the article. Moreover, since his interest has been focused not upon the product but upon the prize which is being offered, it is quite possible that the listener may be highly irritated at not having won anything. In this case the contest becomes an agent of ill will for the manufacturer. There is little doubt that this occurs to some degree in almost every contest. Moreover, the extent of this dissatisfaction is probably greater than usually realized. The danger of its occurrence can be lessened to some degree by the inclusion of a large number of small prizes among the awards.

Another effect of the contest has been to unduly lengthen the announcement in the program and to fill it with cumbersome and uninteresting details. These details have been a source of irritation to listeners who have not been interested in the contest, and, in addition, have taken away from the amount of time which could be devoted to selling the article itself. In the more extreme cases the situation presented itself where the sponsor was advertising the contest rather than the product, which received only incidental mention. Networks and agencies both have been opposed to contests, and for the most part have employed them merely upon the insistence of their clients.

Compared to the contest, the special offer, in its various forms, is a much more effective medium to be used in conjunction with a broadcast advertising program. Every interested listener receives something. In addition, no long and complicated announcement is required to present the details of the offer. Moreover, both the offer and the announcement which it entails are integral parts of the advertiser's sales message. They are not extraneous to the main purpose of selling as much of the product as possible by convincing people of the desirability of its purchase.

The use of the offer also allows greater variation, and consequent greater novelty and distinctiveness, than does the contest. There is a greater opportunity either for direct sampling or, at least, for product tie-in. Fire hats to dramatize the Texaco Fire Chief Gasoline, puzzle pictures for children, mixing spoons for housewives, eye cups for users of borax, bridge score pads, beetle ware glasses to be used in the bathroom, and similar items are examples in point. It is easier to connect the offer with the retail outlet than in the case of the contest, since the store can be made the point of distribution and not merely the place where entry blanks may be received. A combination of the special offer and contest principles is found in the offer which is contingent upon the solution of some problem such as the solving of a puzzle. In such an instance the puzzle is made as simple as possible in order to insure its solution by as large a number of people as possible. The advantage of this type of offer is that it introduces an element of play into the proceedings, and further ministers to the listener's sense of accomplishment. It is estimated that approximately half of the concerns whose business warrants such activity, i.e., manufacturers of convenience goods, are using some form of offer at the present time.[3]

Another aspect of the question of securing the maximum effectiveness from the broadcast advertising program by engaging in various subsidiary activities is the so-called merchandising of the program. The accepted trade meaning of the term includes two groups of closely related activities: (1) various steps taken to promote dealer interest in the program and to point out its value to the individual retailer; and (2) activities having for their purpose the building up of increased listener interest by means other than the program proper. Neither terminology nor practice in this field is clearly defined, though the preceding description will serve as a starting point.

The question of building up increased listener interest in the program, or of calling attention to the program through agencies other than broadcasting, forms the simpler of the two problems and will be considered first. The means open in this field comprise largely other forms of advertising. General newspaper and magazine tie-ins, where the program is mentioned as part of the general advertisement, seem to be the most prevalent form to be used in this field. In the spring of 1931, approximately half of the program sponsors on the National Broadcasting Company

[3] E. P. H. James, manager of sales promotion, National Broadcasting Company.

networks made this part of their advertising procedure. One-third of the companies followed a similar practice with regard to their magazine advertising, while another third made the practice of inserting special "spot-light" advertisements in the newspapers, devoted exclusively to calling attention to their program.[4] Other types of program tie-ins employed in relation to the listener include "Thanks notes" to listeners who write, envelope stuffers, direct mail to selected groups of listeners (usually carried on through the dealer), car cards, the publication of house organs, and similar items.

At times highly ingenious methods are devised. Thus, in the case of a milk company, attention was called to the program by means of a cardboard collar placed around the neck of each milk bottle delivered by the company in seven states. In the case of the Wrigley "Lone Wolf Tribe" program broadcast for children, a number of Indian chiefs were sent to various schools to speak on Indian lore.[5] There was no direct tie-in with the program, either in the way of mentioning the sponsor or even of mentioning the program itself. In spite of its indirectness, the method was generally satisfactory. A variation of this method which has achieved great popularity in recent months has been the public appearance of the program artists in theaters throughout the country and, at times, the actual production of the broadcast from the theater stage. These and similar devices are employed, the specific method varying with the sponsor, his program, and his product. Efforts of this type are more prevalent in the case of network programs than on the part of individual stations, though their use is growing among local advertisers.

Of even greater interest are the steps taken by advertisers to secure dealer co-operation either in pushing the radio program or in building up dealer interest in the program. Radio broadcasting is still a comparatively new advertising medium. As a result, the dealer interest in ventures of this type is high. Agency executives report that a radio program gives a company prestige with its dealer organization which cannot be achieved to a like degree by any other method. Consequently, this becomes an especially important aspect of broadcast

---

[4] *Broadcast Advertising*, Vol. II (National Broadcasting Company).

[5] "Merchandising a Radio Program," by Paul W. Kesten, Columbia Broadcasting System, in *Radio and Education* (1932), pp. 87–89.

advertising and it is imperative that the dealer should be fully
informed regarding the program. This can be accomplished by
means of special portfolios given to salesmen and illustrating
the high lights of the broadcasting series. It can be done through
the use of direct mail to dealers, the presentation of the program at dealers' or salesmen's conventions, the use of house
organs and by like methods. It is surprising, at times, the extent to which so simple a practice is overlooked. In a number of
instances where important companies had sponsored radio programs, surveys indicated that less than 60 per cent of the dealers
seemed to be aware of the fact that the company was broadcasting.[6]

Interesting the dealer in the radio broadcast advertising program on his own part, however, is merely the first step in promoting the program through retail channels. More important
is securing dealer co-operation in the setting up of displays, the
sending of direct mail literature, and similar steps which will
assist in building up the listener audience for the program.
Surveys again indicate a willingness on the part of dealers to
accept material of this type and a lack of enterprise on the part
of advertisers in making the most of their opportunities in this
direction.[7] In a group of 500 druggists surveyed by the National
Broadcasting Company, 76 per cent of those replying to the
questions stated that they wanted pictures of radio personalities
as features for window and counter displays, 56 per cent wanted
pictures of the product to be used for the same purpose, while
51 per cent desired to have the displays so constructed as to
make possible the insertion of the article itself. There seemed to
be a slight preference for window display as against counter display material.

In the case of network broadcasting the activities outlined
thus far comprise the principal features to be used by advertisers.
In their actual use, the network plays a passive part. Both
national networks strongly recommend activities of this type,
and both of them have display rooms showing what other clients
have done. Their own merchandising departments are always
ready to assist the advertiser and his client in any manner pos-

---

[6] *Merchandising Radio to Dealers*, National Broadcasting Company.

[7] "Druggists tell us—," a study by the Merchandising Division of the National
Broadcasting Company.

sible, though confining their activities to a strictly advisory
capacity. There is no attempt in any instance to take an active
and leading part in planning the advertiser's program in this
field.

The advent of spot broadcasting gave rise to interesting developments with regard to the dealer contact and other promotional service rendered by individual stations to their clients.
Stations tended, on the whole, to follow newspaper procedure
in this field, and went a great deal farther than did the networks.
They voluntarily assumed a number of distribution burdens of
the advertiser which hardly could be termed broadcast advertising, and usually performed them at no additional cost. Of a
group of 50 stations questioned as to the form of promotional
service which they rendered in the fall of 1932,[8] 17.5 per cent
replied that they had no service of this type while another 17.5
stated that they participated only in an advisory sense. The
remaining 65 per cent engaged in some type of activity with regard to promoting the program. Of the group carrying on such
service, 64 per cent arranged for the showing of posters and displays in retail outlets, 59 per cent sent letters to the trade telling
of the program—though one third of them charged the sponsor
for the postage—while 58 per cent called on dealers for a similar
purpose.

Other activities mentioned included the broadcasting of preliminary announcements of the program; announcements in
the station's daily news period; including the program in the
station's newspaper advertising; publishing programs in the
station's own news bulletin; securing dealers for the company;
making telephone surveys of the program's effectiveness; conducting market surveys for the sponsor; checking on sales within
the territory; furnishing talent for personal appearances; help-
ing with fan mail; addressing sales meetings and similar items.
Some of the more ambitious stations conduct practically all of
these activities, maintaining a large staff for that purpose, furnishing the advertiser with numerous and complete reports, and
rendering generally valuable service. One station has even gone
so far as to organize a fleet of fourteen motor cars manned
by expert sales promotion men, together with two specially

[8] See Appendix B for detailed questions.

equipped display trucks, to render dealer contact service to their clients. These operate in a territory embracing three middle western states, as well as parts of several others.

Though this service is quite valuable and highly appreciated by the advertiser, there is a grave question as to how far the broadcaster should venture in this field. If newspaper experience is to be repeated, the broadcaster will greatly overexpand his service in this direction, and then will be obliged to contract it. Experienced broadcasters, possessing newspaper advertising and promotion background, state emphatically that this will be the case. As practiced at the present time, the station merchandising service is in substance a form of price-cutting. It performs tasks for the advertiser which are only remotely related to the item for which money is being paid. The distribution of displays and solicitation of the trade regarding a new radio program is an important advertising function, but it is a duty which devolves upon the advertiser and his agency and not upon the station. The function of the station is to furnish the most effective program possible and to broadcast it in the best possible manner. At that point its responsibility ends.

It is quite true that the station may be better situated to contact dealers than is the advertiser himself, or that the program may gain greater prestige from the use of this method. On the other hand, if such service is rendered, it should be charged for accordingly and should not be included in the time revenue. Its inclusion in the time charge is all the more unsound because it tends to hide the cost of the service from both station and advertiser and to promote undue expansion of activities in this field without adequate recompense to the station. Therefore, if any promotional and dealer contact service is to be rendered, it should be carried on only upon due compensation.

The question of getting the greatest possible effectiveness out of the broadcast advertising program is broader than any of the detailed activities hitherto described. Fundamentally, it involves a close correlation of the program, both as to basic idea and details of construction, with the rest of the advertising campaign. At times the radio presentation may dramatize the central theme of the entire campaign, as in the case of Ed Wynn and the Texaco Fire Chief program. In other cases it may be an institutional undertaking designed merely to supplement the main campaign and to build up general goodwill. In some instances it may serve to reach special groups within the community, and in still other cases to accomplish a specific purpose such as winning a hearing for the company's salesmen. The uses to which the broadcast advertising program can be put are many and varied, and its effectiveness depends primarily upon the skill with which it is employed.

PART IV
EVALUATION AND CONCLUSIONS

CHAPTER XV

AMERICAN BROADCASTING AND THE PUBLIC INTEREST

The approach to the discussion of the various phases of American broadcasting has been from the viewpoint of its rôle as an advertising medium. Broadcasting has been considered as being one of a number of media of mass communication by means of which the advertiser could reach the public. Accordingly, the problems involved in its use for that purpose have received primary consideration, though the broader aspects of structure and service have been treated wherever they possessed bearing upon the former question.

Since no medium of mass communication can be considered merely in the light of its ability to carry an advertising message to potential customers, the approach has been a limited one. Media of mass communication, such as radio and the press, possess an element of public interest which transcends their usefulness in advertising. Newspapers and magazines constitute agencies for the dissemination of information and entertainment (the latter is true of magazines more than of newspapers) which are of fundamental importance to the community. The advertising is merely the means by which they are enabled to render this service and, at the same time, to receive a reasonable return on their investment.

In this respect, American broadcasting is in no different a position from that of the press. Like it, broadcasting renders a service more important than the dissemination of advertising messages. Every day it carries entertainment into millions of homes. It constitutes a means of direct and almost instantaneous communication with great portions of the American public, the value of which was strikingly illustrated in the recent financial panic.[1] Furnishing such service constitutes the chief justifi-

[1] Following the closing of the Michigan banks some weeks earlier, American finance reached a state of demoralization by March 3, 1933, where it became necessary to declare banking holidays in practically all of the important financial states of the nation. A state of financial panic existed. Under such conditions, public confidence reaches its

cation of the existence of radio broadcasting in any form. Broadcast advertising is important primarily because it makes possible this service, and only to a secondary extent because it assists in the sale of goods and the carrying on of the processes of trade. Because of this relationship of advertising to American broadcasting, the problems of the former become the concern of advertiser and public alike.

The propriety of magazines and newspapers deriving their main support from advertising revenue has never been questioned very seriously. Likewise, it has seldom been suggested that the insertion of advertising matter in periodicals has had an undesirable effect upon the service rendered the reading public. In the case of radio broadcasting, both questions have been raised to a serious degree and have even found their way into the halls of Congress.[2]

The prominence given to this matter in the field of broadcasting is due to a number of reasons. One of them is the fact that broadcasting wave-lengths are limited in quantity. Thus it is more difficult for a group of individuals to secure a station for themselves than to issue their own newspaper or magazine. The problem of the public interest is therefore more complicated in the case of broadcasting than with respect to the press. A second reason is the fact that broadcasting is the most direct of all advertising media. In it, the sales message stands isolated in point of time. It cannot be glanced over or turned aside as easily as can a page of advertising in a periodical. Consequently, to those who dislike advertising, it will be more irritating than similar material appearing in a magazine and newspaper, even though its message is inherently no more objectionable than is some of

---

low ebb. Yet, before the full force of the news had impressed itself upon the consciousness of the American people, the forceful handling of the emergency in President Roosevelt's inaugural address on March 4, and the reassuring promise for speedy action—brought directly into millions of homes—immediately laid the groundwork for restored public confidence as no other act could possibly have done. The effect of this broadcast was further reinforced when the entire nation heard the passage of emergency legislation direct from the halls of Congress on Thursday, March 9, and when, on the following Sunday, the President explained directly to the people the significance of the measures taken.

[2] The Dill-Couzens Resolution (Senate Resolution 129), instructing the Radio Commission to investigate American broadcast advertising, and the Fess Bill (died in committee), requiring 15 per cent of the wave-lengths to be given to educational interests, are examples in point.

the printed advertising.[3] Moreover, the agitation on this point
has been given considerable impetus by the activities of certain
publishing and educational groups within recent years.[4] Finally,
broadcasting by government-owned or closely controlled mo-
nopolies, financed by taxation, has been the system in vogue in
many European countries. This is in direct contrast to the
United States, where a privately owned and competitively operated broadcasting system is maintained on the basis of revenue
derived from advertising. The records of the principal foreign
broadcasting systems, however, have been advanced by some
as reasons for adopting similar principles in this country.

With these objections being raised against American broadcasting, and with certain groups advocating government ownership and operation of broadcasting stations and networks, it
becomes necessary to inquire as to whether the system in vogue
is the best adapted to meet conditions in the United States, or
whether a superior one might be devised and put into operation.
The chief characteristics of the service rendered to the listener
by broadcasters in this country have been presented, and constitute a partial answer to the problem. It also is necessary to
compare the service afforded by American broadcasting to that
rendered by the systems in operation in the principal foreign

[3] The amount of material which might be objected to on the grounds of content is
probably much less than that appearing in almost any leading magazine, were one to
read the copy completely. Thus, in one issue of a leading women's monthly magazine,
one is told to beware of the "pink toothbrush"; shown pictures of germs which lodge in
the throat; given numerous lengthy instructions regarding the preservation of beauty;
told that "cathartics should be used only as a last resort"; that one will "do it better on
dated coffee"; has pictured for one the unpleasantness of a person with a cold sneezing
near one; is regaled with the sad plight of the young woman whose underthings have
not been washed properly so as to take away perspiration odors; is told of numerous
ways to guard the breath; is informed as to the proper tissues; warned of the danger of
a "lordosis backline"; told of the bases of incompatible marriage in some detail and initiated into other similar problems. As they are presented and attended, the majority of
these advertisements do not seem objectionable. On the other hand, when read in detail,
the effect at times becomes decidedly unpleasant. There is comparatively little material
on the air at the present time which might be termed this type.

[4] The propaganda of the Ventura Free Press and the National Committee on Education by Radio, Washington, D.C., are examples in point. Both organizations have been
extremely violent in their position and have been especially prone to ignore even the
most obvious facts which did not fit into their preconceived viewpoints. Since the latter
has been closely allied to the National Educational Association and various parent-
teacher groups, its repeated expression of bias has done much to hide the true situation
regarding American broadcasting.

nations which might be considered as facing conditions analogous to those in the United States. These systems include those of Great Britain, Germany, and Canada, primarily, though brief mention also should be made of French broadcasting.

Next to the United States and Denmark, Great Britain is the most important country in the world with respect to radio broadcasting. In August, 1932, there were 4,821,436 radio licenses in effect in Great Britain, a number equal to 10.7 per cent of the country's population.[5] Calculated on the same basis, American radio-set ownership equaled 13.0 per cent, and that of Denmark 13.4 per cent,[6] of the total population.

Though presenting entirely different problems from those of the United States, Denmark possesses one of the most interesting broadcasting systems in the world. It is government owned, carries no advertising, and presents a program structure remarkably well adapted to the needs of its people. At half-past ten every morning the fish prices are broadcast from Copenhagen, being quoted for that city, as well as for the Hamburg, Stockholm, Rotterdam, and Amsterdam markets and the English and Baltic ports. Every fisherman has a radio on his boat, and thus is able to convey his catch to the most profitable market. Ample time is given to entertainment as well as to more serious programs. There is one dramatic program called "The Family Hansen" which has achieved great popularity. It is of the "Real Folks" type of entertainment and combines comedy with folk drama. Another program to win a wide following is that of a comedy monologue, wherein the artist satirizes everyone and everything, including the prime minister and ruling family.[7] The system works ideally in Denmark, though there is no indication that it could be applied with equal success to the United States.

The British broadcasting system, likewise, is a form of government monopoly, though in this instance there is a greater similarity between its broadcasting problems and those arising in this country. The maintenance and operation of the system is vested in the British Broadcasting Corporation, a public corporation without share capital, organized under Royal Charter,

---

[5] *B.B.C. Yearbook, 1933*, p. 88.   [6] *Ibid.*

[7] Address by Senator Clarence C. Dill of Washington, rebroadcast by the Columbia Broadcasting System from London, England, May 31, 1931.

and acting as trustees for the national interest. The company is therefore a government-inspired monopoly. Its connection with the government is further enhanced by the fact that it comes under the supervision of the postmaster general, to whom it is required to present an annual report and whose rulings it must obey.

The company likewise is required to broadcast any material which the government desires to have disseminated among the public and to refrain from presenting other items when so ordered.[8]

British broadcasting is financed by means of a license fee on sets amounting to $2.43 annually. Not all of the funds so collected are employed in maintaining broadcasting facilities and producing programs in the interests of the listening public. A large portion of the total revenue goes to the post-office for general expenses and is never expended upon broadcasting. Moreover, as the revenue has increased, it has been the post-office, primarily, which has benefited. Thus, in 1927, out of tax receipts of £800,959, the corporation received 67.2 per cent. In 1929 it was accorded 64.2 per cent of the £944,301 received in that year from listeners.[9] In 1932 it received but slightly in excess of 50.0 per cent of approximately £2,400,000 collected in set taxes in that year.[10] Thus the increased set ownership and consequent revenue which has been built up through the activities of the British Broadcasting Corporation programs is reinvested in listener service to only a very slight degree, and is used for the most part in meeting some of the general expenses of the government.

Besides the amount turned over to the post-office, an additional sum, equaling 18.7 per cent of the total B.B.C. revenue in 1929, was paid to the government in the form of an income tax. Finally, administrative expenses seem to be rising faster than revenue, so that a continually smaller portion of total funds seems to be devoted to programs themselves.[11] How much of this is due to the station construction policy of the B.B.C. is hard to say in view of the limited data.

With regard to the collection of the taxes, the British have

[8] *Broadcasting Abroad*, National Advisory Council on Radio in Education, pp. 27–28.

[9] *B.B.C. Yearbook, 1931*, p. 36.

[10] *Ibid., 1933*, p. 87.   [11] *Ibid., 1931*, p. 37.

experienced difficulties mildly akin to the enforcement of the Prohibition Amendment in this country. In 1931 it was estimated that there were 400,000 bootleg sets in London alone, a figure which at that time equaled almost 10 per cent of the total number of set licenses issued.[12] The corporation's yearbook of that season goes to great lengths to chide listeners who have not paid their fee, devoting one whole section to its discussion. The post-office, however, is more practical and has devised a means of combating the situation. Trucks equipped with set-detecting apparatus are sent periodically to various towns, and the offenders caught in this manner are brought into court and fined. The desired effect is always attained, and for a brief period there is a marked increase in set registrations in that community.

There is no subsidiary revenue derived from advertising programs, since none are broadcast. This does not mean that they may not be broadcast, but that the management of the British Broadcasting Company has consistently refused to accept advertising of any sort. In a supplementary agreement regarding the powers of the B.B.C., made in October, 1923, the corporation was permitted to receive a consideration for broadcasting "commercial information approved for broadcasting by the Postmaster General, subject to such conditions as he may prescribe." As far as can be determined, the issue has never been carried to that official.[13]

Though the various reports of the B.B.C. sedulously avoid mention of the subject, it is by no means certain that all listeners are in favor of prohibiting advertising over British stations. Some of the popular magazines[14] in the radio field have been outspoken on this point, and have even gone so far as to discuss the problems which would be involved in the presentation of advertising programs over the corporation's stations. In the past year the corporation itself seemed to have sensed the seriousness of this tendency (serious at least from its own viewpoint) and devoted six pages of the current yearbook to a discussion of why broadcast advertising should not be allowed.[15] Arguments advanced included the fact that listeners would not like the

[12] Ibid., 1932, p. 29.

[13] Printer's Ink, November 20, 1924, p. 49; Wireless Magazine (London), July, 1931, p. 597.

[14] Wireless Magazine, July, 1931, p. 597.

[15] B.B.C. Yearbook, 1933, pp. 54, 59, 62–64.

programs, that broadcasting is not a satisfactory advertising medium, that it would set up competition with the press, and similar items. One of the most interesting aspects of this whole question is the extent to which British listeners tune in on Radio Paris, a French station over which several English phonograph-record companies advertise consistently, and where a large number of announcements are made in English for the benefit of listeners across the channel.[16]

The structure of British broadcasting is at present in a state of transition. When completed it will include five high-power, twin-wave stations which will blanket the entire United Kingdom. One wave will be for national programs, broadcast over all stations simultaneously, and the other for local programs. At the present time the plan is only partly completed, so that sixteen stations of varying power are being used to cover the country.[17]

Data on the actual composition of British programs are not available later than 1930, a summary of which is found in Table XLVIII.

Careful perusal of the lengthy discussions of various types of programs which appear in the annual editions of the *B.B.C. Yearbook* and of such actual programs as have been available for inspection make possible at least a broad general evaluation of the quality of British programs. It is evident that more time is devoted to classical music than in this country, though there is reason to question whether much of it reaches the high standard available to American audiences in the best broadcasts here. Opera has not been developed to the extent that it has in the weekly Metropolitan Opera broadcasts. Though symphonic concerts are more frequent, nevertheless none of the programs show the admirable balance found in the average offering of the New York Philharmonic, Boston Symphony, and Philadelphia Orchestras.[18] The numbers presented undoubtedly are designed

---

[16] *Variety*, December 6, 1932, p. 35.

[17] *Radio Markets of the World, 1932*, U.S. Department of Commerce, p. 96.

[18] The Promenade Concerts in the 1931 season, under the baton of Sir Henry Wood, showed a tendency toward concentrating completely upon one composer in each program, and of combining numbers on a program which would never appear together in this country. In addition to the natural featuring of British music there was much more of the Bach-Handel type than would be found in the United States, and less modern offerings. However, B.B.C. itself has pioneered admirably in this field.

for the tastes of English audiences, so that comparison on this point is difficult. However, there is a tendency toward less variety in the British concert series than in this country.

With regard to educational programs, the British surpass this country in quantity, and until recently, at least, in quality of presentation. A feature of special interest has been the organiza-

TABLE XLVIII*

PERCENTAGE OF PROGRAMS OF VARIOUS TPYES PRESENTED BY BRITISH BROADCASTING CORPORATION DURING THE SEASON 1929-30

TYPE OF PROGRAM	PERCENTAGE OF TOTAL HOURS	
	National	Regional
Serious music	21.4	22.2
Light music	18.3	34.8
Variety music	4.1	4.7
Dance bands	10.5	19.7
Gramophone records	4.5	2.0
Total music	58.8	83.4
Drama	1.9	1.7
Talks and readings	9.2	1.6
Schools: education	2.8	....
Adult education	2.2	3.1
News and running comments	9.2	8.6
Religious services	5.5	1.1
Appeals	0.2	0.2
Children's hour	5.6	....
Special transmission	0.4	0.1
Pictures	4.4	0.2
Total	100.0	100.0

* B.B.C. Yearbook, 1931, p. 43.

tion of listening groups in connection with the adult educational talks. These groups meet together to hear given programs and later to discuss them. They are under the direction of trained leaders and are given added assistance by means of pamphlets especially prepared for use in conjunction with the broadcasts. This form of activity is based upon the strong adult education movement which originated in Great Britain more than fifty years ago, and which constitutes an important factor in English life.

In serious drama, also, there is a tendency for English programs to excel, though they are correspondingly weak in mystery drama, comedy, and in the historical presentations which are so important in American broadcasting. The folk drama program, of the "Country Doctor" type, likewise is missing. It is interesting to note that in 1931 a negro pair named "Alexander and Mose" appeared on B.B.C. programs and won no little popularity with an act closely resembling "Amos 'n' Andy."[19]

With regard to popular programs, the British broadcasts are much weaker than are those of stations in this country. If there is any criticism to be leveled at English programs it is that they give too little attention to presentations of popular interest, even as the American broadcaster may err in the other direction.

The daily program structure of the B.B.C. does not seem to be any better balanced than those of national networks in this country, even though varying markedly as to the type of material broadcast. This is indicated in the schedule of the National (Daventry) Station on Sunday, August 16, and Wednesday, August 19, 1931.

Sunday, August 16, 1931[20]

A.M.— 10:30 Time signal
P.M.— 3:00 Recital. Soprano, violin, and piano
3:45 Miss Phyllis M. Potter. For the Children. "Fifteen Minutes in Palestine"
4:00 Missionary Talk
4:15 Central Band of H.M. Royal Air Force
5:30 Piano recital
6:00 English Eloquence (Second Series)—VIII—A Speech on The Triumph of Irish Independence, delivered on April 16, 1782, by the Rt. Hon. Henry Grattan
6:30 Welsh Service
8:00 Studio Service conducted by the Rev. H. R. L. Sheppard
8:50 News
9:05 Arthur Benjamin, piano, and the B.B.C. Light Orchestra
10:30 Epilogue (Devotional Period)

Wednesday, August 19, 1931

A.M.— 10:15 Daily service
10:30 Time signal
P.M.— 12:00 Gramophone Records
12:45 Organ Recital

[19] *B.B.C. Yearbook, 1932*, p. 193.   [20] *The Listener*, August 12, 1931, p. 268.

1:30–2:30 Light Music
   3:30 Symphony Concert
   4:45 Organ Recital
   5:15 Children's Hour
   6:00 Dance Orchestra
   6:15 News
   6:40 Foundation of Music
7:00–7:20 Sir Daniel Hall. Talks on Farming—XVIII
   8:00 Promenade Concert
   9:40 News
  10:00 Mr. George Grossmith.—"My Apprenticeship at Holly-
         wood"—II
  10:15 Orchestra
11:00–12:00 Dance Music

These programs are typical of the English daily structure and show little if any superiority over the balance and variety of the American daily broadcasts. The chief disparity between the two lies in the type of programs broadcast rather than in any other feature.

Another question which might arise regarding the program service of the two systems is the extent to which each of them have presented outstanding programs. In this regard the latest data available for the B.B.C. are for the last week in October, 1932, while the American program information available nearest that date is for the last week of November of the same year. In so far as the political broadcasts earlier in the fall would have distorted the picture for this country, the comparison of these two dates is probably a better one than if the same week had been used in both cases.

During the last week of October, the British Broadcasting Company presented the following outstanding programs:[21] *Sunday:* None. *Monday:* First winter concert of the B.B.C. Symphony Orchestra. *Tuesday:* "Nor' West" special radio play by L. duGarde Peach; International String Quartet. *Wednesday:* B.B.C. Symphony Orchestra in Queen's Hall, with Mischa Elman as soloist. *Thursday:* Jack Hubbert and His "Folks." *Friday:* First of Political Debates—"Disarmament." *Saturday:* Public Chamber Music Concert in Broadcasting House Concert Hall; Lionel Fertis and Solomon playing the sonatas of Bax and Brahms.

[21] *B.B.C. Yearbook 1933*, p. 224.

Programs broadcast over the key stations of the three national networks in this country during the week beginning Sunday, November 27, 1932, included the following outstanding events:

Sunday: "Adventures through Fire and Ice," Father Bernard Hubbard, Alaskan explorer and missionary; "The Pasteur Institute and Its Work," Pierre le Comte duNuoy, of the Pasteur Institute, speaking from Paris; "Dangerous Corner," a play by J. B. Priestley; Leon Trotzky, speaking from Copenhagen, Denmark; concert by the New York Philharmonic Orchestra; concert with Ernest Hutcheson, pianist, and the Columbia Symphony Orchestra.

Monday: Dramatization of *David Harum;* Radio Guild Drama—"Tartuffe"; light opera—"The Mikado"; "Balancing the Budget in Europe with Unemployment Insurance," Dr. Fritz Rager, University of Vienna, speaking from Vienna.

Tuesday: "A College Course for the Unemployed," Dr. William Mather Lewis, president of Lafayette College; "Redistributing Functions of State and Local Governments"—Professor Paul W. Wagner, University of North Carolina, O. Max Gardner, governor of North Carolina, and Harry F. Byrd, ex-governor of Virginia; Curtis Institute of Music Symphony Orchestra; Song Fest at Town Hall, New York City, led by ex-Governor Alfred E. Smith; Symphony Orchestra, John Charles Thomas, baritone, soloist.

Wednesday: Mischa Levitzki, pianist and concert orchestra; Eastman School of Music Symphony Orchestra, Dr. Howard Hansen conducting; tribute to Mark Twain on the 97th anniversary of his birth.

Thursday: "The Founding of Vassar College," C. Mildred Thompson, dean; American Museum of Natural History Talk: "Coral Forests."

Friday: Musical Appreciation Hour with Dr. Walter Damrosch; talk by Hendrik Willem Van Loon; "March of Time" program—dramatized news events.

Saturday: Performance of "Elektra" by Richard Strauss—the first performance of this opera by the Metropolitan Opera Company; New York Philharmonic Orchestra Children's Concert; "Should War Debts Be Collected or Cancelled?" talk by Alfred P. Sloan, president of the General Motors Corporation and chairman of the Committee on Consideration of Intergovernmental Debts.

It will be noted that the outstanding events on the American broadcasting program compare very favorably with those on the British schedule. In both cases the weeks chosen are average periods and are fairly representative of the season as a whole. Thus American broadcasters provide program service over longer periods of the day than does the British Broadcasting Corporation; offer a program schedule just as well balanced as the English one though differing greatly as to content; and manage to present, on the average, at least an equal number of outstanding broadcasts of more than ordinary interest.

Two minor differences which should be of interest are, first, the tendency of British programs to have an interval of several minutes between them,[22] and second, the extremely formal method of announcing numbers and artists.[23] With regard to the first of these a B.B.C. report complains of the difficulty of timing programs within a thirty-second limit, which is current practice in this country. and also advances the opinion the listeners do not wish one program to follow too closely upon another in so far as the succeeding presentation may disturb the mood created by the one which went before it. In the case of the latter, it is British practice not to make announcements between numbers, at least on concerts originating elsewhere than in their own studios, so that the listener who has tuned in late remains in ignorance as to the program which he is hearing.[24]

One of the greatest distinctions between British and American broadcasting systems is in the attitude toward the presentation of controversial material. In the United States, the greater freedom of debate is allowed over the air. The bitter political controversy carried on over national networks and individual stations by all parties in the recent presidential election is illustrative of the degree to which all opinions may be broadcast in this country. What is true in the field of politics pertains to other fields as well. Speakers may advocate the cancellation of war debts in spite of the fact that the government has officially opposed such action. Debates take place in the fields of economics, religion, politics, and social theory. Stations exist for the express purpose of battling chain-store development, while the Socialist party has its own station in New York City. Speakers such as Leon Trotzky are brought to the American listening public by a great national network.

All of this is in decided contrast to English practice. "Political, industrial, and religious controversy" were prohibited from the start of British broadcasting,[25] and it was not until after fierce discussions in Parliament in 1928 that the ban was lifted

---

[22] *B.B.C. Yearbook, 1932*, pp. 115–16.   [23] *Ibid.*

[24] Announcement made over the Columbia Broadcasting System on occasion of the rebroadcast of an all-Bach concert from Queen's Hall, London, August 24, 1932.

[25] *B.B.C. Yearbook, 1929*, pp. 39–41.

to any degree at all. Following this, discussions or symposiums were allowed on political and economic questions, though to a limited degree. In its 1929 *Yearbook* the British Broadcasting Corporation stated[26] that "Theoretically it is now possible to broadcast talks upon all controversial subjects, but great care must still be exercised in the choice and handling of subjects. . . . . It would be a misuse of such a privilege to allow it to be a vehicle of unchallenged partisan statements."

The first political broadcast in England occurred in April, 1928, upon the local Government Bill, with the party in power seeing to it that it received the last word upon all occasions. Evidently the bars had not been let down sufficiently to please the British listener, for in its 1932 report the B.B.C. defended its course in this field in the following manner:[27] "Those who think progress is slow, should remember that unless it is gradual it will not find acceptance among the millions of listeners who in the first five years of B.B.C.'s existence became accustomed to a colorless treatment of rather neutral subjects, and the avoidance of controversy altogether." Even now speeches are carefully censored, even when the person in question is a foreign government official,[28] and only recently the head of the British Broadcasting Corporation's speaker's bureau was dismissed for progressive political beliefs.[29]

The retarding influence of such an attitude is well illustrated by the information received by the British and American people with regard to the Geneva Disarmament Conference from their respective broadcasting organizations. During the entire course of the proceedings, seven programs were relayed to England:[30] five by Vernon Bartlett, the B.B.C. commentator, one by the Bishop of York, and one by Arthur Henderson. During the same period approximately sixty programs were relayed by the two national network companies to American listeners. Representatives of China and Japan, the Foreign Minister of Italy, M. Tardieu of France, Chancellor Bruening of Germany, Arthur Henderson of England, and other prominent figures were brought before the microphone. When it was found that Chancellor Bruening had hurriedly left for Berlin, an American broad-

[26] *Ibid.*, p. 59.

[27] *Ibid., 1932*, p. 103.

[28] *Radio in Education, 1932*, p. 210.

[29] *Ibid.*, p. 209.

[30] *Ibid.*, p. 211.

302 A DECADE OF RADIO ADVERTISING

casting representative followed him there and arranged for him
to speak from that point. The difference in service rendered by
the two systems was so pronounced that the *London Daily
Herald* delivered a scathing criticism of the B.B.C. on the subject, demanding to know why it had not done better in reporting
the conference to the British people.[31] Thus, in the field of practical education with regard to public affairs, American broadcasting shows marked superiority and preserves to a much
greater degree the principle of free speech than does British
broadcasting.

The general situation with regard to German broadcasting,
at least prior to the advent of the Hitler régime, was similar to
that in England. The administration of the system was somewhat different. German broadcasting was more decentralized,
being divided into nine districts, one for each major subdivision
of the country. The stations were owned by the post-office,
though private program companies operated the various stations. These companies, in turn, were bound together in the
Reichs-Rundfunk G.m.b.H., the parent company of the system. The actual program policy was further supervised by the
government through the use of advisory committees, so that
probably less freedom of action was to be found in Germany
than in England.[32] Revenue was raised principally by taxation
which amounted to approximately $6.00 a set.[33] Total set regis-
tration was only half as great in proportion to population as in
the case of the United States.[34]

In the case of German broadcasting a limited amount of advertising is allowed. However it is restricted to the period of
from 8:15 to 9:00 o'clock in the morning and is confined to brief
announcements regarding the product. At times advertising
may be continued until the noon hour. Foreign manufacturers
are not allowed to advertise at all.[35]

Recently the administration of German broadcasting was
placed completely in the hands of the government, the Reich
buying such securities as were privately held. It now owns 51
per cent of the stock in the Reichs-Rundfunk and its subsidiaries, while the six largest states hold 49 per cent of the securities.

[31] *Broadcasting*, June 1, 1932.   [33] *Radio Markets of the World, 1932*, p. 4.
[32] *New York Times*, August 14, 1932.   [34] *B.B.C. Yearbook, 1933*, p. 88.
[35] *Radio Broadcasting in Europe*, Bureau of Foreign and Domestic Commerce, p. 9.

The object of the new move was stated to be that of freeing broadcasting from politics, especially interstate.[36] How this is to be accomplished is not clear.

In the field of program service, German broadcasters seem to be enterprising and wide awake. There is a great deal of interchange of programs between the various local stations, as well as with other European countries. Program hours devoted to entertainment and information of different types broadcast during the year of 1931 are as shown in Table XLIX.

TABLE XLIX*

PERCENTAGE OF HOURS OF VARIOUS TYPES OF PROGRAMS BROADCAST BY THE REICHS-RUNDFUNK IN 1931

Type of Program	Percentage of Hours
Music and entertainment	39.0
Phonograph records	19.0
Literature	5.5
News and other reports	13.1
Lectures	14.5
Morning devotions	1.6
Children's programs	4.7
Women's programs	1.6
Agricultural programs	1.0
Total programs	100.0

* *Rundfunk Jahrbuch*, 1932, p. 139.

The exact significance of the table is not quite clear, especially since the proportion of musical entertainment seems uncommonly low. Nor is it in agreement with other program data published by the Reichs-Rundfunk. In this case the program hours broadcast by the Berlin station in 1930 constituted 64.5 per cent music, 22.7 per cent talks, 11.2 per cent literature, and 1.6 per cent miscellaneous.[37] Both program summaries therefore must be interpreted with a certain amount of circumspection.

An examination of German program data as found in the annual yearbooks of the Reichs-Rundfunk indicates the existence of excellent programs of classical music, probably equal to those of any other country in the world, and a similar strength in the field of education. It is estimated that 20,000 German

[36] *Broadcasting*, September 1, 1932.

[37] *Die Entwicklung des deutschen Rundfunks in Zahlen, 1923–1930.*

schools are equipped with radios.[38] Broadcasts to school children totaled eight periods a week in 1930.[39] Adult educational
programs also are presented usually between the hours of six and
eight o'clock at night.

The German broadcasting day is more varied than is the
British, and more closely approximates our own programs in
this respect. The day's program begins at 5:50 A.M. with weather forecasts for the farmers.[40] Following this there is a half-hour
of setting-up exercises. At 6:30 a concert and variety period is
broadcast, and by 8:00 o'clock there comes a second agricultural
period. Since the day in question is Sunday, one hears the
chimes of the Potsdam Church at 8:55, following which there is
an hour of morning devotions. After the services, there is an
organ concert, an open forum for older people, and some more
music. Shortly after noon a sports broadcast is relayed from the
Nürnberg Stadium, and at 3:00 o'clock the Davis Cup Tennis
match between Germany and the United States is broadcast.
While this is being presented, some of the stations carry alter-
nate programs of classical music, folk tales and folk drama, and
other sports broadcasts. This continues until 7:00 P.M., following which dramatic and musical programs are broadcast until
10:00 o'clock when a sports résumé is presented of the day.
From then on, dance music is played until midnight. The program is very similar to the average American broadcasting day
and seems to be neither superior nor inferior to it.

In the field of political broadcasting, Germany has shown even
less tolerance of controversy than has England. While British
policy has been passive and has given no one access to broadcasting facilities, German policy has made the radio stations of
the country available only to the ruling party. In the German
elections of the spring of 1932, Chancellor Bruening used the
broadcasting system to great advantage in promoting the re-elec-
tion of President Hindenburg, while prohibiting any of the opposition from resorting to the radio to reach the voting public.[41]
With the Nazis in power, an even stricter censorship of broadcasting may be expected. With the exception of its political

[38] *Radio in Education, 1932*, p. 199.

[39] *Broadcasting Abroad*, National Advisory Council on Radio in Education, p. 60.

[40] *Rundfunk Jahrbuch, 1930*, pp. 345–54.

[41] *Radio in Education, 1932*, pp. 200–201.

aspects, German broadcasting seems to hold a slight edge over the British system, but does not have any marked advantages as compared with American structure and practice.

Very little information is available regarding French broadcasting, which does not seem to be very highly developed. A dual system of control is in operation in the country, the government maintaining one group of stations and private enterprise another. It is reported that the privately owned stations, which accept advertising, are prosperous.[42] As stated before, several French stations are broadcasting special programs for British listeners, advertising English phonograph records, and that these stations have built up a large audience among the British listening public.

The Canadian system is especially worthy of consideration in an evaluation of the listener service rendered by various systems of broadcasting in use throughout the world. Not only does it represent a compromise between the American system and the European type of broadcasting, but also, because of its being contiguous to the United States, is of the greatest interest to American broadcasters. Until recently the Canadian system was one of private enterprise, similar to this country. However, during the summer of 1932 the report of the Canadian Royal Commission on Radio Broadcasting, recommending government ownership and operation of stations, was passed by the Provincial Parliament. A commission of three members was created to supervise broadcasting and to produce the necessary programs. Advertising was not prohibited, but was limited to 5 per cent of the entire program time.

The Royal Commission's report is an interesting one and reveals the motives which dictated the action of the Royal Commission and Parliament. The report states as its first conclusion that, though there is a diversity of opinion regarding many factors in the radio situation, there is unanimity on one fundamental question—"Canadian radio listeners want Canadian programs."[43] This, says the commission, has not been done by private enterprise. Stations are located in urban centers and do not give rural coverage; there is too much advertising, and a

[42] *Broadcast Advertising in Europe*, U.S. Department of Commerce, p. 6.

[43] "A Proposal for Public Ownership of Radio," *Education by Radio*, May 26, 1932, pp. 69–72.

duplication of service. The Commission continues that the majority of programs heard are from sources outside of Canada, and that their continued reception will tend "to mould the minds of the young people in the home to ideals and opinions that are not Canadian." It therefore suggests the following means whereby broadcasting can be carried on "in the interests of Canadian listeners and in the national interests of Canada": (1) the establishment of one or more groups of stations operated by private enterprise in receipt of a subsidy from the government; (2) the establishment and operation of stations by a government-owned and -financed company; and (3) the establishment and operation of stations by the provincial governments. Out of these three possibilities, only the second category remains.

It is quite easy to see the rising tide of Canadian national consciousness in the report. It was American programs and advertising which crossed the border and entertained the Canadian audience. This, in turn, must have fostered the sale of American goods at a time when Canada was becoming more and more intent upon the development of her home markets. It is rumored that there were other factors operative in the situation. Even more important than the above, was the newspaper opposition to radio broadcasting and the belief on the part of western listeners that they were not receiving adequate service under the private enterprise system.[44] The nationalism theory wins greater credence when one examines the Commission recommendation that the Provincial government insist upon a more equitable division of the broadcast band with the United States.[45] This is proposed in spite of the fact that Canada has three times the facilities per capita and only one-sixth the wattage per channel as does the United States.[46] Thus it is indicated clearly that complete use has not been made of the facilities now possessed by Canada.

The usual governmental restriction upon freedom of speech raises its head in one of the recommendations of the Commission, which states that, "While we are of the opinion that broad-

[44] *Variety*, October 11, 1932, p. 55.

[45] *A Proposal for Public Ownership of Radio*, p. 71.

[46] O. H. Caldwell, former U.S. radio commissioner, present editor *Electronics*, and *Radio Retailing* (*New York Times*, May 15, 1932).

casting of political matters should not be altogether banned, nevertheless, we consider that it should be very carefully restricted under arrangements mutually agreed upon by all political parties concerned."

The early operation of the Canadian system has not been encouraging to its progenitors. In the first place, the expense has been heavy and the revenue disappointingly small. Under the plan finally adopted it is intended to build seven 50,000-watt stations blanketing most of Canada and to supplement these with four or five low-powered stations. The construction cost of such a program is no less than $3,225,000, while the yearly operation, exclusive of talent costs, will amount to $2,500,000.[47] Allowing for 600,000 receiving sets,[48] each of which must pay a tax of $2.00 annually, a revenue amounting to $1,200,000 is possible from this source. With continued depression, the receipts from taxes may fall short of this figure. In addition to this revenue the government has given the broadcasting authorities a subsidy of $1,000,000 with which to begin operations. Some advertising revenue also will be received, the Commission optimistically estimating this at $700,000. These sums total $2,900,000, which is considerably short of the maintenance and capital expenditures which will be required during the next several years. Thus the financial outlook for the new system is not very bright.

The financial restrictions outlined previously came into evidence early in the new régime. In December, 1932, the new Commission announced that it would be impossible for it to carry chain programs as far west as Vancouver,[49] one of the things demanded by western listeners. In March of the current year, however, it bought three stations in that area, though it has indicated no intention of connecting these in a network link at the present time.[50] Other difficulties have beset the new Commission. Its first broadcast brought a protest from the musicians' unions that non-union labor was being used, and from French-Canadian members of Parliament that not enough French had been spoken on the program.[51] There also are ru-

[47] *A Proposal for Public Ownership of Radio*, p. 72.

[48] *Radio Markets of the World, 1932*, p. 54.

[49] *Variety*, December 13, 1932.

[50] *Philadelphia Bulletin*, March 8, 1933.   [51] *Variety*, February 7, 1933.

mors that the press views with disfavor the granting of $1,000,-000 subsidy to a government-owned competitor. Should Canadian broadcasting succeed and a volume of advertising be built up, the press problem will become very much more severe and may even imperil the entire system.

Thus, faced with inadequate funds, limited program resources and newspaper antagonism, the future of the Canadian system promises to be a precarious one. Unless it can secure revenue from advertising, it is almost certain to be unable to raise sufficient funds to carry out the relatively modest plan which it has set for itself. On the other hand, if it does succeed as an advertising medium it will face increasing opposition from the press. Since the press is powerful politically, and the Commission is a minor creature of the state, it is almost certain to lose this contest.

These, then, are the principal systems which could be adopted by the United States in lieu of the system of private enterprise at present operative here. A careful examination of all of them fails to reveal any marked advantages over the American system, and, in addition, indicates several disadvantages, especially in the realm of free speech. Other disadvantages include a tendency to give people the kind of programs which the government thinks they should have rather than the kind which they really desire, less of a variety of programs than is furnished the listener under a system of private enterprise, a tendency to become bound by convention, and a tendency toward less efficient coverage than has been built up in countries where government broadcasting has not been the rule.[52] It seems, therefore, that in spite of its shortcomings the American system of broadcasting is best adapted to meet American conditions. To the degree which its programs lack balance, they do so on the side of the masses. Moreover, such error as exists in this direction can be rectified easily and simply without a fundamental change in structure. In addition to these considerations, American broadcasting leads all of the nations in the extent to which it brings public issues before the people, and in the degree to which it provides a forum for a discussion of the questions of the moment.

[52] L. D. Batson, of the Electrical Equipment Division of the Department of Commerce, sums up these disadvantages in splendid fashion in *Radio Markets of the World, 1932*, pp. 5–6.

Even were a system of governmental ownership and operation desirable, which is by no means the case, the expense involved in setting up and operating such a system would constitute an important obstacle to its ultimate realization. So, also, would the problem of national versus state control. It is estimated that a national system capable of supplying three programs to the entire country would cost no less than $120,000,000 to instal, and another $100,000,000 annually for cost of technical operation.[53] At least another $25,000,000 would be required for programs if they were to be kept up to their present standard of excellence. This would make a cost of $245,000,000 for the first year, exclusive of wire charges and similar miscellaneous expenses. A more simple structure might be reared in the way of a chain of high-powered stations covering the country and a series of less powerful state-operated stations to render local service. Such service would require an initial investment of $50,000,000 and an annual maintenance cost of about the same amount. It is not clear from government estimates whether this cost covers the construction and operation of state stations as well as national units or whether it is confined to the latter. There are other difficulties with this system. Among them are the problems arising out of the control of broadcasting by 49 different governments, the scarcity of adequate talent in certain states and the probability that state and national broadcasting would become one more field in which political patronage might be exercised. Moreover, any system of government control and operation would give rise to the political problems so evident in all European broadcasting. Because of these factors, as well as by reason of its fundamental soundness from the viewpoint of listener service, there is little danger that the American system of broadcasting will be changed radically in the near future.

[53] *Commercial Radio Advertising*, Federal Radio Commission, pp. 2-3.

CHAPTER XVI

PROBLEMS CONFRONTING AMERICAN BROAD-CASTING IN ITS RÔLE AS AN ADVER-TISING MEDIUM

Though American broadcasting has been shown to compare favorably with the systems in vogue in principal foreign countries, there is still ample room for improvement in its use as an advertising medium. This is true both from the viewpoint of the listener service rendered by the American system and with regard to its efficiency as an agency for conveying the advertiser's message to the radio audience. Since the approach throughout this study has been to consider radio broadcasting primarily as a means of advertising, it is necessary to present conclusions regarding the manner in which the problems confronting the medium in this phase of its activity may be handled most effectively. Primarily, these problems are confined to the following fields: (1) the future market for broadcast advertising; (2) the broadcasting structure available for use by advertisers; (3) the program service and technique employed in advertising and sustaining programs; (4) commercial practice with regard to station and network relations with advertisers; and (5) the question of the future regulation of the industry as it relates to advertising.

With regard to the future market for broadcast advertising, several factors stand forth clearly. The first of these is that radio broadcasting has definitely proved its worth, as is indicated by the continuous increase in the expenditures made by advertisers over the medium and by the high degree of success achieved by those who have employed it skilfully. Even more important, however, is the observation that broadcasting has passed through the pioneer stage of its existence.

Every new product or service, which has been soundly conceived from the viewpoint of its basic utility, at the outset of its history experiences a period of phenomenal growth. During this period the segments of the public to whom the new product is of the greatest utility and who are best able to purchase it are turning to it from other products. In this stage of its development the novelty of the new article, together with its basic utility, gives it at least a temporary advantage over more established products. However, when this first market has been exploited, the rate of growth in sales decreases, and the product has reached its normal level in the competitive field. From now on it can win an additional share of the market only by fierce competition with the substitute and unlike products which compete with it for the purchaser's dollar.

This is the position in which radio broadcast advertising finds itself at the present moment. Its first growth is over and it has become an established medium. Its future growth must be won largely at the expense of the other major advertising media with which it competes. This means primarily magazines and newspapers. Competition between radio, newspapers, and magazines will become all the more severe because of the fact that advertising budgets are being scanned more carefully than ever before and more specific results are being demanded of all media. Advertising appropriations have been curtailed severely since 1929 and promise to remain at their new level for some time to come.

In this competition radio must stand squarely upon its own feet. It must organize itself as efficiently as possible and must seek to hold its share of the nation's advertising expenditure by rendering the maximum service possible in keeping with the return which it receives. Radio cannot take halfway steps in this direction. It must be sold—intelligently, courageously, and without apologies regarding competition with other media which have been too frequent in its promotion in the past. Behind this intensive selling effort there must exist a scientifically developed service, which has been brought to the highest possible peak of efficiency through the co-operative effort of the entire industry. This attitude is fundamental to any further extension of the market for radio broadcast advertising in competition with other media.

As to the nature of the industries utilizing radio broadcasting for advertising purposes, little fundamental change can be expected. Convenience goods—such as foodstuffs, cigarettes, soft drinks, cosmetics and many proprietary remedies—will continue to comprise the backbone of broadcast advertising.

This is indeed fortunate; for these industries tend to fluctuate less in sales than does the general run of trade and, because of this, advertise more steadily.

Broadcast advertising need not be confined to products of this type. There is definite room for the cultivation of class markets for high-priced goods by means of radio. The advantage of being able to create goodwill through the program, the ability to dramatize the product, create prestige for the company by the excellence of the presentation; win attention to the advertisement by means of placing attractive entertainment next to it in point of time or of interweaving the two; these are factors which can be adapted to the sale of high-priced specialty goods almost as readily as they can in the convenience goods field. Likewise, the ease of listening as against reading, the effect of the voice personality of the announcer and the ability to build a personal contact between the advertiser and listener, the elasticity of coverage enjoyed by broadcasting, and its efficacy in stimulating dealer interest and co-operation are as important in the sale of articles of class appeal as with regard to a cheaper article of wider distribution.

Moreover, the absolute number of listeners of the class purchasing these more expensive articles who can be reached by means of broadcasting is large enough to warrant the effort, even though they may constitute a relatively small percentage of the total listening audience. The principal problem is that of building the right kind of program for this group, a matter which should be able to be solved by careful study and the exercise of ingenuity.

Another market which possesses important possibilities for future expansion is the field of retail advertising over the radio. In retailing, two items are being sold to the consumer: the product itself and the general service of the store. Radio broadcasting is especially effective in building up store loyalty because of the goodwill which it engenders. It makes possible the development of a personality on the part of the store. When intelligently used, it may be employed effectively as a means of direct selling. This field is an undeveloped one, partly because of retailer reluctance to experiment and partly by reason of the broadcaster's own lack of appreciation of the best manner in which to sell and service retail accounts. The only means by which this market can be tapped in the future is for the broadcaster to study retail problems with the greatest possible care and to learn to adapt the working of his medium to retail needs. In this way new forms of retail utilization of broadcasting facilities will be discovered and the value of radio to the merchant will be enhanced.

The problem of improved program service is of paramount importance to the future of broadcast advertising. It must be admitted that thus far broadcasters have not made the most intelligent use of the program material available to them. There has been a lamentable lack of originality in the program field. The precedents of the stage, concert hall, and motion pictures have been followed too closely. There has been too much of a temptation to build programs for quick resale rather than to experiment with new forms of fundamental importance. It therefore is vitally important that broadcasters experiment in the direction of developing individual forms of music and script programs especially fitted to radio. It is the program which is the chief salable commodity in the possession of the broadcaster today. This is especially true of the network, where the problems of coverage have largely been solved. Nevertheless, the networks thus far have been grossly delinquent in the development of new program material, and have been content for the most part to copy one another and to follow the established routine of other forms of entertainment.

From the viewpoint of the individual broadcasting station the program problem is a more difficult one to solve. In many cases satisfactory talent is not available. Similarly, the financial resources necessary to experimentation are not always present, though there have been several notable examples where this difficulty has been overcome by enterprising management. In this instance the electrical transcription company can render important service. The furnishing of electrical transcriptions for sustaining programs, at prices which small stations can afford to pay, is one of the most important factors which can be developed in the independent field. Its effect would be marked with regard to the improvement of the general level of programs broadcast. It is recognized, however, that the difficulties involved in such an undertaking are numerous.

Another means whereby the program service of the individual

station can be improved is through co-operative action in the construction of programs and in the interchange of program ideas among non-competing stations. It is doubtful whether actual scripts and arrangements could be exchanged, at least at the outset. However, program ideas, such as one for a striking St. Patrick's Day broadcast, or a special feature for Thrift Week, could profitably be circulated among the co-operating stations. Not only would the interchange of such ideas improve the programs themselves, but it would add materially to station advertising revenue. Special groups of advertisers could be persuaded to join in the Thrift Week program, or in other similar presentations. Since an undertaking of this sort involves a large measure of co-operative effort, it may be that the activities of the group could be extended into the field of station representation. On the other hand, the exchange of programs might be carried out by a strong trade association, possessing a comprehensive and carefully planned policy of economic as well as political activity.

The future of the broadcasting structure of the country depends largely upon one factor: namely, the North American Conference which will be held sometime during 1933 for the purpose of reallocating radio broadcasting facilities among the various North American countries. This is of vital importance, since at the present time Mexico is not operating on any assigned frequencies, but is shifting about to suit its taste, while Canada is demanding a larger share of available facilities. Because of these factors it is almost certain that a basic reallocation of wave assignments will take place in this country following the Conference. It may even be that additional frequencies will be added to the portion of the wave spectrum available to broadcasters. On the other hand, it may merely mean that it will be necessary to utilize existing facilities with greater efficiency than has thus far been done. No matter what the outcome, it will have important bearing upon the future of broadcasting as an advertising medium. It therefore is necessary that the broadcasters arrive at a sound plan which may be set before the Conference, and that they, as well as other radio interests, will be adequately represented at the meetings—both by the government and in their own right.

Another matter of fundamental importance, both with regard

to improved listener service and greater advertising efficacy, is the necessity of developing higher-powered stations in the United States. Stations ranging from 100 kilowatts upward to the limit of their technical efficiency, and operating on cleared channels, are necessary for the rendering of adequate service in rural areas. Likewise they are one of the most economical methods covering whole trading areas.

This procedure is costly and requires huge financial resources. It therefore is especially well adapted for development by national networks. High-powered stations, owned by the networks and located strategically throughout the country so as to give maximum coverage, would make of the network a magazine of the air. It also would help to do away with the troublesome problem of station delivery which the network faces at the present time. The affiliated station still could be kept as part of the network structure for purposes of intensive coverage. It might also be that many affiliated stations would desire to secure sustaining programs from the network proper upon payment of a fee such as that recently instituted by the National Broadcasting Company. This would make of the network both an advertising medium and a program service.

Whether high power is developed or not, there are a number of fundamental readjustments which must be made in network structure. Station ownership and control is essential to network stability unless more satisfactory relations can be developed with member stations. The rate structure must be readjusted on sound economic lines, if either high power or better network-station relations are to be achieved. It is essential from every viewpoint that the present unscientific rates, which charge too little for metropolitan outlets and relatively too much for outlying stations, be changed fundamentally in the near future.

In addition to this, networks must be sold to the advertiser on the basis of their total coverage, at least within the basic area. The advertiser must be made to view them as one national medium rather than as a group of stations from which one may be subtracted and another added more or less at will. Networks have been too prone to sell their wares in this manner, and thus have served to aggravate the split-network problem. This attitude of mind on the part of network sales departments also has tended to overemphasize the question of station delivery.

In the field of spot broadcasting, no definite answer is possible. Either the special station representative will grow in strength or else the integrated spot specialist will keep him in the background. On the other hand, the co-operative network may be the answer to the problems in this field.

It is safe to say in summary, therefore, that the radio broadcasting structure of the future will be more elastic even than at present and that it will be more readily adaptable to the specific needs of a given advertiser.

With regard to commercial practices, the principal problem affecting the future development of radio broadcast advertising is the maintenance of rates on the part of the stations of the country. If this is not done, the progress of the industry will be greatly impeded. Since price-cutting brings with it the temptation to cut the quality of the program and to accept business of doubtful value, it tends to cheapen the entire industry and to cause broadcast advertising to lose prestige. Since advertising is founded upon respect for and confidence in the advertiser and the medium, such a tendency would do tremendous harm to the development of broadcasting.

In the immediate future there will be a great temptation for broadcasters to extend service to advertisers to a degree out of keeping with the revenue derived and to engage in activities not logically a part of a station's functions. This tendency must be discouraged, since it amounts in substance to an especially insidious form of price-cutting, and since it unduly inflates station expense. Where service legitimately should be rendered, the station should be ready to do so, but it should not do the work of the advertiser or his agency without charging for it.

Two other problems exist in the field of commercial practice. The first of these relates to the development of adequate coverage and circulation data, and the second to the rise of sound methods of station promotion and sales administration. In the field of broadcasting, the question of circulation is much more complicated than in the case of a newspaper or magazine. The newspaper is limited in delivery only by the extent of the mail service. Likewise, it is supposed that all subscribers read their papers. Therefore, a measure of the number of subscribers to a periodical is usually taken as a satisfactory indication of the number of its readers. This by no means guarantees how many people will read the advertiser's own insertion in the periodical. In the case of broadcasting, no such accurate method has thus far been developed. Scientific methods for measuring station coverage, i.e., where the station can be heard if people care to listen to it, have been devised. A beginning has been made toward the determination of a station's circulation from among the listeners residing in its coverage area. However, much remains to be done with regard to both factors. Eventually it will be necessary to set up an Audit Bureau of Circulation for broadcasting similar to that in the periodical field.

The second problem in this category centers about the question of the selling of radio broadcasting service to the client. In the past there has been little constructive selling and a great deal of order-taking. With increased competition this no longer may be the case. Salesmen must know what broadcast advertising can be expected to accomplish and how it can best be used. They must be aware of its place in the general distributive program. Their efforts must be directed toward the best prospects and they must be supplied with adequate information regarding the station and the medium as a whole.

In addition to the various problems within the industry proper, there also exists the question of the degree of regulation which should be applied to radio broadcasting and the direction which it should take. During the past eighteen months several proposals have been made to regulate the content of the advertising message, especially as to its length. It is doubtful whether such a procedure is sound. In response to a question addressed to them by the Federal Radio Commission as to whether it would be practicable to restrict advertising on a radio program to the mere mention of the sponsor's name, all 51 of the leading advertising agencies of the country replying to the query answered in the negative.[1] The restriction of advertising content with respect to quantity is not the solution of the commercial announcement problem, if such a problem exists. It is not the length itself, but the words used, which causes a commercial announcement to offend the public. Moreover, the field is of a type which cannot be regulated effectively by legislation, but must be guided mainly by the rule of reason. With helpful guidance from the Federal Radio Commission,

---

[1] *Commercial Radio Advertising*, Federal Radio Commission, pp. 165–201.

and with the co-operation of the industry itself, the less desirable features of commercial announcements will be removed without further legislative enactment.

A field of regulation which may look to be important, unless stations exercise more care than is being shown by some of them at the present time, is that of unethical practices in advertising. The advertising of dubious patent medicines on a per inquiry plan and similar practices are examples in point. If stations do not abandon these voluntarily they should be forced to do so by higher authority. Since for the most part these are minor violations and should not be punished immediately by revocation of the broadcaster's license, it may be necessary to devise a new series of penalties including suspension and fine for infraction of regulations.

Another matter of basic importance to the industry is the extension of station licenses for a period longer than six months, for which time they are usually granted at present. This introduces an element of uncertainty into the industry which causes no end of unnecessary confusion. Theoretically, an offending broadcaster may lose his entire business six months after his license has been granted, in spite of the fact that he has built up a profitable undertaking during the period in which his station has been in operation. This penalty is so severe that it is enforced only in extreme cases. A longer period of licenses, three years, for example, would be a much more logical form of regulation. If combined with minor penalties for small infractions, it would insure a higher quality of regulation. Moreover, it would save the broadcaster a great deal of legal expense and would help to curtail the work of the Federal Radio Commission. Finally, the high standard of technical regulation at present in force must be continued.

In facing these problems, the radio broadcasting industry has two choices. The first of these is for each station to proceed along its own lines, and for progress to be achieved by the gradual transmission of information from one station to another. The other is to plan a course of co-operative action, wherein the networks and great majority of stations will combine resources and ability in the solution of their mutual problems.

The basis for co-operation already has been laid in the joint action of broadcasters with regard to the music copyright controversy and in their mutual defense against unwise legislation. These problems were crucial, each in their turn; and, indeed, copyright still remains one of the critical matters to be solved by the industry. The economic problems outlined in the preceding paragraphs are equally important to the continued growth of the industry, even if they are not as spectacular in nature. Broadcasting and broadcast advertising today are at the crossroads. The first lusty growth of the industry is over. If it is to keep its virility and to continue to grow, then the problems of its program service, its structural relations, and commercial practice must be attacked co-operatively. As competition among media grows more severe, radio broadcasting must be sold upon the basis of exact knowledge and actual performance, and its service must be made as efficient as possible. This requires combined, not individual, effort.

Some of the specific problems which must be attacked in a united manner are: standard accounting, coverage and research data, and sales management procedure; the collection of general information regarding the use of radio broadcasting and the success with which it has been employed; the development of statistical indices which will trace the course of spot as well as of network business; the fostering of basic research in the psychological, program, and economic aspects of radio broadcasting; the establishment of a standard order blank, agency recognition and a credit bureau; the creation of program exchanges by non-competing stations; and similar matters.

Problems such as these must be attacked co-operatively if the industry is to achieve the full measure of success possible. With regard to their solution, the individual stations have more in the way of common interest than diversity of purpose. Consequently they constitute a sound basis for unified action. There are approximately 600 broadcasting stations in the United States, providing a splendid opportunity for a compact and well-organized trade body functioning in the economic as well as political field. The basis for an organization of this scope exists in the present association of broadcasters, though its program of activity remains to be enlarged, made more scientific, and less opportunistic.

In any joint action, the rights of all types of broadcasters must be respected. The problems of small independent stations and large regional broadcasters, of independent stations and network companies, must receive equal consideration. At times there may be a temptation for the larger and more important broadcasters to overlook the importance of the small local station. It is this class of station, however, which constitutes the backbone of broadcasting, rendering service to numbers of communities, and actively identifying themselves with the economic social, and political life of the areas which they serve. The improvement of these stations, and the safeguarding of their interests, is every bit as important as is the progress of the larger and more spectacular units of the industry.

What broadcasting needs is a planned program for the next four or five years. Though true with respect to every industry, this is especially advisable for radio broadcasting because the particular characteristics which it possesses make it an ideal field for planned co-operative action. This program should embrace the following major points:

1. The establishment and maintenance of standard trade practices throughout the industry.
2. The setting up of machinery within the industry which will permit the collection of economic and other data capable of being used by stations and networks in selling their services in competition with other media.
3. The encouragement and support of fundamental research in the various technical, economic, psychological, and artistic phases of broadcasting, the results of which will be of assistance in the improvement of the service rendered by the medium to the advertiser and the public.
4. The development of machinery whereby the facts collected by the industry and the results attained from research can be circulated as widely as possible among the various stations, and whereby individual stations may receive special assistance in overcoming their specific problems.
5. Every effort should be made by the industry to perfect the machinery of effective self-government, to the end that the highest possible standards of broadcasting may be maintained and that the minimum of outside regulation will be required. In this manner the maximum degree of freedom for constructive action will be made possible.

With such a program, carefully planned and courageously followed, the future progress of radio broadcasting both as an advertising medium and a constructive social force in the community should largely be insured and any threat of possible stagnation obviated.

APPENDIXES

APPENDIX A

List of stations co-operating in the study, either by answering the questionnaire sent to 165 station managers, furnishing more detailed information, or granting the writer the courtesy of an interview and examination of their plant and methods.

LIST OF STATIONS ANSWERING BROADCAST ADVERTISING QUESTIONNAIRE

Station Call Letters	Location	Nighttime Power in Watts*	Network Affiliation
KTAR	Phoenix, Ariz.	500	NBC
KECA	Los Angeles, Calif.	1,000	NBC
KFAC	Los Angeles, Calif.	1,000	None
KFI	Los Angeles, Calif.	50,000	NBC
KGFJ	Los Angeles, Calif.	100	None
KFBK	Sacramento, Calif.	100	CBS
KJBS	San Francisco, Calif.	100	None
KGEK	Yuma, Colo.	100	None
WDRC	Hartford, Conn.	500	CBS
WRC	Washington, D.C.	500	NBC
WTOC	Savannah, Ga.	500	CBS
WAAF	Chicago, Ill.	500	None
WEBQ	Harrisburg, Ill.	100	None
WHBU	Anderson, Ind.	100	None
WFBM	Indianapolis, Ind.	1,000	CBS
KFNF	Shenandoah, Iowa	500	None
WLBF	Kansas City, Kan.	100	None
WSMB	New Orleans, La.	500	NBC
WCSH	Portland, Me.	1,000	NBC
WEEI	Boston, Mass.	1,000	NBC
WJBK	Detroit, Mich.	50	None
WWJ	Detroit, Mich.	1,000	NBC
WFDF	Flint, Mich.	100	None
WJDX	Jackson, Miss.	1,000	NBC
KGIR	Butte, Mont.	500	NBC
KGVO	Missoula, Mont.	100	None
KFAB	Lincoln, Neb.	5,000	CBS
WJAG	Norfolk, Neb.	1,000	None
WOKO	Albany, N.Y.	500	CBS
WFBL	Syracuse, N.Y.	1,000	CBS
WBT	Charlotte, N.C.	25,000	CBS
KFYR	Bismarck, N.D.	1,000	NBC
KDLR	Devil's Lake, N.D.	100	None
WDAY	Fargo, N.D.	1,000	NBC
WLW	Cincinnati, Ohio	50,000	NBC
WTAM	Cleveland, Ohio	50,000	NBC
WSPD	Toledo, Ohio	1,000	CBS
KOIN	Portland, Ore.	1,000	CBS
WHP	Harrisburg, Pa.	500	CBS
WGAL	Lancaster, Pa.	100	None
WKJC	Lancaster, Pa.	100	None
WFI	Philadelphia, Pa.	500	CBS
KQV	Pittsburgh, Pa.	500	None
WJAS	Pittsburgh, Pa.	1,000	CBS
WGBI	Scranton, Pa.	250	None
WEAN	Providence, R.I.	250	CBS
KGRS	Amarillo, Tex.	1,000	CBS
WOAI	San Antonio, Tex.	50,000	NBC
KDYL	Salt Lake City, Utah	1,000	NBC
KGA	Spokane, Wash.	5,000	NBC
WIBA	Madison, Wis.	500	NBC
KDFN	Caspar, Wyo.	500	None

* As of June 30, 1932.

STATIONS EITHER SUBMITTING DETAILED DATA OR INTERVIEWED

Station Call Letters	Location	Nighttime Power in Watts	Network Affiliation
KMJ	Fresno, Calif.	100	None
KNX	Hollywood, Calif.	5,000	None
WENR	Chicago, Ill.	50,000	NBC
WMAQ	Chicago, Ill.	5,000	NBC
WMBD	Peoria, Ill.	500	CBS
WCAO	Baltimore, Md.	250	CBS
WJR	Detroit, Mich.	50,000	NBC
WMBC	Detroit, Mich.	100	None
WNAC	Boston, Mass.	1,000	CBS
WCCO	Minneapolis, Minn.	5,000	NBC
KFBB	Great Falls, Mont.	1,000	None
WBEN	Buffalo, N.Y.	1,000	NBC
WGR	Buffalo, N.Y.	1,000	CBS
WKBW	Buffalo, N.Y.	5,000	CBS
WABC	New York, N.Y.	50,000	CBS
WEAF	New York, N.Y.	50,000	NBC
WJZ	New York, N.Y.	50,000	NBC
WLW	Cincinnati, Ohio	50,000	NBC
WHK	Cleveland, Ohio	1,000	CBS
WFBG	Altoona, Pa.	100	None
WCAU	Philadelphia, Pa.	10,000	CBS
WFAA	Dallas, Tex.	50,000	NBC
KOMO	Seattle, Wash.	1,000	NBC
WRJN	Racine, Wis.	100	None

SUMMARY OF STATIONS SUPPLYING INFORMATION FOR STUDY OF BROADCAST ADVERTISING

Zone	Network Affiliates			Independent Stations			All Stations		
	Answering Questionnaire	Supplying* Other Data	Total	Answering Questionnaire	Supplying Other Data	Total	Answering Questionnaire	Supplying Other Data	Total
I	8	8	15	1	......	1	8	8	16
II	6	4	10	6	2	8	12	6	18
III	6	1	7	......	......	......	7	......	7
IV	8	4	12	8	1	9	16	5	21
V	9	1	10	1	3	4	10	4	14
Entire country	37	18	54	16	6	22	53	23	76

* Either supplying detailed information or furnishing data by means of an interview.

APPENDIX B[1]

QUESTIONNAIRE AND ACCOMPANYING LETTER SENT TO 165 BROADCASTING STATION MANAGERS

QUESTIONS FOR PURPOSE OF STATION CLASSIFICATION

1. Call letters.....................Power......................watts. Location...
2. Full or part time operation......................If part time, hours operation........................
3. Chain or chains with which affiliated...

QUESTIONS AS TO WHO ARE THE SPONSORS OF RADIO ADVERTISING OVER YOUR STATION

NOTE.—Please confine answers to other than network programs broadcast over your station.

1. Have there been any marked trends or changes in the types of industries or companies sponsoring programs over your station in the past four or five years? If so what are they?

   ....

   ....

   ....

   ....

   ....

2. To what extent, if any, have national advertisers been spotting programs over your station in recent years? Has this been on the increase or not? Has it been largely transcriptions or live talent business?

   ....

   ....

   ....

3. In your opinion or experience, has your local or chain business increased most rapidly during the past four or five years? What reasons do you believe explain this trend? (*This question for chain affiliates only.*)

   ....

   ....

   ....

   ....

   ....

[1] These questions have been kept general in deference to station managers, for whom the supplying of more detailed information would have entailed considerable expense, if it had not been completely impossible.

4. Is it your impression that the turnover among your station clients has been on the increase or decrease during the past four or five years? What do you think are the reasons for this trend?

....

....

....

5. How do your rates compare with those of 1929? Have they increased or decreased, and if so, approximately what percent, using one quarter-hour nighttime program, one broadcast, as the basis of your estimate?

....

....

....

QUESTIONS REGARDING WHEN BROADCASTING IS USED FOR ADVERTISING PURPOSES

1. Approximately what proportion of your local business remains on the air during the summer? Has the amount of summer radio advertising over your station increased, decreased, or remained about the same since 1929? If increased, has it done so faster than winter business?

....

....

....

....

2. Has your summer business tended to concentrate in certain industries or types of business? If so what?

....

....

3. What is your best day of the week as far as volume of advertising is concerned? Your poorest? Has there been any shift in the use of broadcasting for advertising on different days of the week that you have noticed since 1929? If so what?

....

....

....

4. Which is the greater, and by approximately how much, your volume of morning or afternoon commercial broadcasting time? Which of the two has increased the most rapidly during the past year?

....

....

5. Does your daytime broadcasting tend to be concentrated in certain types of industries, and if so what kinds? Have you noticed any special trend in this field during the past several years?

....

....

....

6. Which has increased the more rapidly during the past year, your daytime or night-time business? Why in your opinion?

....

....

7. Has there been any tendency toward increasing sponsorship of programs repeated on more than one night of the week? Has this been confined to any specific kinds of programs? Is the trend keeping up or not?

....

....

....

....

8. Has there been any marked tendency toward sponsors presenting more than one program a day over your station? For instance, a daytime one for housewives and a general entertainment one at night, or is this largely confined to chain broadcasting?

....

....

....

....

QUESTIONS REGARDING THE KIND OF PROGRAMS BROADCAST BY STATIONS

NOTE.—This again is to be confined to non-chain programs since chain information has been collected.

1. What have been the chief trends in the kinds and types of programs broadcast over your station since 1929? For instance, has the proportion of popular music increased; is there a marked trend toward comedy or old-fashioned music; what has been the trend in drama, etc.? Is there a greater variety of programs or more of a concentration on certain types? If so what? (Please be as specific as possible in answering this question.)

....

....

....

....

....

....

....

....

....

2. Is there any marked difference between the commercially sponsored and sustaining programs as to type or characteristics? Do the commercial sponsors as a group sponsor as wide a variety of different kinds of programs as you do in your sustaining periods, or do they tend to concentrate on certain kinds of programs? If the latter, what kind do they prefer to sponsor?

....

....

....

....

....

3. What is the trend in the length of program over your station? Is the quarter-hour continuing in popularity as much as in the past, or is the half-hour tending to come back? What, in your opinion, are the reasons behind such trend as there may be here?

....

....

....

....

4. In your opinion or experience, have the commercial announcements been getting longer or shorter over your station since 1929? What has been the trend especially in the past six or eight months?

....

....

....

....

5. Has there been any marked change or changes in the type of announcement during the above period? If so, what? Are there any special reasons for this change?

....

....

....

....

....

6. What has been the trend in the use of contests and special offers by sponsors over your station, especially during the past year? Approximately what proportion of your local sponsors resort to contests or offers? In your experience, what value, if any, do they have?

....

....

....

....

QUESTIONS REGARDING STATION SERVICES TO SPONSORS

1. What specifically do you do in the way of assisting to merchandise a sponsor's program? Give examples if possible.

....

....

....

....

....

....

2. What program service does your station offer clients? Have you been taking an increasing or lesser part in the preparation of clients' programs during the past several years? What, specifically, do you do in this field?

QUESTIONS REGARDING STATION RELATIONS WITH THE PRESS

1. What has been the attitude of the newspapers of your community toward the publication of station programs since 1929? Please be as specific as possible in describing this trend.

----

2. Is your station affiliated with any newspaper? Does any newspaper broadcast over your station? If so, what is the nature of the arrangement?

QUESTIONS REGARDING ELECTRICAL TRANSCRIPTIONS

1. Has there been an increase or decrease in your electrical transcription business during the past year? Approximately how much?

----

2. Has the commercial sponsorship of electrical transcription programs been principally by local concerns, national advertisers spotting programs on local stations of their own accord, or local dealers advertising national products? Has there been any trend in one direction or another in this field during the past year or so? If so, what?

----

3. Approximately what proportion of your commercially sponsored transcriptions are on evening programs? Is it more or less than a year ago?

----

4. Do you use electrical transcriptions for sustaining periods? Do you broadcast records for this purpose? Are you making increased use of either of these?

----

5. What in your experience is the public reaction to electrical transcriptions? Is it as favorable as to live talent programs? Has there been any change in its reaction over the past year or so? If so, what?

COMMUNITY SERVICE

1. What specifically have you done during the past year in the way of broadcasting programs and carrying on other activities in the community service? (For example, co-operating with the local Board of Education, broadcasting civic events, etc.)

PLEASE RETURN THIS QUESTIONNAIRE TO:
HERMAN S. HETTINGER
Merchandising Department
Wharton School of Finance and Commerce
University of Pennsylvania
Philadelphia, Pennsylvania

APPENDIX C

STATIONS OF THE NATIONAL BROADCASTING COMPANY AND COLUMBIA BROAD-CASTING SYSTEM, INC.

NATIONAL BROADCASTING COMPANY STRUCTURE ANALYSIS

STATIONS AND POWER (IN WATTS) OF THE ORIGINAL WEAF CHAIN*

STATION CALL LETTERS	CITY AND STATE	ZONE	POWER ANNUALLY IN WATTS				
			1922	1923	1924	1925	1926
WEAF............	New York, N.Y.	1	500	500	5,000	5,000	5,000
WEEI............	Boston, Mass.	1	....	....	....	500	500
WTIC............	Hartford, Conn.	1	....	....	....	500	500
WJAR...........	Providence, R.I.	1	....	....	500	500	500
WTAG...........	Worcester, Mass.	1	....	....	....	500	500
WCSH...........	Portland, Me.	1	....	....	....	......	500
WFI(WLIT).......	Philadelphia, Pa.	2	....	....	....	500	500
WCAE..........	Pittsburgh, Pa.	2	....	....	....	500	500
WTAM..........	Cleveland, Ohio	2	....	....	....	1,500	1,500
WWJ............	Detroit, Mich.	2	....	....	....	1,000	1,000
WSAI...........	Cincinnati, Ohio	2	....	....	....	5,000	5,000
WGR...........	Buffalo, N.Y.	1	....	....	750	750	750
WGN...........	Chicago, Ill.	4	....	....	....	......	1,000
KSD............	St. Louis, Mo.	4	....	....	....	......	500
WOC...........	Davenport, Iowa	4	....	....	....	5,000	5,000
WDAF..........	Kansas City, Mo.	4	....	....	....	......	500
WCCO..........	Minneapolis, Minn.	4	....	....	....	......	5,000
Total power...	....	......	500	500	6,250	21,250	28,750
Number of sta-tions.......	....	......	1	1	3	13	18

* Power and station membership is given here as of June 30 annually. Where night and day power vary, night power is used.

Source: *NBC Markets* and various annual issues of *Commercial and Government Broadcasting Stations of the United States*, Radio Division, Bureau of Foreign and Domestic Commerce.

STATIONS AND POWER OF VARIOUS BASIC AND SUBSIDIARY NETWORKS, 1926–32*

(A) THE RED NETWORK (WEAF)

STATION CALL LETTERS	CITY AND STATE	ZONE	1926†	1927	1928	1929	1930	1931	1932
WEAF	New York, N.Y.	1	5,000	50,000	50,000	50,000	50,000	50,000	50,000
WEEI	Boston, Mass.	1	500	500	500	500	1,000	1,000	1,000
WTIC	Hartford, Conn.	1	500	500	500	500	50,000	50,000	50,000
WJAR	Providence, R.I.	1	500	500	500	500	250	250	250
WTAG	Worcester, Mass.	1	500	500	250	250	250	250	250
WCSH	Portland, Me.	1	500	500	500	500	500	1,000	1,000
WGR	Buffalo, N.Y.	1	750	750	750	1,000	1,000	......	......
WFBR	Baltimore, Md.	1	......	......	......	......	......	......	500
WRC	Washington, D.C.	1	......	1,000	1,000	500	500	500	500
WGY	Schenectady, N.Y.	1	......	30,000	50,000	50,000	50,000	50,000	50,000
WBEN	Buffalo, N.Y.	1	......	......	......	......	......	1,000	1,000
WFI	Philadelphia, Pa.	2	500	500	500	500	500	500	500
WLIT	Philadelphia, Pa.	2	500	500	500	500	500	500	500
WCAE	Pittsburgh, Pa.	2	500	500	500	500	1,000	1,000	1,000
WTAM	Cleveland, Ohio	2	1,500	3,500	3,500	3,500	50,000	50,000	50,000
WWJ	Detroit, Mich.	2	1,000	1,000	1,000	1,000	1,000	1,000	1,000
WSAI	Cincinnati, Ohio	2	5,000	5,000	5,000	500	500	500	500
WENR‡	Chicago, Ill.	4	......	......	......	5,000	5,000	5,000	5,000
WLS	Chicago, Ill.	4	......	......	......	5,000	5,000	50,000	50,000
WMAQ	Chicago, Ill.	4	......	......	......	......	......	......	5,000
WGN	Chicago, Ill.	4	1,000	15,000	25,000	25,000	25,000	25,000	......
KYW	Chicago, Ill.	4	......	3,500	2,500	5,000	10,000	10,000	10,000
WCFL	Chicago, Ill.	4	......	......	......	1,500	1,500	1,500	1,500
WIBO	Chicago, Ill.	4	......	......	......	......	1,000	1,000	......
KSD	St. Louis, Mo.	4	500	500	500	500	500	500	500
WOC	Davenport, Iowa	4	5,000	5,000	5,000	5,000	5,000	5,000	5,000
WHO	Des Moines, Iowa	4	......	......	5,000	5,000	5,000	5,000	5,000
WOW	Omaha, Neb.	4	......	......	1,000	1,000	1,000	1,000	1,000
WDAF	Kansas City, Mo.	4	500	1,000	1,000	1,000	1,000	1,000	1,000
WCCO	Minneapolis, Minn.	4	5,000	5,000	5,000	......	......	......	......
Total power			29,250	125,250	160,000	164,250	267,000	312,500	292,000
Number of stations			18	21	23	25	26	26	26

* Power as of June 30, annually. Night power used where day and night power vary.

† The National Broadcasting Company was formed in November, 1926. Figures for that year are of June 30 so as to be comparable to independent station data. Few changes occurred between June and November.

‡ All Chicago stations are used alternately by both Red and Blue networks.

STATIONS AND POWER OF VARIOUS BASIC AND SUBSIDIARY NETWORKS, 1926-32—Continued

(B) THE BLUE NETWORK (WJZ)*

STATION CALL LETTERS	CITY AND STATE	ZONE	WATT POWER 1927	1928	1929	1930	1931	1932
WJZ.................	New York, N.Y.	1	30,000	30,000	30,000	30,000	30,000	30,000
WBZ.................	Boston, Mass.	1	15,000	15,000	15,000	15,000	15,000	15,000
WBZA...............	Springfield, Mass.	1	500	500	500	500	1,000	1,000
WBAL...............	Baltimore, Md.	1	5,000	5,000	5,000	10,000	10,000	10,000
WHAM...............	Rochester, N.Y.	1	5,000	5,000	5,000	5,000	5,000	5,000
KDKA...............	Pittsburgh, Pa.	2	30,000	50,000	50,000	50,000	50,000	50,000
WGAR...............	Cleveland, Ohio	2	....	....	....	....	500	500
WJR.................	Detroit, Mich.	2	5,000	5,000	5,000	5,000	5,000	5,000
WCKY...............	Cincinnati, Ohio	2	....	....	....	5,000	5,000	5,000
WLW.................	Cincinnati, Ohio	2	....	5,000	5,000	50,000	50,000	50,000
KWK.................	St. Louis, Mo.	4	....	1,000	1,000	1,000	1,000	1,000
KOIL...............	Omaha-Council Bluffs..........	4	....	....	....	....	....	1,000
WREN...............	Kansas City, Mo.	4	....	1,000	1,000	1,000	1,000	1,000
KFAB...............	Lincoln, Neb.	4	....	....	....	5,000	5,000	....
Total power† (net —minus Number stations Chicago)	....	....	90,500	117,500	117,500	177,500	178,500	174,500
	....	....	7	10	10	12	13	13
Total power (including Number stations Chicago)	....	....	110,500	141,000	145,000	219,000	260,000	246,000
	....	....	9	13	12	17	18	18

* Power given as of June 30 annually. Where night and day power vary, night power is used. Data from *NBC Markets* and *Commercial and Government Radio Stations*, an annual publication of the Radio Division of the Department of Commerce.

† The use of the Chicago stations is interchangeable with the Red and Blue networks.

(C) SOUTHEASTERN GROUP

STATION CALL LETTERS	CITY AND STATE	ZONE	WATT POWER 1927	1928	1929	1930	1931	1932
WRVA........	Richmond, Va.	2	....	....	1,000	5,000	5,000	5,000
WWNC........	Asheville, N.C.	3	....	....	....	....	....	1,000
WIS...........	Columbia, S.C.	3	....	....	....	....	....	500
WPTF........	Raleigh, N.C.	3	....	....	1,000	1,000	1,000	1,000
WBT.........	Charlotte, N.C.	3	....	5,000	5,000	5,000	....	....
WJAX........	Jacksonville, Fla.	3	1,000	1,000	1,000	1,000	1,000	1,000
WFLA-WSUN..	Tampa, Fla.	3	....	....	....	1,000	1,000	1,000
WIOD.........	Miami, Fla.	3	....	....	1,000	1,000	1,000	1,000
Total power	....	....	1,000	6,000	9,000	14,000	9,000	10,500
Number of stations..	....	....	1	2	5	6	5	7

STATIONS AND POWER OF VARIOUS BASIC AND SUBSIDIARY NETWORKS, 1926–32—*Continued*

(D) SOUTH-CENTRAL GROUP

STATION CALL LETTERS	CITY AND STATE	ZONE	WATT POWER					
			1927	1928	1929	1930	1931	1932
WHAS........	Louisville, Ky.	2	500	500	5,000	10,000	10,000	....
WSM.........	Nashville, Tenn.	3	1,000	5,000	5,000	5,000	5,000	5,000
WMC.........	Memphis, Tenn.	3	500	500	500	500	500	500
WSB.........	Atlanta, Ga.	3	1,000	1,000	1,000	5,000	5,000	5,000
WAPI........	Birmingham, Ala.	3	....	....	5,000	5,000	5,000	5,000
WJDX.......	Jackson, Miss.	3	....	....	....	1,000	1,000	1,000
WSMB.......	New Orleans, La.	3	....	....	500	500	500	500
Total power	....	....	3,000	7,000	17,000	27,000	27,000	17,000
Number of stations..	....	....	4	4	6	7	7	6

(E) SOUTHWESTERN GROUP

STATION CALL LETTERS	CITY AND STATE	ZONE	WATT POWER					
			1927	1928	1929	1930	1931	1932
KTBS........	Shreveport, La.	3	....	....	....	....	....	1,000
KVOO........	Tulsa, Okla.	3	1,000	1,000	5,000	5,000	5,000	5,000
WKY.........	Oklahoma City, Ok.	3	....	....	1,000	1,000	1,000	1,000
KTHS........	Hot Springs, Ark.	3	....	....	10,000	10,000	10,000	10,000
WBAP........	Fort Worth, Tex.	3	....	5,000	10,000	10,000	10,000	10,000
KPRC........	Houston, Tex.	3	....	1,000	1,000	1,000	1,000	1,000
WOAI........	San Antonio, Tex.	3	....	5,000	5,000	5,000	50,000	50,000
Total power	....	....	1,000	12,000	32,000	32,000	77,000	78,000
Number of stations..	....	....	1	4	6	6	6	7

(F) NORTHWESTERN GROUP

STATION CALL LETTERS	CITY AND STATE	ZONE	WATT POWER					
			1927	1928	1929	1930	1931	1932
WTMJ.......	Milwaukee, Wis.	4	....	1,000	1,000	1,000	1,000	1,000
WIBA........	Madison, Wis.	4	....	....	....	....	....	500
KSTP........	St. Paul, Minn.	4	....	....	10,000	10,000	10,000	10,000
WEBC.......	Duluth-Superior, Wis.	4	....	1,000	1,000	1,000	1,000	1,000
WDAY.......	Fargo, N.D.	4	....	....	....	....	1,000	1,000
KFYR........	Bismarck, N.D.	4	....	....	....	....	1,000	1,000
Total power	....	....	....	2,000	12,000	12,000	14,000	14,500
Number of stations..	....	....	....	2	3	3	5	6

STATIONS AND POWER OF VARIOUS BASIC AND SUBSIDIARY NETWORKS, 1926–32—*Continued*

(G) MOUNTAIN GROUP

STATION CALL LETTERS	CITY AND STATE	ZONE	WATT POWER					
			1927	1928	1929	1930	1931	1932
KGIR.........	Butte, Mont.	5	....	....	....	....	....	500
KGHL.........	Billings, Mont.	5	....	....	....	....	....	1,000
KOA..........	Denver, Colo.	5	....	5,000	12,500	12,500	12,500	12,500
KSL...........	Salt Lake City, Utah	5	....	....	5,000	5,000	5,000	5,000
Total power			....	5,000	17,500	17,500	17,500	19,000
Number of stations..				1	2	2	2	4

(H) CANADIAN SUBSIDIARIES

STATION CALL LETTERS	CITY AND STATE	WATT POWER					
		1927	1928	1929	1930	1931	1932
CKGW.........	Toronto	....	....	....	5,000	5,000	5,000
CFCF..........	Montreal	....	....	....	....	1,650	1,650
Total power.		....	....	....	5,000	6,650	6,650
Number of stations...					1	2	2

(I) PACIFIC ORANGE NETWORK

STATION CALL LETTERS	CITY AND STATE	ZONE	WATT POWER					
			1927	1928	1929	1930	1931	1932
KGO..........	San Francisco, Calif.	5	7,500	7,500	7,500	7,500	7,500	7,500
KFI...........	Los Angeles, Calif.	5	5,000	5,000	5,000	5,000	5,000	50,000
KGW.........	Portland, Ore.	5	1,000	1,000	1,000	1,000	1,000	1,000
KOMO........	Seattle, Wash.	5	1,000	1,000	1,000	1,000	1,000	1,000
KFOA........	Seattle, Wash.	5	1,000	....	....	....	....	....
KHQ..........	Spokane, Wash.	5	1,000	1,000	1,000	1,000	1,000	1,000
Total power			16,500	15,500	15,500	15,500	15,500	60,500
Number of stations..			6	5	5	5	5	5

STATIONS AND POWER OF VARIOUS BASIC AND SUBSIDIARY NETWORKS, 1926–32—*Continued*

(J) PACIFIC GOLD NETWORK

STATION CALL LETTERS	CITY AND STATE	ZONE	WATT POWER					
			1927	1928	1929	1930	1931	1932
KPO..........	San Francisco, Calif.	5	1,000	1,000	5,000	5,000	5,000	5,000
KECA.........	Los Angeles, Calif.	5	....	....	....	1,000	1,000	1,000
KEX..........	Portland, Ore.	5	....	....	....	....	....	5,000
KJK..........	Seattle, Wash.	5	....	....	....	....	....	5,000
KGA..........	Spokane, Wash.	5	....	....	....	....	....	5,000
Total power	....	....	1,000	1,000	5,000	6,000	6,000	21,000
Number of stations..	....	....	1	1	1	2	2	5

(K) PACIFIC SUPPLEMENTARY NETWORK

STATION CALL LETTERS	CITY AND STATE	ZONE	WATT POWER					
			1927	1928	1929	1930	1931	1932
KFSD.........	San Diego, Calif.	5	....	....	....	500	500	500
KTAR.........	Phoenix, Ariz.	5	....	....	....	500	500	500
Total power	....	....	....	....	....	1,000	1,000	1,000
Number of stations..	....					2	2	2

(L) HAWAIIAN SUBSIDIARY

STATION CALL LETTERS	CITY	ZONE	WATT POWER					
			1927	1928	1929	1930	1931	1932
KGU..........	Honolulu	5	....	....	....	....	....	1,000

COLUMBIA BROADCASTING SYSTEM

STRUCTURE ANALYSIS

STATIONS AND POWER OF VARIOUS BASIC AND SUBSIDIARY NETWORKS, 1928–32*

(A) BASIC NETWORK

Station Call Letters	City and State	Zone	Watt Power				
			1928	1929	1930	1931	1932
CKOK..........	Detroit-Windsor	.....	......	5,000	....	....	5,000
WABC.........	New York, N.Y.	1	......	5,000	5,000	5,000	50,000
WOR...........	Newark, N.J.	1	5,000	5,000	......	......	....
WOKO.........	Albany, N.Y.	1	......	......	......	......	500
WCAO.........	Baltimore, Md.	1	250	250	250	250	250
WNAC.........	Boston, Mass.	1	500	500	1,000	1,000	1,000
WAAB.........	Boston, Mass.	1	......	......	......	......	500
WGR..........	Buffalo, N.Y.	1	......	......	......	1,000	1,000
WMAK.........	Buffalo, N.Y.	1	900	1,000	750	......	....
WKBW.........	Buffalo, N.Y.	1	......	5,000	5,000	5,000	5,000
WDRC.........	Hartford, Conn.	1	......	......	......	500	500
WEAN.........	Providence, R.I.	1	250	250	250	250	250
WFBL..........	Syracuse, N.Y.	1	750	750	1,000	1,000	1,000
WMAL.........	Washington, D.C.	1	......	250	250	250	250
WCAU.........	Philadelphia, Pa.	2	1,000	1,000	10,000	10,000	10,000
†WIP-WFAN....	Philadelphia, Pa.	2	......	500	500	500	500
‡WXYZ........	Detroit, Mich.	2	750	750	1,000	1,000	......
WADC.........	Akron, Ohio	2	1,000	1,000	1,000	1,000	1,000
WKRC.........	Cincinnati, Ohio	2	500	500	1,000	1,000	1,000
WHK..........	Cleveland, Ohio	2	......	1,000	1,000	1,000	1,000
WJAS..........	Pittsburgh, Pa.	2	1,000	1,000	1,000	1,000	1,000
WSPD..........	Toledo, Ohio	2	......	750	500	500	1,000
WLBW.........	Oil City, Pa.	2	......	500	1,000	......	......
WAIU.........	Columbus, Ohio	2	500	......	......	......	......
WBBM.........	Chicago, Ill.	4	......	25,000	25,000	25,000	25,000
WGN..........	Chicago, Ill.	4	......	......	......	......	25,000
WJJD..........	Chicago, Ill.	4	......	......	20,000	20,000	......
WMAQ.........	Chicago, Ill.	4	5,000	5,000	5,000	5,000	......
WOWO.........	Fort Wayne, Ind.	4	500	5,000	10,000	10,000	10,000
WFBM.........	Indianapolis, Ind.	4	......	......	......	......	1,000
KMBC.........	Kansas City, Mo.	4	500	500	1,000	1,000	1,000
KMOX.........	St. Louis, Mo.	4	5,000	5,000	5,000	50,000	50,000
KOIL...........	Council Bluffs, Iowa	4	1,000	1,000	1,000	1,000	......
WHAS.........	Louisville, Ky.	2	......	......	......	......	10,000
Total power	....	......	24,400	66,500	97,500	142,250	202,750
Number of stations..	....	......	17	24	24	24	26

* As of June 30, annually.
† Prior to 1931—WFAN only.
‡ Prior to 1931—WGHP.

STATIONS AND POWER OF VARIOUS BASIC AND SUBSIDIARY NETWORKS, 1928-32—*Continued*

(B) SUPPLEMENTARY STATIONS

Station Call Letters	City and State	Zone	Watt Power				
			1928	1929	1930	1931	1932
WFEA.........	Manchester, N.H.	1					500
WLBZ.........	Bangor, Me.	1				500	500
WHEC........	Rochester, N.Y.	1			500	500	500
WORC........	Worcester, Mass.	1				100	100
WPG..........	Atlantic City, N.J.	1				5,000	5,000
WOKO........	Albany, N.Y.	1				500	
WBCM........	Bay City, Mich.	2			500	500	500
WHP..........	Harrisburg, Pa.	2			500	500	500
WFIW........	Hopkinsville, Ky.	2			1,000	1,000	1,000
WLBW........	Oil City, Pa.	2				500	500
WDBJ........	Roanoke, Va.	2				250	250
WWVA........	Wheeling, W.Va.	2					5,000
WKBN........	Youngstown, Ohio	2			500	500	500
WCAH........	Columbus, Ohio	2				500	500
WAIU........	Columbus, Ohio	2			500	500	
WGST........	Atlanta, Ga.	3				250	250
WBRC........	Birmingham, Ala.	3		500†	500	500	500
WBT..........	Charlotte, N.C.	3				5,000	5,000
WDOD........	Chattanooga, Tenn.	3		1,000†	1,000†	1,000	1,000
KRLD........	Dallas, Tex.	3		5,000‡	10,000‡	10,000	10,000
WRR..........	Dallas, Tex.	3		500‡	500‡	500	500
WBIG........	Greensboro, N.C.	3					500
KTRH........	Houston, Tex.	3				500	500
WNOX........	Knoxville, Tenn.	3					1,000
KRLA........	Little Rock, Ark.	3		1,000‡	1,000‡	1,000	1,000
WREC........	Memphis, Tenn.	3		500†	500†	500	500
WODX........	Mobile, Ala.	3					500
WSFA........	Montgomery, Ala.	3					500
WLAC........	Nashville, Tenn.	3		5,000†	5,000†	5,000	5,000
WDSU........	New Orleans, La.	3		1,000†	1,000†	1,000	1,000
WTAR........	Norfolk, Va.	2				500	500
KFJF........	Oklahoma City, Okla.	3		5,000‡	5,000‡	5,000	5,000
KTSA........	San Antonio, Tex.	3		1,000‡	1,000‡	1,000	1,000
WACO........	Waco, Tex.	3				1,000	1,000
WWNC........	Asheville, N.C.	3				1,000	
WTAQ........	Eau Claire, Wis.	4				1,000	1,000
WKBH........	La Crosse, Wis.	4					1,000
WISN........	Milwaukee, Wis.	4		250§	250§	250	250
WCCO........	Minneapolis, Minn.	4		7,500§	7,500§	7,500	5,000
WMBD........	Peoria, Ill.	4					500
KSCJ........	Sioux City, Iowa	4			1,000‡	1,000	1,000
WIBW........	Topeka, Kan.	4		500‡	500‡	1,000	1,000
WMT..........	Waterloo, Iowa	4			250	500	500
KFH..........	Wichita, Kan.	4		1,000‡	1,000‡	1,000	1,000
WNAX........	Yankton, S.D.	4				1,000	1,000
WFBM........	Indianapolis, Ind.	4			1,000	1,000	

STATIONS AND POWER OF VARIOUS BASIC AND SUBSIDIARY NETWORKS, 1928–32—*Continued*

(B) SUPPLEMENTARY STATIONS—*Continued*

STATION CALL LETTERS	CITY AND STATE	ZONE	WATT POWER				
			1928	1929	1930	1931	1932
WDAY.........	Fargo, N.D.	4	......	......	......	1,000	......
WRHM........	St. Paul, Minn.	4	......	1,000§	......	......	......
KVOR.........	Colorado Springs, Colo.	5	......	......	......	......	1,000
KLZ...........	Denver, Colo.	5	......	1,000*	1,000‖	1,000	1,000
KOH..........	Reno, Nevada	5	......	......	......	......	500
KDYL.........	Salt Lake City, Utah	5	......	1,000*	1,000‖	1,000	1,000
KYA..........	San Francisco, Calif.	5	......	1,000*	......	......	......
KMTR........	Los Angeles, Calif.	5	......	1,000*	......	......	......
KJR...........	Seattle, Wash.	5	......	5,000*	......	......	......
KEX..........	Portland, Ore.	5	......	5,000*	......	......	......
KGA..........	Spokane, Wash.	5	......	5,000*	......	......	......
KOY..........	Phoenix, Ariz.	5	......	......	......	......	500
KFAB.........	Lincoln, Neb.	4	......	......	......	......	5,000
Total power...............			......	49,750	42,500	61,850	71,850
Number of stations...............			......	22	25	41	48

* Pacic and Mountain Group—1929
† East-South-Central Group—1929–30.   § West-North-Central Group—1929–30.
‡ West-South-Central Group—1929–30.   ‖ Mountain Group—1930.

(C) SOUTH-ATLANTIC GROUP

STATION CALL LETTERS	CITY AND STATE	ZONE	WATT POWER				
			1928	1929	1930	1931	1932
WDBJ..........	Roanoke, Va.	2	......	250	250	......	......
WTAR........	Norfolk, Va.	2	......	500	500	......	......
WWNC........	Asheville, N.C.	3	......	1,000	1,000	......	......
WQAM........	Miami, Fla.	3	......	......	......	1,000	1,000
WDBO........	Orlando, Fla.	3	......	......	......	500	250
WTOC........	Savannah, Ga.	3	......	......	......	500	500
WDAE........	Tampa, Fla.	3	......	......	......	1,000	1,000
Total power...............			......	1,750	1,750	3,000	2,750
Number of stations...............			......	3	3	4	4

STATIONS AND POWER OF VARIOUS BASIC AND SUBSIDIARY
NETWORKS, 1928–32—*Continued*

(D) DON LEE COAST UNIT

STATION CALL LETTERS	CITY AND STATE	ZONE	WATT POWER				
			1928	1929	1930	1931	1932
KHJ............	Los Angeles, Calif.	5	....	....	1,000	1,000	1,000
KOIN.........	Portland, Ore.	5	....	....	1,000	1,000	1,000
KFRC.........	San Francisco, Calif.	5	....	....	1,000	1,000	1,000
KVI............	Seattle-Tacoma, Wash.	5	....	....	1,000	1,000	1,000
KFPY.........	Spokane, Wash.	5	....	....	1,000	1,000	1,000
KOL...........	Seattle, Wash.	5	....	....	......	1,000	1,000
KGB...........	San Diego, Calif.	5	....	....	......	......	500
Total power	....	......	....	....	5,000	6,000	6,500
Number of stations..	....	......	....	....	5	6	7

(E) CANADIAN SUPPLEMENTARIES

STATION CALL LETTERS	CITY AND STATE	WATT POWER				
		1928	1929	1930	1931	1932
CKAC.............	Montreal	....	....	5,000	5,000	5,000
CFRB.............	Toronto.........	....	....	4,000	4,000	4,000
Total power.....	....	....	....	9,000	9,000	9,000
Number of stations........	....	....	....	2	2	2

BIBLIOGRAPHY

BOOKS

ARNOLD, FRANK A. *Broadcast Advertising.* Wiley, 1931.

BRITISH BROADCASTING CORPORATION. *The B.B.C. Yearbook: 1929–33.* The British Broadcasting Corporation.

CANNON, WALTER B. *Bodily Changes in Pain, Hunger, Fear, and Rage.* 2d ed. Appleton, 1929.

CODEL, MARTIN (ed.). *Radio and Its Future.* Harper, 1930.

DISERENS, C. M. *Influence of Music on Behavior.* Princeton University Press, 1926.

DUNLAP, ORRIN E. *Advertising by Radio.* Ronald Press, 1929.

———. *Radio in Advertising.* Harper, 1931.

———. *Story of Radio.* Dial Press, 1927.

FARNSWORTH, C. H. *Short Studies in Musical Psychology.* Oxford University Press, 1930.

FELIX, EDGAR H. *Using Radio in Sales Promotion.* McGraw-Hill, 1927.

GEHRING, ALBERT. *Basis of Musical Pleasure.* Putnam, 1910.

GOLDSMITH, ALFRED N., and LESCABOURA, AUSTIN C. *This Thing Called Broadcasting.* Holt, 1930.

HESS, HERBERT W. *Advertising: Its Economics, Philosophy and Technique.* Lippincott, 1931.

HOWES, FRANK. *Borderland of Music and Psychology.* Kegan, Paul, 1927.

JAMES, ALDEN (ed.). *Careers in Advertising: and the Jobs Behind Them.* Macmillan, 1932.

KLEPPNER, OTTO. *Advertising Procedure.* Prentice-Hall, 1925.

O'NEILL, NEVILLE (ed.). *The Advertising Agency Looks at Radio.* Appleton, 1932.

PEAR, T. H. *Voice and Personality as Applied to Radio Broadcasting.* Wiley, 1931.

PILLSBURY, W. B. *Fundamentals of Psychology.* Rev. ed. Macmillan, 1923.

PILLSBURY, W. B., and MEADER, C. L. *Psychology of Language.* Appleton, 1928.

Recent Social Trends in the United States. Report of the President's Research Committee on Social Trends. McGraw-Hill, 1933.

REICHS-RUNDFUNK GESELLSCHAFT. *Rundfunk Jahrbuch: 1929–33.* Union Deutsche Verlagsgesellschaft.

SCHOEN, MAX (ed.). *Effects of Music.* Kegan, Paul, 1927.

SCHMECKBIER, LAURENCE F. *Federal Radio Commission; Its History, Activities, and Organization.* Brookings Institutions, 1932. (Service Monographs of the United States Government, No. 65.)

SCOTT, WALTER DILL. *Psychology of Advertising.* Rev. ed. Dodd, 1931.

SEASHORE, C. E. *Psychology of Musical Talent.* Silver, 1919.

SEYMOUR, KATHARINE, and MARTIN, J. T. W. *How To Write for Radio.* Longmans, 1931.

STORM, THEODORE. *Immensee*. Heath, 1902.

TROTTER, T. T. Y. *Music and Mind*. Doran, 1924.

TYSON, LEVERING (ed.). *Radio and Education*. Proceedings of the Second Annual Assembly of National Advisory Council on Radio in Education, Inc., 1932. University of Chicago Press, 1932.

MAGAZINES AND PERIODICALS

Broadcast Advertising. Chicago, Ill.

Broadcast Reporter.

Broadcasting. Washington, D.C.

Education by Radio. National Committee on Education by Radio, Washington, D.C.

Electronics. New York: McGraw-Hill Publishing Co.

The Listener. London, England: British Broadcasting Corporation.

NAB Reports. Washington, D.C.: National Association of Broadcasters. (Formerly *NAB News Bulletin*.)

National Advertising Records. New York: Denny Publishing Co.

New York Times. New York City.

Printers' Ink. New York: Printers' Ink Publishing Co.

Radio-Magazine. Paris, France.

Radio Retailing. New York: McGraw-Hill Publishing Co.

United States Census. 1930 ed. Washington, D.C.: Government Printing Office.

Variety. New York: Variety, Inc.

Wireless Magazine. London, England: Bernard Jones Publications, Ltd.

PAMPHLETS

COLUMBIA BROADCASTING SYSTEM. *Where They Listen to Columbia and How Many Do, Steadily, Regularly, to Wit: Habitually; in Each County of the Forty-Eight States*. Author, 1932.

CURTIS PUBLISHING COMPANY. *Sales Opportunities. Handbook for Salesmen*. Author, 1932.

"Druggists Tell Us." National Broadcasting Corporation, Merchandising Division, 1931.

ELDER, ROBERT F. *Does Radio Sell Goods?* Columbia Broadcasting System, 1931.

———. *Has Radio Sold Goods in 1932?* Columbia Broadcasting System, 1932.

FEDERAL RADIO COMMISSION. *Annual Reports; No. 1.* 1928 to date. Author.

———. *Commercial Radio Advertising*. Author, 1931.

———. *Radio Broadcast Stations of the U.S.* Author, 1932.

———. *Rules and Regulations*. Author, 1931.

FELIX, EDGAR H. *Recent Developments in Electrical Transcription Broadcasting*. Federal Radio Commission, 1931.

HETTINGER, HERMAN S. *Merchandising Interpretation of Listener-in Reaction and Habits with Respect to Radio Broadcasting*. Manuscript, 1929.

———. *Study of Habits and Preferences of Radio Listeners in Philadelphia*. Manuscript, 1930.

HETTINGER, HERMAN S., AND MEAD, RICHARD R. *Radio Broadcasting as a Medium for Summer Advertising.* Columbia Broadcasting System, 1931.
———. *Summer Radio Audience.* Manuscript, 1931.
JANSKY, C. M., AND BAILEY, L. T. *Coverage and Market Data for Radio Broadcast Station WJAR, Providence, R.I.* WJAR, 1932.
———. *Station Market Data Issued for WBEN, Buffalo, N.Y.* WBEN, 1932.
———. *Station Market Data Issued for WMT, Waterloo, Iowa.* WMT, 1931.
KOON, CLINE M. *How To Broadcast: the Art of Teaching by Radio.* U.S. Office of Education, n.d.
Listener Area. Columbia Broadcasting System, n.d.
Merchandising Radio to Dealers. National Broadcasting Corporation, 1932.
NATIONAL ADVISORY COUNCIL ON RADIO IN EDUCATION, INC. *Broadcasting Abroad, 1932.* Author, 1932. ("Information Series," No. 7.)
———. *Present and Impending Applications to Education of Radio and Allied Art.* 2d ed., rev. Author, 1932.
NATIONAL ASSOCIATION OF BROADCASTERS. *Proceedings of Annual Conventions.* Eighth, 1930, to date. Author, 1930–31.
NATIONAL BROADCASTING CORPORATION. *Analysis of History Making NBC Contributions to the Art of Radio in 1932—Pointing to Even Greater Achievements in 1933.* Author, 1932.
———. *Broadcast Advertising. Merchandising of a Broadcast Advertising Campaign.* Author, 1930.
———. *Markets. A Presentation of Basic Market Facts on the Key Sales Territories of the United States.* Author, 1931.
PALEY, WILLIAM S. *Statement to Advertisers and Advertising Agencies.* Columbia Broadcasting System, 1932.
PRICE, WATERHOUSE AND CO. *Studies of Radio Network Popularity Based on a Nation-wide Audit.* Columbia Broadcasting System, 1930–33.
RADIO DIVISION, DEPARTMENT OF COMMERCE. *Commercial and Government Radio Stations of the United States.* Author, 1927–31.
RIEGEL, ROBERT. *The Buffalo Radio Audience.* WBEN, 1932.
SHEPARD BROADCASTING SERVICE, INC. *Yankee Network of New England.* Author, 1932.
STARCH, DANIEL. *Studies of Radio Broadcasting.* National Broadcasting Corporation, 1929, 1930.
U.S. DEPARTMENT OF COMMERCE. *Radio Markets of the World.* Author, 1932.
WESTINGHOUSE ELECTRIC AND MANUFACTURING CO. *Pamphlet A-04914.*
WITMER, ROY C. *Applying the Singularities of Radio.* National Broadcasting Corporation, 1932. (Little Books on Broadcasting, N.S.F.)

INDEX

INDEX

Dramatized announcements, 264, 268–72

Drug and toilet goods companies as users of broadcast advertising, 129

"Dubbed" programs, 146

Early advertising on the air, 261

Economic bases of broadcast advertising, 1 ff., 41 ff., 64 ff.

Editorial material, control of, in broadcasting, 24

Education, open to radio, 256–57

Educational programs: adult, 223; children's, 222–23

Electrical transcription manufacturing companies as middlemen, 165

Electrical transcriptions, 142 ff. 164–65, 313; advertisers using, 150–51; care needed in presenting records by, 146; compared to live talent, 143, 146–47; early use of, 143; network attitude toward, 150, 154–55; public acceptance of, 153–54; reason for decline of, 147–48; reason for use of, 151–52; stations equipped to use, 147; steps in recording program by, 143–45; trend in use of, 147–49; as type of broadcasting, 142; use of by local advertisers, 179; use of in spot broadcasting, 140

Elements of music, 6 ff.

Emotion, 10

Entertainment chief reason for any broadcasting, 5 ff.

Esso, Five Star Theatre of the Air, 260

Expenditure for broadcast advertising: for drug and toilet goods, 129; for food, 129; by national concerns, 135; on national networks, 113–17; for radio manufacturers, 131–32; on regional networks, 135–36; seasonal variations in, over networks, 185–93; by various groups, 122 ff.

Factors conditioning station service, 70–71

Farm programs, 216, 226

Father Justin's Rosary, on informal network, 103

Features influencing broadcast advertising, 32

Federal Radio Commission, 66, 67, 108–109, 111, 317, 318; allocation of stations by, 76–77; duties of, 74–75; establishment of, 74; favorable to higher power for stations, 69; ruling on

announcements for electrical transcriptions, 155–56

Fels naptha soap, dramatized announcements, 264

Fifteen-minute programs, advantages and disadvantages of, 259

Financial losses to stations from network affiliations, 91

Financial requirements: of broadcast stations, 68–69; of government ownership of broadcasting facilities, 293–94, 307, 309

First program broadcast, 216

Fluctuation lessening in broadcasting advertising ,132

Food companies: seasonal variations in advertising expenditures by, 191; use of broadcast advertising by, 129

Form in music, 6–7, 9

Fosdick, Harry Emerson, 215

French broadcasting, 305

Frequency monitoring, 72

General Motors Corporation, 131, 191

Geneva Disarmament Conference, on the air, 301–2

German broadcasting, 302–5; maintained by taxation, 302; programs, 303–4; typical day, 304

Good will early object of broadcast advertising, 19

Great Atlantic and Pacific Tea Company, 129

Griffith, David Wark, 35–36

Grigsby Grunow Company, 230

Growth of broadcast advertising expenditures, 113–14

Haggard, Howard W., 257

Hale, Florence, 223

Happiness Candy Stores, 262

Hard, William, 16, 215

High-powered stations needed, 315

High-pressure selling in announcements, 265

Hours of commercial programs, second week of November, 1931, 111

Hours of the day of broadcast advertising, variations in, 200–201

Hours of the day most popular for broadcast advertising, 201–3

Howes, Frank, 9

HISTORY OF BROADCASTING:
Radio To Television
An Arno Press/New York Times Collection

Archer, Gleason L.
Big Business and Radio. 1939.

Archer, Gleason L.
History of Radio to 1926. 1938.

Arnheim, Rudolf.
Radio. 1936.

Blacklisting: Two Key Documents. 1952–1956.

Cantril, Hadley and Gordon W. Allport.
The Psychology of Radio. 1935.

Codel, Martin, editor.
Radio and Its Future. 1930.

Cooper, Isabella M.
Bibliography on Educational Broadcasting. 1942.

Dinsdale, Alfred.
First Principles of Television. 1932.

Dunlap, Orrin E., Jr.
Marconi: The Man and His Wireless. 1938.

Dunlap, Orrin E., Jr.
The Outlook for Television. 1932.

Fahie, J. J.
A History of Wireless Telegraphy. 1901.

Federal Communications Commission.
Annual Reports of the Federal Communications Commission.
1934/1935–1955.

Federal Radio Commission.
Annual Reports of the Federal Radio Commission. 1927–1933.

Frost, S. E., Jr.
Education's Own Stations. 1937.

Grandin, Thomas.
The Political Use of the Radio. 1939.

Harlow, Alvin.
Old Wires and New Waves. 1936.

Hettinger, Herman S.
A Decade of Radio Advertising. 1933.

Huth, Arno.
Radio Today: The Present State of Broadcasting. 1942.

Jome, Hiram L.
Economics of the Radio Industry. 1925.

Lazarsfeld, Paul F.
Radio and the Printed Page. 1940.

Lumley, Frederick H.
Measurement in Radio. 1934.

Maclaurin, W. Rupert.
Invention and Innovation in the Radio Industry. 1949.

Radio: Selected A.A.P.S.S. Surveys. 1929–1941.

Rose, Cornelia B., Jr.
National Policy for Radio Broadcasting. 1940.

Rothafel, Samuel L. and Raymond Francis Yates.
Broadcasting: Its New Day. 1925.

Schubert, Paul.
The Electric Word: The Rise of Radio. 1928.

Studies in the Control of Radio: Nos. 1–6. 1940–1948.

Summers, Harrison B., editor.
Radio Censorship. 1939.

Summers, Harrison B., editor.
A Thirty-Year History of Programs Carried on National Radio Networks in the United States, 1926–1956. 1958.

Waldrop, Frank C. and Joseph Borkin.
Television: A Struggle for Power. 1938.

White, Llewellyn.
The American Radio. 1947.

World Broadcast Advertising: Four Reports. 1930–1932.

He led them into his queer mansion

(See page 259)

THE EMERALD CITY OF OZ

BY

L. FRANK BAUM

AUTHOR OF THE ROAD TO OZ, DOROTHY AND THE WIZARD IN OZ,
THE LAND OF OZ, ETC.

ILLUSTRATED BY

JOHN R. NEILL

BOOKS OF WONDER
HARPERCOLLINSPUBLISHERS

This Book
Belongs to

LIST OF CHAPTERS

THE
EMERALD CITY
OF
OZ

TO
HER ROYAL HIGHNESS
CYNTHIA II
OF SYRACUSE;
AND TO EACH AND EVERY ONE
OF THE CHILDREN WHOSE LOYAL
APPRECIATION HAS ENCOURAGED
ME TO WRITE THE OZ BOOKS
THIS VOLUME IS AFFECTIONATELY
DEDICATED.

PERHAPS I should admit on the title page that this book is "By L. Frank Baum and his correspondents," for I have used many suggestions conveyed to me in letters from children. Once on a time I really imagined myself "an author of fairy tales," but now I am merely an editor **or** private secretary for a host of youngsters whose ideas I am requested to weave into the thread of my stories.

These ideas are often clever. They are also logical and interesting. So I have used them whenever I could find an opportunity, and it is but just that I acknowledge my indebtedness to my little friends.

My, what imaginations these children have developed! Sometimes I am fairly astounded by their daring and genius. There will be no lack of fairy-tale authors in the future, I am sure. My readers have told me what to do with Dorothy, and Aunt Em and Uncle Henry, and I have obeyed their mandates. They have also given me a variety of subjects to write about in the future: enough, in fact, to keep me busy for some time. I am very proud of this alliance. Children love these stories because children have helped to create them. My readers know what they want and realize that I try to please them. The result is very satisfactory to the publishers, to me, and (I am quite sure) to the children.

I hope, my dears, it will be a long time before we are obliged to dissolve partnership.

Coronado, 1910   L. FRANK BAUM.

The Emerald City of Oz
Afterword copyright © 1993 by Peter Glassman

HarperCollins*Publishers* and Books of Wonder www.harperchildrens.com
Library of Congress Catalog Card Number: 92-061765
ISBN 0-688-11558-6
Manufactured in China.

6 7 8 9 10

Books of Wonder is a registered trademark of Ozma, Inc.

HOW THE NOME KING BECAME ANGRY

CHAPTER ONE

THE Nome King was in an angry mood, and at such times he was very disagreeable. Every one kept away from him, even his Chief Steward Kaliko.

Therefore the King stormed and raved all by himself, walking up and down in his jewel-studded cavern and getting angrier all the time. Then he remembered that it was no fun being angry unless he had some one to frighten and make miserable, and he rushed to his big gong and made it clatter as loud as he could.

In came the Chief Steward, trying not to show the Nome King how frightened he was.

"Send the Chief Counselor here!" shouted the angry monarch.

11

Kaliko ran out as fast as his spindle legs could carry his fat round body, and soon the Chief Counselor entered the cavern. The King scowled and said to him:

"I'm in great trouble over the loss of my Magic Belt. Every little while I want to do something magical, and find I can't because the Belt is gone. That makes me angry, and when I'm angry I can't have a good time. Now, what do you advise?"

"Some people," said the Chief Counselor, "enjoy getting angry."

"But not all the time," declared the King. "To be angry once in a while is really good fun, because it makes others so miserable. But to be angry morning, noon and night, as I am, grows monotonous and prevents my gaining any other pleasure in life. Now, what do you advise?"

"Why, if you are angry because you want to do magical things and can't, and if you don't want to get angry at all, my advice is not to want to do magical things."

Hearing this, the King glared at his Counselor with a furious expression and tugged at his own long white whiskers until he pulled them so hard that he yelled with pain.

"You are a fool!" he exclaimed.

"I share that honor with your Majesty," said the Chief Counselor.

The King roared with rage and stamped his foot.

12

"Ho, there, my guards!" he cried. "Ho" is a royal way of saying, "Come here." So, when the guards had hoed, the King said to them:

"Take this Chief Counselor and throw him away."

Then the guards took the Chief Counselor, and bound him with chains to prevent his struggling, and threw him away. And the King paced up and down his cavern more angry than before.

Finally he rushed to his big gong and made it clatter like a fire-alarm. Kaliko appeared again, trembling and white with fear.

"Fetch my pipe!" yelled the King.

"Your pipe is already here, your Majesty," replied Kaliko.

"Then get my tobacco!" roared the King.

"The tobacco is in your pipe, your Majesty," returned the Steward.

"Then bring a live coal from the furnace!" commanded the King.

"The tobacco is lighted, and your Majesty is already smoking your pipe," answered the Steward.

"Why, so I am!" said the King, who had forgotten this fact; "but you are very rude to remind me of it."

"I am a lowborn, miserable villain," declared the Chief Steward, humbly.

Chapter One

The Nome King could think of nothing to say next, so he puffed away at his pipe and paced up and down the room. Finally he remembered how angry he was, and cried out:

"What do you mean, Kaliko, by being so contented when your monarch is unhappy?"

"What makes you unhappy?" asked the Steward.

"I 've lost my Magic Belt. A little girl named Dorothy, who was here with Ozma of Oz, stole my Belt and carried it away with her," said the King, grinding his teeth with rage.

"She captured it in a fair fight," Kaliko ventured to say.

"But I want it! I must have it! Half my power is gone with that Belt!" roared the King.

"You will have to go to the Land of Oz to recover it, and your Majesty can't get to the Land of Oz in any possible way," said the Steward, yawning because he had been on duty ninety-six hours, and was sleepy.

"Why not?" asked the King.

"Because there is a deadly desert all around that fairy country, which no one is able to cross. You know that fact as well as I do, your Majesty. Never mind the lost Belt. You have plenty of power left, for you rule this underground kingdom like a tyrant, and thousands of Nomes obey your commands. I advise you to drink a glass of melted silver, to quiet your nerves, and then go to bed."

The Emerald City of Oz

The King grabbed a big ruby and threw it at Kaliko's head. The Steward ducked to escape the heavy jewel, which crashed against the door just over his left ear.

"Get out of my sight! Vanish! Go away — and send General Blug here," screamed the Nome King.

Kaliko hastily withdrew, and the Nome King stamped up and down until the General of his armies appeared.

This Nome was known far and wide as a terrible fighter and a cruel, desperate commander. He had fifty thousand Nome soldiers, all well drilled, who feared nothing but their stern master. Yet General Blug was a trifle uneasy when he arrived and saw how angry the Nome King was.

"Ha! So you're here!" cried the King.

"So I am," said the General.

"March your army at once to the Land of Oz, capture and destroy the Emerald City, and bring back to me my Magic Belt!" roared the King.

"You're crazy," calmly remarked the General.

"What's that? What's that? What's that?" And the Nome King danced around on his pointed toes, he was so enraged.

"You don't know what you're talking about," continued the General, seating himself upon a large cut diamond. "I advise you to stand in a corner and count sixty before you speak again. By that time you may be more sensible."

Chapter One

The King looked around for something to throw at General Blug, but as nothing was handy he began to consider that perhaps the man was right and he had been talking foolishly. So he merely threw himself into his glittering throne and tipped his crown over his ear and curled his feet up under him and glared wickedly at Blug.

"In the first place," said the General, "we cannot march across the deadly desert to the Land of Oz; and, if we could, the Ruler of that country, Princess Ozma, has certain fairy powers that would render my army helpless. Had you not lost your Magic Belt we might have some chance of defeating Ozma; but the Belt is gone."

"I want it!" screamed the King. "I must have it."

"Well, then, let us try in a sensible way to get it," replied the General. "The Belt was captured by a little girl named Dorothy, who lives in Kansas, in the United States of America."

"But she left it in the Emerald City, with Ozma," declared the King.

"How do you know that?" asked the General.

"One of my spies, who is a Blackbird, flew over the desert to the Land of Oz, and saw the Magic Belt in Ozma's palace," replied the King with a groan.

"Now, that gives me an idea," said General Blug,

thoughtfully. "There are two ways to get to the Land of Oz without traveling across the sandy desert."

"What are they?" demanded the King, eagerly.

"One way is *over* the desert, through the air; and the other way is *under* the desert, through the earth."

Hearing this the Nome King uttered a yell of joy and leaped from his throne, to resume his wild walk up and down the cavern.

"That's it, Blug!" he shouted. That's the idea, General! I'm King of the Under World, and my subjects are all miners. I'll make a secret tunnel under the desert to the

18

Land of Oz — yes! right up to the Emerald City — and you will march your armies there and capture the whole country!"

"Softly, softly, your Majesty. Don't go too fast," warned the General. "My Nomes are good fighters, but they are not strong enough to conquer the Emerald City."

"Are you sure?" asked the King.

"Absolutely certain, your Majesty."

"Then what am I to do?"

"Give up the idea and mind your own business," advised the General. "You have plenty to do trying to rule your underground kingdom."

"But I want that Magic Belt — and I'm going to have it!" roared the Nome King.

"I'd like to see you get it," replied the General, laughing maliciously.

The King was by this time so exasperated that he picked up his scepter, which had a heavy ball, made from a sapphire, at the end of it, and threw it with all his force at General Blug. The sapphire hit the General upon his forehead and knocked him flat upon the ground, where he lay motionless. Then the King rang his gong and told his guards to drag out the General and throw him away; which they did.

This Nome King was named Roquat the Red, and no one loved him. He was a bad man and a powerful monarch, and he had resolved to destroy the Land of Oz and its magnificent Emerald City, to enslave Princess Ozma and little Dorothy and all the Oz people, and recover his Magic Belt. This same Belt had once enabled Roquat the Red to carry out many wicked plans; but that was before Ozma and her people marched to the underground cavern and captured it. The Nome King could not forgive Dorothy or Princess Ozma, and he had determined to be revenged upon them.

But they, for their part, did not know they had so dangerous an enemy. Indeed, Ozma and Dorothy had both almost forgotten that such a person as the Nome King yet lived under the mountains of the Land of Ev — which lay just across the deadly desert to the south of the Land of Oz.

An unsuspected enemy is doubly dangerous.

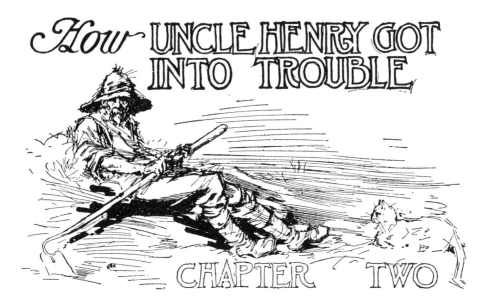

How UNCLE HENRY GOT INTO TROUBLE

CHAPTER TWO

DOROTHY GALE lived on a farm in Kansas, with her Aunt Em and her Uncle Henry. It was not a big farm, nor a very good one, because sometimes the rain did not come when the crops needed it, and then everything withered and dried up. Once a cyclone had carried away Uncle Henry's house, so that he was obliged to build another; and as he was a poor man he had to mortgage his farm to get the money to pay for the new house. Then his health became bad and he was too feeble to work. The doctor ordered him to take a sea voyage and he went to Australia and took Dorothy with him. That cost a lot of money, too.

Uncle Henry grew poorer every year, and the crops raised on the farm only bought food for the family. Therefore the mortgage could not be paid. At last the banker who had loaned him the money said that if he did not pay on a certain day, his farm would be taken away from him.

This worried Uncle Henry a good deal, for without the farm he would have no way to earn a living. He was a good man, and worked in the fields as hard as he could; and Aunt Em did all the housework, with Dorothy's help. Yet they did not seem to get along.

This little girl, Dorothy, was like dozens of little girls you know. She was loving and usually sweet-tempered, and had a round rosy face and earnest eyes. Life was a serious thing to Dorothy, and a wonderful thing, too, for she had encountered more strange adventures in her short life than many other girls of her age.

Aunt Em once said she thought the fairies must have marked Dorothy at her birth, because she had wandered into strange places and had always been protected by some unseen power. As for Uncle Henry, he thought his little niece merely a dreamer, as her dead mother had been, for he could not quite believe all the curious stories Dorothy told them of the Land of Oz, which she had several times visited. He did not think that she tried to deceive her uncle and aunt, but he imagined that she had dreamed all of those astonishing adventures, and that the dreams had been so real to her that she had come to believe them true.

Whatever the explanation might be, it was certain that

Chapter Two

Dorothy had been absent from her Kansas home for several long periods, always disappearing unexpectedly, yet always coming back safe and sound, with amazing tales of where she had been and the unusual people she had met. Her uncle and aunt listened to her stories eagerly and in spite of their doubts began to feel that the little girl had gained a lot of experience and wisdom that were unaccountable in this age, when fairies are supposed no longer to exist.

Most of Dorothy's stories were about the Land of Oz, with its beautiful Emerald City and a lovely girl Ruler named Ozma, who was the most faithful friend of the little Kansas girl. When Dorothy told about the riches of this fairy country Uncle Henry would sigh, for he knew that a single one of the great emeralds that were so common there would pay all his debts and leave his farm free. But Dorothy never brought any jewels home with her, so their poverty became greater every year.

When the banker told Uncle Henry that he must pay the money in thirty days or leave the farm, the poor man was in despair, as he knew he could not possibly get the money. So he told his wife, Aunt Em, of his trouble, and she first cried a little and then said that they must be brave and do the best they could, and go away somewhere and try to earn an honest living. But they were getting old and feeble and she feared that they could not take care of Dorothy as well as they had formerly done. Probably the little girl would also be obliged to go to work.

They did not tell their niece the sad news for several days, not wishing to make her unhappy; but one morning the little girl found Aunt Em softly crying while Uncle Henry tried to comfort her. Then Dorothy asked them to tell her what was the matter.

"We must give up the farm, my dear," replied her uncle, sadly, "and wander away into the world to work for our living."

The girl listened quite seriously, for she had not known before how desperately poor they were.

"We don't mind for ourselves," said her aunt, stroking the little girl's head tenderly; "but we love you as if you were our own child, and we are heart-broken to think that you must also endure poverty, and work for a living before you have grown big and strong."

"What could I do to earn money?" asked Dorothy.

"You might do housework for some one, dear, you are so handy; or perhaps you could be a nurse-maid to little children. I'm sure I don't know exactly what you *can* do to earn money, but if your uncle and I are able to support you we will do it willingly, and send you to school. We fear, though, that we shall have much trouble in earning a living for ourselves. No one wants to employ old people who are broken down in health, as we are."

Dorothy smiled.

"Would n't it be funny," she said, "for me to do housework in Kansas, when I'm a Princess in the Land of Oz?"

"A Princess!" they both exclaimed, astonished.

"Yes; Ozma made me a Princess some time ago, and she has often begged me to come and live always in the Emerald City," said the child.

Her uncle and aunt looked at each other in amazement. Then the man said:

"Do you suppose you could manage to return to your fairyland, my dear?"

"Oh, yes," replied Dorothy; "I could do that easily."

"How?" asked Aunt Em.

"Ozma sees me every day at four o'clock, in her Magic Picture. She can see me wherever I am, no matter what I am doing. And at that time, if I make a certain secret sign, she will send for me by means of the Magic Belt, which I once captured from the Nome King. Then, in the wink of an eye, I shall be with Ozma in her palace."

The elder people remained silent for some time after Dorothy had spoken. Finally Aunt Em said, with another sigh of regret:

"If that is the case, Dorothy, perhaps you 'd better go and

live in the Emerald City. It will break our hearts to lose
you from our lives, but you will be so much better off with
your fairy friends that it seems wisest and best for you to go."

"I'm not so sure about that," remarked Uncle Henry,
shaking his gray head doubtfully. "These things all seem
real to Dorothy, I know; but I'm afraid our little girl won't
find her fairyland just what she has dreamed it to be. It
would make me very unhappy to think that she was wandering among strangers who might be unkind to her."

Dorothy laughed merrily at this speech, and then she became very sober again, for she could see how all this trouble
was worrying her aunt and uncle, and knew that unless she
found a way to help them their future lives would be quite
miserable and unhappy. She knew that she *could* help them.
She had thought of a way already. Yet she did not tell them
at once what it was, because she must ask Ozma's consent
before she would be able to carry out her plans.

So she only said:

"If you will promise not to worry a bit about me, I'll go
to the Land of Oz this very afternoon. And I'll make a
promise, too; that you shall both see me again before the
day comes when you must leave this farm."

"The day is n't far away, now," her uncle sadly replied.
"I did not tell you of our trouble until I was obliged to, dear
Dorothy, so the evil time is near at hand. But if you are

quite sure your fairy friends will give you a home, it will be best for you to go to them, as your aunt says."

That was why Dorothy went to her little room in the attic that afternoon, taking with her a small dog named Toto. The dog had curly black hair and big brown eyes and loved Dorothy very dearly.

The child had kissed her uncle and aunt affectionately before she went upstairs, and now she looked around her little room rather wistfully, gazing at the simple trinkets and worn calico and gingham dresses, as if they were old friends. She was tempted at first to make a bundle of them, yet she knew very well that they would be of no use to her in her future life.

She sat down upon a broken-backed chair — the only one the room contained — and holding Toto in her arms waited patiently until the clock struck four.

Then she made the secret signal that had been agreed upon between her and Ozma.

Uncle Henry and Aunt Em waited downstairs. They were uneasy and a good deal excited, for this is a practical humdrum world, and it seemed to them quite impossible that their little niece could vanish from her home and travel instantly to fairyland.

So they watched the stairs, which seemed to be the only way that Dorothy could get out of the farmhouse, and they watched them a long time. They heard the clock strike four but there was no sound from above.

Half-past four came, and now they were too impatient to wait any longer. Softly they crept up the stairs to the door of the little girl's room.

"Dorothy! Dorothy!" they called.

There was no answer.

They opened the door and looked in.

The room was empty.

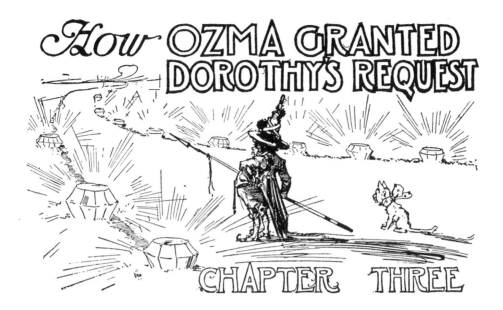

How OZMA GRANTED DOROTHY'S REQUEST

CHAPTER THREE

I SUPPOSE you have read so much about the magnificent Emerald City that there is little need for me to describe it here. It is the Capital City of the Land of Oz, which is justly considered the most attractive and delightful fairyland in all the world.

The Emerald City is built all of beautiful marbles in which are set a profusion of emeralds, every one exquisitely cut and of very great size. There are other jewels used in the decorations inside the houses and palaces, such as rubies, diamonds, sapphires, amethysts and turquoises. But in the streets and upon the outside of the buildings only emeralds appear, from which circumstance the place is named the Emerald City of Oz. It has nine thousand, six hundred and fifty-four buildings, in which lived fifty-seven thousand three hundred and eighteen people, up to the time my story opens.

29

The Emerald City of Oz

All the surrounding country, extending to the borders of the desert which enclosed it upon every side, was full of pretty and comfortable farmhouses, in which resided those inhabitants of Oz who preferred country to city life.

Altogether there were more than half a million people in the Land of Oz — although some of them, as you will soon learn, were not made of flesh and blood as we are — and every inhabitant of that favored country was happy and prosperous.

No disease of any sort was ever known among the Ozites, and so no one ever died unless he met with an accident that prevented him from living. This happened very seldom, indeed. There were no poor people in the Land of Oz, because there was no such thing as money, and all property of every sort belonged to the Ruler. The people were her children, and she cared for them. Each person was given freely by his neighbors whatever he required for his use, which is as much as any one may reasonably desire. Some tilled the lands and raised great crops of grain, which was divided equally among the entire population, so that all had enough. There were many tailors and dressmakers and shoemakers and the like, who made things that any who desired them might wear. Likewise there were jewelers who made ornaments for the person, which pleased and beautified the people, and these ornaments also were free to those who asked for them. Each man and woman, no matter what he or she produced for the good of the community, was supplied by the neighbors with food and clothing and a house and furniture and ornaments and games. If by chance the supply ever ran short, more was taken from the great storehouses of the Ruler, which were afterward filled up again when there was more of any article than the people needed.

Every one worked half the time and played half the time, and the people enjoyed the work as much as they did the play, because it is good to be occupied and to have something to do. There were no cruel overseers set to watch them, and no one to rebuke them or to find fault with them. So each one was proud to do all he could for his friends and neighbors, and was glad when they would accept the things he produced.

You will know, by what I have here told you, that the Land of Oz was a remarkable country. I do not suppose such an arrangement would be practical with us, but Dorothy assures me that it works finely with the Oz people.

Oz being a fairy country, the people were, of course, fairy people; but that does not mean that all of them were very unlike the people of our own world. There were all sorts of queer characters among them, but not a single one who was evil, or who possessed a selfish or violent nature. They were peaceful, kind-hearted, loving and merry, and every inhabitant adored the beautiful girl who ruled them, and delighted to obey her every command.

In spite of all I have said in a general way, there were some parts of the Land of Oz not quite so pleasant as the farming country and the Emerald City which was its center. Far away in the South Country there lived in the mountains a band of strange people called Hammer-Heads, because they had no arms and used their flat heads to pound any one who came near them. Their necks were like rubber, so that they could shoot out their heads to quite a distance, and afterward draw them back again to their shoulders. The Hammer-Heads were called the "Wild People," but never harmed any but those who disturbed them in the mountains where they lived.

In some of the dense forests there lived great beasts of every sort; yet these were for the most part harmless and even sociable, and conversed agreeably with those who visited their haunts. The Kalidahs—beasts with bodies like bears and heads like tigers—had once been fierce and bloodthirsty, but even they were now nearly all tamed, although at times one or another of them would get cross and disagreeable.

Not so tame were the Fighting Trees, which had a forest of their own. If any one approached them these curious trees would bend down their branches, twine them around the intruders, and hurl them away.

Chapter Three

But these unpleasant things existed only in a few remote parts of the Land of Oz. I suppose every country has some drawbacks, so even this almost perfect fairyland could not be quite perfect. Once there had been wicked witches in the land, too; but now these had all been destroyed; so, as I said, only peace and happiness reigned in Oz.

For some time Ozma has ruled over this fair country, and never was Ruler more popular or beloved. She is said to be the most beautiful girl the world has ever known, and her heart and mind are as lovely as her person.

Dorothy Gale had several times visited the Emerald City and experienced adventures in the Land of Oz, so that she and Ozma had now become firm friends. The girl Ruler had even made Dorothy a Princess of Oz, and had often implored her to come to Ozma's stately palace and live there always; but Dorothy had been loyal to her Aunt Em and Uncle Henry, who had cared for her since she was a baby, and she had refused to leave them because she knew they would be lonely without her.

However, Dorothy now realized that things were going to be different with her uncle and aunt from this time forth, so after giving the matter deep thought she decided to ask Ozma to grant her a very great favor.

A few seconds after she had made the secret signal in her little bedchamber, the Kansas girl was seated in a lovely room

in Ozma's palace in the Emerald City of Oz. When the first loving kisses and embraces had been exchanged, the fair Ruler inquired:

"What is the matter, dear? I know something unpleasant has happened to you, for your face was very sober when I saw it in my Magic Picture. And whenever you signal me to transport you to this safe place, where you are always welcome, I know you are in danger or in trouble."

Dorothy sighed.

"This time, Ozma, it is n't I," she replied. "But it 's worse, I guess, for Uncle Henry and Aunt Em are in a heap of trouble, and there seems no way for them to get out of it — anyhow, not while they live in Kansas."

"Tell me about it, Dorothy," said Ozma, with ready sympathy.

"Why, you see Uncle Henry is poor; for the farm in Kansas does n't 'mount to much, as farms go. So one day Uncle Henry borrowed some money, and wrote a letter saying that if he did n't pay the money back they could take his farm for pay. Course he 'spected to pay by making money from the farm; but he just could n't. An' so they 're going to take the farm, and Uncle Henry and Aunt Em won't have any place to live. They 're pretty old to do much hard work, Ozma; so I' ll have to work for them, unless — "

Ozma had been thoughtful during the story, but now she smiled and pressed her little friend's hand.

"Unless what, dear?" she asked.

Dorothy hesitated, because her request meant so much to them all.

"Well," said she, "I'd like to live here in the Land of Oz, where you've often 'vited me to live. But I can't, you know, unless Uncle Henry and Aunt Em could live here too."

"Of course not," exclaimed the Ruler of Oz, laughing gaily. "So, in order to get you, little friend, we must invite your Uncle and Aunt to live in Oz, also."

"Oh, will you, Ozma?" cried Dorothy, clasping her chubby little hands eagerly. "Will you bring them here with the Magic Belt, and give them a nice little farm in the Munchkin Country, or the Winkie Country — or some other place?"

"To be sure," answered Ozma, full of joy at the chance to please her little friend. "I have long been thinking of this very thing, Dorothy dear, and often I have had it in my mind to propose it to you. I am sure your uncle and aunt must be good and worthy people, or you would not love them so much; and for *your* friends, Princess, there is always room in the Land of Oz."

Dorothy was delighted, yet not altogether surprised, for

she had clung to the hope that Ozma would be kind enough to grant her request. When, indeed, had her powerful and faithful friend refused her anything?

"But you must not call me 'Princess,' " she said; "for after this I shall live on the little farm with Uncle Henry and Aunt Em, and princesses ought not to live on farms."

"Princess Dorothy will not," replied Ozma, with her sweet smile. "You are going to live in your own rooms in this palace, and be my constant companion."

"But Uncle Henry — " began Dorothy.

"Oh, he is old, and has worked enough in his lifetime," interrupted the girl Ruler; "so we must find a place for your uncle and aunt where they will be comfortable and happy and need not work more than they care to. When shall we transport them here, Dorothy?"

"I promised to go and see them again before they were turned out of the farmhouse," answered Dorothy; "so—perhaps next Saturday — "

"But why wait so long?" asked Ozma. "And why make the journey back to Kansas again? Let us surprise them, and bring them here without any warning."

"I'm not sure that they believe in the Land of Oz," said Dorothy, "though I've told 'em 'bout it lots of times."

"They'll believe when they see it," declared Ozma; "and if they are told they are to make a magical journey to our fairyland, it may make them nervous. I think the best way will be to use the Magic Belt without warning them, and when they have arrived you can explain to them whatever they do not understand."

"Perhaps that 's best," decided Dorothy. "There is n't

much use in their staying at the farm until they are put out, 'cause it 's much nicer here."

"Then to-morrow morning they shall come here," said Princess Ozma. "I will order Jellia Jamb, who is the palace housekeeper, to have rooms all prepared for them, and after breakfast we will get the Magic Belt and by its aid transport your uncle and aunt to the Emerald City."

"Thank you, Ozma!" cried Dorothy, kissing her friend gratefully.

"And now," Ozma proposed, "let us take a walk in the gardens before we dress for dinner. Come, Dorothy dear!"

How THE NOME KING PLANNED REVENGE

CHAPTER FOUR

THE reason most people are bad is because they do not try to be good. Now, the Nome King had never tried to be good, so he was very bad indeed. Having decided to conquer the Land of Oz and to destroy the Emerald City and enslave all its people, King Roquat the Red kept planning ways to do this dreadful thing, and the more he planned the more he believed he would be able to accomplish it.

About the time Dorothy went to Ozma the Nome King called his Chief Steward to him and said:

"Kaliko, I think I shall make you the General of my armies."

"I think you won't," replied Kaliko, positively.

"Why not?" inquired the King, reaching for his scepter with the big sapphire.

"Because I 'm your Chief Steward, and know nothing of

39

warfare," said Kaliko, preparing to dodge if anything were thrown at him. "I manage all the affairs of your kingdom better than you could yourself, and you 'll never find another Steward as good as I am. But there are a hundred Nomes better fitted to command your army, and your Generals get thrown away so often that I have no desire to be one of them."

"Ah, there is some truth in your remarks, Kaliko," remarked the King, deciding not to throw the scepter. "Summon my army to assemble in the Great Cavern."

Kaliko bowed and retired, and in a few minutes returned to say that the army was assembled. So the King went out upon a balcony that overlooked the Great Cavern, where fifty thousand Nomes, all armed with swords and pikes, stood marshaled in military array.

When they were not required as soldiers all these Nomes were metal workers and miners, and they had hammered so much at the forges and dug so hard with pick and shovel that they had acquired great muscular strength. They were strangely formed creatures, rather round and not very tall. Their toes were curly and their ears broad and flat.

In time of war every Nome left his forge or mine and became part of the great army of King Roquat. The soldiers wore rock-colored uniforms and were excellently drilled.

The King looked upon this tremendous army, which

stood silently arrayed before him, and a cruel smile curled
the corners of his mouth, for he saw that his legions were
very powerful. Then he addressed them from the balcony,
saying:

"I have thrown away General Blug, because he did not
please me. So I want another General to command this
army. Who is next in command?"

"I am," replied Colonel Crinkle, a dapper-looking Nome,
as he stepped forward to salute his monarch.

The King looked at him carefully and said:

"I want you to march this army through an underground
tunnel, which I am going to bore, to the Emerald City of Oz.
When you get there I want you to conquer the Oz people,
destroy them and their city, and bring all their gold and
silver and precious stones back to my cavern. Also you are
to recapture my Magic Belt and return it to me. Will you
do this, General Crinkle?"

"No, your Majesty," replied the Nome; "for it can't be
done."

"Oh, indeed!" exclaimed the King. Then he turned to
his servants and said: "Please take General Crinkle to the
torture chamber. There you will kindly slice him into thin
slices. Afterward you may feed him to the seven-headed
dogs."

"Anything to oblige your Majesty," replied the servants, politely, and led the condemned man away.

When they had gone the King addressed the army again.

"Listen!" said he. "The General who is to command my armies must promise to carry out my orders. If he fails he will share the fate of poor Crinkle. Now, then, who will volunteer to lead my hosts to the Emerald City?"

For a time no one moved and all were silent. Then an old Nome with white whiskers so long that they were tied around his waist to prevent their tripping him up, stepped out of the ranks and saluted the King.

"I'd like to ask a few questions, your Majesty," he said.

"Go ahead," replied the King.

"These Oz people are quite good, are they not?"

"As good as apple pie," said the King.

"And they are happy, I suppose?" continued the old Nome.

"Happy as the day is long," said the King.

"And contented and prosperous?" inquired the Nome.

"Very much so," said the King.

"Well, your Majesty," remarked he of the white whiskers, "I think I should like to undertake the job, so I'll be your General. I hate good people; I detest happy people; I'm opposed to any one who is contented and prosperous. That is why I am so fond of your Majesty. Make me your General and I 'll promise to conquer and destroy the Oz people. If I fail I 'm ready to be sliced thin and fed to the seven-headed dogs."

"Very good! Very good, indeed! That 's the way to talk!" cried Roquat the Red, who was greatly pleased.

"What is your name, General?"

"I 'm called Guph, your Majesty."

"Well, Guph, come with me to my private cave and we 'll talk it over." Then he turned to the army. "Nomes and soldiers," said he, "you are to obey the commands of General Guph until he becomes dog-feed. Any man who fails to obey

43

his new General will be promptly thrown away. You are now dismissed."

Guph went to the King's private cave and sat down upon an amethyst chair and put his feet on the arm of the King's ruby throne. Then he lighted his pipe and threw the live coal he had taken from his pocket upon the King's left foot and puffed the smoke into the King's eyes and made himself comfortable. For he was a wise old Nome, and he knew that the best way to get along with Roquat the Red was to show that he was not afraid of him.

"I 'm ready for the talk, your Majesty," he said.

The King coughed and looked at his new General fiercely.

"Do you not tremble to take such liberties with your monarch?" he asked.

"Oh, no," said Guph, calmly, and he blew a wreath of smoke that curled around the King's nose and made him sneeze. "You want to conquer the Emerald City, and I 'm the only Nome in all your dominions who can conquer it. So you will be very careful not to hurt me until I have carried out your wishes. After that——"

"Well, what then?" inquired the King.

"Then you will be so grateful to me that you won't care to hurt me," replied the General.

"That is a very good argument," said Roquat. "But suppose you fail?"

Chapter Four

"Then it 's the slicing machine. I agree to that," announced Guph. "But if you do as I tell you there will be no failure. The trouble with you, Roquat, is that you don't think carefully enough. I do. You would go ahead and march through your tunnel into Oz, and get defeated and

driven back. I won't. And the reason I won't is because when I march I 'll have all my plans made, and a host of allies to assist my Nomes."

"What do you mean by that?" asked the King.

"I 'll explain, King Roquat. You 're going to attack a fairy country, and a mighty fairy country, too. They haven't much of an army in Oz, but the Princess who rules them has

45

a fairy wand; and the little girl Dorothy has your Magic Belt; and at the North of the Emerald City lives a clever sorceress called Glinda the Good, who commands the spirits of the air. Also I have heard that there is a wonderful Wizard in Ozma's palace, who is so skillful that people used to pay him money in America to see him perform. So you see it will be no easy thing to overcome all this magic."

"We have fifty thousand soldiers!" cried the King, proudly.

"Yes; but they are Nomes," remarked Guph, taking a silk handkerchief from the King's pocket and wiping his own pointed shoes with it. "Nomes are immortals, but they are not strong on magic. When you lost your famous Belt the greater part of your own power was gone from you. Against Ozma you and your Nomes would have no show at all."

Roquat's eyes flashed angrily.

"Then away you go to the slicing machine!" he cried.

"Not yet," said the General, filling his pipe from the King's private tobacco pouch.

"What do you propose to do?" asked the monarch.

"I propose to obtain the power we need," answered Guph. "There are a good many evil creatures who have magic powers sufficient to destroy and conquer the Land of Oz. We will get them on our side, band them all together, and then take Ozma and her people by surprise. It's all very simple

46

and easy when you know how. Alone we should be helpless to injure the Ruler of Oz, but with the aid of the evil powers we can summon we shall easily succeed."

King Roquat was delighted with this idea, for he realized how clever it was.

"Surely, Guph, you are the greatest General I have ever had!" he exclaimed, his eyes sparkling with joy. "You must go at once and make arrangements with the evil powers to assist us, and meantime I 'll begin to dig the tunnel."

"I thought you 'd agree with me, Roquat," replied the new General. "I 'll start this very afternoon to visit the Chief of the Whimsies."

How DOROTHY BECAME A PRINCESS

CHAPTER FIVE

WHEN the people of the Emerald City heard that Dorothy had returned to them every one was eager to see her, for the little girl was a general favorite in the Land of Oz. From time to time some of the folk from the great outside world had found their way into this fairyland, but all except one had been companions of Dorothy and had turned out to be very agreeable people. The exception I speak of was the wonderful Wizard of Oz, a sleight-of-hand performer from Omaha who went up in a balloon and was carried by a current of air to the Emerald City. His queer and puzzling tricks made the people of Oz believe him a great wizard for a time, and he ruled over them until Dorothy arrived on her first visit and showed the Wizard to be a mere humbug. He was a gentle, kindly-hearted little man, and Dorothy grew to like him afterward. When, after an absence, the Wizard

48

Chapter Five

returned to the Land of Oz, Ozma received him graciously and gave him a home in a part of the palace.

In addition to the Wizard two other personages from the outside world had been allowed to make their home in the Emerald City. The first was a quaint Shaggy Man, whom Ozma had made the Governor of the Royal Store-houses, and the second a Yellow Hen named Billina, who had a fine house in the gardens back of the palace, where she looked after a large family. Both these had been old comrades of Dorothy, so you see the little girl was quite an important personage in Oz, and the people thought she had brought them good luck, and loved her next best to Ozma. During her several visits this little girl had been the means of destroying two wicked witches who oppressed the people, and she had discovered a live scarecrow who was now one of the most popular personages in all the fairy country. With the Scarecrow's help she had rescued Nick Chopper, a Tin Woodman, who had rusted in a lonely forest, and the tin man was now the Emperor of the Country of the Winkies and much beloved because of his kind heart. No wonder the people thought Dorothy had brought them good luck! Yet, strange as it may seem, she had accomplished all these wonders not because she was a fairy or had any magical pow-ers whatever, but because she was a simple, sweet and true little girl who was honest to herself and to all whom she met. In this world in which we live simplicity and kindness are the only magic wands that work wonders, and in the Land of Oz Dorothy found these same qualities had won for her the love and admiration of the people. Indeed, the little girl had made many warm friends in the fairy country, and the only real grief the Ozites had ever experienced was when Dorothy left them and returned to her Kansas home.

Now she received a joyful welcome, although no one except Ozma knew at first that she had finally come to stay for good and all.

That evening Dorothy had many callers, and among them were such important people as Tiktok, a machine man who thought and spoke and moved by clockwork; her old companion the genial Shaggy Man; Jack Pumpkinhead, whose body was brush-wood and whose head was a ripe pumpkin with a face carved upon it; the Cowardly Lion and the Hungry Tiger, two great beasts from the forest, who served Princess Ozma, and Professor H. M. Wogglebug, T. E. This wogglebug was a remarkable creature. He had once been a tiny little bug, crawling around in a school-room, but he was discovered and highly magnified so that he could be seen more plainly, and while in this magnified condition he had escaped. He had always remained big, and he dressed like a dandy and was so full of knowledge and information (which

are distinct acquirements), that he had been made a Professor
and the head of the Royal College.

Dorothy had a nice visit with these old friends, and also
talked a long time with the Wizard, who was little and old
and withered and dried up, but as merry and active as a
child. Afterward she went to see Billina's fast growing
family of chicks.

Toto, Dorothy's little black dog, also met with a cordial
reception. Toto was an especial friend of the Shaggy Man,
and he knew every one else. Being the only dog in the Land
of Oz, he was highly respected by the people, who believed
animals entitled to every consideration if they behaved
themselves properly.

Dorothy had four lovely rooms in the palace, which were
always reserved for her use and were called "Dorothy's
rooms." These consisted of a beautiful sitting room, a dressing room, a dainty bedchamber and a big marble bathroom.
And in these rooms were everything that heart could desire,
placed there with loving thoughtfulness by Ozma for her
little friend's use. The royal dressmakers had the little
girl's measure, so they kept the closets in her dressing room
filled with lovely dresses of every description and suitable
for every occasion. No wonder Dorothy had refrained from
bringing with her her old calico and gingham dresses! Here
everything that was dear to a little girl's heart was supplied

in profusion, and nothing so rich and beautiful could ever have been found in the biggest department stores in America. Of course Dorothy enjoyed all these luxuries, and the only reason she had heretofore preferred to live in Kansas was because her uncle and aunt loved her and needed her with them.

Now, however, all was to be changed, and Dorothy was really more delighted to know that her dear relatives were to share in her good fortune and enjoy the delights of the Land of Oz, than she was to possess such luxury for herself.

Next morning, at Ozma's request, Dorothy dressed herself in a pretty sky-blue gown of rich silk, trimmed with real pearls. The buckles of her shoes were set with pearls, too, and more of these priceless gems were on a lovely coronet which she wore upon her forehead.

"For," said her friend Ozma, "from this time forth, my dear, you must assume your rightful rank as a Princess of Oz, and being my chosen companion you must dress in a way befitting the dignity of your position."

Dorothy agreed to this, although she knew that neither gowns nor jewels could make her anything else than the simple, unaffected little girl she had always been.

As soon as they had breakfasted—the girls eating together in Ozma's pretty boudoir—the Ruler of Oz said:

"Now, dear friend, we will use the Magic Belt to transport your uncle and aunt from Kansas to the Emerald City. But I think it would be fitting, in receiving such distinguished guests, for us to sit in my Throne Room."

"Oh, they 're not very 'stinguished, Ozma," said Dorothy. "They 're just plain people, like me."

"Being your friends and relatives, Princess Dorothy, they are certainly distinguished," replied the Ruler, with a smile.

"They—they won't hardly know what to make of all your splendid furniture and things," protested Dorothy, gravely. "It may scare 'em to see your grand Throne Room, an' p'raps we 'd better go into the back yard, Ozma, where the cabbages grow an' the chickens are playing. Then it would seem more natural to Uncle Henry and Aunt Em."

"No: they shall first see me in my Throne Room," replied Ozma, decidedly; and when she spoke in that tone Dorothy knew it was not wise to oppose her, for Ozma was accustomed to having her own way.

So together they went to the Throne Room, an immense domed chamber in the center of the palace. Here stood the royal throne, made of solid gold and encrusted with enough precious stones to stock a dozen jewelry stores in our country.

Ozma, who was wearing the Magic Belt, seated herself in the throne, and Dorothy sat at her feet. In the room were assembled many ladies and gentlemen of the court, clothed in rich apparel and wearing fine jewelry. Two immense animals squatted, one on each side of the throne—the Cowardly Lion and the Hungry Tiger. In a balcony high up in the dome an orchestra played sweet music, and beneath the dome two electric fountains sent sprays of colored perfumed water shooting up nearly as high as the arched ceiling.

"Are you ready, Dorothy?" asked the Ruler.

"I am," replied Dorothy; "but I don't know whether Aunt Em and Uncle Henry are ready."

"That won't matter," declared Ozma. "The old life can have very little to interest them, and the sooner they begin the new life here the happier they will be. Here they come, my dear!"

As she spoke, there before the throne appeared Uncle Henry and Aunt Em, who for a moment stood motionless, glaring with white and startled faces at the scene that confronted them. If the ladies and gentlemen present had not been so polite I am sure they would have laughed at the two strangers.

Aunt Em had her calico dress skirt "tucked up," and she wore a faded blue-checked apron. Her hair was rather straggly and she had on a pair of Uncle Henry's old slippers. In one hand she held a dish-towel and in the other a cracked earthenware plate, which she had been engaged in wiping when so suddenly transported to the Land of Oz.

Chapter Five

Uncle Henry, when the summons came, had been out in the barn "doin' chores." He wore a ragged and much soiled straw hat, a checked shirt without any collar and blue overalls tucked into the tops of his old cowhide boots.

"By gum!" gasped Uncle Henry, looking around as if bewildered.

"Well, I swan!" gurgled Aunt Em, in a hoarse, frightened voice. Then her eyes fell upon Dorothy, and she said: "D-d-d-don't that look like our little girl—our Dorothy, Henry?"

"Hi, there—look out, Em!" exclaimed the old man, as Aunt Em advanced a step; "take care o' the wild beastses, or you 're a goner!"

But now Dorothy sprang forward and embraced and kissed her aunt and uncle affectionately, afterward taking their hands in her own.

"Don't be afraid," she said to them. "You are now in the Land of Oz, where you are to live always, and be comfer'ble an' happy. You 'll never have to worry over anything again, 'cause there won't be anything to worry about. And you owe it all to the kindness of my friend Princess Ozma."

Here she led them before the throne and continued:

"Your Highness, this is Uncle Henry. And this is Aunt Em. They want to thank you for bringing them here from Kansas."

Aunt Em tried to "slick" her hair, and she hid the dish-towel and dish under her apron while she bowed to the lovely Ozma. Uncle Henry took off his straw hat and held it awkwardly in his hands.

But the Ruler of Oz rose and came from her throne to greet her newly arrived guests, and she smiled as sweetly upon them as if they had been a king and a queen.

"You are very welcome here, where I have brought you for Princess Dorothy's sake," she said, graciously, "and I hope you will be quite happy in your new home." Then she turned to her courtiers, who were silently and gravely regarding the scene, and added: "I present to my people our Princess Dorothy's beloved Uncle Henry and Aunt Em, who will hereafter be subjects of our kingdom. It will please me to have you show them every kindness and honor in your power, and to join me in making them happy and contented."

Hearing this, all those assembled bowed low and respectfully to the old farmer and his wife, who bobbed their own heads in return.

"And now," said Ozma to them, "Dorothy will show you the rooms prepared for you. I hope you will like them, and shall expect you to join me at luncheon."

So Dorothy led her relatives away, and as soon as they were out of the Throne Room and alone in the corridor Aunt Em squeezed Dorothy's hand and said:

"Child, child! How in the world did we ever get here so quick? And is it all real? And are we to stay here, as she says? And what does it all mean, anyhow?"

Dorothy laughed.

"Why did n't you tell us what you were goin' to do?"

inquired Uncle Henry, reproachfully. "If I 'd known about it I 'd 'a put on my Sunday clothes."

"I 'll 'splain ever'thing as soon as we get to your rooms," promised Dorothy. "You 're in great luck, Uncle Henry and Aunt Em; an' so am I! And oh! I 'm so happy to have got you here, at last!"

As he walked by the little girl's side Uncle Henry stroked his whiskers thoughtfully.

"'Pears to me, Dorothy, we won't make bang-up fairies," he remarked.

"An' my back hair looks like a fright!" wailed Aunt Em.

"Never mind," returned the little girl, reassuringly. "You won't have anything to do now but to look pretty, Aunt Em; an' Uncle Henry won't have to work till his back aches, that 's certain."

"Sure?" they asked, wonderingly, and in the same breath.

"Course I 'm sure," said Dorothy. "You 're in the Fairy-land of Oz, now; an' what 's more, you belong to it!"

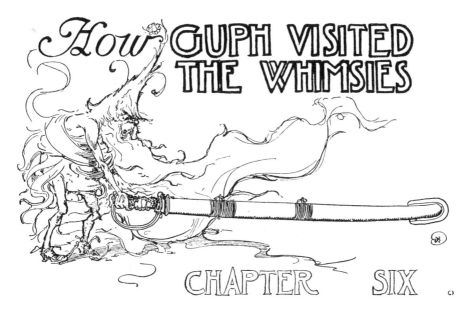

How GUPH VISITED THE WHIMSIES

CHAPTER SIX

THE new General of the Nome King's army knew perfectly well that to fail in his plans meant death for him. Yet he was not at all anxious or worried. He hated every one who was good and longed to make all who were happy unhappy. Therefore he had accepted this dangerous position as **General** quite willingly, feeling sure in his **evil mind** that he would be able to do a lot of mischief and finally conquer the Land of Oz.

Yet Guph determined to be careful, and to lay his plans well, so as not to fail. He argued that only careless people fail in what they attempt to do.

The mountains underneath which the Nome King's extensive caverns were located lay grouped just north of the Land of Ev, which lay directly across the deadly desert to the east of the Land of Oz. As the mountains were also on

59

the edge of the desert the Nome King found that he had only to tunnel underneath the desert to reach Ozma's dominions. He did not wish his armies to appear above ground in the Country of the Winkies, which was the part of the Land of Oz nearest to King Roquat's own country, as then the people would give the alarm and enable Ozma to fortify the Emerald City and assemble an army. He wanted to take all the Oz people by surprise; so he decided to run the tunnel clear through to the Emerald City, where he and his hosts could break through the ground without warning and conquer the people before they had time to defend themselves.

Roquat the Red began work at once upon his tunnel, setting a thousand miners at the task and building it high and broad enough for his armies to march through it with ease. The Nomes were used to making tunnels, as all the kingdom in which they lived was under ground; so they made rapid progress.

While this work was going on General Guph started out alone to visit the Chief of the Whimsies.

These Whimsies were curious people who lived in a retired country of their own. They had large, strong bodies, but heads so small that they were no bigger than door-knobs. Of course, such tiny heads could not contain any great amount of brains, and the Whimsies were so ashamed of their personal appearance and lack of commonsense that they wore big heads, made of pasteboard, which they fastened over their own little heads. On these pasteboard heads they sewed sheep's wool for hair, and the wool was colored many tints—pink, green and lavender being the favorite colors.

The faces of these false heads were painted in many ridiculous ways, according to the whims of the owners, and these big, burly creatures looked so whimsical and absurd in their queer masks that they were called "Whimsies." They foolishly imagined that no one would suspect the little heads that were inside the imitation ones, not knowing that it is folly to try to appear otherwise than as nature has made us.

The Chief of the Whimsies had as little wisdom as the others, and had been chosen chief merely because none among them was any wiser or more capable of ruling. The Whimsies were evil spirits and could not be killed. They were hated and feared by every one and were known as terrible fighters because they were so strong and muscular and had not sense enough to know when they were defeated.

General Guph thought the Whimsies would be a great help to the Nomes in the conquest of Oz, for under his leadership they could be induced to fight as long so they could stand up. So he traveled to their country and asked to see the Chief, who lived in a house that had a picture of his grotesque false head painted over the doorway.

The Chief's false head had blue hair, a turned-up nose, and a mouth that stretched half across the face. Big green eyes had been painted upon it, but in the center of the chin were two small holes made in the pasteboard, so that the Chief could see through them with his own tiny eyes; for when the big head was fastened upon his shoulders the eyes in his own natural head were on a level with the false chin.

Said General Guph to the Chief of the Whimsies:

"We Nomes are going to conquer the Land of Oz and capture our King's Magic Belt, which the Oz people stole from him. Then we are going to plunder and destroy the whole country. And we want the Whimsies to help us."

"Will there be any fighting?" asked the Chief.

"Plenty," replied Guph.

That must have pleased the Chief, for he got up and danced around the room three times. Then he seated himself again, adjusted his false head, and said:

"We have no quarrel with Ozma of Oz."

"But you Whimsies love to fight, and here is a splendid chance to do so," urged Guph.

"Wait till I sing a song," said the Chief. Then he lay back in his chair and sang a foolish song that did not seem to the General to mean anything, although he listened carefully. When he had finished, the Chief Whimsie looked at him through the holes in his chin and asked:

"What reward will you give us if we help you?"

The General was prepared for this question, for he had been thinking the matter over on his journey. People often

do a good deed without hope of reward, but for an evil deed they always demand payment.

"When we get our Magic Belt," he made reply, "our King, Roquat the Red, will use its power to give every Whimsie a natural head as big and fine as the false head he now wears. Then you will no longer be ashamed because your big strong bodies have such teenty-weenty heads."

"Oh! Will you do that?" asked the Chief, eagerly.

"We surely will," promised the General.

"I'll talk to my people," said the Chief.

So he called a meeting of all the Whimsies and told them of the offer made by the Nomes. The creatures were de-

lighted with the bargain, and at once agreed to fight for the Nome King and help him to conquer Oz.

One Whimsie alone seemed to have a glimmer of sense, for he asked:

"Suppose we fail to capture the Magic Belt? What will happen then, and what good will all our fighting do?"

64

But they threw him into the river for asking foolish questions, and laughed when the water ruined his pasteboard head before he could swim out again.

So the compact was made and General Guph was delighted with his success in gaining such powerful allies.

But there were other people, too, just as important as the Whimsies, whom the clever old Nome had determined to win to his side.

How AUNT EM CONQUERED THE LION

CHAPTER SEVEN

"THESE are your rooms," said Dorothy, opening a door.

Aunt Em drew back at sight of the splendid furniture and draperies.

"Ain't there any place to wipe my feet?" she asked.

"You will soon change your slippers for new shoes," replied Dorothy. "Don't be afraid, Aunt Em. Here is where you are to live, so walk right in and make yourself at home."

Aunt Em advanced hesitatingly.

"It beats the Topeka Hotel!" she cried, admiringly. "But this place is too grand for us, child. Can't we have some back room in the attic, that's more in our class?"

"No," said Dorothy. "You've got to live here, 'cause Ozma says so. And all the rooms in this palace are just as fine as these, and some are better. It won't do any good to fuss, Aunt Em. You've got to be swell and high-toned

66

in the Land of Oz, whether you want to or not; so you may as well make up your mind to it."

"It 's hard luck," replied her aunt, looking around with an awed expression; "but folks can get used to anything, if they try. Eh, Henry?"

"Why, as to that," said Uncle Henry, slowly, "I b'lieve in takin' what 's pervided us, an' askin' no questions. I 've traveled some, Em, in my time, and you hain't; an' that makes a difference atween us."

Then Dorothy showed them through the rooms. The first was a handsome sitting-room, with windows opening upon the rose gardens. Then came separate bedrooms for Aunt Em and Uncle Henry, with a fine bathroom between them. Aunt Em had a pretty dressing room, besides, and Dorothy opened the closets and showed several exquisite costumes that had been provided for her aunt by the royal dressmakers, who had worked all night to get them ready. Everything that Aunt Em could possibly need was in the drawers and closets, and her dressing-table was covered with engraved gold toilet articles.

Uncle Henry had nine suits of clothes, cut in the popular Munchkin fashion, with knee-breeches, silk stockings and low shoes with jeweled buckles. The hats to match these costumes had pointed tops and wide brims with small gold bells around the edges. His shirts were of fine linen with frilled bosoms, and his vests were richly embroidered with colored silks.

Uncle Henry decided that he would first take a bath and then dress himself in a blue satin suit that had caught his fancy. He accepted his good fortune with calm composure and refused to have a servant to assist him. But Aunt Em was "all of a flutter," as she said, and it took Dorothy and Jellia Jamb, the housekeeper, and two maids a long time to dress her and do up her hair and get her "rigged like a popinjay," as she quaintly expressed it. She wanted to stop and admire everything that caught her eye, and she sighed continually and declared that such finery was too good for an old country woman, and that she never thought she would have to "put on airs" at her time of life.

Finally she was dressed, and when they went into the sitting-room there was Uncle Henry in his blue satin, walking gravely up and down the room. He had trimmed his beard and mustache and looked very dignified and respectable.

"Tell me, Dorothy," he said; "do all the men here wear duds like these?"

"Yes," she replied; "all 'cept the Scarecrow and the Shaggy Man—and of course the Tin Woodman and Tiktok, who are made of metal. You 'll find all the men at Ozma's court dressed just as you are—only perhaps a little finer."

"Henry, you look like a play-actor," announced Aunt Em, looking at her husband critically.

"An' you, Em, look more highfalutin' than a peacock,"
he replied.

"I guess you 're right," she said, regretfully; "but we 're
helpless victims of high-toned royalty."

Dorothy was much amused.

"Come with me," she said, "and I 'll show you 'round the
palace."

She took them through the beautiful rooms and introduced them to all the people they chanced to meet. Also
she showed them her own pretty rooms, which were not far
from their own.

"So it's all true," said Aunt Em, wide-eyed with amazement, "and what Dorothy told us of this fairy country was plain facts instead of dreams! But where are all the strange creatures you used to know here?"

"Yes; where's the Scarecrow?" inquired Uncle Henry.

"Why, he's just now away on a visit to the Tin Woodman, who is Emp'ror of the Winkie Country," answered the little girl. "You'll see him when he comes back, and you're sure to like him."

"And where's the Wonderful Wizard?" asked Aunt Em.

"You'll see him at Ozma's luncheon, for he lives in this palace," was the reply.

"And Jack Pumpkinhead?"

"Oh, he lives a little way out of town, in his own pumpkin field. We'll go there some time and see him, and we'll call on Professor Wogglebug, too. The Shaggy Man will be at the luncheon, I guess, and Tiktok. And now I'll take you out to see Billina, who has a house of her own."

So they went into the back yard, and after walking along winding paths some distance through the beautiful gardens they came to an attractive little house where the Yellow Hen sat on the front porch sunning herself.

"Good morning, my dear Mistress," called Billina, fluttering down to meet them. "I was expecting you to call, for I heard you had come back and brought your uncle and aunt with you."

"We 're here for good and all, this time, Billina," cried Dorothy, joyfully. "Uncle Henry and Aunt Em belong in Oz now as much as I do!"

"Then they are very lucky people," declared Billina; "for there could n't be a nicer place to live. But come, my dear; I must show you all my Dorothys. Nine are living and have grown up to be very respectable hens; but one took cold at Ozma's birthday party and died of the pip, and the other two turned out to be horrid roosters, so I had to change their names from Dorothy to Daniel. They all had the letter 'D' engraved upon their gold lockets, you remember, with your picture inside, and 'D' stands for Daniel as well as for Dorothy."

"Did you call both the roosters Daniel?" asked Uncle Henry.

"Yes, indeed. I 've nine Dorothys and two Daniels; and the nine Dorothys have eighty-six sons and daughters and over three hundred grandchildren," said Billina, proudly.

"What names do you give 'em all, dear?" inquired the little girl.

"Oh, they are all Dorothys and Daniels, some being Juniors and some Double-Juniors. Dorothy and Daniel are two good names, and I see no object in hunting for others," declared the Yellow Hen. "But just think, Dorothy, what a big chicken family we 've grown to be, and our numbers increase nearly every day! Ozma does n't know what to do with all the eggs we lay, and we are never eaten or harmed in any way, as chickens are in your country. They give us everything to make us contented and happy, and I, my dear, am the acknowledged Queen and Governor of every chicken in Oz, because I 'm the eldest and started the whole colony."

"You ought to be very proud, ma'am," said Uncle Henry, who was astonished to hear a hen talk so sensibly.

"Oh, I am," she replied. "I 've the loveliest pearl necklace you ever saw. Come in the house and I 'll show it to you. And I 've nine leg bracelets and a diamond pin for each wing. But I only wear them on state occasions."

They followed the Yellow Hen into the house, which Aunt Em declared was neat as a pin. They could not sit down, because all Billina's chairs were roosting-poles made of silver; so they had to stand while the hen fussily showed them her treasures.

Then they had to go into the back rooms occupied by Billina's nine Dorothys and two Daniels, who were all plump yellow chickens and greeted the visitors very politely. It was easy to see that they were well bred and that Billina had looked after their education.

In the yards were all the children and grandchildren of these eleven elders and they were of all sizes, from well-grown hens to tiny chickens just out of the shell. About

Chapter Seven

fifty fluffy yellow youngsters were at school, being taught good manners and good grammar by a young hen who wore spectacles. They sang in chorus a patriotic song of the Land of Oz, in honor of their visitors, and Aunt Em was much impressed by these talking chickens.

Dorothy wanted to stay and play with the young chickens for awhile, but Uncle Henry and Aunt Em had not seen the palace grounds and gardens yet and were eager to get better acquainted with the marvelous and delightful land in which they were to live.

"I'll stay here, and you can go for a walk," said Dorothy. "You'll be perfec'ly safe anywhere, and may do whatever you want to. When you get tired, go back to the palace and find your rooms, and I'll come to you before luncheon is ready."

So Uncle Henry and Aunt Em started out alone to explore the grounds, and Dorothy knew that they could n't get lost, because all the palace grounds were enclosed by a high wall of green marble set with emeralds.

It was a rare treat to these simple folk, who had lived in the country all their lives and known little enjoyment of any sort, to wear beautiful clothes and live in a palace and be treated with respect and consideration by all around them. They were very happy indeed as they strolled up the shady walks and looked upon the gorgeous flowers and shrubs, feeling that their new home was more beautiful than any tongue could describe.

Suddenly, as they turned a corner and walked through a gap in a high hedge, they came face to face with an enormous Lion, which crouched upon the green lawn and seemed surprised by their appearance.

They stopped short, Uncle Henry trembling with horror and Aunt Em too terrified to scream. Next moment the poor woman clasped her husband around the neck and cried:

"Save me, Henry, save me!"

"Can't even save myself, Em," he returned, in a husky voice, "for the animile looks as if it could eat both of us, an' lick its chops for more! If I only had a gun—"

"Have n't you, Henry? Have n't you?" she asked anxiously.

"Nary gun, Em. So let 's die as brave an' graceful as we can. I knew our luck could n't last!"

"I won't die. I won't be eaten by a lion!" wailed Aunt Em, glaring upon the huge beast. Then a thought struck her, and she whispered: "Henry, I 've heard as savage beastses can be conquered by the human eye. I 'll eye that lion out o' countenance an' save our lives."

"Try it, Em," he returned, also in a whisper. "Look at him as you do at me when I 'm late to dinner."

Aunt Em turned upon the Lion a determined countenance

and a wild dilated eye. She glared at the immense beast steadily, and the Lion, who had been quietly blinking at them, began to appear uneasy and disturbed.

"Is anything the matter, ma'am?" he asked, in a mild voice.

At this speech from the terrible beast Aunt Em and Uncle Henry both were startled, and then Uncle Henry remembered that this must be the Lion they had seen in Ozma's Throne Room.

"Hold on, Em!" he exclaimed. "Quit the eagle eye conquest an' take courage. I guess this is the same Cowardly Lion Dorothy has told us about."

"Oh, is it?" she asked, much relieved.

"When he spoke, I got the idea; and when he looked so 'shamed like, I was sure of it," Uncle Henry continued.

Aunt Em regarded the animal with new interest.

"Are you the Cowardly Lion?" she inquired. "Are you Dorothy's friend?"

"Yes 'm," answered the Lion, meekly. "Dorothy and I are old chums and are very fond of each other. I 'm the King of Beasts, you know, and the Hungry Tiger and I serve Princess Ozma as her body guards."

"To be sure," said Aunt Em, nodding. "But the King of Beasts should n't be cowardly."

"I 've heard that said before," remarked the Lion, yawning till he showed his two great rows of sharp white teeth; "but that does not keep me from being frightened whenever I go into battle."

"What do you do, run?" asked Uncle Henry.

"No; that would be foolish, for the enemy would run after me," declared the Lion. "So I tremble with fear and pitch in as hard as I can; and so far I have always won my fight."

"Ah, I begin to understand," said Uncle Henry.

"Were you scared when I looked at you just now?" inquired Aunt Em.

"Terribly scared, madam," answered the Lion, "for at first I thought you were going to have a fit. Then I noticed you were trying to overcome me by the power of your eye, and your glance was so fierce and penetrating that I shook with fear."

This greatly pleased the lady, and she said quite cheerfully:

"Well, I won't hurt you, so don't be scared any more. I just wanted to see what the human eye was good for."

"The human eye is a fearful weapon," remarked the Lion, scratching his nose softly with his paw to hide a smile. "Had I not known you were Dorothy's friends I might have torn you both into shreds in order to escape your terrible gaze."

Aunt Em shuddered at hearing this, and Uncle Henry said hastily:

"I'm glad you knew us. Good morning, Mr. Lion; we'll hope to see you again—by and by—some time in the future."

"Good morning," replied the Lion, squatting down upon the lawn again. "You are likely to see a good deal of me, if you live in the Land of Oz."

How THE GRAND GALLIPOOT JOINED THE NOMES

CHAPTER EIGHT

AFTER leaving the Whimsies, Guph continued on his journey and penetrated far into the Northwest. He wanted to get to the Country of the Growleywogs, and in order to do that he must cross the Ripple Land, which was a hard thing to do. For the Ripple Land was a succession of hills and valleys, all very steep and rocky, and they changed places constantly by rippling. While Guph was climbing a hill it sank down under him and became a valley, and while he was descending into a valley it rose up and carried him to the top of a hill. This was very perplexing to the traveler, and a stranger might have thought he could never cross the Ripple Land at all. But Guph knew that if he kept steadily on he would get to the end at last; so he paid no attention to the changing hills and valleys and plodded along as calmly as if walking upon the level ground.

Chapter Eight

The result of this wise persistence was that the General finally reached firmer soil and, after penetrating a dense forest, came to the Dominion of the Growleywogs.

No sooner had he crossed the border of this domain when two guards seized him and carried him before the Grand Gallipoot of the Growleywogs, who scowled upon him ferociously and asked him why he dared intrude upon his territory.

"I 'm the Lord High General of the Invincible Army of the Nomes, and my name is Guph," was the reply. "All the world trembles when that name is mentioned."

The Growleywogs gave a shout of jeering laughter at this, and one of them caught the Nome in his strong arms and tossed him high into the air. Guph was considerably shaken when he fell upon the hard ground, but he appeared to take no notice of the impertinence and composed himself to speak again to the Grand Gallipoot.

"My master, King Roquat the Red, has sent me here to confer with you. He wishes your assistance to conquer the Land of Oz."

Here the General paused, and the Grand Gallipoot scowled upon him more terribly than ever and said:

"Go on!"

The voice of the Grand Gallipoot was partly a roar and partly a growl. He mumbled his words badly and Guph had to listen carefully in order to understand him.

These Growleywogs were certainly remarkable creatures. They were of gigantic size, yet were all bone and skin and muscle, there being no meat or fat upon their bodies at all. Their powerful muscles lay just underneath their skins, like bunches of tough rope, and the weakest Growleywog was so strong that he could pick up an elephant and toss it seven miles away.

It seems unfortunate that strong people are usually so disagreeable and overbearing that no one cares for them. In fact, to be different from your fellow creatures is always a misfortune. The Growleywogs knew that they were disliked and avoided by every one, so they had become surly and unsociable even among themselves. Guph knew that they hated all people, including the Nomes; but he hoped to win them over, nevertheless, and knew that if he succeeded they would afford him very powerful assistance.

"The Land of Oz is ruled by a namby-pamby girl who is disgustingly kind and good," he continued. "Her people are all happy and contented and have no care or worries whatever."

"Go on!" growled the Grand Gallipoot.

"Once the Nome King enslaved the Royal Family of Ev —another goody-goody lot that we detest," said the General. "But Ozma interfered, although it was none of her business, and marched her army against us. With her was a Kansas

girl named Dorothy, and a Yellow Hen, and they marched directly into the Nome King's cavern. There they liberated our slaves from Ev and stole King Roquat's Magic Belt, which they carried away with them. So now our King is making a tunnel under the deadly desert, so we can march through it to the Emerald City. When we get there we mean to conquer and destroy all the land and recapture the Magic Belt."

Again he paused, and again the Grand Gallipoot growled:

"Go on!"

Guph tried to think what to say next, and a happy thought soon occurred to him.

"We want you to help us in this conquest," he announced, "for we need the mighty aid of the Growleywogs in order to make sure that we shall not be defeated. You are the strongest people in all the world, and you hate good and happy creatures as much as we Nomes do. I am sure it will be a real pleasure to you to tear down the beautiful Emerald City, and in return for your valuable assistance we will allow you to bring back to your country ten thousand people of Oz, to be your slaves."

"Twenty thousand!" growled the Grand Gallipoot.

"All right, we promise you twenty thousand," agreed the General.

The Gallipoot made a signal and at once his attendants picked up General Guph and carried him away to a prison, where the jailor amused himself by sticking pins in the round fat body of the old Nome, to see him jump and hear him yell.

But while this was going on the Grand Gallipoot was talking with his counselors, who were the most important officials of the Growleywogs. When he had stated to them the proposition of the Nome King he said:

"My advice is to offer to help them. Then, when we have conquered the Land of Oz, we will take not only our twenty thousand prisoners but all the gold and jewels we want."

"Let us take the Magic Belt. too," suggested one counselor.

"And rob the Nome King and make him our slave," said another.

"That is a good idea," declared the Grand Gallipoot. "I 'd like King Roquat for my own slave. He could black my boots and bring me my porridge every morning while I am in bed."

"There is a famous Scarecrow in Oz. I 'll take him for my slave," said a counselor.

"I 'll take Tiktok, the machine man," said another.

"Give me the Tin Woodman," said a third.

They went on for some time, dividing up the people and the treasure of Oz in advance of the conquest. For they had no doubt at all that they would be able to destroy Ozma's domain. Were they not the strongest people in all the world?

"The deadly desert has kept us out of Oz before," remarked the Grand Gallipoot, "but now that the Nome King is building a tunnel we shall get into the Emerald City very easily. So let us send the little fat General back to his King with our promise to assist him. We will not say that we intend to conquer the Nomes after we have conquered Oz, but we will do so, just the same."

This plan being agreed upon, they all went home to dinner, leaving General Guph still in prison. The Nome had no idea that he had succeeded in his mission, for finding himself in prison he feared the Growleywogs intended to put him to death.

By this time the jailor had tired of sticking pins in the General, and was amusing himself by carefully pulling the Nome's whiskers out by the roots, one at a time. This enjoyment was interrupted by the Grand Gallipoot sending for the prisoner.

"Wait a few hours," begged the jailor. "I have n't pulled out a quarter of his whiskers yet."

"If you keep the Grand Gallipoot waiting he 'll break your back," declared the messenger.

"Perhaps you 're right," sighed the jailor. "Take the prisoner away, if you will, but I advise you to kick him at every step he takes. It will be good fun, for he is as soft as a ripe peach."

So Gupn was led away to the royal castle, where the Grand Gallipoot told him that the Growleywogs had decided to assist the Nomes in conquering the Land of Oz.

"Whenever you are ready," he added, "send me word and I will march with eighteen thousand of my most powerful warriors to your aid."

Guph was so delighted that he forgot all the smarting caused by the pins and the pulling of whiskers. He did not even complain of the treatment he had received, but thanked the Grand Gallipoot and hurried away upon his journey.

He had now secured the assistance of the Whimsies and the Growleywogs; but his success made him long for still more allies. His own life depended upon his conquering Oz, and he said to himself:

"I'll take no chances. I'll be certain of success. Then, when Oz is destroyed, perhaps I shall be a greater man than old Roquat, and I can throw him away and be King of the Nomes myself. Why not? The Whimsies are stronger than the Nomes, and they are my friends. The Growleywogs are stronger than the Whimsies, and they also are my friends. There are some people still stronger than the Growleywogs, and if I can but induce them to aid me I shall have nothing more to fear."

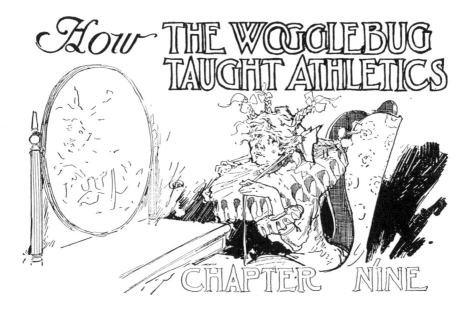

How THE WOGGLEBUG TAUGHT ATHLETICS

CHAPTER NINE

IT did not take Dorothy long to establish herself in her new home, for she knew the people and the manners and customs of the Emerald City just as well as she knew the old Kansas farm.

But Uncle Henry and Aunt Em had some trouble in getting used to the finery and pomp and ceremony of Ozma's palace, and felt uneasy because they were obliged to be "dressed up" all the time. Yet every one was very courteous and kind to them and endeavored to make them happy. Ozma, especially, made much of Dorothy's relatives, for her little friend's sake, and she well knew that the awkwardness and strangeness of their new mode of life would all wear off in time.

The old people were chiefly troubled by the fact that there was no work for them to do.

"Ev'ry day is like Sunday, now," declared Aunt Em, solemnly, "and I can't say I like it. If they 'd only let me do up the dishes after meals, or even sweep an' dust my own rooms, I 'd be a deal happier. Henry don't know what to do with himself either, and once when he stole out an' fed the chickens Billina scolded him for letting 'em eat between meals. I never knew before what a hardship it is to be rich and have everything you want."

These complaints began to worry Dorothy; so she had a long talk with Ozma upon the subject.

"I see I must find them something to do," said the girlish Ruler of Oz, seriously. "I have been watching your uncle and aunt, and I believe they will be more contented if occupied with some light tasks. While I am considering this matter, Dorothy, you might make a trip with them through the Land of Oz, visiting some of the odd corners and introducing your relatives to some of our curious people."

"Oh, that would be fine!" exclaimed Dorothy, eagerly.

"I will give you an escort befitting your rank as a Princess," continued Ozma; "and you may go to some of the places you have not yet visited yourself, as well as some others that you know. I will mark out a plan of the trip for you and have everything in readiness for you to start to-morrow morning. Take your time, dear, and be gone as long as you wish. By the time you return I shall have found some occupation for Uncle Henry and Aunt Em that will keep them from being restless and dissatisfied."

Dorothy thanked her good friend and kissed the lovely Ruler gratefully. Then she ran to tell the joyful news to her uncle and aunt.

Next morning, after breakfast, everything was found ready for their departure.

The escort included Omby Amby, the Captain General of Ozma's army, which consisted merely of twenty-seven officers besides the Captain General. Once Omby Amby had been a private soldier—the only private in the army—but as there was never any fighting to do Ozma saw no need of a private, so she made Omby Amby the highest officer of them all. He was very tall and slim and wore a gay uniform and a fierce mustache. Yet the mustache was the only fierce thing about Omby Amby, whose nature was as gentle as that of a child.

The wonderful Wizard had asked to join the party, and with him came his friend the Shaggy Man, who was shaggy but not ragged, being dressed in fine silks with satin shags and bobtails. The Shaggy Man had shaggy whiskers and hair, but a sweet disposition and a soft, pleasant voice.

There was an open wagon, with three seats for the passengers, and the wagon was drawn by the famous wooden Sawhorse which had once been brought to life by Ozma by means of a magic powder. The Sawhorse wore golden shoes to keep his wooden legs from wearing away, and he was strong and swift. As this curious creature was Ozma's own favorite steed, and very popular with all the people of the Emerald City, Dorothy knew that she had been highly favored by being permitted to use the Sawhorse on her journey.

In the front seat of the wagon sat Dorothy and the Wizard. Uncle Henry and Aunt Em sat in the next seat and the Shaggy Man and Omby Amby in the third seat. Of course Toto was with the party, curled up at Dorothy's feet, and just as they were about to start Billina came fluttering along the path and begged to be taken with them. Dorothy readily agreed, so the Yellow Hen flew up and perched herself upon the dashboard. She wore her pearl necklace and three bracelets upon each leg, in honor of the occasion.

Dorothy kissed Ozma good-bye, and all the people standing around waved their handkerchiefs, and the band in an upper balcony struck up a military march. Then the Wizard clucked to the Sawhorse and said: "Gid-dap!" and the wooden animal pranced away and drew behind him the big red wagon and all the passengers, without any effort at all. A servant threw open a gate of the palace enclosure, that they might pass out; and so, with music and shouts following them, the journey was begun.

"It 's almost like a circus," said Aunt Em, proudly. "I can't help feelin' high an' mighty in this kind of a turn-out."

Indeed, as they passed down the street, all the people cheered them lustily, and the Shaggy Man and the Wizard and the Captain General all took off their hats and bowed politely in acknowledgment.

When they came to the great wall of the Emerald City the gates were opened by the Guardian who always tended them. Over the gateway hung a dull-colored metal magnet shaped like a horse-shoe, placed against a shield of polished gold.

"That," said the Shaggy Man, impressively, "is the wonderful Love Magnet. I brought it to the Emerald City myself, and all who pass beneath this gateway are both loving and beloved."

"It 's a fine thing," declared Aunt Em, admiringly. "If we 'd had it in Kansas I guess the man who held a mortgage on the farm would n't have turned us out."

"Then I 'm glad we did n't have it," returned Uncle Henry. "I like Oz better than Kansas, even; an' this little wood Sawhorse beats all the critters I ever saw. He don't have to be curried, or fed, or watered, an' he 's strong as an ox. Can he talk, Dorothy?"

"Yes, Uncle," replied the child. "But the Sawhorse never says much. He told me once that he can't talk and think at the same time, so he prefers to think."

"Which is very sensible," declared the Wizard, nodding approvingly. "Which way do we go, Dorothy?"

"Straight ahead into the Quadling Country," she answered. "I 've got a letter of interduction to Miss Cuttenclip."

"Oh!" exclaimed the Wizard, much interested. "Are we going there? Then I 'm glad I came, for I 've always wanted to meet the Cuttenclips."

"Who are they?" inquired Aunt Em.

"Wait till we get there," replied Dorothy, with a laugh; "then you 'll see for yourself. I 've never seen the Cuttenclips, you know, so I can't 'zactly 'splain 'em to you."

Once free of the Emerald City the Sawhorse dashed away at tremendous speed. Indeed, he went so fast that Aunt Em had hard work to catch her breath, and Uncle Henry held fast to the seat of the red wagon.

"Gently—gently, my boy!" called the Wizard, and at this the Sawhorse slackened his speed.

"What 's wrong?" asked the animal, slightly turning his wooden head to look at the party with one eye, which was a knot of wood.

"Why, we wish to admire the scenery, that 's all," answered the Wizard.

"Some of your passengers," added the Shaggy Man,

"have never been out of the Emerald City before, and the country is all new to them."

"If you go too fast you'll spoil all the fun," said Dorothy. "There's no hurry."

"Very well; it is all the same to me," observed the Sawhorse; and after that he went at a more moderate pace.

Uncle Henry was astonished.

"How can a wooden thing be so intelligent?" he asked.

"Why, I gave him some sawdust brains the last time I fitted his head with new ears," explained the Wizard. "The sawdust was made from hard knots, and now the Sawhorse is able to think out any knotty problem he meets with."

"I see," said Uncle Henry.

"I don't," remarked Aunt Em; but no one paid any attention to this statement.

Before long they came to a stately building that stood upon a green plain with handsome shade trees grouped here and there.

"What is that?" asked Uncle Henry.

"That," replied the Wizard, "is the Royal Athletic College of Oz, which is directed by Professor H. M. Wogglebug, T. E.

"Let's stop and make a call," suggested Dorothy.

So the Sawhorse drew up in front of the great building and they were met at the door by the learned Wogglebug himself. He seemed fully as tall as the Wizard, and was dressed in a red and white checked vest and a blue swallow-tailed coat, and had yellow knee breeches and purple silk stockings upon his slender legs. A tall hat was jauntily set upon his head and he wore spectacles over his big bright eyes.

"Welcome, Dorothy," said the Wogglebug; "and welcome to all your friends. We are indeed pleased to receive you at this great Temple of Learning."

"I thought it was an Athletic College," said the Shaggy Man.

"It is, my dear sir," answered the Wogglebug, proudly. "Here it is that we teach the youth of our great land scientific College Athletics—in all their purity."

"Don't you teach them anything else?" asked Dorothy. "Don't they get any reading, writing and 'rithmetic?"

"Oh, yes; of course. They get all those, and more," returned the Professor. "But such things occupy little of their time. Please follow me and I will show you how my scholars are usually occupied. This is a class hour and they are all busy."

They followed him to a big field back of the college building, where several hundred young Ozites were at their classes. In one place they played football, in another baseball. Some played tennis, some golf; some were swimming in a big pool. Upon a river which wound through the grounds several crews in racing boats were rowing with great enthusiasm. Other groups of students played basketball and cricket, while in one place a ring was roped in to permit boxing and wrestling by the energetic youths. All the collegians seemed busy and there was much laughter and shouting.

"This college," said Professor Wogglebug, complacently, "is a great success. It 's educational value is undisputed, and we are turning out many great and valuable citizens every year."

"But when do they study?" asked Dorothy.

"Study?" said the Wogglebug, looking perplexed at the question.

"Yes; when do they get their 'rithmetic, and jogerfy, and such things?"

"Oh, they take doses of those every night and morning," was the reply.

"What do you mean by doses?" Dorothy inquired, wonderingly.

"Why, we use the newly invented School Pills, made by your friend the Wizard. These pills we have found to be very effective, and they save a lot of time. Please step this way and I will show you our Laboratory of Learning."

He led them to a room in the building where many large bottles were standing in rows upon shelves.

Chapter Nine

"These are the Algebra Pills," said the Professor, taking down one of the bottles. "One at night, on retiring, is equal to four hours of study. Here are the Geography Pills—one at night and one in the morning. In this next bottle are the Latin Pills—one three times a day. Then we have the

Grammar Pills—one before each meal—and the Spelling Pills, which are taken whenever needed."

"Your scholars must have to take a lot of pills," remarked Dorothy, thoughtfully. "How do they take 'em, in apple-sauce?"

"No, my dear. They are sugar-coated and are quickly

and easily swallowed. I believe the students would rather take the pills than study, and certainly the pills are a more effective method. You see, until these School Pills were invented we wasted a lot of time in study that may now be better employed in practising athletics."

"Seems to me the pills are a good thing," said Omby Amby, who remembered how it used to make his head ache as a boy to study arithmetic.

"They are, sir," declared the Wogglebug, earnestly. "They give us an advantage over all other colleges, because at no loss of time our boys become thoroughly conversant with Greek and Latin, Mathematics and Geography, Grammar and Literature. You see they are never obliged to interrupt their games to acquire the lesser branches of learning."

"It's a great invention, I'm sure," said Dorothy, looking admiringly at the Wizard, who blushed modestly at this praise.

"We live in an age of progress," announced Professor Wogglebug, pompously. "It is easier to swallow knowledge than to acquire it laboriously from books. Is it not so, my friends?"

"Some folks can swallow anything," said Aunt Em, "but to me this seems too much like taking medicine."

"Young men in college always have to take their medicine, one way or another," observed the Wizard, with a smile; "and, as our Professor says, these School Pills have proved to be a great success. One day while I was making them I happened to drop one of them, and one of Billina's chickens gobbled it up. A few minutes afterward this chick got upon a roost and recited 'The Boy Stood on the Burning Deck' without making a single mistake. Then it recited 'The Charge of the Light Brigade' and afterwards 'Excelsior.' You see, the chicken had eaten an Elocution Pill."

They now bade good bye to the Professor, and thanking him for his kind reception mounted again into the red wagon and continued their journey.

How THE CUTTENCLIPS LIVED

CHAPTER TEN

THE travelers had taken no provisions with them because they knew that they would be welcomed wherever they might go in the Land of Oz, and that the people would feed and lodge them with genuine hospitality. So about noon they stopped at a farm-house and were given a delicious luncheon of bread and milk, fruits and wheat cakes with maple syrup. After resting a while and strolling through the orchards with their host—a round, jolly farmer—they got into the wagon and again started the Sawhorse along the pretty, winding road.

There were sign-posts at all the corners, and finally they came to one which read:

☛ TAKE THIS ROAD TO THE CUTTENCLIPS

Chapter Ten

There was also a hand pointing in the right direction, so they turned the Sawhorse that way and found it a very good road, but seemingly little traveled.

"I 've never been to see the Cuttenclips before," remarked Dorothy.

"Nor I," said the Captain General.

"Nor I," said the Wizard.

"Nor I," said Billina.

"I 've hardly been out of the Emerald City since I arrived in this country," added the Shaggy Man.

"Why, none of us has been there, then," exclaimed the little girl. "I wonder what the Cuttenclips are like."

"We shall soon find out," said the Wizard, with a sly laugh. "I 've heard they are rather flimsy things."

The farm-houses became fewer as they proceeded, and the path was at times so faint that the Sawhorse had hard work to keep in the road. The wagon began to jounce, too; so they were obliged to go slowly.

After a somewhat wearisome journey they came in sight of a high wall, painted blue with pink ornaments. This wall was circular, and seemed to enclose a large space. It was so high that only the tops of the trees could be seen above it.

The path led up to a small door in the wall, which was closed and latched. Upon the door was a sign in gold letters reading as follows:

VISITORS are requested to MOVE SLOWLY and CAREFULLY, and to avoid COUGHING or making any BREEZE or DRAUGHT

"That 's strange," said the Shaggy Man, reading the sign aloud. "Who *are* the Cuttenclips, anyhow?"

"Why, they 're paper dolls," answered Dorothy. "Did n't you know that?"

"Paper dolls! Then let 's go somewhere else," said Uncle Henry. "We 're all too old to play with dolls, Dorothy."

"But these are different," declared the girl. "They 're alive.

"Alive!" gasped Aunt Em, in amazement.

"Yes. Let 's go in," said Dorothy.

So they all got out of the wagon, since the door in the wall was not big enough for them to drive the Sawhorse and wagon through it.

"You stay here, Toto!" commanded Dorothy, shaking her finger at the little dog. "You 're so careless that you might make a breeze if I let you inside."

Toto wagged his tail as if disappointed at being left behind; but he made no effort to follow them. The Wizard unlatched the door, which opened outward, and they all looked eagerly inside.

Chapter Ten

Just before the entrance was drawn up a line of tiny soldiers, with uniforms brightly painted and paper guns upon their shoulders. They were exactly alike, from one end of the line to the other, and all were cut out of paper and joined together in the centers of their bodies.

As the visitors entered the enclosure the Wizard let the door swing back into place, and at once the line of soldiers tumbled over, fell flat upon their backs, and lay fluttering upon the ground.

"Hi, there!" called one of them; "what do you mean by slamming the door and blowing us over?"

"I beg your pardon, I 'm sure," said the Wizard, regretfully. "I did n't know you were so delicate."

"We 're not delicate!" retorted another soldier, raising his head from the ground. "We are strong and healthy; but we can't stand draughts."

"May I help you up?" asked Dorothy.

"If you please," replied the end soldier. "But do it gently, little girl."

Dorothy carefully stood up the line of soldiers, who first dusted their painted clothes and then saluted the visitors with their paper muskets. From the end it was easy to see that the entire line had been cut out of paper, although from the front the soldiers looked rather solid and imposing.

"I 've a letter of introduction from Princess Ozma to Miss Cuttenclip," announced Dorothy.

"Very well," said the end soldier, and blew upon a paper whistle that hung around his neck. At once a paper soldier in a Captain's uniform came out of a paper house near by and approached the group at the entrance. He was not very big, and he walked rather stiffly and uncertainly on his paper legs; but he had a pleasant face, with very red cheeks and very blue eyes, and he bowed so low to the strangers that Dorothy laughed, and the breeze from her mouth nearly blew the Captain over. He wavered and struggled and finally managed to remain upon his feet.

"Take care, Miss!" he said, warningly. "You 're breaking the rules, you know, by laughing."

"Oh, I did n't know that," she replied.

"To laugh in this place is nearly as dangerous as to cough," said the Captain. "You 'll have to breathe very quietly, I assure you."

"We 'll try to," promised the girl. "May we see Miss Cuttenclip, please?"

"You may," promptly returned the Captain. "This is one of her reception days. Be good enough to follow me."

He turned and led the way up a path, and as they followed slowly, because the paper Captain did not move very swiftly, they took the opportunity to gaze around them at this strange paper country.

Beside the path were paper trees, all cut out very neatly and painted a brilliant green color. And back of the trees were rows of cardboard houses, painted in various colors but most of them having green blinds. Some were large and some small, and in the front yards were beds of paper flowers quite natural in appearance. Over some of the porches paper vines were twined, giving them a cosy and shady look.

As the visitors passed along the street a good many paper dolls came to the doors and windows of their houses to look at them curiously. These dolls were nearly all the same height, but were cut into various shapes, some being fat and some lean. The girl dolls wore many beautiful costumes of tissue paper, making them quite fluffy; but their heads and hands were no thicker than the paper of which they were made.

Some of the paper people were on the street, walking along or congregated in groups and talking together; but as soon as they saw the strangers they all fluttered into the houses as fast as they could go, so as to be out of danger.

"Excuse me if I go edgewise," remarked the Captain, as they came to a slight hill. "I can get along faster that way and not flutter so much."

"That's all right," said Dorothy. "We don't mind how you go, I'm sure."

At one side of the street was a paper pump, and a paper boy was pumping paper water into a paper pail. The Yellow Hen happened to brush against this boy with her wing, and he flew into the air and fell into a paper tree, where he stuck until the Wizard gently pulled him out. At the same time the pail went soaring into the air, spilling the paper water, while the paper pump bent nearly double.

"Goodness me!" said the Hen. "If I should flop my wings I believe I'd knock over the whole village!"

"Then don't flop them—please don't!" entreated the Captain. "Miss Cuttenclip would be very much distressed if her village was spoiled."

"Oh, I'll be careful," promised Billina.

"Are not all these paper girls and women named Miss Cuttenclips?" inquired Omby Amby.

"No, indeed," answered the Captain, who was walking better since he began to move edgewise. "There is but one Miss Cuttenclip, who is our Queen, because she made us all. These girls are Cuttenclips, to be sure, but their names are Emily and Polly and Sue and Betty and such things. Only the Queen is called Miss Cuttenclip."

"I must say that this place beats anything I ever heard of," observed Aunt Em. "I used to play with paper dolls myself, an' cut 'em out; but I never thought I 'd ever see such things alive."

"I don't see as it 's any more curious than hearing hens talk," returned Uncle Henry.

"You 're likely to see many queer things in the Land of Oz, sir," said the Wizard. "But a fairy country is extremely interesting when you get used to being surprised."

"Here we are!" called the Captain, stopping before a cottage.

This house was made of wood, and was remarkably pretty in design. In the Emerald City it would have been considered a tiny dwelling, indeed; but in the midst of this paper village it seemed immense. Real flowers were in the garden and real trees grew beside it. Upon the front door was a sign reading:

MISS CUTTENCLIP.

Just as they reached the porch the front door opened and a little girl stood before them. She appeared to be about the same age as Dorothy, and smiling upon her visitors she said, sweetly:

"You are welcome."

All the party seemed relieved to find that here was a real girl, of flesh and blood. She was very dainty and pretty as she stood there welcoming them. Her hair was a golden blonde and her eyes turquoise blue. She had rosy cheeks and lovely white teeth. Over her simple white lawn dress she wore an apron with pink and white checks, and in one hand she held a pair of scissors.

"May we see Miss Cuttenclip, please?" asked Dorothy.

"I am Miss Cuttenclip," was the reply. "Won't you come in?"

She held the door open while they all entered a pretty sitting-room that was littered with all sorts of paper—some stiff, some thin, and some tissue. The sheets and scraps were of all colors. Upon a table were paints and brushes, while several pair of scissors, of different sizes, were lying about.

"Sit down, please," said Miss Cuttenclip, clearing the paper scraps off some of the chairs. "It is so long since I have had any visitors that I am not properly prepared to receive them. But I'm sure you will pardon my untidy room, for this is my workshop."

"Do you make all the paper dolls?" inquired Dorothy.

"Yes; I cut them out with my scissors, and paint the faces and some of the costumes. It is very pleasant work, and I am happy making my paper village grow."

"But how do the paper dolls happen to be alive?" asked Aunt Em.

"The first dolls I made were not alive," said Miss Cuttenclip. " I used to live near the castle of a great Sorceress named Glinda the Good, and she saw my dolls and said they were very pretty. I told her I thought I would like them better if they were alive, and the next day the Sorceress brought me a lot of magic paper. 'This is live paper,' she said, 'and all the dolls you cut out of it will be alive, and able to think and to talk. When you have used it all up, come to me and I will give you more.'

"Of course I was delighted with this present," continued Miss Cuttenclip, "and at once set to work and made several paper dolls, which, as soon as they were cut out, began to walk around and talk to me. But they were so thin that I found that any breeze would blow them over and scatter them dreadfully; so Glinda found this lonely place for me, where few people ever come. She built the wall to keep any wind from blowing away my people, and told me I could build a paper village here and be its Queen. That is why I came here and settled down to work and started the village you now see. It was many years ago that I built the first houses, and I've kept pretty busy and made my village grow finely; and I need not tell you that I am very happy in my work."

"Many years ago!" exclaimed Aunt Em. "Why, how old are you, child?"

"I never keep track of the years," said Miss Cuttenclip, laughing. "You see, I don't grow up at all, but stay just the same as I was when first I came here. Perhaps I 'm older even than you are, madam; but I could n't say for sure."

They looked at the lovely little girl wonderingly, and the Wizard asked:

"What happens to your paper village when it rains?"

"It does not rain here," replied Miss Cuttenclip. "Glinda keeps all the rain storms away; so I never worry about my dolls getting wet. But now, if you will come with me, it will give me pleasure to show you over my paper kingdom. Of course you must go slowly and carefully, and avoid making any breeze."

They left the cottage and followed their guide through the various streets of the village. It was indeed an amazing place, when one considered that it was all made with scissors, and the visitors were not only greatly interested but full of admiration for the skill of little Miss Cuttenclip.

In one place a large group of especially nice paper dolls assembled to greet their Queen, whom it was easy to see they loved dearly. These dolls marched and danced before the visitors, and then they all waved their paper handkerchiefs and sang in a sweet chorus a song called "The Flag of Our Native Land."

At the conclusion of the song they ran up a handsome paper flag on a tall flagpole, and all of the people of the village gathered around to cheer as loudly as they could—although, of course, their voices were not especially strong.

Miss Cuttenclip was about to make her subjects a speech in reply to this patriotic song, when the Shaggy Man happened to sneeze.

He was a very loud and powerful sneezer at any time, and he had tried so hard to hold in this sneeze that when it suddenly exploded the result was terrible.

The paper dolls were mowed down by dozens, and flew and fluttered in wild confusion in every direction, tumbling this way and that and getting more or less wrinkled and bent.

A wail of terror and grief came from the scattered throng, and Miss Cuttenclip exclaimed:

"Dear me! dear me!" and hurried at once to the rescue of her overturned people.

"Oh, Shaggy Man! How could you?" asked Dorothy, reproachfully.

"I could n't help it—really I could n't," protested the Shaggy Man, looking quite ashamed. "And I had no idea it took so little to upset these paper dolls."

"So little!" said Dorothy. "Why, it was 'most as bad as a Kansas cyclone." And then she helped Miss Cuttenclip rescue the paper folk and stand them on their feet again. Two of the cardboard houses had also tumbled over, and the little Queen said she would have to repair them and paste them together before they could be lived in again.

And now, fearing they might do more damage to the flimsy paper people, they decided to go away. But first they thanked Miss Cuttenclip very warmly for her courtesy and kindness to them.

"Any friend of Princess Ozma is always welcome here—unless he sneezes," said the Queen, with a rather severe look at the Shaggy Man, who hung his head. "I like to have visitors admire my wonderful village, and I hope you will call again."

Miss Cuttenclip ✂

Chapter Ten

Miss Cuttenclip herself led them to the door in the wall, and as they passed along the street the paper dolls peeped at them half fearfully from the doors and windows. Perhaps they will never forget the Shaggy Man's awful sneeze, and I am sure they were all glad to see the meat people go away.

How THE GENERAL MET THE FIRST AND FOREMOST

CHAPTER ELEVEN

ON leaving the Growleywogs General Guph had to recross the Ripple Lands, and he did not find it a pleasant thing to do. Perhaps having his whiskers pulled out one by one and being used as a pin-cushion for the innocent amusement of a good natured jailor had not improved the quality of Guph's temper, for the old Nome raved and raged at the recollection of the wrongs he had suffered, and vowed to take vengeance upon the Growleywogs after he had used them for his purposes and Oz had been conquered. He went on in this furious way until he was half across the Ripple Land. Then he became seasick, and the rest of the way this naughty Nome was almost as miserable as he deserved to be.

But when he reached the plains again and the ground was firm under his feet he began to feel better, and instead of going back home he turned directly west. A squirrel, perched in a tree, saw him take this road and called to him warningly: "Look out!" But he paid no attention. An eagle paused in its flight through the air to look at him wonderingly and say: "Look out!" But on he went.

No one can say that Guph was not brave, for he had determined to visit those dangerous creatures the Phanfasms, who resided upon the very top of the dread Mountain of Phantastico. The Phanfasms were Erbs, and so dreaded by mortals and immortals alike that no one had been near their mountain home for several thousand years. Yet General Guph hoped to induce them to join in his proposed warfare against the good and happy Oz people.

Guph knew very well that the Phanfasms would be almost as dangerous to the Nomes as they would to the Ozites, but he thought himself so clever that he believed that he could manage these strange creatures and make them obey him. And there was no doubt at all that if he could enlist the services of the Phanfasms their tremendous power, united to the strength of the Growleywogs and the cunning of the Whimsies would doom the Land of Oz to absolute destruction.

So the old Nome climbed the foothills and trudged along the wild mountain paths until he came to a big gully that encircled the Mountain of Phantastico and marked the boundary line of the dominion of the Phanfasms. This gully was about a third of the way up the mountain, and it was filled to the brim with red-hot molten lava, in which swam fire-serpents and poisonous salamanders. The heat from this mass and its poisonous smell were both so unbearable that even birds hesitated to fly over the gully, but circled around it. All living things kept away from the mountain.

Now Guph had heard, during his long lifetime, many tales of these dreaded Phanfasms; so he had heard of this barrier of melted lava, and also he had been told that there was a narrow bridge that spanned it in one place. So he walked along the edge until he found the bridge. It was a single arch of gray stone, and lying flat upon this bridge was a scarlet alligator, seemingly fast asleep.

When Guph stumbled over the rocks in approaching the bridge the creature opened its eyes, from which tiny flames shot in all directions, and after looking at the intruder very wickedly the scarlet alligator closed its eyelids again and lay still.

Guph saw there was no room for him to pass the alligator on the narrow bridge, so he called out to it:

"Good morning, friend. I don't wish to hurry you, but please tell me if you are coming down, or going up?"

"Neither," snapped the alligator, clicking its cruel jaws together.

The General hesitated.

"Are you likely to stay there long?" he asked.

"A few hundred years or so," said the alligator.

Guph softly rubbed the end of his nose and tried to think what to do.

"Do you know whether the First and Foremost Phanfasm of Phantastico is at home or not?" he presently inquired.

"I expect he is, seeing he is always at home," replied the alligator.

"Ah; who is that coming down the mountain?" asked the Nome, gazing upward.

The alligator turned to look over its shoulder, and at once Guph ran to the bridge and leaped over the sentinel's back before it could turn back again. The scarlet monster made a snap at the Nome's left foot, but missed it by fully an inch.

"Ah ha!" laughed the General, who was now on the mountain path. "I fooled you that time."

"So you did; and perhaps you fooled yourself," retorted the alligator. "Go up the mountain, if you dare, and find out what the First and Foremost will do to you!"

"I will," declared Guph, boldly; and on he went up the path.

At first the scene was wild enough, but gradually it grew more and more awful in appearance. All the rocks had the shapes of frightful beings and even the tree trunks were gnarled and twisted like serpents.

Suddenly there appeared before the Nome a man with the head of an owl. His body was hairy, like that of an ape, and his only clothing was a scarlet scarf twisted around his waist. He bore a huge club in his hand and his round owl eyes blinked fiercely upon the intruder.

"What are you doing here?" he demanded, threatening Guph with his club.

"I've come to see the First and Foremost Phanfasm of Phantastico," replied the General, who did not like the way this creature looked at him, but still was not afraid.

"Ah; you shall see him!" the man said, with a sneering laugh. "The First and Foremost shall decide upon the best way to punish you."

"He will not punish me," returned Guph, calmly, "for I have come here to do him and his people a rare favor. Lead on, fellow, and take me directly to your master."

The owl-man raised his club with a threatening gesture.

"If you try to escape," he said, "beware—"

But here the General interrupted him.

"Spare your threats," said he, "and do not be impertinent, or I will have you severely punished. Lead on, and keep silent!"

This Guph was really a clever rascal, and it seems a pity he was so bad, for in a good cause he might have accomplished much. He realized that he had put himself into a dangerous position by coming to this dreadful mountain, but he also knew that if he showed fear he was lost. So he adopted a bold manner as his best defense. The wisdom of this plan was soon evident, for the Phanfasm with the owl's head turned and led the way up the mountain.

At the very top was a level plain, upon which were heaps of rock that at first glance seemed solid. But on looking closer Guph discovered that these rock heaps were dwellings, for each had an opening.

Not a person was to be seen outside the rock huts. All was silent.

The owl-man led the way among the groups of dwellings to one standing in the center. It seemed no better and no worse than any of the others. Outside the entrance to this rock heap the guide gave a low wail that sounded like "Lee-ow-ah!"

Suddenly there bounded from the opening another hairy man. This one wore the head of a bear. In his hand he bore a brass hoop. He glared at the stranger in evident surprise.

"Why have you captured this foolish wanderer and brought him here?" he demanded, addressing the owl-man.

"I did not capture him," was the answer. "He passed the scarlet alligator and came here of his own free will and accord."

The First and Foremost looked at the General.

"Have you tired of life, then?" he asked.

"No, indeed," answered Guph. "I am a Nome, and the Chief General of King Roquat the Red's great army of Nomes. I come of a long-lived race, and I may say that I expect to live a long time yet. Sit down, you Phanfasms—if you can find a seat in this wild haunt—and listen to what I have to say."

With all his knowledge and bravery General Guph did not know that the steady glare from the bear eyes was reading his inmost thoughts as surely as if they had been put into words. He did not know that these despised rock heaps of the Phanfasms were merely deceptions to his own eyes, nor could he guess that he was standing in the midst of one of the most splendid and luxurious cities ever built by magic power. All that he saw was a barren waste of rock heaps, a hairy man with an owl's head and another with a bear's head. The sorcery of the Phanfasms permitted him to see no more.

Suddenly the First and Foremost swung his brass hoop and caught Guph around the neck with it. The next instant, before the General could think what had happened to him, he was dragged inside the rock hut. Here, his eyes still blinded to realities, he perceived only a dim light, by which the hut seemed as rough and rude inside as it was outside. Yet he had a strange feeling that many bright eyes were fastened upon him and that he stood in a vast and extensive hall.

The First and Foremost now laughed grimly and released his prisoner.

"If you have anything to say that is interesting," he remarked, "speak out, before I strangle you."

So Guph spoke out. He tried not to pay any attention to a strange rustling sound that he heard, as of an unseen multitude drawing near to listen to his words. His eyes could see only the fierce bear-man, and to him he addressed his speech. First he told of his plan to conquer the Land of Oz and plunder the country of its riches and enslave its people, who, being fairies, could not be killed. After relating all this, and telling of the tunnel the Nome King was building, he said he had come to ask the First and Foremost to join the Nomes, with his band of terrible warriors, and help them to defeat the Oz people.

The General spoke very earnestly and impressively, but when he had finished the bear-man began to laugh as if much amused, and his laughter seemed to be echoed by a chorus of merriment from an unseen multitude. Then, for the first time, Guph began to feel a trifle worried.

"Who else has promised to help you?" finally asked the First and Foremost.

"The Whimsies," replied the General.

Again the bear-headed Phanfasm laughed.

"Any others?" he inquired.

Chapter Eleven

"Only the Growleywogs," said Guph.

This answer set the First and Foremost laughing anew.

"What share of the spoils am I to have?" was the next question.

"Anything you like, except King Roquat's Magic Belt," replied Guph.

At this the Phanfasm set up a roar of laughter, which had its echo in the unseen chorus, and the bear-man seemed so amused that he actually rolled upon the ground and shouted with merriment.

"Oh, these blind and foolish Nomes!" he said. "How big they seem to themselves and how small they really are!"

Suddenly he arose and seized Guph's neck with one hairy paw, dragging him out of the hut into the open.

Here he gave a curious wailing cry, and, as if in answer, from all the rocky huts on the mountain-top came flocking a horde of Phanfasms, all with hairy bodies, but wearing heads of various animals, birds and reptiles. All were ferocious and repulsive-looking to the deceived eyes of the Nome, and Guph could not repress a shudder of disgust as he looked upon them.

The First and Foremost slowly raised his arms, and in a twinkling his hairy skin fell from him and he appeared before the astonished Nome as a beautiful woman, clothed in a flowing gown of pink gauze. In her dark hair flowers were entwined, and her face was noble and calm.

At the same instant the entire band of Phanfasms was transformed into a pack of howling wolves, running here and there as they snarled and showed their ugly yellow fangs.

The woman now raised her arms, even as the man-bear had done, and in a twinkling the wolves became crawling lizards, while she herself changed into a huge butterfly.

Guph had only time to cry out in fear and take a step backward to avoid the lizards when another transformation occurred, and all returned instantly to the forms they had originally worn.

Then the First and Foremost, who had resumed his hairy body and bear head, turned to the Nome and asked:

"Do you still demand our assistance?"

"More than ever," answered the General, firmly.

"Then tell me: what can you offer the Phanfasms that they have not already?" inquired the First and Foremost.

Guph hesitated. He really did not know what to say. The Nome King's vaunted Magic Belt seemed a poor thing compared to the astonishing magical powers of these people. Gold, jewels and slaves they might secure in any quantity without especial effort. He felt that he was dealing with powers greatly beyond him. There was but one argument that might influence the Phanfasms, who were creatures of evil.

Chapter Eleven

"Permit me to call your attention to the exquisite joy of making the happy unhappy," said he at last. "Consider the pleasure of destroying innocent and harmless people."

"Ah! you have answered me," cried the First and Foremost. "For that reason alone we will aid you. Go home,

and tell your bandy-legged king that as soon as his tunnel is finished the Phanfasms will be with him and lead his legions to the conquest of Oz. The deadly desert alone has kept us from destroying Oz long ago, and your underground tunnel is a clever thought. Go home, and prepare for our coming!"

Guph was very glad to be permitted to go with this promise. The owl-man led him back down the mountain path and ordered the scarlet alligator to crawl away and allow the Nome to cross the bridge in safety.

After the visitor had gone a brilliant and gorgeous city appeared upon the mountain top, clearly visible to the eyes of the gaily dressed multitude of Phanfasms that lived there. And the First and Foremost, beautifully arrayed, addressed the others in these words:

"It is time we went into the world and brought sorrow and dismay to its people. Too long have we remained by ourselves upon this mountain top, for while we are thus secluded many nations have grown happy and prosperous, and the chief joy of the race of Phanfasms is to destroy happiness. So I think it is lucky that this messenger from the Nomes arrived among us just now, to remind us that the opportunity has come for us to make trouble. We will use King Roquat's tunnel to conquer the Land of Oz. Then we will destroy the Whimsies, the Growleywogs and the Nomes, and afterward go out to ravage and annoy and grieve the whole world."

The multitude of evil Phanfasms eagerly applauded this plan, which they fully approved.

I am told that the Erbs are the most powerful and merciless of all the evil spirits, and the Phanfasms of Phantastico belong to the race of Erbs.

How THEY MATCHED THE FUDDLES

CHAPTER TWELVE

DOROTHY and her fellow travelers rode away from the Cuttenclip village and followed the indistinct path as far as the sign-post. Here they took the main road again and proceeded pleasantly through the pretty farming country. When evening came they stopped at a dwelling and were joyfully welcomed and given plenty to eat and good beds for the night.

Early next morning, however, they were up and eager to start, and after a good breakfast they bade their host good-bye and climbed into the red wagon, to which the Sawhorse had been hitched all night. Being made of wood, this horse never got tired nor cared to lie down. Dorothy was not quite sure whether he ever slept or not, but it was certain that he never did when anybody was around.

The weather is always beautiful in Oz, and this morning

127

the air was cool and refreshing and the sunshine brilliant and delightful.

In about an hour they came to a place where another road branched off. There was a sign-post here which read:

☛ THIS WAY TO FUDDLECUMJIG

"Oh, here is where we turn," said Dorothy, observing the sign.

"What! Are we going to Fuddlecumjig?" asked the Captain General.

"Yes; Ozma thought we would enjoy the Fuddles. They are said to be very interesting," she replied.

"No one would suspect it from their name," said Aunt Em. "Who are they, anyhow? More paper things?"

"I think not," answered Dorothy, laughing; "but I can't say 'zactly, Aunt Em, what they are. We'll find out when we get there."

"Perhaps the Wizard knows," suggested Uncle Henry.

"No; I've never been there before," said the Wizard. "But I've often heard of Fuddlecumjig and the Fuddles, who are said to be the most peculiar people in all the Land of Oz."

"In what way?" asked the Shaggy Man.

"I don't know, I'm sure," said the Wizard.

Just then, as they rode along the pretty green lane to-

ward Fuddlecumjig, they espied a kangaroo sitting by the roadside. The poor animal had its face covered with both its front paws and was crying so bitterly that the tears coursed down its cheeks in two tiny streams and trickled across the road, where they formed a pool in a small hollow.

The Sawhorse stopped short at this pitiful sight, and Dorothy cried out, with ready sympathy:

"What 's the matter, Kangaroo?"

"Boo-hoo! Boo-hoo!" wailed the kangaroo; "I 've lost my mi—mi—mi—Oh, boo-hoo! Boo-hoo!" —

"Poor thing," said the Wizard, "she 's lost her mister. It 's probably her husband, and he 's dead."

'No, no, no!" sobbed the kangaroo. "It—it is n't that. I 've lost my mi—mi— Oh, boo, boo-hoo!"

"I know," said the Shaggy Man; "she 's lost her mirror."

"No; it 's my mi—mi—mi—Boo-hoo! My mi—Oh, Boo-hoo!" and the kangaroo cried harder than ever.

"It must be her mince-pie," suggested Aunt Em.

"Or her milk-toast," proposed Uncle Henry.

"I 've lost my mi—mi—mittens!" said the kangaroo, getting it out at last.

"Oh!" cried the Yellow Hen, with a cackle of relief. "Why did n't you say so before?"

"Boo-hoo! I—I—could n't," answered the kangaroo.

"But, see here," said Dorothy, "you don't need mittens in this warm weather."

"Yes, indeed I do," replied the animal, stopping her sobs and removing her paws from her face to look at the little girl reproachfully. "My hands will get all sunburned and tanned without my mittens, and I 've worn them so long that I 'll probably catch cold without them."

"Nonsense!" said Dorothy. "I never heard before of any kangaroo wearing mittens."

"Did n't you?" asked the animal, as if surprised

130

Chapter Twelve

"Never!" repeated the girl. "And you 'll probably make yourself sick if you don't stop crying. Where do you live?"

"About two miles beyond Fuddlecumjig," was the answer. "Grandmother Gnit made me the mittens, and she 's one of the Fuddles."

"Well, you 'd better go home now, and perhaps the old lady will make you another pair," suggested Dorothy. "We 're on our way to Fuddlecumjig, and you may hop along beside us."

So they rode on, and the kangaroo hopped beside the red wagon and seemed quickly to have forgotten her loss. By and by the Wizard said to the animal:

"Are the Fuddles nice people?"

"Oh, very nice," answered the kangaroo; "that is, when they 're properly put together. But they get dreadfully scattered and mixed up, at times, and then you can't do anything with them."

"What do you mean by their getting scattered?" inquired Dorothy.

"Why, they 're made in a good many small pieces," explained the kangaroo; "and whenever any stranger comes near them they have a habit of falling apart and scattering themselves around. That 's when they get so dreadfully mixed, and its a hard puzzle to put them together again."

"Who usually puts them together?" asked Omby Amby.

"Any one who is able to match the pieces. I sometimes put Grandmother Gnit together myself, because I know her so well I can tell every piece that belongs to her. Then, when she's all matched, she knits for me, and that's how she made my mittens. But it took a good many days hard knitting, and I had to put Grandmother together a good many times, because every time I came near she'd scatter herself."

"I should think she would get used to your coming, and not be afraid," said Dorothy.

"It is n't that," replied the kangaroo. "They 're not a bit afraid, when they 're put together, and usually they 're very jolly and pleasant. It 's just a habit they have, to scatter themselves, and if they did n't do it they would n't be Fuddles."

The travelers thought upon this quite seriously for a time, while the Sawhorse continued to carry them rapidly forward. Then Aunt Em remarked:

"I don't see much use our visitin' these Fuddles. If we find them scattered, all we can do is to sweep 'em up, and then go about our business."

"Oh, I b'lieve we 'd better go on," replied Dorothy. "I 'm getting hungry, and we must try to get some luncheon at Fuddlecumjig. Perhaps the food won't be scattered as badly as the people."

"You 'll find plenty to eat there," declared the kangaroo,

hopping along in big bounds because the Sawhorse was going so fast; "and they have a fine cook, too, if you can manage to put him together. There 's the town now—just ahead of us!"

They looked ahead and saw a group of very pretty houses standing in a green field a little apart from the main road.

"Some Munchkins came here a few days ago and matched a lot of people together," said the kangaroo. "I think they are together yet, and if you go softly, without making any noise, perhaps they won't scatter."

"Let 's try it," suggested the Wizard.

So they stopped the Sawhorse and got out of the wagon, and, after bidding good bye to the kangaroo, who hopped away home, they entered the field and very cautiously approached the group of houses.

So silently did they move that soon they saw through the windows of the houses, people moving around, while others were passing to and fro in the yards between the buildings. They seemed much like other people, from a distance, and apparently they did not notice the little party so quietly approaching.

They had almost reached the nearest house when Toto saw a large beetle crossing the path and barked loudly at it. Instantly a wild clatter was heard from the houses and yards. Dorothy thought it sounded like a sudden hailstorm, and the visitors, knowing that caution was no longer necessary, hurried forward to see what had happened.

After the clatter an intense stillness reigned in the town. The strangers entered the first house they came to, which was also the largest, and found the floor strewn with pieces of the people who lived there. They looked much like fragments of wood neatly painted, and were of all sorts of curious and fantastic shapes, no two pieces being in any way alike.

They picked up some of these pieces and looked at them carefully. On one which Dorothy held was an eye, which looked at her pleasantly but with an interested expression, as if it wondered what she was going to do with it. Quite near by she discovered and picked up a nose, and by matching the two pieces together found that they were part of a face.

"If I could find the mouth," she said, "this Fuddle might be able to talk, and tell us what to do next."

"Then let us find it," replied the Wizard, and so all got down on their hands and knees and began examing the scattered pieces.

"I've found it!" cried the Shaggy Man, and ran to Dorothy with a queer-shaped piece that had a mouth on it. But when they tried to fit it to the eye and nose they found the parts would n't match together.

"That mouth belongs to some other person," said Dorothy. "You see we need a curve here and a point there, to make it fit the face."

"Well, it must be here some place," declared the Wizard; "so if we search long enough we shall find it."

Dorothy fitted an ear on next, and the ear had a little patch of red hair above it. So while the others were searching for the mouth she hunted for pieces with red hair, and found several of them which, when matched to the other pieces, formed the top of a man's head. She had also found the other eye and the ear by the time Omby Amby in a far corner discovered the mouth. When the face was thus completed all the parts joined together with a nicety that was astonishing.

"Why, it 's like a picture puzzle!" exclaimed the little girl. "Let 's find the rest of him, and get him all together."

"What 's the rest of him like?" asked the Wizard. "Here are some pieces of blue legs and green arms, but I don't know whether they are his or not."

"Look for a white shirt and a white apron," said the head which had been put together, speaking in a rather faint voice. "I 'm the cook."

"Oh, thank you," said Dorothy. "It 's lucky we started you first, for I 'm hungry, and you can be cooking something for us to eat while we match the other folks together."

It was not so very difficult, now that they had a hint as to how the man was dressed, to find the other pieces belonging to him, and as all of them now worked on the cook, trying piece after piece to see if it would fit, they finally had the cook set up complete.

When he was finished he made them a low bow and said:

"I will go at once to the kitchen and prepare your dinner. You will find it something of a job to get all the Fuddles together, so I advise you to begin on the Lord High Chigglewitz, whose first name is Larry. He 's a bald-headed fat man and is dressed in a blue coat with brass buttons, a pink vest and drab breeches. A piece of his left knee is missing, having been lost years ago when he scattered himself too carelessly. That makes him limp a little, but he gets along very well with half a knee. As he is the chief personage in this town of Fuddlecumjig, he will be able to welcome you and assist you with the others. So it will be best to work on him while I 'm getting your dinner."

"We will," said the Wizard; "and thank you very much, Cook, for the suggestion."

Aunt Em was the first to discover a piece of the Lord High Chigglewitz.

"It seems to me like a fool business, this matching folks together," she remarked; "but as we have n't anything to do till dinner 's ready we may as well get rid of some of this rubbish. Here, Henry, get busy and look for Larry's bald head. I 've got his pink vest, all right."

They worked with eager interest, and Billina proved a great help to them. The Yellow Hen had sharp eyes and could put her head close to the various pieces that lay scattered around. She would examine the Lord High Chigglewitz and see which piece of him was next needed, and then hunt around until she found it. So before an hour had passed old Larry was standing complete before them.

"I congratulate you, my friends," he said, speaking in a cheerful voice. "You are certainly the cleverest people who ever visited us. I was never matched together so quickly in my life. I 'm considered a great puzzle, usually."

"Well," said Dorothy, "there used to be a picture puzzle craze in Kansas, and so I 've had some 'sperience matching puzzles. But the pictures were flat, while you are round, and that makes you harder to figure out."

"Thank you, my dear," replied old Larry, greatly pleased. "I feel highly complimented. Were I not a really good puzzle there would be no object in my scattering myself."

"Why do you do it?" asked Aunt Em, severely. "Why don't you behave yourself, and stay put together?"

The Lord High Chigglewitz seemed annoyed **by** this speech; but he replied, politely:

"Madam, you have perhaps noticed that every **person**

has some peculiarity. Mine is to scatter myself. What your own peculiarity is I will not venture to say; but I shall never find fault with you, whatever you do."

"Now, you 've got your diploma, Em," said Uncle Henry, with a laugh, "and I 'm glad of it. This is a queer country, and we may as well take people as we find them."

"If we did, we 'd leave these folks scattered," she returned, and this retort made everybody laugh good-naturedly.

Just then Omby Amby found a hand with a knitting needle in it, and they decided to put Grandmother Gnit together. She proved an easier puzzle than old Larry, and when she was completed they found her a pleasant old lady who welcomed them cordially. Dorothy told her how the kangaroo had lost her mittens, and Grandmother Gnit promised to set to work at once and make the poor animal another pair.

Then the cook came to call them to dinner, and they found an inviting meal prepared for them. The Lord High Chigglewitz sat at the head of the table and Grandmother Gnit at the foot, and the guests had a merry time and thoroughly enjoyed themselves.

After dinner they went out into the yard and matched several other people together, and this work was so interesting that they might have spent the entire day at Fuddlecumjig had not the Wizard suggested that they resume their journey.

"But I don't like to leave all these poor people scattered," said Dorothy, undecided what to do.

"Oh, don't mind us, my dear," returned old Larry.

"Every day or so some of the Gillikins, or Munchkins, or Winkies come here to amuse themselves by matching us together, so there will be no harm in leaving these pieces where they are for a time. But I hope you will visit us again, and if you do you will always be welcome, I assure you."

"Don't you ever match each other?" she inquired.

"Never; for we are no puzzles to ourselves, and so there would n't be any fun in it."

They now said goodbye to the queer Fuddles and got into their wagon to continue their journey.

"Those are certainly strange people," remarked Aunt Em, thoughfully, as they drove away from Fuddlecumjig, "but I really can't see what use they are, at all."

"Why, they amused us all for several hours," replied the Wizard. "That is being of use to us, I 'm sure."

"I think they 're more fun than playing solitaire or mumbletypeg," declared Uncle Henry, soberly. "For my part, I 'm glad we visited the Fuddles."

How THE GENERAL TALKED TO THE KING

CHAPTER THIRTEEN

WHEN General Guph returned to the cavern of the Nome King his Majesty asked:

"Well, what luck? Will the Whimsies join us?"

"They will," answered the General. "They will fight for us with all their strength and cunning."

"Good!" exclaimed the King. "What reward did you promise them?"

"Your Majesty is to use the Magic Belt to give each Whimsie a large, fine head, in place of the small one he is now obliged to wear."

"I agree to that," said the King. "This is good news, Guph, and it makes me feel more certain of the conquest of Oz."

"But I have other news for you," announced the General.

"Good or bad?"

141

"Good, your Majesty."

"Then I will hear it," said the King, with interest.

"The Growleywogs will join us."

"No!" cried the astonished King.

"Yes, indeed," said the General. "I have their promise."

"But what reward do they demand?" inquired the King, suspiciously, for he knew how greedy the Growleywogs were.

"They are to take a few of the Oz people for their slaves," replied Guph. He did not think it necessary to tell Roquat that the Growleywogs demanded twenty thousand slaves. It would be time enough for that when Oz was conquered.

"A very reasonable request, I 'm sure," remarked the King. "I must congratulate you, Guph, upon the wonderful success of your journey."

"But that is not all," said the General, proudly.

The King seemed astonished.

"Speak out, sir!" he commanded.

"I have seen the First and Foremost Phanfasm of the Mountain of Phantastico, and he will bring his people to assist us."

"What!" cried the King. "The Phanfasms! You don't mean it, Guph!"

"It is true," declared the General, proudly.

The King became thoughtful, and his brows wrinkled.

Chapter Thirteen

"I'm afraid, Guph," he said rather anxiously, "that the First and Foremost may prove as dangerous to us as to the Oz people. If he and his terrible band come down from the mountain they may take the notion to conquer the Nomes!"

"Pah! That is a foolish idea," retorted Guph, irritably, but he knew in his heart that the King was right. "The First and Foremost is a particular friend of mine, and will do us no harm. Why, when I was there, he even invited me into his house."

The General neglected to tell the King how he had been jerked into the hut of the First and Foremost by means of the brass hoop. So Roquat the Red looked at his General admiringly and said:

"You are a wonderful Nome, Guph. I'm sorry I did not make you my General before. But what reward did the First and Foremost demand?"

"Nothing at all," answered Guph. "Even the Magic Belt itself could not add to his powers of sorcery. All the Phanfasms wish is to destroy the Oz people, who are good and happy. This pleasure will amply repay them for assisting us."

"When will they come?" asked Roquat, half fearfully.

"When the tunnel is completed," said the General.

"We are nearly half way under the desert now," announced the King; "and that is fast work, because the tunnel has to be drilled through solid rock. But after we have passed the desert it will not take us long to extend the tunnel to the walls of the Emerald City."

"Well, whenever you are ready, we shall be joined by the Whimsies, the Growleywogs and the Phanfasms," said Guph; "so the conquest of Oz is assured without a doubt."

Again the King seemed thoughtful.

"I 'm almost sorry we did not undertake the conquest alone," said he. "All of these allies are dangerous people, and they may demand more than you have promised them. It might have been better to have conquered Oz without any outside assistance."

"We could not do it," said the General, positively.

"Why not, Guph?"

"You know very well. You have had one experience with the Oz people, and they defeated you."

"That was because they rolled eggs at us," replied the King, with a shudder. "My Nomes cannot stand eggs, any more than I can myself. They are poison to all who live underground."

"That is true enough," agreed Guph.

"But we might have taken the Oz people by surprise, and conquered them before they had a chance to get any eggs. Our former defeat was due to the fact that the girl Dorothy had a Yellow Hen with her. I do not know what ever be-

"I'M THE COOK".

came of that hen, but I believe there are no hens at all in the Land of Oz, and so there could be no eggs there."

"On the contrary," said Guph, "there are now hundreds of chickens in Oz, and they lay heaps of those dangerous eggs. I met a goshawk on my way home, and the bird informed me that he had lately been to Oz to capture and devour some of

the young chickens. But they are protected by magic, so tne hawk did not get a single one of them."

"That is a very bad report," said the King, nervously. "Very bad, indeed. My Nomes are willing to fight, but they simply can't face hen's eggs—and I don't blame them."

'They won't need to face them," replied Guph. "I 'm afraid of eggs myself, and don't propose to take any chances of being poisoned by them. My plan is to send the Whimsies through the tunnel first, and then the Growleywogs and the Phanfasms. By the time we Nomes get there the eggs will all be used up, and we may then pursue and capture the inhabitants at our leisure."

"Perhaps you are right," returned the King, with a dismal sigh. "But I want it distinctly understood that I claim Ozma and Dorothy as my own prisoners. They are rather nice girls, and I do not intend to let any of those dreadful creatures hurt them, or make them their slaves. When I have captured them I will bring them here and transform them into china ornaments to stand on my mantle. They will look very pretty—Dorothy on one end of the mantle and Ozma on the other—and I shall take great care to see they are not broken when the maids dust them."

"Very well, your Majesty. Do what you will with the girls, for all I care. Now that our plans are arranged, and we have the three most powerful bands of evil spirits in the world to assist us, let us make haste to get the tunnel finished as soon as possible."

"It will be ready in three days," promised the King, and hurried away to inspect the work and see that the Nomes kept busy.

How THE WIZARD PRACTICED SORCERY

CHAPTER FOURTEEN

"WHERE next?" asked the Wizard, when they had left the town of Fuddlecumjig and the Sawhorse had started back along the road.

"Why, Ozma laid out this trip," replied Dorothy, "and she 'vised us to see the Rigmaroles next, and then visit the Tin Woodman."

"That sounds good," said the Wizard. "But what road do we take to get to the Rigmaroles?"

"I don't know, 'zactly," returned the little girl; "but it must be somewhere just southwest from here."

"Then why need we go way back to the crossroads?" asked the Shaggy Man. "We might save a lot of time by branching off here."

"There is n't any path," asserted Uncle Henry.

"Then we 'd better go back to the signposts, and make sure of our way," decided Dorothy.

But after they had gone a short distance farther the Sawhorse, who had overheard their conversation, stopped and said:

"Here is a path."

Sure enough, a dim path seemed to branch off from the road they were on, and it led across pretty green meadows and past leafy groves, straight toward the southwest.

"That looks like a good path," said Omby Amby. "Why not try it?"

"All right," answered Dorothy. "I 'm anxious to see what the Rigmaroles are like, and this path ought to take us there the quickest way."

No one made any objection to the plan, so the Sawhorse turned into the path, which proved to be nearly as good as the one they had taken to get to the Fuddles.

At first they passed a few retired farm houses, but soon these scattered dwellings were left behind and only the meadows and the trees were before them. But they rode along in cheerful contentment, and Aunt Em got into an argument with Billina about the proper way to raise chickens.

"I do not care to contradict you," said the Yellow Hen, with dignity, "but I have an idea I know more about chickens than human beings do."

"Pshaw!" replied Aunt Em, "I 've raised chickens for nearly forty years, Billina, and I know you 've got to starve 'em to make 'em lay lots of eggs, and stuff 'em if you want good broilers."

"Broilers!" exclaimed Billina, in horror. "Broil my chickens!"

"Why, that 's what they 're for, ain't it?" asked Aunt Em, astonished.

"No, Aunt, not in Oz," said Dorothy. "People do not eat chickens here. You see, Billina was the first hen that was ever seen in this country, and I brought her here myself. Everybody liked her an' respected her, so the Oz people would n't any more eat her chickens than they would eat Billina."

"Well, I declare," gasped Aunt Em. "How about the eggs?"

"Oh, if we have more eggs than we want to hatch, we allow people to eat them," said Billina. "Indeed, I am very glad the Oz folks like our eggs, for otherwise they would spoil."

"This certainly is a queer country," sighed Aunt Em.

"Excuse me," called the Sawhorse, "the path has ended and I 'd like to know which way to go."

They looked around and, sure enough, there was no path to be seen.

"Well," said Dorothy, "we 're going southwest, and it seems just as easy to follow that direction without a path as with one."

"Certainly," answered the Sawhorse. "It is not hard to draw the wagon over the meadow. I only want to know where to go."

"There 's a forest over there across the prairie," said the Wizard, "and it lies in the direction we are going. Make straight for the forest, Sawhorse, and you 're bound to go right."

So the wooden animal trotted on again and the meadow grass was so soft under the wheels that it made easy riding. But Dorothy was a little uneasy at losing the path, because now there was nothing to guide them.

No houses were to be seen at all, so they could not ask their way of any farmer; and although the Land of Oz was always beautiful, wherever one might go, this part of the country was strange to all the party.

"Perhaps we 're lost," suggested Aunt Em, after they had proceeded quite a way in silence.

"Never mind," said the Shaggy Man; "I've been lost many a time—and so has Dorothy—and we 've always been found again."

"But we may get hungry," remarked Omby Amby.

"That is the worst of getting lost in a place where there are no houses near."

"We had a good dinner at the Fuddle town," said Uncle Henry, "and that will keep us from starving to death for a long time."

"No one ever starved to death in Oz," declared Dorothy, positively; "but people may get pretty hungry sometimes."

The Wizard said nothing, and he did not seem especially anxious. The Sawhorse was trotting along briskly, yet the forest seemed farther away than they had thought when they first saw it. So it was nearly sundown when they finally came to the trees; but now they found themselves in a most beautiful spot, the wide-spreading trees being covered with flowering vines and having soft mosses underneath them.

"This will be a good place to camp," said the Wizard, as the Sawhorse stopped for further instructions.

"Camp!" they all echoed.

"Certainly," asserted the Wizard. "It will be dark before very long and we cannot travel through this forest at night. So let us make a camp here, and have some supper, and sleep until daylight comes again."

They all looked at the little man in astonishment, and Aunt Em said, with a sniff:

"A pretty camp we'll have, I must say! I suppose you intend us to sleep under the wagon."

"And chew grass for our supper," added the Shaggy Man, laughing.

But Dorothy seemed to have no doubts and was quite cheerful.

"It 's lucky we have the wonderful Wizard with us," she said; "because he can do 'most anything he wants to."

"Oh, yes; I forgot we had a Wizard," said Uncle Henry, looking at the little man curiously.

"I did n't," chirped Billina, contentedly.

The Wizard smiled and climbed out of the wagon, and all the others followed him.

"In order to camp," said he, "the first thing we need is tents. Will some one please lend me a handkerchief?"

The Shaggy Man offered him one, and Aunt Em another. He took them both and laid them carefully upon the grass near to the edge of the forest. Then he laid his own handkerchief down, too, and standing a little back from them he waved his left hand toward the handkerchiefs and said:

"Tents of canvas, white as snow,
Let me see how fast you grow!"

Then, lo and behold! the handkerchiefs became tiny tents, and as the travelers looked at them the tents grew bigger and bigger until in a few minutes each one was large enough to contain the entire party.

"This," said the Wizard, pointing to the first tent, "is

for the accomodation of the ladies. Dorothy, you and your Aunt may step inside and take off your things."

Every one ran to look inside the tent, and they saw two pretty white beds, all ready for Dorothy and Aunt Em, and a silver roost for Billina. Rugs were spread upon the grassy floor and some camp chairs and a table completed the furniture.

"Well, well, well! This beats anything I ever saw or heard of!" exclaimed Aunt Em, and she glanced at the Wizard almost fearfully, as if he might be dangerous because of his great powers.

"Oh, Mr. Wizard! How did you manage to do it?" asked Dorothy.

"It's a trick Glinda the Sorceress taught me, and it is much better magic than I used to practise in Omaha, or when I first came to Oz," he answered. "When the Good Glinda found I was to live in the Emerald City always, she promised to help me, because she said the Wizard of Oz ought really to be a clever Wizard, and not a humbug. So we have been much together and I am learning so fast that I expect to be able to accomplish some really wonderful things in time."

"You've done it now!" declared Dorothy. "These tents are just wonderful!"

"But come and see the men's tent," said the Wizard. So

they went to the second tent, which had shaggy edges because it had been made from the Shaggy Man's handkerchief, and found that completely furnished also. It contained four neat beds for Uncle Henry, Omby Amby, the Shaggy Man' and the Wizard. Also there was a soft rug for Toto to lie upon.

"The third tent," explained the Wizard, "is our dining room and kitchen."

They visited that next, and found a table and dishes in the dining tent, with plenty of those things necessary to use in cooking. The Wizard carried out a big kettle and set it swinging on a crossbar before the tent. While he was doing this Omby Amby and the Shaggy Man brought a supply of twigs from the forest and then they built a fire underneath the kettle.

"Now, Dorothy," said the Wizard, smiling, "I expect you to cook our supper."

"But there is nothing in the kettle," she cried.

"Are you sure?" inquired the Wizard.

"I did n't see anything put in, and I 'm almost sure it was empty when you brought it out," she replied.

"Nevertheless," said the little man, winking slyly at Uncle Henry, "you will do well to watch our supper, my dear, and see that it does n't boil over."

Then the men took some pails and went into the forest

to search for a spring of water, and while they were gone Aunt Em said to Dorothy:

"I believe the Wizard is fooling us. I saw the kettle myself, and when he hung it over the fire there was n't a thing in it but air."

"Don't worry," remarked Billina, confidently, as she

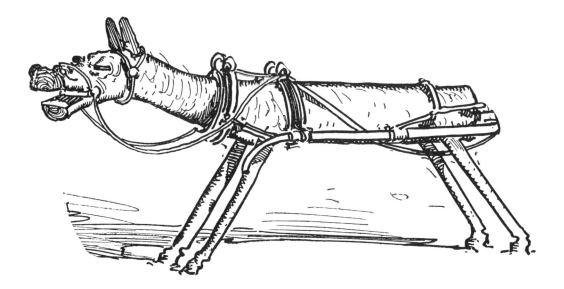

nestled in the grass before the fire. "You 'll find something in the kettle when it 's taken off—and it won't be poor, innocent chickens, either."

"Your hen has very bad manners, Dorothy," said Aunt Em, looking somewhat disdainfully at Billina. "It seems too bad she ever learned how to talk."

155

There might have been another unpleasant quarrel between Aunt Em and Billina had not the men returned just then with their pails filled with clear, sparkling water. The Wizard told Dorothy that she was a good cook and he believed their supper was ready.

So Uncle Henry lifted the kettle from the fire and poured its contents into a big platter which the Wizard held for him. The platter was fairly heaped with a fine stew, smoking hot, with many kinds of vegetables and dumplings and a rich, delicious gravy.

The Wizard triumphantly placed the platter upon the table in the dining tent and then they all sat down in camp chairs to the feast.

There were several other dishes on the table, all carefully covered, and when the time came to remove these covers they found bread and butter, cakes, cheese, pickles and fruits— including some of the luscious strawberries of Oz.

No one ventured to ask a question as to how these things came there. They contented themselves by eating heartily the good things provided, and Toto and Billina had their full share, you may be sure. After the meal was over Aunt Em whispered to Dorothy:

"That may have been magic food, my dear, and for that reason perhaps it won't be very nourishing; but I 'm willing to say it tasted as good as anything I ever et." Then she added, in a louder tone: "Who 's going to do the dishes?"

"No one, madam," answered the Wizard. "The dishes have 'done' themselves."

"La sakes!" ejaculated the good lady, holding up her hands in amazement. For, sure enough, when she looked at the dishes they had a moment before left upon the table, she found them all washed and dried and piled up into neat stacks.

How DOROTHY HAPPENED TO GET LOST

CHAPTER FIFTEEN

IT was a beautiful evening, so they drew their camp chairs in a circle before one of the tents and began to tell stories to amuse themselves and pass away the time before they went to bed.

Pretty soon a zebra was seen coming out of the forest, and he trotted straight up to them and said politely:

"Good evening, people."

The zebra was a sleek little animal and had a slender head, a stubby mane and a paint-brush tail—very like a donkey's. His neatly shaped white body was covered with regular bars of dark brown, and his hoofs were delicate as those of a deer.

"Good evening, friend Zebra," said Omby Amby, in reply to the creature's greeting. "Can we do anything for you?"

Chapter Fifteen

"Yes," answered the zebra. "I should like you to settle a dispute that has long been a bother to me, as to whether there is more water or land in the world."

"Who are you disputing with?" asked the Wizard.

"With a soft-shell crab," said the zebra. "He lives in a pool where I go to drink every day, and he is a very impertinent crab, I assure you. I have told him many times that the land is much greater in extent than the water, but he will not be convinced. Even this very evening, when I told him he was an insignificant creature who lived in a small pool, he asserted that the water was greater and more important than the land. So, seeing your camp, I decided to ask you to settle the dispute for once and all, that I may not be further annoyed by this ignorant crab."

When they had listened to this explanation Dorothy inquired:

"Where is the soft-shell crab?"

"Not far away," replied the zebra. "If you will agree to judge between us I will run and get him."

"Run along, then," said the little girl.

So the animal pranced into the forest and soon came trotting back to them. When he drew near they found a soft-shell crab clinging fast to the stiff hair of the zebra's head, where it held on by one claw.

"Now then, Mr. Crab," said the zebra, "here are the people I told you about; and they know more than you do, who live in a pool, and more than I do, who live in a forest. For they have been travelers all over the world, and know every part of it."

"There's more of the world than Oz," declared the crab, in a stubborn voice.

"That is true," said Dorothy; "but I used to live in Kansas, in the United States, and I've been to California and to Australia—and so has Uncle Henry."

"For my part," added the Shaggy Man, "I've been to Mexico and Boston and many other foreign countries."

"And I," said the Wizard, "have been to Europe and Ireland."

"So you see," continued the zebra, addressing the crab, "here are people of real consequence, who know what they are talking about."

"Then they know there's more water in the world than there is land," asserted the crab, in a shrill, petulant voice.

"They know you are wrong to make such an absurd statement, and they will probably think you are a lobster instead of a crab," retorted the animal.

At this taunt the crab reached out its other claw and seized the zebra's ear, and the creature gave a cry of pain and began prancing up and down, trying to shake off the crab, which clung fast.

"HALT!"

Chapter Fifteen

"Stop pinching!" cried the zebra. "You promised not to pinch if I would carry you here!"

"And you promised to treat me respectfully," said the crab, letting go the ear.

"Well, have n't I?" demanded the zebra.

"No; you called me a lobster," said the crab.

"Ladies and gentlemen," continued the zebra, "please pardon my poor friend, because he is ignorant and stupid, and does not understand. Also the pinch of his claw is very annoying. So pray tell him that the world contains more land than water, and when he has heard your judgment I will carry him back and dump him into his pool, where I hope he will be more modest in the future."

"But we cannot tell him that," said Dorothy, gravely, "because it would not be true."

"What!" exclaimed the zebra, in astonishment; "do I hear you aright?"

"The soft-shell crab is correct," declared the Wizard. "There is considerably more water than there is land in the world."

"Impossible!" protested the zebra. "Why, I can run for days upon the land, and find but little water."

"Did you ever see an ocean?" asked Dorothy.

"Never," admitted the zebra. "There is no such thing as an ocean in the Land of Oz."

"Well, there are several oceans in the world," said Dorothy, "and people sail in ships upon these oceans for weeks and weeks, and never see a bit of land at all. And the joggerfys will tell you that all the oceans put together are bigger than all the land put together."

At this the crab began laughing in queer chuckles that reminded Dorothy of the way Billina sometimes cackled.

"*Now* will you give up, Mr. Zebra?" it cried, jeeringly; "now will you give up?"

The zebra seemed much humbled.

"Of course I cannot read geographys," he said.

"You could take one of the Wizard's School Pills," suggested Billina, "and that would make you learned and wise without studying."

The crab began laughing again, which so provoked the zebra that he tried to shake the little creature off. This resulted in more ear-pinching, and finally Dorothy told them that if they could not behave they must go back to the forest.

"I'm sorry I asked you to decide this question," said the zebra, crossly. "So long as neither of us could prove we were right we quite enjoyed the dispute; but now I can never drink at that pool again without the soft-shell crab laughing at me. So I must find another drinking place."

"Do! Do, you ignoramus!" shouted the crab, as loudly

as his little voice would carry. "Rile some other pool with your clumsy hoofs, and let your betters alone after this!"

Then the zebra trotted back to the forest, bearing the crab with him, and disappeared amid the gloom of the trees. And as it was now getting dark the travelers said good night to one another and went to bed.

Dorothy awoke just as the light was beginning to get strong next morning, and not caring to sleep any later she quietly got out of bed, dressed herself, and left the tent where Aunt Em was yet peacefully slumbering.

Outside she noticed Billina busily pecking around to secure bugs or other food for breakfast, but none of the men in the other tent seemed awake. So the little girl decided to take a walk in the woods and try to discover some path or road that they might follow when they again started upon their journey.

She had reached the edge of the forest when the Yellow Hen came fluttering along and asked where she was going.

"Just to take a walk, Billina; and maybe I'll find some path," said Dorothy.

"Then I'll go along," decided Billina, and scarcely had she spoken when Toto ran up and joined them.

Toto and the Yellow Hen had become quite friendly by this time, although at first they did not get along well together. Billina had been rather suspicious of dogs, and Toto had had an idea that it was every dog's duty to chase a hen on sight. But Dorothy had talked to them and scolded them for not being agreeable to one another until they grew better acquainted and became friends.

I won't say they loved each other dearly, but at least they had stopped quarreling and now managed to get on together very well.

The day was growing lighter every minute and driving the black shadows out of the forest; so Dorothy found it very pleasant walking under the trees. She went some distance in one direction, but not finding a path, presently turned in a different direction. There was no path here, either, although she advanced quite a way into the forest, winding here and there among the trees and peering through the bushes in an endeavor to find some beaten track.

"I think we'd better go back," suggested the Yellow Hen, after a time. "The people will all be up by this time and breakfast will be ready."

"Very well," agreed Dorothy. "Let 's see—the camp must be over this way."

She had probably made a mistake about that, for after they had gone far enough to have reached the camp they still found themselves in the thick of the woods. So the little girl stopped short and looked around her, and Toto glanced up into her face with his bright little eyes and wagged his tail as if he knew something was wrong. He could n't tell much about direction himself, because he had spent his time prowling among the bushes and running here and there; nor had Billina paid much attention to where they were going, being interested in picking bugs from the moss as they passed along. The Yellow Hen now turned one eye up toward the little girl and asked:

"Have you forgotten where the camp is, Dorothy?"

"Yes," she admitted; "have you, Billina?"

"I did n't try to remember," returned Billina. "I 'd no idea you would get lost, Dorothy."

"It 's the thing we don't expect, Billina, that usually happens," observed the girl, thoughtfully. "But it 's no use standing here. Let 's go in that direction," pointing a finger at random. "It may be we 'll get out of the forest over there."

So on they went again, but this way the trees were closer together, and the vines were so tangled that often they tripped Dorothy up.

Suddenly a voice cried sharply:

"Halt!"

At first Dorothy could see nothing, although she looked around very carefully. But Billina exclaimed:

"Well, I declare!"

"What is it?" asked the little girl: for Toto began barking at something, and following his gaze she discovered what it was.

A row of spoons had surrounded the three, and these spoons stood straight up on their handles and carried swords and muskets. Their faces were outlined in the polished bowls and they looked very stern and severe.

Dorothy laughed at the queer things.

"Who are you?" she asked.

"We 're the Spoon Brigade," said one.

"In the service of his Majesty King Kleaver," said another.

"And you are our prisoners," said a third.

Chapter Fifteen

Dorothy sat down on an old stump and looked at them, her eyes twinkling with amusement.

"What would happen," she inquired, "if I should set my dog on your Brigade?"

"He would die," replied one of the spoons, sharply. "One shot from our deadly muskets would kill him, big as he is."

"Don't risk it, Dorothy," advised the Yellow Hen. "Remember this is a fairy country, yet none of us three happens to be a fairy."

Dorothy grew sober at this.

"P'raps you 're right, Billina," she answered. "But how funny it is, to be captured by a lot of spoons!"

"I do not see anything very funny about it," declared a spoon. "We 're the regular military brigade of the kingdom."

"What kingdom?" she asked.

"Utensia," said he.

"I never heard of it before," asserted Dorothy. Then she added, thoughtfully, "I don't believe Ozma ever heard of Utensia, either. Tell me, are you not subjects of Ozma of Oz?"

"We never have heard of her," retorted a spoon. "We are subjects of King Kleaver, and obey only his orders, which are to bring all prisoners to him as soon as they are captured. So step lively, my girl, and march with us, or we may be tempted to cut off a few of your toes with our swords."

This threat made Dorothy laugh again. She did not believe she was in any danger; but here was a new and interesting adventure, so she was willing to be taken to Utensia that she might see what King Kleaver's kingdom was like.

CHAPTER SIXTEEN

THERE must have been from six to eight dozen spoons in the Brigade, and they marched away in the shape of a hollow square, with Dorothy, Billina and Toto in the center of the square. Before they had gone very far Toto knocked over one of the spoons by wagging his tail, and then the Captain of the Spoons told the little dog to be more careful, or he would be punished. So Toto was careful, and the Spoon Brigade moved along with astonishing swiftness, while Dorothy really had to walk fast to keep up with it.

By and by they left the woods and entered a big clearing, in which was the Kingdom of Utensia.

Standing all around the clearing were a good many cookstoves, ranges and grills, of all sizes and shapes, and besides these there were several kitchen cabinets and cupboards and a few kitchen tables. These things were crowded with uten-

169

sils of all sorts: frying pans, sauce pans, kettles, forks, knives, basting and soup spoons, nutmeg graters, sifters, colenders, meat saws, flat irons, rolling pins and many other things of a like nature.

When the Spoon Brigade appeared with the prisoners a wild shout arose and many of the utensils hopped off their stoves or their benches and ran crowding around Dorothy and the hen and the dog.

"Stand back!" cried the Captain, sternly, and he led his captives through the curious throng until they came before a big range that stood in the center of the clearing. Beside this range was a butcher's block upon which lay a great cleaver with a keen edge. It rested upon the flat of its back, its legs were crossed and it was smoking a long pipe.

"Wake up, your Majesty," said the Captain. "Here are prisoners."

Hearing this, King Kleaver sat up and looked at Dorothy sharply.

"Gristle and fat!" he cried. "Where did this girl come from?"

"I found her in the forest and brought her here a prisoner," replied the Captain.

"Why did you do that?" inquired the King, puffing his pipe lazily.

"To create some excitement," the Captain answered.

"It is so quiet here that we are all getting rusty for want of amusement. For my part, I prefer to see stirring times."

"Naturally," returned the cleaver, with a nod. "I have always said, Captain, without a bit of irony, that you are a sterling officer and a solid citizen, bowled and polished to a degree. But what do you expect me to do with these prisoners?"

"That is for you to decide," declared the Captain. "You are the King."

"To be sure; to be sure," muttered the cleaver, musingly. "As you say, we have had dull times since the steel and grindstone eloped and left us. Command my Counselors and the Royal Courtiers to attend me, as well as the High Priest and the Judge. We'll then decide what can be done."

The Captain saluted and retired and Dorothy sat down on an overturned kettle and asked:

"Have you anything to eat in your kingdom?"

"Here! Get up! Get off from me!" cried a faint voice, at which his Majesty the cleaver said:

"Excuse me, but you're sitting on my friend the Ten-quart Kettle."

Dorothy at once arose, and the kettle turned right side up and looked at her reproachfully.

"I'm a friend of the King, so no one dares sit on me," said he.

Chapter Sixteen

"I 'd prefer a chair, anyway," she replied.

"Sit on that hearth," commanded the King.

So Dorothy sat on the hearth-shelf of the big range, and the subjects of Utensia began to gather around in a large and inquisitive throng. Toto lay at Dorothy's feet and Billina flew upon the range, which had no fire in it, and perched there as comfortably as she could.

When all the Counselors and Courtiers had assembled—and these seemed to include most of the inhabitants of the kingdom—the King rapped on the block for order and said:

"Friends and Fellow Utensils! Our worthy Commander of the Spoon Brigade, Captain Dipp, has captured the three prisoners you see before you and brought them here for—for—I don't know what for. So I ask your advice how to act in this matter, and what fate I should mete out to these captives. Judge Sifter, stand on my right. It is your business to sift this affair to the bottom. High Priest Colender, stand on my left and see that no one testifies falsely in this matter."

As these two officials took their places Dorothy asked:

"Why is the colender the High Priest?"

"He 's the holiest thing we have in the kindgom," replied King Kleaver.

"Except me," said a sieve. "I 'm the whole thing when it comes to holes."

"What we need," remarked the King, rebukingly, "is a wireless sieve. I must speak to Marconi about it. These old fashioned sieves talk too much. Now, it is the duty of the King's Counselors to counsel the King at all times of emergency, so I beg you to speak out and advise me what to do with these prisoners."

"I demand that they be killed several times, until they are dead!" shouted a pepperbox, hopping around very excitedly.

"Compose yourself, Mr. Paprica," advised the King. "Your remarks are piquant and highly-seasoned, but you need a scattering of commonsense. It is only necessary to kill a person once to make him dead; but I do not see that it is necessary to kill this little girl at all."

"I don't, either," said Dorothy.

"Pardon me, but you are not expected to advise me in this matter," replied King Kleaver.

"Why not?" asked Dorothy.

"You might be prejudiced in your own favor, and so mislead us," he said. "Now then, good subjects, who speaks next?"

"I 'd like to smooth this thing over, in some way," said a flatiron, earnestly. "We are supposed to be useful to mankind, you know."

"But the girl is n't mankind! She 's womankind!" yelled a corkscrew.

"What do you know about it?" inquired the King.

"I 'm a lawyer," said the corkscrew, proudly. "I am accustomed to appear at the bar."

"But you 're crooked," retorted the King, "and that debars you. You may be a corking good lawyer, Mr. Popp, but I must ask you to withdraw your remarks."

"Very well," said the corkscrew, sadly; "I see I have n't any pull at this court."

"Permit me," continued the flatiron, "to press my suit, your Majesty. I do not wish to gloss over any fault the prisoner may have committed, if such a fault exists; but we owe her some consideration, and that 's flat!"

"I 'd like to hear from Prince Karver," said the King.

At this a stately carvingknife stepped forward and bowed.

"The Captain was wrong to bring this girl here, and she was wrong to come," he said. "But now that the foolish deed is done let us all prove our mettle and have a slashing good time."

"That 's it! that 's it!" screamed a fat choppingknife. "We 'll make mincemeat of the girl and hash of the chicken and sausage of the dog!"

There was a shout of approval at this and the King had to rap again for order.

"Gentlemen, gentlemen!" he said, "your remarks are somewhat cutting and rather disjointed, as might be expected from such acute intellects. But you give no reasons for your demands."

"See here, Kleaver; you make me tired," exclaimed a saucepan, strutting before the King very impudently. "You 're about the worst King that ever reigned in Utensia, and that 's saying a good deal. Why don't you run things yourself, instead of asking everybody's advice, like the big, clumsy idiot you are?"

The King sighed.

"I wish there was n't a saucepan in my kingdom," he said. "You fellows are always stewing, over something, and every once in a while you slop over and make a mess of it. Go hang yourself, sir—by the handle—and don't let me hear from you again."

Dorothy was much shocked by the dreadful language the untesils employed, and she thought that they must have had very little proper training. So she said, addressing the King, who seemed very unfit to rule his turbulent subjects:

"I wish you 'd decide my fate right away. I can't stay here all day, trying to find out what you 're going to do with me."

Chapter Sixteen

"This thing is becoming a regular broil, and it 's time I took part in it," observed a big gridiron, coming forward.

"What I 'd like to know," said a can-opener, in a shrill voice, "is why the girl came to our forest, anyhow, and why she intruded upon Captain Dipp—who ought to be called Dippy—and who she is, and where she came from, and where she is going, and why and wherefore and therefore and when."

"I 'm sorry to see, Sir Jabber," remarked the King to the can-opener, "that you have such a prying disposition. As a matter of fact, all the things you mention are none of our business."

Having said this the King relighted his pipe, which had gone out.

"Tell me, please, what *is* our business?" inquired a potato-masher, winking at Dorothy somewhat impertinently. "I 'm fond of little girls, myself, and it seems to me she has as much right to wander in the forest as we have."

"Who accuses the little girl, anyway?" inquired a rolling-pin. "What has she done?"

"I don't know," said the King. "What has she done, Captain Dipp?"

"That 's the trouble, your Majesty. She has n't done anything," replied the Captain.

"What do you want me to do?" asked Dorothy.

This question seemed to puzzle them all. Finally a chafingdish, exclaimed, irritably:

"If no one can throw any light on this subject you must excuse me if I go out."

At this a big kitchen fork pricked up its ears and said in a tiny voice:

"Let 's hear from Judge Sifter."

"That 's proper," returned the King.

So Judge Sifter turned around slowly several times and then said:

"We have nothing against the girl except the stove-hearth upon which she sits. Therefore I order her instantly discharged."

"Discharged!" cried Dorothy. "Why, I never was discharged in my life, and I don't intend to be. If its all the same to you, I 'll resign."

"It 's all the same," declared the King. "You are free —you and your companions—and may go wherever you like."

"Thank you," said the little girl. "But have n't you anything to eat in your kingdom? I 'm hungry."

"Go into the woods and pick blackberries," advised the King, lying down upon his back again and preparing to go to sleep. "There is n't a morsel to eat in all Utensia, that I know of."

Chapter Sixteen

So Dorothy jumped up and said:

"Come on, Toto and Billina. If we can't find the camp we may find some blackberries."

The untensils drew back and allowed them to pass without protest, although Captain Dipp marched the Spoon Brigade in close order after them until they had reached the edge of the clearing.

There the spoons halted; but Dorothy and her companions entered the forest again and began searching diligently for a way back to the camp, that they might rejoin their party.

How THEY CAME TO BUNBURY

CHAPTER SEVENTEEN

WANDERING through the woods, without knowing where you are going or what adventure you are about to meet next, is not as pleasant as one might think. The woods are always beautiful and impressive, and if you are not worried or hungry you may enjoy them immensely; but Dorothy was worried and hungry that morning, so she paid little attention to the beauties of the forest, and hurried along as fast as she could go. She tried to keep in one direction and not circle around, but she was not at all sure that the direction she had chosen would lead her to the camp.

By and by, to her great joy, she came upon a path. It ran to the right and to the left, being lost in the trees in both directions, and just before her, upon a big oak, were fastened two signs, with arms pointing both ways. One sign read:

Chapter Seventeen

☞ TAKE THE OTHER ROAD TO BUNBURY

and the second sign read:

☞ TAKE THE OTHER ROAD TO BUNNYBURY

"Well!" exclaimed Billina, eyeing the signs, "this looks as if we were getting back to civilization again."

"I 'm not sure about the civil'zation, dear," replied the little girl; "but it looks as if we might get *somewhere*, and that 's a big relief, anyhow."

"Which path shall we take?" inquired the Yellow Hen.

Dorothy stared at the signs thoughtfully.

"Bunbury sounds like something to eat," she said. "Let 's go there."

"It 's all the same to me," replied Billina. She had picked up enough bugs and insects from the moss as she went along to satisfy her own hunger, but the hen knew Dorothy could not eat bugs; nor could Toto.

The path to Bunbury seemed little traveled, but it was distinct enough and ran through the trees in a zigzag course until it finally led them to an open space filled with the queerest houses Dorothy had ever seen. They were all made of crackers, laid out in tiny squares, and were of many pretty and ornamental shapes, having balconies and porches with posts of bread-sticks and roofs shingled with wafer-crackers.

There were walks of bread-crusts leading from house to

house and forming streets, and the place seemed to have many inhabitants.

When Dorothy, followed by Billina and Toto, entered the place, they found people walking the streets or assembled in groups talking together, or sitting upon the porches and balconies.

And what funny people they were!

Men, women and children were all made of buns and bread. Some were thin and others fat; some were white, some light brown and some very dark of complexion. A few of the buns, which seemed to form the more important class of the people, were neatly frosted. Some had raisins for eyes and currant buttons on their clothes; others had eyes of cloves and legs of stick cinnamon, and many wore hats and bonnets frosted pink and green.

There was something of a commotion in Bunbury when the strangers suddenly appeared among them. Women caught up their children and hurried into their houses, shutting the cracker doors carefully behind them. Some men ran so hastily that they tumbled over one another, while others, more brave, assembled in a group and faced the intruders defiantly.

Dorothy at once realized that she must act with caution in order not to frighten these shy people, who were evidently unused to the presence of strangers. There was a delightful fragrant odor of fresh bread in the town, and this made the little girl more hungry than ever. She told Toto and Billina to stay back while she slowly advanced toward the group that stood silently awaiting her.

"You must 'scuse me for coming unexpected," she said, softly, "but I really did n't know I was coming here until I arrived. I was lost in the woods, you know, and I 'm as hungry as anything."

"Hungry!" they murmured, in a horrified chorus.

"Yes; I have n't had anything to eat since last night's supper," she explained. "Are there any eatables in Bunbury?"

They looked at one another undecidedly, and then one portly bun man, who seemed a person of consequence, stepped forward and said:

"Little girl, to be frank with you, we are all eatables. Everything in Bunbury is eatable to ravenous human creatures like you. But it is to escape being eaten and destroyed that we have secluded ourselves in this out-of-the-way place, and there is neither right nor justice in your coming here to feed upon us."

Dorothy looked at him longingly.

"You 're bread, are n't you?" she asked.

"Yes; bread and butter. The butter is inside me, so it won't melt and run. I do the running myself."

At this joke all the others burst into a chorus of laughter, and Dorothy thought they could n't be much afraid if they could laugh like that.

"Could n't I eat something besides people?" she asked. "Could n't I eat just one house, or a side-walk, or something? I would n't mind much what it was, you know."

"This is not a public bakery, child," replied the man, sternly. "It 's private property."

"I know Mr.—Mr.—"

"My name is C. Bunn, Esquire," said the man. "C stands for Cinnamon, and this place is called after my family, which is the most aristocratic in the town."

"Oh, I don't know about that," objected another of the queer people. "The Grahams and the Browns and Whites are all excellent families, and there are none better of their kind. I 'm a Boston Brown, myself."

"I admit you are all desirable citizens," said Mr. Bunn, rather stiffly; "but the fact remains that our town is called Bunbury."

" 'Scuse me," interrupted Dorothy; "but I'm getting hungrier every minute. Now, if you 're polite and kind, as I 'm sure you ought to be, you 'll let me eat *something*. There 's so much to eat here that you never will miss it."

Then a big, puffed-up man, of a delicate brown color, stepped forward and said:

"I think it would be a shame to send this child away hungry, especially as she agrees to eat whatever we can spare and not touch our people."

"So do I, Pop," replied a Roll who stood near.

"What, then, do you suggest, Mr. Over?" inquired Mr. Bunn.

"Why, I 'll let her eat my back fence, if she wants to. It 's made of waffles, and they 're very crisp and nice."

"She may also eat my wheelbarrow," added a pleasant looking Muffin. "It 's made of nabiscos with a zuzu wheel."

"Very good; very good," remarked Mr. Bunn. "That is certainly very kind of you. Go with Pop Over and Mr. Muffin, little girl, and they will feed you."

"Thank you very much," said Dorothy, gratefully. "May I bring my dog Toto, and the Yellow Hen? They 're hungry, too."

"Will you make them behave?" asked the Muffin.

"Of course," promised Dorothy.

"Then come along," said Pop Over.

So Dorothy and Billina and Toto walked up the street and the people seemed no longer to be at all afraid of them. Mr. Muffin's house came first, and as his wheelbarrow stood in the front yard the little girl ate that first. It did n't seem very fresh, but she was so hungry that she was not particular. Toto ate some, too, while Billina picked up the crumbs.

185

While the strangers were engaged in eating, many of the people came and stood in the street curiously watching them. Dorothy noticed six roguish looking brown children standing all in a row, and she asked:

"Who are you, little ones?"

"We 're the Graham Gems," replied one; "and we' re all twins."

"I wonder if your mother could spare one or two of you?" asked Billina, who decided that they were fresh baked; but at this dangerous question the six little gems ran away as fast as they could go.

"You must n't say such things, Billina," said Dorothy, reprovingly. "Now let 's go into Pop Over's back yard and get the waffles."

"I sort of hate to let that fence go," remarked Mr. Over, nervously, as they walked toward his house. "The neighbors back of us are Soda Biscuits, and I don't care to mix with them."

"But I 'm hungry yet," declared the girl. "That wheelbarrow was n't very big."

"I 've got a shortcake piano, but none of my family can play on it," he said, reflectively. "Suppose you eat that."

"All right," said Dorothy; "I don't mind. Anything to be accomodating."

So Mr. Over led her into the house, where she ate the piano, which was of an excellent flavor.

"Is there anything to drink here?" she asked .

"Yes; I 've a milk pump and a water pump; which will you have?" he asked.

"I guess I 'll try 'em both," said Dorothy.

So Mr. Over called to his wife, who brought into the yard a pail made of some kind of baked dough, and Dorothy pumped the pail full of cool, sweet milk and drank it eagerly.

The wife of Pop Over was several shades darker than her husband.

"Are n't you overdone?" the little girl asked her.

"No indeed," answered the woman. "I 'm neither overdone nor done over; I 'm just Mrs. Over, and I 'm the President of the Bunbury Breakfast Band."

Dorothy thanked them for their hospitality and went away. At the gate Mr. Cinnamon Bunn met her and said he would show her around the town.

"We have some very interesting inhabitants," he remarked, walking stiffly beside her on his stick-cinnamon legs; "and all of us who are in good health are well bred. If you are no longer hungry we will call upon a few of the most important citizens."

Toto and Billina followed behind them, behaving very well, and a little way down the street they came to a handsome residence where Aunt Sally Lunn lived. The old lady was glad to meet the little girl and gave her a slice of white bread and butter which had been used as a door-mat. It was almost fresh and tasted better than anything Dorothy had eaten in the town.

"Where do you get the butter?" she inquired.

"We dig it out of the ground, which, as you may have observed, is all flour and meal," replied Mr. Bunn. "There is a butter mine just at the opposite side of the village. The trees which you see here are all doughleanders and doughderas, and in the season we get quite a crop of dough-nuts off them."

"I should think the flour would blow around and get into your eyes," said Dorothy.

"No," said he; "we are bothered with cracker dust sometimes, but never with flour."

Then he took her to see Johnny Cake, a cheerful old gentleman who lived near by.

"I suppose you 've heard of me," said old Johnny, with an air of pride. "I 'm a great favorite all over the world."

"Are n't you rather yellow?" asked Dorothy, looking at him critically.

"Maybe, child. But don't think I 'm bilious, for I was never in better health in my life," replied the old gentleman. "If anything ailed me, I 'd willingly acknowledge the corn."

"Johnny 's a trifle stale," said Mr. Bunn, as they went away; "but he 's a good mixer and never gets cross-grained. I will now take you to call upon some of my own relatives."

They visited the Sugar Bunns, the Currant Bunns and the Spanish Bunns, the latter having a decidedly foreign appearance. Then they saw the French Rolls, who were very polite to them, and made a brief call upon the Parker H. Rolls, who seemed a bit proud and overbearing.

"But they 're not as stuck up as the Frosted Jumbles," declared Mr. Bunn, "who are people I really can't abide. I don't like to be suspicious or talk scandal, but sometimes I think the Jumbles have too much baking powder in them."

Just then a dreadful scream was heard, and Dorothy turned hastily around to find a scene of great excitement a little way down the street. The people were crowding around Toto and throwing at him everything they could find at hand. They pelted the little dog with hard-tack, crackers, and even articles of furniture which were hard baked and heavy enough for missiles.

Toto howled a little as the assortment of bake stuff struck him; but he stood still, with head bowed and tail between his legs, until Dorothy ran up and inquired what the matter was.

"Matter!" cried a rye loafer, indignantly, "why the horrid beast has eaten three of our dear Crumpets, and is now devouring a Salt-rising Biscuit!"

"Oh, Toto! How could you?" exclaimed Dorothy, much distressed.

Toto's mouth was full of his salt-rising victim; so he only whined and wagged his tail. But Billina, who had flown to the top of a cracker house to be in a safe place, called out:

"Don't blame him, Dorothy; the Crumpets dared him to do it."

"Yes, and you pecked out the eyes of a Raisin Bunn— one of our best citizens!" shouted a bread pudding, shaking its fist at the Yellow Hen.

"What 's that! What 's that?" wailed Mr. Cinnamon Bunn, who had now joined them. "Oh, what a misfortune —what a terrible misfortune!"

"See here," said Dorothy, determined to defend her pets, "I think we 've treated you all pretty well, seeing you 're eatables, an' reg 'lar food for us. I 've been kind to you, and eaten your old wheelbarrows and pianos and rubbish, an' not said a word. But Toto and Billina can't be 'spected to go hungry when the town 's full of good things they like to eat, 'cause they can't understand your stingy ways as I do."

"You must leave here at once!" said Mr. Bunn, sternly.

Chapter Seventeen

"Suppose we won't go?" asked Dorothy, who was now much provoked.

"Then," said he, "we will put you into the great ovens where we are made, and bake you."

Dorothy gazed around and saw threatening looks upon the faces of all. She had not noticed any ovens in the town, but they might be there, nevertheless, for some of the inhabitants seemed very fresh. So she decided to go, and calling to Toto and Billina to follow her she marched up the street with as much dignity as possible, considering that she was followed by the hoots and cries of the buns and biscuits and other bake stuff.

How OZMA LOOKED INTO THE MAGIC PICTURE

CHAPTER EIGHTEEN

PRINCESS Ozma was a very busy little ruler, for she looked carefully after the comfort and welfare of her people and tried to make them happy. If any quarrels arose she decided them justly; if any one needed counsel or advice she was ready and willing to listen to them.

For a day or two after Dorothy and her companions had started on their trip, Ozma was occupied with the affairs of her kingdom. Then she began to think of some manner of occupation for Uncle Henry and Aunt Em that would be light and easy and yet give the old people something to do.

She soon decided to make Uncle Henry the Keeper of the Jewels, for some one really was needed to count and look after the bins and barrels of emeralds, diamonds, rubies and other precious stones that were in the Royal Storehouses. That would keep Uncle Henry busy enough, but it was

HIS MAJESTY WAS THOUGHTFUL

harder to find something for Aunt Em to do. The palace was full of servants, so there was no detail of housework that Aunt Em could look after.

While Ozma sat in her pretty room engaged in thought she happened to glance at her Magic Picture.

This was one of the most important treasures in all the Land of Oz. It was a large picture, set in a beautiful gold frame, and it hung in a prominent place upon a wall of Ozma's private room.

Usually this picture seemed merely a country scene, but whenever Ozma looked at it and wished to know what any of her friends or acquaintances were doing, the magic of this wonderful picture was straightway disclosed. For the country scene would gradually fade away and in its place would appear the likeness of the person or persons Ozma might wish to see, surrounded by the actual scenes in which they were then placed. In this way the Princess could view any part of the world she wished, and watch the actions of any one in whom she was interested.

Ozma had often seen Dorothy in her Kansas home by this means, and now, having a little leisure, she expressed a desire to see her little friend again. It was while the travelers were at Fuddlecumjig, and Ozma laughed merrily as she watched in the picture her friends trying to match the pieces of Grandmother Gnit.

"They seem happy and are doubtless having a good time," the girl Ruler said to herself; and then she began to think of the many adventures she herself had encountered with Dorothy.

The images of her friends now faded from the Magic Picture and the old landscape slowly reappeared.

Ozma was thinking of the time when with Dorothy and her army she marched to the Nome King's underground cavern, beyond the Land of Ev, and forced the old monarch to liberate his captives, who belonged to the Royal Family of Ev. That was the time when the Scarecrow nearly frightened the Nome King into fits by throwing one of Billina's eggs at him, and Dorothy had captured King Roquat's Magic Belt and brought it away with her to the Land of Oz.

The pretty Princess smiled at the recollection of this adventure, and then she wondered what had become of the Nome King since then. Merely because she was curious and had nothing better to do, Ozma glanced at the Magic Picture and wished to see in it the King of the Nomes.

Roquat the Red went every day into his tunnel to see how the work was getting along and to hurry his workmen as much as possible. He was there now, and Ozma saw him plainly in the Magic Picture.

She saw the underground tunnel, reaching far underneath the Deadly Desert which separated the Land of Oz from the mountains beneath which the Nome King had his extensive caverns. She saw that the tunnel was being made in the direction of the Emerald City, and knew at once it was being dug so that the army of Nomes could march through it and attack her own beautiful and peaceful country.

"I suppose King Roquat is planning revenge against us," she said, musingly, "and thinks he can surprise us and make us his captives and slaves. How sad it is that any one can have such wicked thoughts! But I must not blame King Roquat too severely, for he is a Nome, and his nature is not so gentle as my own."

Then she dismissed from her mind further thought of the tunnel, for that time, and began to wonder if Aunt Em would not be happy as Royal Mender of the Stockings of the Ruler of Oz. Ozma wore few holes in her stockings; still, they sometimes needed mending. Aunt Em ought to be able to do that very nicely.

Next day the Princess watched the tunnel again in her Magic Picture, and every day afterward she devoted a few minutes to inspecting the work. It was not especially interesting, but she felt that it was her duty.

Slowly but surely the big arched hole crept through the rocks underneath the deadly desert, and day by day it drew nearer and nearer to the Emerald City.

How BUNNYBURY WELCOMED THE STRANGERS

CHAPTER NINETEEN

DOROTHY left Bunbury the same way she had entered it and when they were in the forest again she said to Billina:

"I never thought that things good to eat could be so dis'gree'ble."

"Often I've eaten things that tasted good but were disagreeable afterward," returned the Yellow Hen. "I think, Dorothy, if eatables are going to act badly, it's better before than after you eat them."

"P'raps you're right," said the little girl, with a sigh. "But what shall we do now?"

"Let us follow the path back to the signpost," suggested Billina. "That will be better than getting lost again."

"Why, we're lost anyhow," declared Dorothy; "but I guess you're right about going back to that signpost, Billina."

Chapter Nineteen

They returned along the path to the place where they had first found it, and at once took "the other road" to Bunnybury. This road was a mere narrow strip, worn hard and smooth but not wide enough for Dorothy's feet to tread. Still it was a guide, and the walking through the forest was not at all difficult.

Before long they reached a high wall of solid white marble, and the path came to an end at this wall.

At first Dorothy thought there was no opening at all in the marble, but on looking closely she discovered a small square door about on a level with her head, and underneath this closed door was a bell-push. Near the bell-push a sign was painted in neat letters upon the marble, and the sign read:

No Admittance
Except on Business

This did not discourage Dorothy, however, and she rang the bell.

Pretty soon a bolt was cautiously withdrawn and the marble door swung slowly open. Then she saw it was not really a door, but a window, for several brass bars were placed across it, being set fast in the marble and so close together that the little girl's fingers might barely go between them. Back of the bars appeared the face of a white rabbit

—a very sober and sedate face—with an eye-glass held in his left eye and attached to a cord in his button-hole.

"Well! what is it?" asked the rabbit, sharply.

"I 'm Dorothy," said the girl, "and I 'm lost, and—"

"State your business, please," interrupted the rabbit.

"My business," she replied, "is to find out where I am, and to—"

"No one is allowed in Bunnybury without an order or a letter of introduction from either Ozma of Oz or Glinda the Good," announced the rabbit; "so that that settles the matter," and he started to close the window.

"Wait a minute!" cried Dorothy. "I 've got a letter from Ozma."

"From the Ruler of Oz?" asked the rabbit, doubtingly.

"Of course. Ozma 's my best friend, you know; and I 'm a Princess myself," she announced, earnestly.

"Hum—ha! Let me see your letter," returned the rabbit, as if he still doubted her.

So she hunted in her pocket and found the letter Ozma had given her. Then she handed it through the bars to the rabbit, who took it in his paws and opened it. He read it aloud in a pompous voice, as if to let Dorothy and Billina see that he was educated and could read writing. The letter was as follows:

Chapter Nineteen

"It will please me to have my subjects greet Princess Dorothy, the bearer of this royal missive, with the same courtesy and consideration they would extend to me."

"Ha—hum! It is signed 'Ozma of Oz,'" continued the rabbit, "and is sealed with the Great Seal of the Emerald City. Well, well, well! How strange! How remarkable!"

"What are you going to do about it?" inquired Dorothy, impatiently.

"We must obey the royal mandate," replied the rabbit. "We are subjects of Ozma of Oz, and we live in her country. Also we are under the protection of the great Sorceress Glinda the Good, who made us promise to respect Ozma's commands."

"Then may I come in?" she asked.

"I'll open the door," said the rabbit. He shut the window and disappeared, but a moment afterward a big door in the wall opened and admitted Dorothy to a small room, which seemed to be a part of the wall and built into it.

Here stood the rabbit she had been talking with, and now that she could see all of him she gazed at the creature in surprise. He was a good sized white rabbit with pink eyes, much like all other white rabbits. But the astonishing thing about him was the manner in which he was dressed. He wore a white satin jacket embroidered with gold, and having diamond buttons. His vest was rose-colored satin, with tourmaline buttons. His trousers were white, to correspond with the jacket, and they were baggy at the knees—like those of a zouave—being tied with knots of rose ribbons. His shoes were of white plush with diamond buckles, and his stockings were rose silk.

The richness and even magnificence of the rabbit's clothing made Dorothy stare at the little creature wonderingly. Toto and Billina had followed her into the room and when he saw them the rabbit ran to a table and sprang upon it nimbly. Then he looked at the three through his monocle and said:

"These companions, Princess, cannot enter Bunnybury with you."

"Why not?" asked Dorothy.

"In the first place they would frighten our people, who dislike dogs above all things on earth; and, secondly, the letter of the Royal Ozma does not mention them."

"But they 're my friends," persisted Dorothy, "and go wherever I go."

"Not this time," said the rabbit, decidedly. "You, yourself, Pincess, are a welcome visitor, since you come so highly recommended; but unless you consent to leave the dog and the hen in this room I cannot permit you to enter the town."

Chapter Nineteen

"Never mind us, Dorothy," said Billina. "Go inside and see what the place is like. You can tell us about it afterward, and Toto and I will rest comfortably here until you return."

This seemed the best thing to do, for Dorothy was curious to see how the rabbit people lived and she was aware of the fact that her friends might frighten the timid little creatures. She had not forgotten how Toto and Billina had misbehaved in Bunbury, and perhaps the rabbit was wise to insist on their staying outside the town.

"Very well," she said, "I 'll go in alone. I s'pose you 're the King of this town, are n't you?"

"No," answered the rabbit, "I 'm merely the Keeper of the Wicket, and a person of little importance, although I try to do my duty. I must now inform you, Princess, that before you enter our town you must consent to reduce."

"Reduce what?" asked Dorothy.

"Your size. You must become the size of the rabbits, although you may retain your own form."

"Would n't my clothes be too big for me?" she inquired.

"No; they will reduce when your body does."

"Can *you* make me smaller?" asked the girl.

"Easily," returned the rabbit.

"And will you make me big again, when I 'm ready to go away?"

"I will," said he.

"All right, then; I 'm willing," she announced.

The rabbit jumped from the table and ran—or rather hopped—to the further wall, where he opened a door so tiny that even Toto could scarcely have crawled through it.

"Follow me," he said.

Now, almost any other little girl would have declared that she could not get through so small a door; but Dorothy had already encountered so many fairy adventures that she believed nothing was impossible in the Land of Oz. So she quietly walked toward the door, and at every step she grew smaller and smaller until, by the time the opening was reached, she could pass through it with ease. Indeed, as she stood beside the rabbit, who sat upon his hind legs and used his paws as hands, her head was just about as high as his own.

Then the Keeper of the Wicket passed through and she followed, after which the door swung shut and locked itself with a sharp click.

Dorothy now found herself in a city so strange and beautiful that she gave a gasp of surprise. The high marble wall extended all around the place and shut out all the rest of the world. And here were marble houses of curious forms, most of them resembling overturned kettles but with delicate slender spires and minarets running far up into the sky. The streets were paved with white marble and in front of each house was a lawn of rich green clover. Everything was as neat as wax, the green and white contrasting prettily together.

But the rabbit people were, after all, the most amazing things Dorothy saw. The streets were full of them, and

their costumes were so splendid that the rich dress of the Keeper of the Wicket was commonplace when compared with the others. Silks and satins of delicate hues seemed always used for material, and nearly every costume sparkled with exquisite gems.

But the lady rabbits outshone the gentlemen rabbits in

splendor, and the cut of their gowns was really wonderful. They wore bonnets, too, with feathers and jewels in them, and some wheeled baby carriages in which the girl could see wee bunnies. Some were lying asleep while others lay sucking their paws and looking around them with big pink eyes.

As Dorothy was no bigger in size than the grown-up rabbits she had a chance to observe them closely before they noticed her presence. Then they did not seem at all alarmed, although the little girl naturally became the center of attraction and all regarded her with great curiosity.

"Make way!" cried the Keeper of the Wicket, in a pompous voice; "make way for Princess Dorothy, who comes from Ozma of Oz."

Hearing this announcement, the throng of rabbits gave place to them on the walks, and as Dorothy passed along they all bowed their heads respectfully.

Walking thus through several handsome streets they came to a square in the center of the City. In this square were some pretty trees and a statue in bronze of Glinda the Good, while beyond it were the portals of the Royal Palace —an extensive and imposing building of white marble covered with a filigree of frosted gold.

How DOROTHY LUNCHED WITH A KING

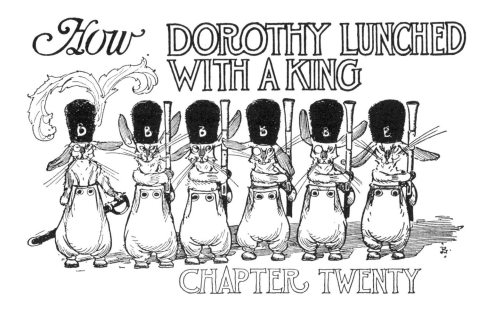

CHAPTER TWENTY

A LINE of rabbit soldiers was drawn up before the palace entrance, and they wore green and gold uniforms with high shakos upon their heads and held tiny spears in their hands. The Captain had a sword and a white plume in his shako.

"Salute!" cried the Keeper of the Wicket. "Salute Princess Dorothy, who comes from Ozma of Oz!"

"Salute!" yelled the Captain, and all the soldiers promptly saluted.

They now entered the great hall of the palace, where they met a gaily dressed attendant, from whom the Keeper of the Wicket inquired if the King were at leisure.

"I think so," was the reply. "I heard his Majesty blubbering and wailing as usual only a few minutes ago. If he does n't stop acting like a cry-baby I 'm going to resign my position here and go to work."

"What 's the matter with your King?" asked Dorothy, surprised to hear the rabbit attendant speak so disrespectfully of his monarch.

"Oh, he does n't want to be King, that 's all; and he simply *has* to," was the reply.

"Come!" said the Keeper of the Wicket, sternly; "lead us to his Majesty; and do not air our troubles before strangers, I beg of you."

"Why, if this girl is going to see the King, he 'll air his own troubles," returned the attendant.

"That is his royal privilege," declared the Keeper.

So the attendant led them into a room all draped with cloth-of-gold and furnished with satin-covered gold furniture. There was a throne in this room, set on a dais and having a big cushioned seat, and on this seat reclined the Rabbit King. He was lying on his back, with his paws in the air, and whining very like a puppy-dog.

"Your Majesty! your Majesty! Get up. Here 's a visitor," called out the attendant.

The King rolled over and looked at Dorothy with one watery pink eye. Then he sat up and wiped his eyes carefully with a silk handkerchief and put on his jeweled crown, which had fallen off.

"Excuse my grief, fair stranger," he said, in a sad voice.

"You behold in me the most miserable monarch in all the world. What time is it, Blinkem?"

"One o'clock, your Majesty," replied the attendant to whom the question was addressed.

"Serve luncheon at once!" commanded the King. "Luncheon for two—that 's for my visitor and me—and see that the human has some sort of food she 's accustomed to."

"Yes, your Majesty," answered the attendant, and went away.

"Tie my shoe, Bristle," said the King to the Keeper of the Wicket. "Ah, me! how unhappy I am!"

"What seems to be worrying your Majesty?" asked Dorothy.

"Why, it 's this king business, of course," he returned, while the Keeper tied his shoe. "I did n't want to be King of Bunnybury at all, and the rabbits all knew it. So they elected me—to save themselves from such a dreadful fate, I suppose—and here I am, shut up in a palace, when I might be free and happy."

"Seems to me," said Dorothy, "it 's a great thing to be a King."

"Were you ever a King?" inquired the monarch.

"No," she answered, laughing.

"Then you know nothing about it," he said. "I have n't inquired who you are, but it does n't matter. While we 're at luncheon, I 'll tell you all my troubles. They 're a great deal more interesting than anything you can say about yourself."

"Perhaps they are, to you," replied Dorothy.

"Luncheon is served!" cried Blinkem, throwing open the door, and in came a dozen rabbits in livery, all bearing trays which they placed upon the table, where they arranged the dishes in an orderly manner.

"Now clear out—all of you!" exclaimed the King. "Bristle, you may wait outside, in case I want you."

When they had gone and the King was alone with Dorothy he came down from his throne, tossed his crown into a corner and kicked his ermine robe under the table.

"Sit down," he said, "and try to be happy. It 's useless for me to try, because I 'm always wretched and miserable. But I 'm hungry, and I hope you are."

"I am," said Dorothy. "I 've only eaten a wheelbarrow and a piano to-day—oh, yes! and a slice of bread and butter that used to be a door-mat."

"That sounds like a square meal," remarked the King, seating himself opposite her; "but perhaps it was n't a square piano. Eh?"

Dorothy laughed.

"You don't seem so very unhappy now," she said.

"But I am," protested the King, fresh tears gathering in his eyes. "Even my jokes are miserable. I'm wretched, woeful, afflicted, distressed and dismal as an individual can be. Are you not sorry for me?"

"No," answered Dorothy, honestly, "I can't say I am. Seems to me that for a rabbit you're right in clover. This is the prettiest little city I ever saw."

"Oh, the city is good enough," he admitted. "Glinda, the Good Sorceress, made it for us because she was fond of rabbits. I don't mind the City so much, although I would n't live here if I had my choice. It is being King that has absolutely ruined my happiness."

"Why would n't you live here by choice?" she asked.

"Because it is all unnatural, my dear. Rabbits are out of place in such luxury. When I was young I lived in a burrow in the forest. I was surrounded by enemies and often had to run for my life. It was hard getting enough to eat, at times, and when I found a bunch of clover I had to listen and look for danger while I ate it. Wolves prowled around the hole in which I lived and sometimes I did n't dare stir out for days at a time. Oh, how happy and contented I was then! I was a real rabbit, as nature made me—wild and free! —and I even enjoyed listening to the startled throbbing of my own heart!"

"I 've often thought," said Dorothy, who was busily eating, "that it would be fun to be a rabbit."

"It *is* fun—when you 're the genuine article," agreed his Majesty. "But look at me now! I live in a marble palace instead of a hole in the ground. I have all I want to eat, without the joy of hunting for it. Every day I must dress in fine clothes and wear that horrible crown till it makes my head ache. Rabbits come to me with all sorts of troubles, when my own troubles are the only ones I care about. When I walk out I can't hop and run; I must strut on my rear legs and wear an ermine robe! And the soldiers salute me and the band plays and the other rabbits laugh and clap their paws and cry out: 'Hail to the King!' Now let me ask you, as a friend and a young lady of good judgment: is n't all this pomp and foolishness enough to make a decent rabbit miserable?"

"Once," said Dorothy, reflectively, "men were wild and unclothed and lived in caves and hunted for food as wild beasts do. But they got civ'lized, in time, and now they 'd hate to go back to the old days."

"That is an entirely different case," replied the King. "None of you Humans were civilized in one lifetime. It came to you by degrees. But I have known the forest and the free life, and that is why I resent being civilized all at once, against my will, and being made a King with a crown and an ermine robe. Pah!"

"If you don't like it, why don't you resign?" she asked.

"Impossible!" wailed the Rabbit, wiping his eyes again with his handkerchief. "There 's a beastly law in this town that forbids it. When one is elected a King there 's no getting out of it."

"Who made the laws?" inquired Dorothy.

"The same Sorceress who made the town—Glinda the Good. She built the wall, and fixed up the City, and gave us several valuable enchantments, and made the laws. Then she invited all the pink-eyed white rabbits of the forest to come here, after which she left us to our fate."

"What made you 'cept the invitation, and come here?" asked the child.

"I did n't know how dreadful city life was, and I 'd no idea I would be elected King," said he, sobbing bitterly. "And—and—now I 'm It—with a capital I—and can't escape!"

"I know Glinda," remarked Dorothy, eating for dessert a dish of charlotte russe, "and when I see her again I 'll ask her to put another King in your place."

"Will you? Will you, indeed?" asked the King, joyfully.

"I will if you want me to," she replied.

Chapter Twenty

"Hurroo—hurray!" shouted the King; and then he jumped up from the table and danced wildly about the room, waving his napkin like a flag and laughing with glee.

After a time he managed to control his delight and returned to the table.

"When are you likely to see Glinda?" he inquired.

"Oh, p'raps in a few days," said Dorothy.

'And you won't forget to ask her?"

"Of course not."

"Princess," said the Rabbit King, earnestly, "you have relieved me of a great unhappiness, and I am very grateful. Therefore I propose to entertain you, since you are my guest and I am the King, as a slight mark of my appreciation. Come with me to my reception hall."

He then summoned Bristle and said to him: "Assemble all the nobility in the great reception hall, and also tell Blinkem that I want him immediately."

The Keeper of the Wicket bowed and hurried away, and his Majesty turned to Dorothy and continued: "We'll have time for a walk in the gardens before the people get here."

The gardens were back of the palace and were filled with beautiful flowers and fragrant shrubs, with many shade and fruit trees and marble paved walks running in every direction. As they entered this place Blinkem came running to the King, who gave him several orders in a low voice. Then his Majesty rejoined Dorothy and led her through the gardens, which she admired very much.

"What lovely clothes your Majesty wears!" she said, glancing at the rich blue satin costume, embroidered with pearls, in which the King was dressed.

"Yes," he returned, with an air of pride, "this is one of my favorite suits; but I have a good many that are even more elaborate. We have excellent tailors in Bunnybury, and Glinda supplies all the material. By the way, you might ask the Sorceress, when you see her, to permit me to keep my wardrobe."

"But if you go back to the forest you will not need clothes," she said.

"N—o!" he faltered; "that may be so. But I 've dressed up so long that I 'm used to it, and I don't imagine I 'd care to run around naked again. So perhaps the Good Glinda will let me keep the costumes."

"I 'll ask her," agreed Dorothy.

Then they left the gardens and went into a fine big reception hall, where rich rugs were spread upon the tiled floors and the furniture was exquisitely carved and studded with jewels. The King's chair was an especially pretty piece of furniture, being in the shape of a silver lily with one leaf bent over to form the seat. The silver was everywhere

thickly encrusted with diamonds and the seat was upholstered in white satin.

"Oh, what a splendid chair!" cried Dorothy, clasping her
hands admiringly.

"Is n't it?" answered the King, proudly. "It is my favorite seat, and I think it especially becoming to my complexion. While I think of it, I wish you 'd ask Glinda to
let me keep this lily chair when I go away."

"It would n't look very well in a hole in the ground,
would it?" she suggested.

"Maybe not; but I 'm used to sitting in it and I 'd like
to take it with me," he answered. "But here come the ladies
and gentlemen of the court; so please sit beside me and be
presented."

How THE KING CHANGED HIS MIND

CHAPTER TWENTY-ONE

JUST then a rabbit band of nearly fifty pieces marched in, playing upon golden instruments and dressed in neat uniforms. Following the band came the nobility of Bunnybury, all richly dressed and hopping along on their rear legs. Both the ladies and the gentlemen wore white gloves upon their paws, with their rings on the outside of the gloves, as this seemed to be the fashion here. Some of the lady rabbits carried lorgnettes, while many of the gentlemen rabbits wore monocles in their left eyes.

The courtiers and their ladies paraded past the King, who introduced Princess Dorothy to each couple in a very graceful manner. Then the company seated themselves in chairs and on sofas and looked expectantly at their monarch.

"It is our royal duty, as well as our royal pleasure," he

216

said, "to provide fitting entertainment for our distinguished guest. We will now present the Royal Band of Whiskered Friskers."

As he spoke the musicians, who had arranged themselves in a corner, struck up a dance melody while into the room pranced the Whiskered Friskers. They were eight pretty rabbits dressed only in gauzy purple skirts fastened around their waists with diamond bands. Their whiskers were colored a rich purple, but otherwise they were pure white.

After bowing before the King and Dorothy the Friskers began their pranks, and these were so comical that Dorothy laughed with real enjoyment. They not only danced together, whirling and gyrating around the room, but they leaped over one another, stood upon their heads and hopped and skipped here and there so nimbly that it was hard work to keep track of them. Finally they all made double somersaults and turned handsprings out of the room.

The nobility enthusiastically applauded, and Dorothy applauded with them.

"They 're fine!" she said to the King.

"Yes, the Whiskered Friskers are really very clever," he replied. "I shall hate to part with them when I go away, for they have often amused me when I was very miserable. I wonder if you would ask Glinda—"

"No, it would n't do at all," declared Dorothy, positively. "There would n't be room in your hole in the ground for so many rabbits, 'spec'ly when you get the lily chair and your clothes there. Don't think of such a thing, your Majesty."

The King sighed. Then he stood up and announced to the company:

"We will now behold a military drill by my picked Bodyguard of Royal Pikemen."

Now the band played a march and a company of rabbit soldiers came in. They wore green and gold uniforms and marched very stiffly but in perfect time. Their spears, or pikes, had slender shafts of polished silver with golden heads, and during the drill they handled these weapons with wonderful dexterity.

"I should think you 'd feel pretty safe with such a fine Bodyguard," remarked Dorothy.

"I do," said the King. "They protect me from every harm. I suppose Glinda would n't—"

"No," interrupted the girl; "I 'm sure she would n't. It s the King's own Bodyguard, and when you are no longer King you can 't have 'em."

The King did not reply, but he looked rather sorrowful for a time.

When the soldiers had marcned out he said to the company:

Chapter Twenty-One

"The Royal Jugglers will now appear."

Dorothy had seen many jugglers in her lifetime, but never any so interesting as these. There were six of them, dressed in black satin embroidered with queer symbols in silver—a costume which contrasted strongly with their snow-white fur.

First they pushed in a big red ball and three of the rabbit jugglers stood upon its top and made it roll. Then two of them caught up a third and tossed him into the air, all vanishing, until only the two were left. Then one of these tossed the other upward and remained alone of all his fellows. This last juggler now touched the red ball, which fell apart, being hollow, and the five rabbits who had disappeared in the air scrambled out of the hollow ball.

Next they all clung together and rolled swiftly upon the floor. When they came to a stop only one fat rabbit juggler was seen, the others seeming to be inside him. This one leaped lightly into the air and when he came down he exploded and separated into the original six. Then four of them rolled themselves into round balls and the other two tossed them around and played ball with them.

These were but a few of the tricks the rabbit jugglers performed, and they were so skillful that all the nobility and even the King applauded as loudly as did Dorothy.

"I suppose there are no rabbit jugglers in all the world to compare with these," remarked the King. "And since I may not have the Whiskered Friskers or my Bodyguard, you might ask Glinda to let me take away just two or three of these jugglers. Will you?"

"I 'll ask her," replied Dorothy, doubtfully.

"Thank you," said the King; "thank you very much. And now you shall listen to the Winsome Waggish Warblers, who have often cheered me in my moments of anguish."

The Winsome Waggish Warblers proved to be a quartette of rabbit singers, two gentlemen and two lady rabbits. The gentlemen Warblers wore full-dress swallow-tailed suits of white satin, with pearls for buttons, while the lady Warblers were gowned in white satin dresses with long trails.

The first song they sang began in this way:

"When a rabbit gets a habit
  Of living in a city
And wearing clothes and furbelows
  And jewels rare and pretty,
He scorns the Bun who has to run
  And burrow in the ground
And pities those whose watchful foes
  Are man and gun and hound."

Chapter Twenty-One

Dorothy looked at the King when she heard this song and noticed that he seemed disturbed and ill at ease.

"I don't like that song," he said to the Warblers. "Give us something jolly and rollicking."

So they sang to a joyous, tinkling melody as follows:

"Bunnies gay
Delight to play
In their fairy town secure;
Ev'ry frisker
Flirts his whisker
At a pink-eyed girl demure.
Ev'ry maid
In silk arrayed
At her partner shyly glances,
Paws are grasped,
Waists are clasped
As they whirl in giddy dances.
Then together
Through the heather
'Neath the moonlight soft they stroll;
Each is very
Blithe and merry,
Gamboling with laughter droll.
Life is fun
To ev'ry one

Guarded by our magic charm
    For to dangers
    We are strangers,
Safe from any thought of harm."

"You see," said Dorothy to the King, when the song ended, "the rabbits all seem to like Bunnybury except you. And I guess you 're the only one that ever has cried or was unhappy and wanted to get back to your muddy hole in the ground."

His Majesty seemed thoughtful, and while the servants passed around glasses of nectar and plates of frosted cakes their King was silent and a bit nervous.

When the refreshments had been enjoyed by all and the servants had retired Dorothy said:

"I must go now, for it 's getting late and I 'm lost. I 've got to find the Wizard and Aunt Em and Uncle Henry and all the rest sometime before night comes, if I poss'bly can."

"Won't you stay with us?" asked the King. "You will be very welcome."

"No, thank you," she replied. "I must get back to my friends. And I want to see Glinda just as soon as I can, you know."

So the King dismissed his court and said he would himself walk with Dorothy to the gate. He did not weep nor groan any more, but his long face was quite solemn and his big ears hung dejectedly on each side of it. He still wore his crown and his ermine and walked with a handsome gold-headed cane.

When they arrived at the room in the wall the little girl found Toto and Billina waiting for her very patiently. They had been liberally fed by some of the attendants and were in no hurry to leave such comfortable quarters.

The Keeper of the Wicket was by this time back in his old place, but he kept a safe distance from Toto. Dorothy bade good bye to the King as they stood just inside the wall.

"You 've been good to me," she said, "and I thank you ever so much. As soon as poss'ble I 'll see Glinda and ask her to put another King in your place and send you back into the wild forest. And I 'll ask her to let you keep some of your clothes and the lily chair and one or two jugglers to amuse you. I 'm sure she will do it, 'cause she 's so kind she does n't like any one to be unhappy."

"Ahem!" said the King, looking rather downcast. "I don't like to trouble you with my misery; so you need n't see Glinda."

"Oh, yes I will," she replied. "It won't be any trouble at all."

"But, my dear," continued the King, in an embarrassed way, "I 've been thinking the subject over carefully, and I find there are a lot of pleasant things here in Bunnybury that I would miss if I went away. So perhaps I 'd better stay."

Dorothy laughed. Then she looked grave.

"It won't do for you to be a King and a cry-baby at the same time," she said. "You 've been making all the other rabbits unhappy and discontented with your howls about being so miserable. So I guess its better to have another King."

"Oh, no indeed!" exclaimed the King, earnestly. "If you won't say anything to Glinda I 'll promise to be merry and gay all the time, and never cry or wail again."

"Honor bright?" she asked.

"On the royal word of a King I promise it!" he answered.

"All right," said Dorothy. "You 'd be a reg'lar lunatic to want to leave Bunnybury for a wild life in the forest, and I 'm sure any rabbit outside the city would be glad to take your place."

"Forget it, my dear; forget all my foolishness," pleaded the King, earnestly. "Hereafter I 'll try to enjoy myself and do my duty by my subjects."

So then she left him and entered through the little door into the room in the wall, where she grew gradually bigger and bigger until she had resumed her natural size.

The Keeper of the Wicket let them out into the forest and told Dorothy that she had been of great service to

"BUT I HAVEN'T CUT OFF A FINGER!" SHE SOBBED.

Bunnybury because she had brought their dismal King to a realization of the pleasure of ruling so beautiful a city.

"I shall start a petition to have your statue erected beside Glinda's in the public square," said the Keeper. "I hope you will come again, some day, and see it."

"Perhaps I shall," she replied.

Then, followed by Toto and Billina, she walked away from the high marble wall and started back along the narrow path toward the sign-post.

How THE WIZARD FOUND DOROTHY

CHAPTER TWENTY-TWO

WHEN they came to the signpost, there, to their joy, were the tents of the Wizard pitched beside the path and the kettle bubbling merrily over a fire. The Shaggy Man and Omby Amby were gathering firewood while Uncle Henry and Aunt Em sat in their camp chairs talking with the Wizard.

They all ran forward to greet Dorothy, as she approached, and Aunt Em exclaimed: "Goodness gracious, child! Where have you been?"

"You 've played hookey the whole day," added the Shaggy Man, reproachfully.

"Well, you see, I 've been lost," explained the little girl, "and I 've tried awful hard to find the way back to you, but just could n't do it."

"Did you wander in the forest all day?" asked Uncle Henry.

226

Chapter Twenty-Two

"You must be a'most starved!" said Aunt Em.

"No," said Dorothy, "I 'm not hungry. I had a wheelbarrow and a piano for breakfast, and lunched with a King."

"Ah!" exclaimed the Wizard, nodding with a bright smile. "So you 've been having adventures again."

"She 's stark crazy!" cried Aunt Em. "Whoever heard of eating a wheelbarrow?"

"It was n't very big," said Dorothy; "and it had a zuzu wheel."

"And I ate the crumbs," added Billina, soberly.

"Sit down and tell us about it," begged the Wizard. "We 've hunted for you all day, and at last I noticed your footsteps in this path—and the tracks of Billina. We found the path by accident, and seeing it only led to two places I decided you were at either one or the other of those places. So we made camp and waited for you to return. And now, Dorothy, tell us where you have been—to Bunbury or to Bunnybury?"

"Why, I 've been to both," she replied; "but first I went to Utensia, which is n't on any path at all."

She then sat down and related the day's adventures, and you may be sure Aunt Em and Uncle Henry were much astonished at the story.

"But after seeing the Cuttenclips and the Fuddles," remarked her uncle, "we ought not to wonder at anything in this strange country.

"Seems like the only common and ordinary folks here are ourselves," rejoined Aunt Em, diffidently.

"Now that we 're together again, and one reunited party," observed the Shaggy Man, "what are we to do next?"

"Have some supper and a night 's rest," answered the Wizard promptly, "and then proceed upon our journey."

"Where to?" asked the Captain General.

"We have n't visited the Rigmaroles or the Flutterbudgets yet," said Dorothy. "I 'd like to see them—would n't you?"

"They don't sound very interesting," objected Aunt Em. "But perhaps they are."

"And then," continued the little Wizard, "we will call upon the Tin Woodman and Jack Pumpkinhead and our old friend the Scarecrow, on our way home."

"That will be nice!" cried Dorothy, eagerly.

"Can't say *they* sound very interesting, either," remarked Aunt Em.

"Why, they 're the best friends I have!" asserted the little girl, "and you 're sure to like them, Aunt Em, 'cause *ever'*-body likes them."

By this time twilight was approaching, so they ate the

Chapter Twenty-Two

fine supper which the Wizard magically produced from the kettle and then went to bed in the cosy tents.

They were all up bright and early next morning, but Dorothy did n't venture to wander from the camp again for fear of more accidents.

"Do you know where there 's a road?" she asked the little man.

"No, my dear," replied the Wizard; "but I 'll find one."

After breakfast he waved his hand toward the tents and they became handkerchiefs again, which were at once returned to the pockets of their owners. Then they all climbed into the red wagon and the Sawhorse inquired:

"Which way?"

"Never mind which way," replied the Wizard. "Just go as you please and you 're sure to be right. I 've enchanted the wheels of the wagon, and they will roll in the right direction, never fear."

As the Sawhorse started away through the trees Dorothy said:

"If we had one of those new-fashioned airships we could float away over the top of the forest, and look down and find just the places we want.

"Airship? Pah!" retorted the little man, scornfully. "I hate those things, Dorothy, although they are nothing new to either you or me. I was a balloonist for many years, and once my balloon carried me to the Land of Oz, and once to the Vegetable Kingdom. And once Ozma had a Gump that flew all over this kingdom and had sense enough to go where it was told to—which airships won't do. The house which the cyclone brought to Oz all the way from Kansas, with you and Toto in it—was a real airship at the time; so you see we've had plenty of experience flying with the birds."

"Airships are not so bad, after all," declared Dorothy. "Some day they'll fly all over the world, and perhaps bring people even to the Land of Oz."

"I must speak to Ozma about that," said the Wizard, with a slight frown. "It would n't do at all, you know, for the Emerald City to become a way-station on an airship line."

"No," said Dorothy, "I don't s'pose it would. But what can we do to prevent it?"

"I'm working out a magic recipe to fuddle men's brains, so they'll never make an airship that will go where they want it to go," the Wizard confided to her. "That won't keep the things from flying, now and then, but it'll keep them from flying to the Land of Oz."

Just then the Sawhorse drew the wagon out of the forest and a beautiful landscape lay spread before the travelers' eyes. Moreover, right before them was a good road that wound away through the hills and valleys.

"Now," said the Wizard, with evident delight, "we are

on the right track again, and there is nothing more to worry about."

"It's a foolish thing to take chances in a strange country," observed the Shaggy Man. "Had we kept to the roads we

never would have been lost. Roads always leads to some place, else they would n't be roads."

"This road," added the Wizard, "leads to Rigmarole Town. I 'm sure of that because I enchanted the wagon wheels."

Sure enough, after riding along the road for an hour or two they entered a pretty valley where a village was nestled among the hills. The houses were Munchkin shaped, for they were all domes, with windows wider than they were high, and pretty balconies over the front doors.

Aunt Em was greatly relieved to find this town "neither paper nor patch-work," and the only surprising thing about it was that it was so far distant from all other towns.

As the Sawhorse drew the wagon into the main street the travelers noticed that the place was filled with people, standing in groups and seeming to be engaged in earnest conversation. So occupied with themselves were the inhabitants that they scarcely noticed the strangers at all. So the Wizard stopped a boy and asked:

"Is this Rigmarole Town?"

"Sir," replied the boy, "if you have traveled very much you will have noticed that every town differs from every other town in one way or another and so by observing the methods of the people and the way they live as well as the style of their dwelling places it ought not to be a difficult thing to make up your mind without the trouble of asking questions whether the town bears the appearance of the one you intended to visit or whether perhaps having taken a different road from the one you should have taken you have made an error in your way and arrived at some point where—"

Chapter Twenty-Two

"Land sakes!" cried Aunt Em, impatiently; "what's all this rigmarole about?"

"That's it!" said the Wizard, laughing merrily. "It's a rigmarole because the boy is a Rigmarole and we've come to Rigmarole Town."

"Do they all talk like that?" asked Dorothy, wonderingly.

"He might have said 'yes' or 'no' and settled the question," observed Uncle Henry.

"Not here," said Omby Amby. "I don't believe the Rigmaroles know what 'yes' or 'no' means."

While the boy had been talking several other people had approached the wagon and listened intently to his speech. Then they began talking to one another in long, deliberate speeches, where many words were used but little was said. But when the strangers criticised them so frankly one of the women, who had no one else to talk to, began an address to them, saying:

"It is the easiest thing in the world for a person to say 'yes' or 'no' when a question that is asked for the purpose of gaining information or satisfying the curiosity of the one who has given expression to the inquiry has attracted the attention of an individual who may be competent either from personal experience or the experience of others to answer it with more or less correctness or at least an attempt to satisfy the desire for information on the part of the one who has made the inquiry by—"

"Dear me!" exclaimed Dorothy, interrupting the speech. "I 've lost all track of what you are saying."

"Don't let her begin over again, for goodness sake!" cried Aunt Em.

But the woman did not begin again. She did not even stop talking, but went right on as she had begun, the words flowing from her mouth in a stream.

"I 'm quite sure that if we waited long enough and listened carefully, some of these people might be able to tell us something, in time," said the Wizard.

"Don't let 's wait," returned Dorothy. "I 've heard of the Rigmaroles, and wondered what they were like; but now I know, and I 'm ready to move on."

"So am I," declared Uncle Henry; "we 're wasting time here."

"Why, we 're all ready to go," added the Shaggy Man, putting his fingers to his ears to shut out the monotonous babble of those around the wagon.

So the Wizard spoke to the Sawhorse, who trotted nimbly through the village and soon gained the open country on the other side of it. Dorothy looked back, as they rode away, and noticed that the woman had not yet finished her speech but was talking as glibly as ever, although no one was near to hear her.

"If those people wrote books," Omby Amby remarked with a smile, "it would take a whole library to say the cow jumped over the moon."

'Perhaps some oᵣ em do write books," asserted the little Wizard. "I 've read a few rigmaroles that might have come from this very town."

"Some of the college lecturers and ministers are certainly related to these people," observed the Shaggy Man; "and it seems to me the Land of Oz is a little ahead of the United

States in some of its laws. For here, if one can't talk clearly, and straight to the point, they send him to Rigmarole Town; while Uncle Sam lets him roam around wild and free, to torture innocent people."

Dorothy was thoughtful. The Rigmaroles had made a strong impression upon her. She decided that whenever she spoke, after this, she would use only enough words to express what she wanted to say.

HOW THEY ENCOUNTERED THE FLUTTERBUDGETS

CHAPTER TWENTY-THREE

THEY were soon among the pretty hills and valleys again, and the Sawhorse sped up hill and down at a fast and easy pace, the roads being hard and smooth. Mile after mile was speedily covered, and before the ride had grown at all tiresome they sighted another village. The place seemed even larger than Rigmarole Town, but was not so attractive in appearance.

"This must be Flutterbudget Center," declared the Wizard. "You see, it 's no trouble at all to find places if you keep to the right road."

"What are the Flutterbudgets like?" inquired Dorothy.

"I do not know, my dear. But Ozma has given them a town all their own, and I 've heard that whenever one of the people becomes a Flutterbudget he is sent to this place to live."

"That is true," Omby Amby added; "Flutterbudget Center and Rigmarole Town are called 'the Defensive Settlements of Oz.'"

The village they now approached was not built in a valley, but on top of a hill, and the road they followed wound around the hill like a corkscrew, ascending the hill easily until it came to the town.

"Look out!" screamed a voice. "Look out, or you'll run over my child!"

They gazed around and saw a woman standing upon the sidewalk nervously wringing her hands as she gazed at them appealingly.

"Where is your child?" asked the Sawhorse.

"In the house," said the woman, bursting into tears; "but if it should happen to be in the road, and you ran over it, those great wheels would crush my darling to jelly. Oh, dear! oh dear! Think of my darling child being crushed to jelly by those great wheels!"

"Gid-dap!" said the Wizard, sharply, and the Sawhorse started on.

They had not gone far before a man ran out of a house shouting wildly: "Help! Help!"

The Sawhorse stopped short and the Wizard and Uncle Henry and the Shaggy Man and Omby Amby jumped out of the wagon and ran to the poor man's assistance. Dorothy followed them as quickly as she could.

"What 's the matter?" asked the Wizard.

"Help! help!" screamed the man; "my wife has cut her finger off and she 's bleeding to death!"

Then he turned and rushed back to the house, and all the party went with him. They found a woman in the front dooryard moaning and groaning as if in great pain.

"Be brave, madam!" said the Wizard, consolingly. "You won't die just because you have cut off a finger, you may be sure."

"But I have n't cut off a finger!" she sobbed.

"Then what *has* happened?" asked Dorothy.

"I—I pricked my finger with a needle while I was sewing, and—and the blood came!" she replied. "And now I 'll have blood-poisoning, and the doctors will cut off my finger, and that will give me a fever and I shall die!"

"Pshaw!" said Dorothy; "I 've pricked my finger many a time, and nothing happened."

"Really?" asked the woman, brightening and wiping her eyes upon her apron.

"Why, it 's nothing at all," declared the girl. "You 're more scared than hurt."

"Ah, that 's because she 's a Flutterbudget," said the

Wizard, nodding wisely. "I think I know now what these people are like."

"So do I," announced Dorothy.

"Oh, boo-hoo-hoo!" sobbed the woman, giving way to a fresh burst of grief.

"What 's wrong now?" asked the Shaggy Man.

"Oh, suppose I had pricked my foot!" she wailed. "Then the doctors would have cut my foot off, and I 'd be lamed for life!"

"Surely, ma'am," replied the Wizard, "and if you 'd pricked your nose they might cut your head off. But you see you did n't."

"But I might have!" she exclaimed, and began to cry again. So they left her and drove away in their wagon. And her husband came out and began calling "Help!" as he had before; but no one seemed to pay any attention to him.

As the travelers turned into another street they found a man walking excitedly up and down the pavement. He appeared to be in a very nervous condition and the Wizard stopped him to ask:

"Is anything wrong, sir?"

"Everything is wrong," answered the man, dismally. "I can't sleep."

"Why not?" inquird Omby Amby.

"If I go to sleep I 'll have to shut my eyes," he explained;

"and if I shut my eyes they may grow together, and then I 'd be blind for life!"

"Did you ever hear of any one's eyes growing together?" asked Dorothy.

"No," said the man, "I never did. But it would be a dreadful thing, would n't it? And the thought of it makes me so nervous I 'm afraid to go to sleep."

"There 's no help for this case," declared the Wizard; and they went on.

At the next street corner a woman rushed up to them crying:

"Save my baby! Oh, good, kind people, save my baby!"

"Is it in danger?" asked Dorothy, noticing that the child was clasped in her arms and seemed sleeping peacefully.

"Yes, indeed," said the woman, nervously. "If I should go into the house and throw my child out of the window, it would roll way down to the bottom of the hill; and then if there were a lot of tigers and bears down there, they would tear my darling babe to pieces and eat it up!"

"Are there any tigers and bears in this neighborhood?" the Wizard asked.

"I 've never heard of any," admitted the woman; "but if there were—"

"Have you any idea of throwing your baby out of the window?" questioned the little man.

"None at all," she said; "but if—"

"All your troubles are due to those 'ifs'," declared the Wizard. "If you were not a Flutterbudget you would n't worry."

"There 's another 'if'," replied the woman. "Are you a Flutterbudget, too?"

"I will be, if I stay here long," exclaimed the Wizard, nervously.

"Another 'if'!" cried the woman.

But the Wizard did not stop to argue with her. He made the Sawhorse canter all the way down the hill, and only breathed easily when they were miles away from the village.

After they had ridden in silence for a while Dorothy turned to the little man and asked:

"Do 'ifs' really make Flutterbudgets?"

"I think the 'ifs' help," he answered seriously . "Foolish fears, and worries over nothing, with a mixture of nerves and ifs, will soon make a Flutterbudget of any one."

Then there was another long silence, for all the travelers were thinking over this statement, and nearly all decided it must be true.

The country they were now passing through was everywhere tinted purple, the prevailing color of the Gillikin Country; but as the Sawhorse ascended a hill they found that upon the other side everything was of a rich yellow hue.

Chapter Twenty-Three

"Aha!" cried the Captain General; "here is the Country of the Winkies. We are just crossing the boundary line."

"Then we may be able to lunch with the Tin Woodman," announced the Wizard, joyfully.

"Must we lunch on tin?" asked Aunt Em.

"Oh, no;" replied Dorothy. "Nick Chopper knows how to feed meat people, and he will give us plenty of good things to eat, never fear. I 've been to his castle before."

"Is Nick Chopper the Tin Woodman's name?" asked Uncle Henry.

"Yes; that 's one of his names," answered the little girl; "and another of his names is 'Emp'ror of the Winkies.' He 's the King of this country, you know, but Ozma rules over all the countries of Oz."

"Does the Tin Woodman keep any Flutterbudgets or Rigmaroles at his castle?" inquired Aunt Em, uneasily.

"No, indeed," said Dorothy, positively. "He lives in a new tin castle, all full of lovely things."

"I should think it would rust," said Uncle Henry.

"He has thousands of Winkies to keep it polished for him," explained the Wizard. "His people love to do anything in their power for their beloved Emperor, so there is n't a particle of rust on all the big castle."

"I suppose they polish their Emperor, too," said Aunt Em.

"Why, some time ago he had himself nickel-plated," the Wizard answered; "so he only needs rubbing up once in a while. He's the brightest man in all the world, is dear Nick Chopper; and the kindest-hearted."

"I helped find him," said Dorothy, reflectively. "Once the Scarecrow and I found the Tin Woodman in the woods, and he was just rusted still, that time, an' no mistake. But we oiled his joints, an' got 'em good and slippery, and after that he went with us to visit the Wizard at the Em'rald City."

"Was that the time the Wizard scared you?" asked Aunt Em.

"He did n't treat us well, at first," acknowledged Dorothy; "for he made us go away and destroy the Wicked Witch. But after we found out he was only a humbug wizard we were not afraid of him."

The Wizard sighed and looked a little ashamed.

"When we try to deceive people we always make mistakes," he said. "But I 'm getting to be a real wizard now, and Glinda the Good's magic, that I am trying to practice, can never harm any one."

"You were always a good man," declared Dorothy, "even when you were a bad wizard."

"He 's a good wizard now," asserted Aunt Em, looking at the little man admiringly. "The way he made those tents grow out of handkerchiefs was just wonderful! And did n't he enchant the wagon wheels so they 'd find the road?"

"All the people of Oz," said the Captain General, "are very proud of their Wizard. He once made some soap-bubbles that astonished the world."

The Wizard blushed at this praise, yet it pleased him. He no longer looked sad, but seemed to have recovered his usual good humor.

The country through which they now rode was thickly dotted with farmhouses, and yellow grain waved in all the fields. Many of the Winkies could be seen working on their farms and the wild and unsettled parts of Oz were by this time left far behind.

These Winkies appeared to be happy, light-hearted folk, and all removed their caps and bowed low when the red wagon with its load of travelers passed by.

It was not long before they saw something glittering in the sunshine far ahead.

"See!" cried Dorothy; "that's the Tin Castle, Aunt Em!"

And the Sawhorse, knowing his passengers were eager to arrive, broke into a swift trot that soon brought them to their destination.

How THE TIN WOODMAN TOLD THE SAD NEWS

CHAPTER TWENTY-FOUR

THE Tin Woodman received Princess Dorothy's party with much grace and cordiality, yet the little girl decided that something must be worrying her old friend, because he was not so merry as usual.

But at first she said nothing about this, for Uncle Henry and Aunt Em were fairly bubbling over with admiration for the beautiful tin castle and its polished tin owner. So her suspicion that something unpleasant had happened was for a time forgotten.

"Where is the Scarecrow?" she asked, when they had all been ushered into the big tin drawing-room of the castle, the Sawhorse being led around to the tin stable in the rear.

"Why, our old friend has just moved into his new mansion," explained the Tin Woodman. "It has been a long time in building, although my Winkies and many other peo-

247

ple from all parts of the country have been busily working upon it. At last, however, it is completed, and the Scarecrow took possession of his new home just two days ago."

"I had n't heard that he wanted a home of his own," said Dorothy. "Why does n't he live with Ozma in the Emerald City? He used to, you know; and I thought he was happy there."

"It seems," said the Tin Woodman, "that our dear Scarecrow cannot be contented with city life, however beautiful his surroundings might be. Originally he was a farmer, for he passed his early life in a cornfield, where he was supposed to frighten away the crows."

"I know," said Dorothy, nodding. "I found **him**, and lifted him down from his pole."

"So now, after a long residence in the Emerald City, his tastes have turned to farm life again," continued the Tin Man. "He feels that he cannot be happy without a farm of his own, so Ozma gave him some land and every one helped him build his mansion, and now he is settled there for good."

"Who designed his house?" asked the Shaggy Man.

"I believe it was Jack Pumpkinhead, who is also a farmer," was the reply.

They were now invited to enter the tin dining room, where luncheon was served.

Aunt Em found, to her satisfaction, that Dorothy's promise was more than fulfilled; for, although the Tin Woodman had no appetite of his own, he respected the appetites of his guests and saw that they were bountifully fed.

They passed the afternoon in wandering through the beautiful gardens and grounds of the palace. The walks were all paved with sheets of tin, brightly polished, and there were tin fountains and tin statues here and there among the trees. The flowers were mostly natural flowers and grew in the regular way; but their host showed them one flower bed which was his especial pride.

"You see, all common flowers fade and die in time," he explained, "and so there are seasons when the pretty blooms are scarce. Therefore I decided to make one tin flower bed all of tin flowers, and my workmen have created them with rare skill. Here you see tin camelias, tin marigolds, tin carnations, tin poppies and tin hollyhocks growing as naturally as if they were real."

Indeed, they were a pretty sight, and glistened under the sunlight like spun silver.

"Is n't this tin hollyhock going to seed?" asked the Wizard, bending over the flowers.

"Why, I believe it is!" exclaimed the Tin Woodman, as if surprised. "I had n't noticed that before. But I shall plant the tin seeds and raise another bed of tin hollyhocks."

In one corner of the gardens Nick Chopper had established

a fish-pond, in which they saw swimming and disporting themselves many pretty tin fishes.

"Would they bite on hooks?" asked Aunt Em, curiously.

The Tin Woodman seemed hurt at this question.

"Madam," said he, "do you suppose I would allow any-one to catch my beautiful fishes, even if they were foolish enough to bite on hooks? No, indeed! Every created thing is safe from harm in my domain, and I would as soon think of killing my little friend Dorothy as killing one of my tin fishes."

"The Emperor is very kind-hearted, ma'am," explained the Wizard. "If a fly happens to light upon his tin body he does n't rudely brush it off, as some people might do; he asks it politely to find some other resting place."

"What does the fly do then?" enquired Aunt Em.

"Usually it begs his pardon and goes away," said the Wizard, gravely. "Flies like to be treated politely as well as other creatures, and here in Oz they understand what we say to them, and behave very nicely."

"Well," said Aunt Em, "the flies in Kansas, where I came from, don't understand anything but a swat. You have to smash 'em to make 'em behave; and it 's the same way with 'skeeters. Do you have 'skeeters in Oz?"

"We have some very large mosquitoes here, which sing as beautifully as song birds," replied the Tin Woodman.

"But they never bite or annoy our people, because they are well fed and taken care of. The reason they bite people in your country is because they are hungry—poor things!"

"Yes," agreed Aunt Em; "they 're hungry, all right. An' they ain't very particular who they feed on. I 'm glad you 've got the 'skeeters educated in Oz."

That evening after dinner they were entertained by the Emperor's Tin Cornet Band, which played for them several sweet melodies. Also the Wizard did a few sleight-of-hand tricks to amuse the company; after which they all retired to their cosy tin bedrooms and slept soundly until morning.

After breakfast Dorothy said to the Tin Woodman:

"If you 'll tell us which way to go we 'll visit the Scarecrow on our way home."

"I will go with you, and show you the way," replied the Emperor; "for I must journey to-day to the Emerald City."

He looked so anxious, as he said this, that the little girl asked:

"There is n't anything wrong with Ozma, is there?"

He shook his tin head.

"Not yet," said he; "but I 'm afraid the time has come when I must tell you some very bad news, little friend."

"Oh, what is it?" cried Dorothy.

"Do you remember the Nome King?" asked the Tin Woodman.

"I remember him very well," she replied.

"The Nome King has not a kind heart," said the Emperor, sadly, "and he has been harboring wicked thoughts of revenge, because we once defeated him and liberated his slaves and you took away his Magic Belt. So he has ordered his Nomes to dig a long tunnel underneath the deadly desert, so that he may march his hosts right into the Emerald City. When he gets there he intends to destroy our beautiful country."

Dorothy was much surprised to hear this.

"How did Ozma find out about the tunnel?" she asked.

"She saw it in her Magic Picture."

"Of course," said Dorothy; "I might have known that. And what is she going to do?"

"I cannot tell," was the reply.

"Pooh!" cried the Yellow Hen. "We 're not afraid of the Nomes. If we roll a few of our eggs down the tunnel they 'll run away back home as fast as they can go."

"Why, that 's true enough!" exclaimed Dorothy. "The Scarecrow once conquered all the Nome King's army with some of Billina's eggs."

"But you do not understand all of the dreadful plot," continued the Tin Woodman. "The Nome King is clever, and he knows his Nomes would run from eggs; so he has bargained with many terrible creatures to help him. These evil spirits are not afraid of eggs or anything else, and they are very powerful. So the Nome King will send them through the tunnel first, to conquer and destroy, and then the Nomes will follow after to get their share of the plunder and slaves."

They were all startled to hear this, and every face wore a troubled look.

"Is the tunnel all ready?" asked Dorothy.

"Ozma sent me word yesterday that the tunnel was all completed except for a thin crust of earth at the end. When our enemies break through this crust they will be in the gardens of the royal palace, in the heart of the Emerald City. I offered to arm all my Winkies and march to Ozma's assistance; but she said no."

"I wonder why?" asked Dorothy.

"She answered that all the inhabitants of Oz, gathered together, were not powerful enough to fight and overcome the evil forces of the Nome King. Therefore she refuses to fight at all."

"But they will capture and enslave us, and plunder and ruin all our lovely land!" exclaimed the Wizard, greatly disturbed by this statement.

"I fear they will," said the Tin Woodman, sorrowfully. "And I also fear that those who are not fairies, such as the Wizard, and Dorothy, and her uncle and aunt, as well as

Toto and Billina, will be speedily put to death by the conquerors."

"What can be done?" asked Dorothy, shuddering a little at the prospect of this awful fate.

"Nothing can be done!" gloomily replied the Emperor of the Winkies. "But since Ozma refuses my army I will go myself to the Emerald City. The least I may do is to perish beside my beloved Ruler."

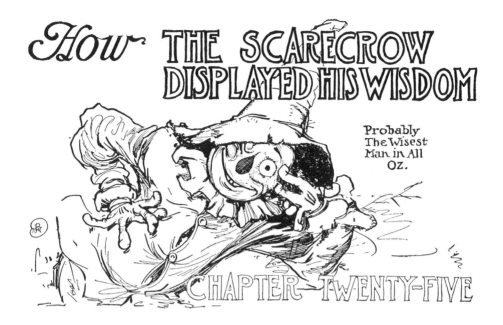

How THE SCARECROW DISPLAYED HIS WISDOM

Probably The Wisest Man in All Oz.

CHAPTER TWENTY-FIVE

THIS amazing news had saddened every heart and all were now anxious to return to the Emerald City and share Ozma's fate. So they started without loss of time, and as the road led past the Scarecrow's new mansion they determined to make a brief halt there and confer with him.

"The Scarecrow is probably the wisest man in all Oz," remarked the Tin Woodman, when they had started upon their journey. "His brains are plentiful and of excellent quality, and often he has told me things I might never have thought of myself. I must say I rely a good deal upon the Scarecrow's brains in this emergency."

The Tin Woodman rode on the front seat of the wagon, where Dorothy sat between him and the Wizard.

"Has the Scarecrow heard of Ozma's trouble?" asked the Captain General.

255

"I do not know, sir," was the reply.

"When I was a private," said Omby Amby, "I was an excellent army, as I fully proved in our war against the Nomes. But now there is not a single private left in our army, since Ozma made me the Captain General, so there is no one to fight and defend our lovely Ruler."

"True," said the Wizard. "The present army is composed only of officers, and the business of an officer is to order his men to fight. Since there are no men there can be no fighting."

"Poor Ozma!" whispered Dorothy, with tears in her sweet eyes. "It's dreadful to think of all her lovely fairy country being destroyed. I wonder if we couldn't manage to escape and get back to Kansas by means of the Magic Belt? And we might take Ozma with us and all work hard to get money for her, so she wouldn't be so *very* lonely and unhappy about the loss of her fairyland."

"Do you think there would be any work for *me* in Kansas?" asked the Tin Woodman.

"If you are hollow, they might use you in a canning factory," suggested Uncle Henry. "But I can't see the use of your working for a living. You never eat or sleep or need a new suit of clothes."

"I was not thinking of myself," replied the Emperor, with

dignity. "I merely wondered if I could not help to support Dorothy and Ozma."

As they indulged in these sad plans for the future they journeyed in sight of the Scarecrow's new mansion, and even though filled with care and worry over the impending fate of Oz, Dorothy could not help a feeling of wonder at the sight she saw.

The Scarecrow's new house was shaped like an immense ear of corn. The rows of kernels were made of solid gold, and the green upon which the ear stood upright was a mass of sparkling emeralds. Upon the very top of the structure was perched a figure representing the Scarecrow himself, and upon his extended arms, as well as upon his head, were several crows carved out of ebony and having ruby eyes. You may imagine how big this ear of corn was when I tell you that a single gold kernal formed a window, swinging outward upon hinges, while a row of four kernals opened to make the front entrance. Inside there were five stories, each story being a single room.

The gardens around the mansion consisted of cornfields, and Dorothy acknowledged that the place was in all respects a very appropriate home for her good friend the Scarecrow.

"He would have been very happy here, I 'm sure," she said, "if only the Nome King had left us alone. But if Oz is destroyed of course this place will be destroyed too."

"Yes," replied the Tin Woodman, "and also my beautiful tin castle, that has been my joy and pride."

"Jack Pumpkinhead's house will go too," remarked the Wizard, "as well as Professor Wogglebug's Athletic College, and Ozma's royal palace, and all our other handsome buildings."

"Yes, Oz will indeed become a desert when the Nome King gets through with it," sighed Omby Amby.

The Scarecrow came out to meet them and gave them all a hearty welcome.

"I hear you have decided always to live in the Land of Oz, after this," he said to Dorothy; "and that will delight my heart, for I have greatly disliked our frequent partings. But why are you all so downcast?"

"Have you heard the news?" asked the Tin Woodman.

"No news to make me sad," replied the Scarecrow.

Then Nick Chopper told his friend of the Nome King's tunnel, and how the evil creatures of the North had allied themselves with the underground monarch for the purpose of conquering and destroying Oz. "Well," said the Scarecrow, "it certainly looks bad for Ozma, and all of us. But I believe it is wrong to worry over anything before it happens. It is surely time enough to be sad when our country is despoiled and our people made slaves. So let us not deprive ourselves of the few happy hours remaining to us."

"Ah! that is real wisdom," declared the Shaggy Man, approvingly. "After we become really unhappy we shall regret these few hours that are left to us, unless we enjoy them to the utmost."

"Nevertheless," said the Scarecrow, "I shall go with you to the Emerald City and offer Ozma my services."

"She says we can do nothing to oppose our enemies," announced the Tin Woodman.

"And doubtless she is right, sir," answered the Scarecrow. "Still, she will appreciate our sympathy, and it is the duty of Ozma's friends to stand by her side when the final disaster occurs."

He then led them into his queer mansion and showed them the beautiful rooms in all the five stories. The lower room was a grand reception hall, with a hand-organ in one corner. This instrument the Scarecrow, when alone, could turn to amuse himself, as he was very fond of music. The walls were hung with white silk, upon which flocks of black crows were embroidered in black diamonds. Some of the chairs were made in the shape of big crows and upholstered with cushions of corn-colored silk.

The second story contained a fine banquet room, where the Scarecrow might entertain his guests, and the three stories above that were bed-chambers exquisitely furnished and decorated.

"From these rooms," said the Scarecrow, proudly, "one may obtain fine views of the surrounding cornfields. The corn I grow is always husky, and I call the ears my regiments, because they have so many kernels. Of course I cannot ride my cobs, but I really don't care shucks about that. Taken altogether, my farm will stack up with any in the neighborhood."

The visitors partook of some light refreshment and then hurried away to resume the road to the Emerald City. The Scarecrow found a seat in the wagon between Omby Amby and the Shaggy Man, and his weight did not add much to the load because he was stuffed with straw.

"You will notice I have one oat-field on my property," he remarked, as they drove away. "Oat-straw is, I have found, the best of all straws to re-stuff myself with when my interior gets musty or out of shape."

"Are you able to re-stuff youreslf without help?" asked Aunt Em. "I should think that after the straw was taken out of you there would n't be anything left but your clothes."

"You are almost correct, madam," he answered. "My servants do the stuffing, under my direction. For my head, in which are my excellent brains, is a bag tied at the bottom. My face is neatly painted upon one side of the bag, as you may see. My head does not need re-stuffing, as my body does, for all that it requires is to have the face touched up with fresh paint occasionally."

It was not far from the Scarecrow's mansion to the farm of Jack Pumpkinhead, and when they arived there both Uncle Henry and Aunt Em were much impressed. The farm was one vast pumpkin field, and some of the pumpkins were of

enormous size. In one of them, which had been neatly hollowed out, Jack himself lived, and he declared that it was a very comfortable residence. The reason he grew so many pumpkins was in order that he might change his head as often as it became wrinkled or threatened to spoil.

The pumpkin-headed man welcomed his visitors joyfully and offered them several delicious pumpkin pies to eat.

"I don't indulge in pumpkin pies myself, for two reasons," he said. "One reason is that were I to eat pumpkins I would become a cannibal, and the other reason is that I never eat, not being hollow inside."

"Very good reasons," agreed the Scarecrow.

They told Jack Pumpkinhead the dreadful news about the Nome King, and he decided to go with them to the Emerald City and help comfort Ozma.

"I had expected to live here in ease and comfort for many centuries," said Jack, dolefully; "but of course if the Nome King destroys everything in Oz I shall be destroyed too. Really, it seems too bad, does n't it?"

They were soon on their journey again, and so swiftly did the Sawhorse draw the wagon over the smooth roads that before twilight fell that had reached the royal palace in the Emerald City, and were at their journey's end.

How OZMA REFUSED TO FIGHT FOR HER KINGDOM

CHAPTER TWENTY-SIX

OZMA was in her rose garden picking a bouquet when the party arrived, and she greeted all her old and new friends as smilingly and sweetly as ever.

Dorothy's eyes were full of tears as she kissed the lovely Ruler of Oz, and she whispered to her:

"Oh, Ozma, Ozma! I'm *so* sorry!"

Ozma seemed surprised.

"Sorry for what, Dorothy?" she asked.

"For all your trouble about the Nome King," was the reply.

Ozma laughed with genuine amusement.

"Why, that has not troubled me a bit, dear Princess," she replied. Then, looking around at the sad faces of her friends, she added: "Have you all been worrying about this tunnel?"

"We have!" they exclaimed in a chorus.

263

"Well, perhaps it is more serious than I imagined," admitted the fair Ruler; "but I have n't given the matter much thought. After dinner we will all meet together and talk it over."

So they went to their rooms and prepared for dinner, and Dorothy dressed herself in her prettiest gown and put on her coronet, for she thought that this might be the last time she would ever appear as a Princess of Oz.

The Scarecrow, the Tin Woodman and Jack Pumpkinhead all sat at the dinner table, although none of them was made so he could eat. Usually they served to enliven the meal with their merry talk, but to-night all seemed strangely silent and uneasy.

As soon as the dinner was finished Ozma led the company to her own private room in which hung the Magic Picture. When they had seated themselves the Scarecrow was the first to speak.

"Is the Nome King's tunnel finished, Ozma?" he asked.

"It was completed to-day," she replied. "They have built it right under my palace grounds, and it ends in front of the Forbidden Fountain. Nothing but a crust of earth remains to separate our enemies from us, and when they march here they will easily break through this crust and rush upon us."

"Who will assist the Nome King?" inquired the Scarecrow.

"The Whimsies, the Growleywogs and the Phanfasms," she replied. "I watched to-day in my Magic Picture the messengers whom the Nome King sent to all these people to summon them to assemble in his great caverns."

"Let us see what they are doing now," suggested the Tin Woodman.

So Ozma wished to see the Nome King's cavern, and at once the landscape faded from the Magic Picture and was replaced by the scene then being enacted in the jeweled cavern of King Roquat.

A wild and startling scene it was which the Oz people beheld.

Before the Nome King stood the Chief of the Whimsies and the Grand Gallipoot of the Groweywogs, surrounded by their most skillful generals. Very fierce and powerful they looked, so that even the Nome King and General Guph, who stood beside his master, seemed a bit fearful in the presence of their allies.

Now a still more formidable creature entered the cavern. It was the First and Foremost of the Phanfasms and he proudly sat down in King Roquat's own throne and demanded the right to lead his forces through the tunnel in advance of all the others. The First and Foremost now appeared to all eyes in his hairy skin and the bear's head. What his real form was even Roquat did not know.

The Emerald City of Oz

Through the arches leading into the vast series of caverns that lay beyond the throne room of King Roquat, could be seen ranks upon ranks of the invaders—thousands of Phanfasms, Growleywogs and Whimsies standing in serried lines, while behind them were massed the thousands upon thousands of General Guph's own army of Nomes.

"Listen!" whispered Ozma. "I think we can hear what they are saying."

So they kept still and listened.

"Is all ready?" demanded the First and Foremost, haughtily.

"The tunnel is finally completed," replied General Guph.

"How long will it take us to march to the Emerald City?" asked the Grand Gallipoot of the Growleywogs.

"If we start at midnight," replied the Nome King, "we shall arrive at the Emerald City by daybreak. Then, while all the Oz people are sleeping, we will capture them and make them our slaves. After that we will destroy the city itself and march through the Land of Oz, burning and devastating as we go."

"Good!" cried the First and Foremost. "When we get through with Oz it will be a desert wilderness. Ozma shall be my slave."

"She shall be *my* slave!" shouted the Grand Gallipoot, angrily.

"We'll decide that by and by," said King Roquat, hastily. "Don't let us quarrel now, friends. First let us conquer Oz, and then we will divide the spoils of war in a satisfactory manner."

The First and Foremost smiled wickedly; but he only said:

"I and my Phanfasms go first, for nothing on earth can oppose our power."

They all agreed to that, knowing the Phanfasms to be the mightiest of the combined forces. King Roquat now invited them to attend a banquet he had prepared, where they might occupy themselves in eating and drinking until midnight arrived.

As they had now seen and heard all of the plot against them that they cared to, Ozma allowed her Magic Picture to fade away. Then she turned to her friends and said:

"Our enemies will be here sooner than I expected. What do you advise me to do?"

"It is now too late to assemble our people," said the Tin Woodman, despondently. "If you had allowed me to arm and drill my Winkies we might have put up a good fight and destroyed many of our enemies before we were conquered."

"The Munchkins are good fighters, too," said Omby Amby; "and so are the Gillikins."

"But I do not wish to fight," declared Ozma, firmly. "No one has the right to destroy any living creatures, however evil they may be, or to hurt them or make them unhappy. I will not fight—even to save my kingdom."

"The Nome King is not so particular," remarked the Scarecrow. "He intends to destroy us all and ruin our beautiful country."

"Because the Nome King intends to do evil is no excuse for my doing the same," replied Ozma.

"Self-preservation is the first law of nature," quoted the Shaggy Man.

"True," she said, readily. "I would like to discover a plan to save ourselves without fighting."

That seemed a hopeless task to them, but realizing that Ozma was determined not to fight, they tried to think of some means that might promise escape.

"Could n't we bribe our enemies, by giving them a lot of emeralds and gold?" asked Jack Pumpkinhead.

"No, because they believe they are able to take everything we have," replied the Ruler.

"I have thought of something," said Dorothy.

"What is it, dear?" asked Ozma.

"Let us use the Magic Belt to wish all of us in Kansas. We will put some emeralds in our pockets, and can sell them in Topeka for enough to pay off the mortgage on Uncle Henry's farm. Then we can all live together and be happy."

"A clever idea!" exclaimed the Scarecrow.

"Kansas is a very good country. I 've been there," said the Shaggy Man.

"That seems to me an excellent plan," approved the Tin Woodman.

"No!" said Ozma, decidedly. "Never will I desert my people and leave them to so cruel a fate. I will use the Magic Belt to send the rest of you to Kansas, if you wish, but if my beloved country must be destroyed and my people enslaved I will remain and share their fate."

"Quite right," asserted the Scarecrow, sighing. "I will remain with you."

"And so will I," declared the Tin Woodman and the Shaggy Man and Jack Pumpkinhead, in turn. Tiktok, the machine man, also said he intended to stand by Ozma. "For," said he, "I should be of no use at all in Kansas."

"For my part," announced Dorothy, gravely, "if the Ruler of Oz must not desert her people, a Princess of Oz has no right to run away, either. I 'm willing to become a slave with the rest of you; so all we can do with the Magic Belt is to use it to send Uncle Henry and Aunt Em back to Kansas."

"I 've been a slave all my life," Aunt Em replied, with

considerable cheerfulness, "and so has Henry. I guess we won't go back to Kansas, anyway. I 'd rather take my chances with the rest of you."

Ozma smiled upon them all gratefully.

"There is no need to despair just yet," she said. "I 'll get up early to-morrow morning and be at the Forbidden Fountain when the fierce warriors break through the crust of earth. I will speak to them pleasantly and perhaps they won't be so very bad, after all."

"Why do they call it the Forbidden Fountain?" asked Dorothy, thoughtfully.

"Don't you know, dear?" returned Ozma, surprised.

"No," said Dorothy. "Of course I 've seen the fountain in the palace grounds, ever since I first came to Oz; and I 've read the sign which says: 'All Persons are Forbidden to Drink at this Fountain.' But I never knew *why* they were forbidden. The water seems clear and sparkling and it bubbles up in a golden basin all the time."

"That water," declared Ozma, gravely, "is the most dangerous thing in all the Land of Oz. It is the Water of Oblivion."

"What does that mean?" asked Dorothy.

"Whoever drinks at the Forbidden Fountain at once forgets everything he has ever known," Ozma asserted.

"It would n't be a bad way to forget our troubles," suggested Uncle Henry.

"That is true; but you would forget everything else, and become as ignorant as a baby," returned Ozma.

"Does it make one crazy?" asked Dorothy.

"No; it only makes one forget," replied the girl Ruler. "It is said that once—long, long ago—a wicked King ruled

Oz, and made himself and all his people very miserable and unhappy. So Glinda, the Good Sorceress, placed this fountain here, and the King drank of its water and forgot all his wickedness. His mind became innocent and vacant, and when he learned the things of life again they were all good things. But the people remembered how wicked their King had been, and were still afraid of him. Therefore he made them all drink of the Water of Oblivion and forget everything they had known, so that they became as simple and innocent as their King. After that they all grew wise together, and their wisdom was good, so that peace and happiness reigned in the land. But for fear some one might drink of the water again, and in an instant forget all he had learned, the King put that sign upon the fountain, where it has remained for many centuries up to this very day."

They had all listened intently to Ozma's story, and when she finished speaking there was a long period of silence while all thought upon the curious magical power of the Water of Oblivion.

Finally the Scarecrow's painted face took on a broad smile that stretched the cloth as far as it would go.

"How thankful I am," he said, "that I have such an excellent assortment of brains!"

"I gave you the best brains I ever mixed," declared the Wizard, with an air of pride.

"You did, indeed!" agreed the Scarecrow, "and they work so splendidly that they have found a way to save Oz— to save us all!"

"I 'm glad to hear that," said the Wizard. "We never needed saving more than we do just now."

"Do you mean to say you can save us from those awful

Chapter Twenty-Six

Phanfasms, and Growleywogs and Whimsies?'' asked Dorothy eagerly.

"I 'm sure of it, my dear,'' asserted the Scarecrow, still smiling genially.

"Tell us how!'' cried the Tin Woodman.

"Not now,'' said the Scarecrow. "You may all go to bed, and I advise you to forget your worries just as completely as if you had drunk of the Water of Oblivion in the Forbidden Fountain. I 'm going to stay here and tell my plan to Ozma alone, but if you will all be at the Forbidden Fountain at daybreak, you 'll see how easily we will save the kingdom when our enemies break through the crust of earth and come from the tunnel."

So they went away and left the Scarecrow and Ozma alone; but Dorothy could not sleep a wink all night.

"He is only a Scarecrow," she said to herself, "and I 'm not sure that his mixed brains are as clever as he thinks they are."

But she knew that if the Scarecrow's plan failed they were all lost; so she tried to have faith in him.

How THE FIERCE WARRIORS INVADED OZ

CHAPTER TWENTY-SEVEN

THE Nome King and his terrible allies sat at the banquet table until midnight. There was much quarreling between the Growleywogs and Phanfasms, and one of the wee-headed Whimsies got angry at General Guph and choked him until he nearly stopped breathing. Yet no one was seriously hurt, and the Nome King felt much relieved when the clock struck twelve and they all sprang up and seized their weapons.

"Aha!" shouted the First and Foremost. "Now to conquer the Land of Oz!"

He marshaled his Phanfasms in battle array and at his word of command they marched into the tunnel and began the long journey through it to the Emerald City. The First and Foremost intended to take all the treasures in Oz for himself; to kill all who could be killed and enslave the rest; to destroy and lay waste the whole country, and afterward

275

to conquer and enslave the Nomes, the Growleywogs and the Whimsies. And he knew his power was sufficient to enable him to do all these things easily.

Next marched into the tunnel the army of gigantic Growleywogs, with their Grand Gallipoot at their head. They were dreadful beings, indeed, and longed to get to Oz that they might begin to pilfer and destroy. The Grand Gallipoot was a little afraid of the First and Foremost, but had a cunning plan to murder or destroy that powerful being and secure the wealth of Oz for himself. Mighty little of the plunder would the Nome King get, thought the Grand Gallipoot.

The Chief of the Whimsies now marched his false-headed forces into the tunnel. In his wicked little head was a plot to destroy both the First and Foremost and the Grand Gallipoot. He intended to let them conquer Oz, since they insisted on going first; but he would afterward treacherously destroy them, as well as King Roquat, and keep all the slaves and treasure of Ozma's kingdom for himself.

After all his dangerous allies had marched into the tunnel the Nome King and General Guph started to follow them, at the head of fifty thousand Nomes, all fully armed.

"Guph," said the King, "those creatures ahead of us mean mischief. They intend to get everything for themselves and leave us nothing."

"I know," replied the General; "but they are not as clever as they think they are. When you get the Magic Belt you must at once wish the Whimsies and Growleywogs and Phanfasms all back into their own countries—and the Belt will surely take them there."

"Good!" cried the King. "An excellent plan, Guph. I'll do it. While they are conquering Oz I'll get the Magic Belt, and then only the Nomes will remain to ravage the country."

So you see there was only one thing that all were agreed upon—that Oz should be destroyed.

On, on, on the vast ranks of invaders marched, filling the

tunnel from side to side. With a steady tramp, tramp, they advanced, every step taking them nearer to the beautiful Emerald City.

"Nothing can save the Land of Oz!" thought the First and Foremost, scowling until his bear face was as black as the tunnel.

"The Emerald City is as good as destroyed already!" muttered the Grand Gallipoot, shaking his war club fiercely.

"In a few hours Oz will be a desert!" said the Chief of the Whimsies, with an evil laugh.

"My dear Guph," remarked the Nome King to his General, "at last my vengeance upon Ozma of Oz and her people is about to be accomplished."

"You are right!" declared the General. "Ozma is surely lost."

And now the First and Foremost, who was in advance and nearing the Emerald City, began to cough and to sneeze.

"This tunnel is terribly dusty," he growled, angrily. "I'll punish that Nome King for not having it swept clean. My throat and eyes are getting full of dust and I'm as thirsty as a fish!"

The Grand Gallipoot was coughing too, and his throat was parched and dry.

"What a dusty place!" he cried. "I'll be glad when we reach Oz, where we can get a drink."

Chapter Twenty-Seven

"Who has any water?" asked the Whimsie Chief, gasping and choking. But none of his followers carried a drop of water, so he hastened on to get through the dusty tunnel to the Land of Oz.

"Where did all this dust come from?" demanded General Guph, trying hard to swallow but finding his throat so dry he could n't.

"I don't know," answered the Nome King. "I 've been in the tunnel every day while it was being built, but I never noticed any dust before."

"Let 's hurry!" cried the General. "I 'd give half the gold in Oz for a drink of water."

The dust grew thicker and thicker, and the throats and eyes and noses of the invaders were filled with it. But not one halted or turned back. They hurried forward more fierce and vengeful than ever.

How THEY DRANK AT THE FORBIDDEN FOUNTAIN

CHAPTER TWENTY-EIGHT

THE Scarecrow had no need to sleep; neither had the Tin Woodman or Tiktok or Jack Pumpkinhead. So they all wandered out into the palace grounds and stood beside the sparkling water of the Forbidden Fountain until daybreak. During this time they indulged in occasional conversation.

"Nothing could make me forget what I know," remarked the Scarecrow, gazing into the fountain, "for I cannot drink the Water of Oblivion or water of any kind. And I am glad that this is so, for I consider my wisdom unexcelled."

"You are cer-tain-ly- ve-ry wise," agreed Tiktok. "For my part, I can on-ly think by ma-chin-er-y, so I do not pre-tend to know as much as you do."

"My tin brains are very bright, but that is all I claim for them," said Nick Chopper, modestly. "Yet I do not aspire to being very wise, for I have noticed that the happiest people are those who do not let their brains oppress them."

"Mine never worry me," Jack Pumpkinhead acknowledged. "There are many seeds of thought in my head, but they do not sprout easily. I am glad that it is so, for if I occupied my days in thinking I should have no time for anything else."

In this cheery mood they passed the hours until the first golden streaks of dawn appeared in the sky. Then Ozma joined them, as fresh and lovely as ever and robed in one of her prettiest gowns.

"Our enemies have not yet arrived," said the Scarecrow, after greeting affectionately the sweet and girlish Ruler.

"They will soon be here," she said, "for I have just glanced at my Magic Picture, and have seen them coughing and choking with the dust in the tunnel."

"Oh, is there dust in the tunnel?" asked the Tin Woodman.

"Yes; Ozma placed it there by means of the Magic Belt," explained the Scarecrow, with one of his broad smiles.

Then Dorothy came to them, Uncle Henry and Aunt Em following close after her. The little girl's eyes were heavy because she had had a sleepless and anxious night. Toto walked by her side, but the little dog's spirits were very much subdued. Billina, who was always up by daybreak, was not long in joining the group by the fountain.

The Wizard and the Shaggy Man next arrived, and soon after appeared Omby Amby, dressed in his best uniform.

"There lies the tunnel," said Ozma, pointing to a part of the ground just before the Forbidden Fountain, "and in a few moments the dreadful invaders will break through the earth and swarm over the land. Let us all stand on the other side of the Fountain and watch to see what happens."

At once they followed her suggestion and moved around the fountain of the Water of Oblivion. There they stood silent and expectant until the earth beyond gave way with a sudden crash and up leaped the powerful form of the First and Foremost, followed by all his grim warriors.

As the leader sprang forward his gleaming eyes caught the play of the fountain and he rushed toward it and drank eagerly of the sparkling water. Many of the other Phanfasms drank, too, in order to clear their dry and dusty throats. Then they stood around and looked at one another with simple, wondering smiles.

The First and Foremost saw Ozma and her companions beyond the fountain, but instead of making an effort to capture her he merely stared at her in pleased admiration of her beauty—for he had forgotten where he was and why he had come there.

But now the Grand Gallipoot arrived, rushing from the

Chapter Twenty-Eight

tunnel with a hoarse cry of mingled rage and thirst. He too saw the fountain and hastened to drink of its forbidden waters. The other Growleywogs were not slow to follow suit, and even before they had finished drinking the Chief of the Whimsies and his people came to push them away, while they one and all cast off their false heads that they might slake their thirst at the fountain.

When the Nome King and General Guph arrived they both made a dash to drink, but the General was so mad with thirst that he knocked his King over, and while Roquat lay sprawling upon the ground the General drank heartily of the Water of Oblivion.

This rude act of his General made the Nome King so angry that for a moment he forgot he was thirsty and rose to his feet to glare upon the group of terrible warriors he had brought here to assist him. He saw Ozma and her people, too, and yelled out:

"Why don't you capture them? Why don't you conquer Oz, you idiots? Why do you stand there like a lot of dummies?"

But the great warriors had become like little children. They had forgotten all their enmity against Ozma and against Oz. They had even forgotten who they themselves were, or why they were in this strange and beautiful country. As for the Nome King, they did not recognize him, and wondered who he was.

The sun came up and sent its flood of silver rays to light the faces of the invaders. The frowns and scowls and evil looks were all gone. Even the most monstrous of the creatures there assembled smiled innocently and seemed light-hearted and content merely to be alive.

Not so with Roquat, the Nome King. He had not drunk from the Forbidden Fountain and all his former rage against Ozma and Dorothy now inflamed him as fiercely as ever. The sight of General Guph babbling like a happy child and playing with his hands in the cool waters of the fountain astonished and maddened Red Roquat. Seeing that his terrible allies and his own General refused to act, the Nome King turned to order his great army of Nomes to advance from the tunnel and seize the helpless Oz people.

But the Scarecrow suspected what was in the King's mind and spoke a word to the Tin Woodman. Together they ran at Roquat and grabbing him up tossed him into the great basin of the fountain.

The Nome King's body was round as a ball, and it bobbed up and down in the Water of Oblivion while he spluttered and screamed with fear lest he should drown. And when he cried out his mouth filled with water, which ran down his throat, so that straightway he forgot all he had formerly known just as completely as had all the other invaders.

Ozma and Dorothy could not refrain from laughing to see their dreaded enemies become as harmless as babes. There was no danger now that Oz would be destroyed. The only question remaining to solve was how to get rid of this horde of intruders.

The Shaggy Man kindly pulled the Nome King out of the fountain and set him upon his thin legs. Roquat was dripping wet, but he chattered and laughed and wanted to drink more of the water. No thought of injuring any person was now in his mind.

285

Before he left the tunnel he had commanded his fifty thousand Nomes to remain there until he ordered them to advance, as he wished to give his allies time to conquer Oz before he appeared with his own army. Ozma did not wish all these Nomes to overrun her land, so she advanced to King Roquat and taking his hand in her own said gently:

"Who are you? What is your name?"

"I don't know," he replied, smiling at her. "Who are you, my dear?"

"My name is Ozma," she said; "and your name is Roquat."

"Oh, is it?" he replied, seeming pleased.

"Yes; you are King of the Nomes," she said.

"Ah; I wonder what the Nomes are!" returned the King, as if puzzled.

"They are underground elves, and that tunnel over there is full of them," she answered. "You have a beautiful cavern at the other end of the tunnel, so you must go to your Nomes and say: 'March home!' Then follow after them and in time you will reach the pretty cavern where you live."

The Nome King was much pleased to learn this, for he had forgotten he had a cavern. So he went to the tunnel and said to his army: "March home!" At once the Nomes turned and marched back through the tunnel, and the King followed after them, laughing with delight to find his orders so readily obeyed.

Chapter Twenty-Eight

The Wizard went to General Guph, who was trying to count his fingers, and told him to follow the Nome King, who was his master. Guph meekly obeyed, and so all the Nomes quitted the Land of Oz forever.

But there were still the Phanfasms and Whimsies and

Growleywogs standing around in groups, and they were so many that they filled the gardens and trampled upon the flowers and grass because they did not know that the tender plants would be injured by their clumsy feet. But in all other respects they were perfectly harmless and played together like children or gazed with pleasure upon the pretty sights of the royal gardens.

After counseling with the Scarecrow Ozma sent Omby Amby to the palace for the Magic Belt, and when the Captain General returned with it the Ruler of Oz at once clasped the precious Belt around her waist.

"I wish all these strange people—the Whimsies and the Growleywogs and the Phanfasms—safe back in their own homes!" she said.

It all happened in a twinkling, for of course the wish was no sooner spoken than it was granted.

All the hosts of the invaders were gone, and only the trampled grass showed that they had ever been in the Land of Oz.

How GLINDA WORKED A MAGIC SPELL

CHAPTER TWENTY-NINE

"THAT was better than fighting," said Ozma, when all our friends were assembled in the palace after the exciting events of the morning; and each and every one agreed with her.

"No one was hurt," said the Wizard, delightedly.

"And no one hurt us," added Aunt Em.

"But, best of all," said Dorothy, "the wicked people have all forgotten their wickedness, and will not wish to hurt any one after this."

"True, Princess," declared the Shaggy Man. "It seems to me that to have reformed all those evil characters is more important than to have saved Oz."

"Nevertheless," remarked the Scarecrow, "I am glad Oz is saved. I can now go back to my new mansion and live happily."

"And I am glad and grateful that my pumpkin farm is saved," said Jack.

"For my part," added the Tin Woodman, "I cannot express my joy that my lovely tin castle is not to be demolished by wicked enemies."

"Still," said Tiktok, "o-ther en-e-mies may come to Oz some day."

"Why do you allow your clock-work brains to interrupt our joy?" asked Omby Amby, frowning at the machine man.

"I say what I am wound up to say," answered Tiktok.

"And you are right," declared Ozma. "I myself have been thinking of this very idea, and it seems to me there are entirely too many ways for people to get to the Land of Oz. We used to think the deadly desert that surrounds us was enough protection; but that is no longer the case. The Wizard and Dorothy have both come here through the air, and I am told the earth people have invented airships that can fly anywhere they wish them to go."

"Why, sometimes they do, and sometimes they don't," asserted Dorothy.

"But in time the airships may cause us trouble," continued Ozma, "for if the earth folk learn how to manage them we would be overrun with visitors who would ruin our lovely, secluded fairyland."

"That is true enough," agreed the Wizard.

Chapter Twenty-Nine

"Also the desert fails to protect us in other ways," Ozma went on, thoughtfully. "Johnny Dooit once made a sand-boat that sailed across it, and the Nome King made a tunnel under it. So I believe something ought to be done to cut us off from the rest of the world entirely, so that no one in the future will ever be able to intrude upon us."

"How will you do that?" asked the Scarecrow.

"I do not know; but in some way I am sure it can be accomplished. To-morrow I will make a journey to the castle of Glinda the Good, and ask her advice."

"May I go with you?" asked Dorothy, eagerly.

"Of course, my dear Princess; and also I invite any of our friends here who would like to undertake the journey."

They all declared they wished to accompany their girl Ruler, for this was indeed an important mission, since the future of the Land of Oz to a great extent depended upon it. So Ozma gave orders to her servants to prepare for the journey on the morrow.

That day she watched her Magic Picture, and when it showed her that all the Nomes had returned through the tunnel to their underground caverns, Ozma used the Magic Belt to close up the tunnel, so that the earth underneath the desert sands became as solid as it was before the Nomes began to dig.

Early the following morning a gay cavalcade set out to

visit the famous Sorceress, Glinda the Good. Ozma and Dorothy rode in a chariot drawn by the Cowardly Lion and the Hungry Tiger, while the Sawhorse drew the red wagon in which rode the rest of the party.

With hearts light and free from care they traveled merrily along through the lovely and fascinating Land of Oz, and in good season reached the stately castle in which resided the Sorceress.

Glinda knew that they were coming.

"I have been reading about you in my Magic Book," she said, as she greeted them in her gracious way.

"What is your Magic Book like?" inquired Aunt Em, curiously.

"It is a record of everything that happens," replied the Sorceress. "As soon as an event takes place, anywhere in the world, it is immediately found printed in my Magic Book. So when I read its pages I am well informed."

"Did it tell how our enemies drank the Water of 'Blivion?" asked Dorothy.

"Yes, my dear; it told all about it. And also it told me you were all coming to my castle, and why."

"Then," said Ozma, "I suppose you know what is in my mind, and that I am seeking a way to prevent any one in the future from discovering the Land of Oz."

"Yes; I know that. And while you were on your journey I have thought of a way to accomplish your desire. For it seems to me unwise to allow too many outside people to come here. Dorothy, with her uncle and aunt, has now returned to Oz to live always, and there is no reason why we should leave any way open for others to travel uninvited to our fairyland. Let us make it impossible for any one ever to communicate with us in any way, after this. Then we may live peacefully and contentedly."

"Your advice is wise," returned Ozma. "I thank you, Glinda, for your promise to assist me."

"But how can you do it?" asked Dorothy. "How can you keep every one from ever finding Oz?"

"By making our country invisible to all eyes but our own," replied the Sorceress, smiling. "I have a magic charm powerful enough to accomplish that wonderful feat, and now that we have been warned of our danger by the Nome King's invasion, I believe we must not hesitate to separate ourselves forever from all the rest of the world."

"I agree with you," said the Ruler of Oz.

"Won't it make any difference to us?" asked Dorothy, doubtfully.

"No, my dear," Glinda answered, assuringly. "We shall still be able to see each other and everything in the Land of Oz. It won't affect us at all; but those who fly through the air over our country will look down and see nothing at all.

The Emerald City of Oz

Those who come to the edge of the desert, or try to cross it, will catch no glimpse of Oz, or know in what direction it lies. No one will try to tunnel to us again because we cannot be seen and therefore cannot be found. In other words, the Land of Oz will entirely disappear from the knowledge of the rest of the world."

"That's all right," said Dorothy, cheerfully. "You may make Oz invis'ble as soon as you please, for all I care."

"It is already invisible," Glinda stated. "I knew Ozma's wishes, and performed the Magic Spell before you arrived."

Ozma seized the hand of the Sorceress and pressed it gratefully.

"Thank you!" she said.

How THE STORY OF OZ CAME TO AN END

CHAPTER THIRTY

THE writer of these Oz stories has received a little note from Princess Dorothy of Oz which, for a time, has made him feel rather discontented. The note was written on a broad white feather from a stork's wing, and it said:

> *"You will never hear anything more about Oz, because we are now cut off forever from all the rest of the world. But Toto and I will always love you and all the other children who love us.*
>
> "DOROTHY GALE."

This seemed to me too bad, at first, for Oz is a very interesting fairyland. Still, we have no right to feel grieved, for we have had enough of the history of the Land of Oz to fill six story books, and from its quaint people and their strange adventures we have been able to learn many useful and amusing things.

So good luck to little Dorothy and her companions. May they live long in their invisible country and be very happy!

THE END

Afterword

The last Oz book. Could it be? Was this *really* the last Oz story? L. Frank Baum had hinted that he was tired of writing about Oz and wished to tell other stories in his preface to the fourth, *Dorothy and the Wizard in Oz*. He had warned us that the next Oz book might be the last in his preface to the fifth, *The Road to Oz*. But despite this, readers were surprised and saddened when after six adventures in the land of Oz, Baum brought the fun to a close by making Oz completely invisible.

But if Baum were going to end the Oz series, then *The Emerald City of Oz* certainly did so with a bang. Baum filled this marvelous tale with enough magic, imagination, and suspense for two books, ensuring that his last Oz story would be one of his best.

The Emerald City of Oz shows just how much L. Frank Baum had grown as a writer in the ten years since *The Wonderful Wizard of Oz* had first been published. In Baum's previous Oz books, the

Afterword

stories had basically followed the adventures of one character (usually Dorothy) and introduced us to new people and places only as that character encountered them. But in *The Emerald City of Oz*, we follow two plots at one time—the Nome King's nefarious plan to conquer Oz and Dorothy's permanent move to Oz with her aunt and uncle. In this way, Baum is able to introduce us to twice as many fantastic places and peoples.

Certainly Baum grants the deepest wish of all his readers when he allows them to accompany Dorothy and her friends on a tour of Oz. The diversity found throughout Baum's fairy-tale kingdom is one of its most endearing qualities and undoubtedly one of the main reasons it continues to fascinate readers today.

The idea of sending Dorothy and her friends on a tour of Oz was truly an inspired plot device. One can almost imagine Baum thinking to himself that if this was going to be his last story about Oz, then he would show his readers just how fantastic a place Oz could be. In just a few short chapters he introduces us to the Cuttenclips and the Flutterbudgets; the people of Fuddlecumjig, Utensia, Bunbury, Bunnybury, and Rigmarole Town; plus gives us a tour of the Wogglebug's College of Athletics, the Tin Woodman's castle, and the Scarecrow's mansion. Surely these are some of his most colorful, imaginative, and humorous creations. Baum's ability to create this neverending parade of new and unusual people is unmatched in children's literature.

Afterword

Yet in stark contrast, Baum also created for this book some of his most wicked and scary peoples—the Whimsies, the Growleywogs, and the Phanfasms. While there is some humor in the Whimsies outrageously colored paperboard heads and very small brains, the cruelty of the Growleywogs and the truly evil disposition of the Phanfasms are unusually frightful for characters in an Oz tale. By juxtaposing the introduction of these evil people between Dorothy and her friends' lighthearted adventures, Baum created just the right touch of suspense without ever making his story too scary.

Of course, darkness is hardly the mood of *The Emerald City of Oz*. After all, *The Emerald City of Oz* is filled with the sort of puns in which Baum always took such delight. The chapters about Utensia and Bunbury, in particular, are a veritable pun-fest.

Though *The Emerald City of Oz* is noted as one of the best written Oz stories, it is the magnificent illustrations of John R. Neill that make this title one of the most eagerly sought by Oz collectors. For *The Emerald City of Oz*, Neill once again used the beautifully detailed pen-and-ink style he first used in *The Road to Oz* and then added seventeen fabulous watercolor paintings—one to be used for the cover and dust jacket and the remaining sixteen to be used as color plates. And each of these paintings was embellished on press with a sparkling metallic green ink.

Only the first two printings of *The Emerald City of Oz* used this metallic green ink. All subsequent printings dropped this fifth

Afterword

color, leaving white space where the metallic ink had been, and included only twelve of the original sixteen color plates. And only the first issue of *The Emerald City of Oz* included the original watercolor cover design with metallic green ink. For the second and all subsequent printings, a different, less ornate, design was used.

That is why we are especially pleased to release this facsimile edition of *The Emerald City of Oz* with all of the original color plates as well as the original cover design—every one embellished with metallic green ink and gold glitter—re-creating all the magic of the 1910 first edition.

So now you hold in your hands the first printing of *The Emerald City of Oz* to be published in over 80 years the way Baum and Neill intended. But is this truly the last Oz book? After all, Oz is a fairyland and is filled with the most remarkable magic. And if Ozma's Magic Picture can see us and Glinda's Magic Book can tell her whatever is happening anywhere in the world, surely someone in Oz will find a way to send us more stories!

—Peter Glassman

Oz Titles in the
Books of Wonder Series
∾⊶∿

BY L. FRANK BAUM

The Wonderful Wizard of Oz
with illustrations by W. W. Denslow

ILLUSTRATED BY JOHN R. NEILL

The Marvelous Land of Oz · Ozma of Oz
Dorothy and the Wizard in Oz · The Road to Oz · The Emerald City of Oz
The Patchwork Girl of Oz · Tik-Tok of Oz
The Scarecrow of Oz · Rinkitink in Oz · The Lost Princess of Oz
The Tin Woodman of Oz
The Magic of Oz · Glinda of Oz · Little Wizard Stories of Oz

BY ROGER S. BAUM

Dorothy of Oz
with illustrations by Elizabeth Miles

⊶∾

Oz: The Hundredth Anniversary Celebration
edited by Peter Glassman
with art and text in appreciation of Oz
by thirty favorite artists and writers

⊶∾

If you enjoy the Oz books and want to know more about Oz,
you may be interested in The Royal Club of Oz. Devoted to America's
favorite fairyland, it is a club for everyone who loves the Oz books.
For free information, please send a first-class stamp to:

The Royal Club of Oz
P.O. Box 714
New York, New York 10011
or call toll free: (800) 207-6968

Oz Titles in the Books of Wonder Series

❧○❧

BY L. FRANK BAUM

The Wonderful Wizard of Oz
with illustrations by W. W. Denslow

ILLUSTRATED BY JOHN R. NEILL

The Marvelous Land of Oz · *Ozma of Oz*
Dorothy and the Wizard in Oz · *The Road to Oz* · *The Emerald City of Oz*
The Patchwork Girl of Oz · *Tik-Tok of Oz*
The Scarecrow of Oz · *Rinkitink in Oz* · *The Lost Princess of Oz*
The Tin Woodman of Oz
The Magic of Oz · *Glinda of Oz* · *Little Wizard Stories of Oz*

BY ROGER S. BAUM

Dorothy of Oz
with illustrations by Elizabeth Miles

❧❧❧

Oz: The Hundredth Anniversary Celebration
edited by Peter Glassman
with art and text in appreciation of Oz
by thirty favorite artists and writers

❧❧❧

If you enjoy the Oz books and want to know more about Oz,
you may be interested in The Royal Club of Oz. Devoted to America's
favorite fairyland, it is a club for everyone who loves the Oz books.
For free information, please send a first-class stamp to:

The Royal Club of Oz
P.O. Box 714
New York, New York 10011
or call toll free: (800) 207-6968

DOROTHY